PRINNY'S TAYLOR

The Life and Times of Louis Bazalgette (1750-1830)

Charles Bazalgette

© 2015 Charles Bazalgette
All rights reserved. Apart from any use under UK copyright law no part of this publication may be reproduced, stored in a retrieval system, or transmitted, in any form or by any means, without prior written permission of the publisher, nor be otherwise circulated in any form of binding or cover other than that in which it is published and without a similar condition being imposed on the subsequent publisher.

ISBN: 978-0-9879692-0-0

Front cover design by Margaret Anderson, with image by courtesy of the Victoria and Albert Museum, London.

Rear cover and book layout by Sarah Jean Waldock.

Illustrations on rear cover:
Photographic image of a portrait of Louis Bazalgette, probably painted in Paris in 1802. The whereabouts of the original is unknown.

Miniature of the Prince of Wales by Richard Cosway, 1780, in a coquelicot coat that was very likely to have been made by Louis Bazalgette.

Tara Books, PO Box 91, Salmo, BC, V0G 1Z0, Canada
Email: bazalgettec@gmail.com

Contents

Author's Note	v
Preface	vi
Prologue: A morning at Carlton House	1
Chapter 1: A Cévenol Family	5
Chapter 2: 1750-75	12
Chapter 3: 1775-78	19
Chapter 4: 18th Century Tailoring and its Ancillary Trades	32
Chapter 5: 1779-84	40
Chapter 6: 18th Century Tailoring Techniques and Apprenticeship	52
Chapter 7: 1785-86	61
Chapter 8: Organization and Working Conditions in the 18th Century Tailoring Trade	72
Chapter 9: 1787	79
Chapter 10: 1788	94
Chapter 11: 1789	109
Chapter 12: 1790-91	121
Chapter 13: 1792-93	136
Chapter 14: 1794-95	149
Chapter 15: 1796-98	165
Chapter 16: 1799-1802	174
Chapter 17: 1803-06	187
Chapter 18: 1807-12	199
Chapter 19: 1813-16	215

Chapter 20: 1817-19	233
Chapter 21: 1820-28	242
Chapter 22: 1829-32	261
Chapter 23: 1833-36	276
Chapter 24: Louis' Children	284
Postscript	299
Acknowledgements	300
Appendix 1: Glossary of Fabrics and Colours	303
Appendix 2: Georgian Tailoring Stitches	314
Appendix 3: List of London Master Tailors in 1799	321
Appendix 4: Louis Bazalgette's Accounts to the Prince of Wales for 1790	329
Bibliography	365
Descendants of Claude Bazalgette	369
About the author	372

Author's Note

The title is a little anachronistic because the bulk of Louis Bazalgette's service to the Prince of Wales was before the latter came to be known as 'Prinny'. He got that nickname in about 1805, from Minney Seymour, the orphaned daughter of Admiral Lord Hugh Seymour, who was for many years the ward of Mrs. Fitzherbert. When the Prince used to visit Mrs. Fitzherbert he often played with little Minney while he was there. She was only about four or five then, and she called him 'Prinny' to rhyme with her own first name. He told a number of his friends about it, and soon many of them were calling him Prinny too. However, although I do not much like the use of the name it is immediately recognizable, and is much shorter than 'The Prince of Wales, later George IV'. I used the old spelling 'Taylor' as a differentiator and to make the title easier to search for. I rather liked the title 'Rags to Riches', but it is not descriptive enough and there are other books with that title.

So 'Prinny's Taylor' it had to be.

There are three chapters which cover various aspects of Georgian gentlemen's tailoring. During my research I gathered a great deal of material on the subject, which will not be found elsewhere in one place, so for this reason I included it. The reader who finds this as fascinating as I do will find that these chapters enrich the story, but the less-interested can of course skip these chapters and not interfere with the chronological flow. They are always available for reference.

The reader will also come across a couple of passages in italics, which are semi-fictional, but firmly based on fact. This is a device that I had come across in a couple of other biographies and I rather like it. I hope you do too.

Preface

This biography had its origins in my genealogical research into the British branch of the Bazalgette family, whose patriarch was Jean Louis Bazalgette (1750-1830). I had carried out a great deal of genealogical research into my families before I started to concentrate on my great-great-great-great-grandfather Jean Louis. He was born in a village in the Cévennes, in the South of France, into a family who had been tailors for several generations, but then left home, found his way to London and rapidly rose to the top of his profession, serving as tailor to the Prince of Wales for over thirty-two years. I was intrigued because he was regarded in the family as a mysterious figure, the commonest question about him being: 'Where did he get his money and property?'

Several people had already tried to find out more about him, with varying success. The waters were muddied by a French relative who wrote an account of Louis' life which was based on a few facts but was otherwise utter fantasy. This author had Louis sailing across to America in 1777 with the Marquis de Lafayette, fighting in the Revolutionary War, establishing a string of fur-trading posts across the North American continent and finally marrying the daughter of a rich New York fur merchant before sailing to England. There still seem to be people who believe this version of events, but I hope in this book to dispel this myth.

When researching Louis' life, apart from finding the usual vital records, I hit the proverbial brick wall. He was an unknown man. He never got his name in the newspapers, apart from the odd modest donation to charity, and was never mentioned in contemporary accounts, diaries etc., of which I ploughed through a great number. He never advertised, probably because the Prince's orders for clothes took up all of his manufacturing capacity. The fact that over many years I have been able to piece together his life story is owing mainly to the 'snapping up of unconsidered trifles' and to painstaking detective work, plus those few measures of luck that lead the researcher up the right path, against the run of the play, which usually consists of Dame Fortune blithely pointing him down the garden variety.

It is very clear that Louis was a self-effacing, discreet and even secretive man. He did not have any particular vices that we know of. Having become the Prince's tailor when the latter was as young as sixteen, he was able to visit him to take and deliver orders almost clandestinely, which of course suited both of them very well, and although the quantity of clothes he supplied was colossal, he passed unobserved. His name *did* appear in the royal accounts as being owed far more than any other creditor, but otherwise, apart from amassing a large fortune, and then lending money or giving credit to the Prince and his brothers, as well as to other prominent figures such as Richard Sheridan, he avoided the spotlight of history. So unless, like the author, you had followed him like a bloodhound for twenty years, you would never have found this out.

Louis was therefore the right man at the right time, providing an exclusive service of great quality and efficiency to Prinny and almost imperceptibly making himself a millionaire, in modern terms, as a result. He was then able, in his unnoticed way, to become a propertied gentleman and to enjoy his dotage as lord of the manor of Great Bookham.

Prologue: A Morning at Carlton House

On Tuesday 29 November 1787, at about 8 a.m., a rather boxy brown town coach is rolled out of its coach-house at 22, Brooks Mews, Mayfair, which backs on to, and is connected to, a far grander house, 22 Lower Grosvenor Street, the London home of Louis and Frances Bazalgette and their children. This coach is of a lightweight construction, since it is only used in town, and was built to Louis' specifications by William Leader of 37, Liquorpond Street, Holborn, who also made coaches for the Prince of Wales. In looks it is most like a larger precursor of the brougham. The coach's plain and functional appearance is only relieved by the discreet Prince of Wales feathers painted in gold on each door. Once the coachman and his grooms have brought out and hitched up a pair of equally glossy chestnut horses, an ordered but rapid activity commences. Under the supervision of the master tailor, Thomas Smith, three 'imperials' - light but strongly-made boxes measuring about 5½' x 2½' x 1½' - are loaded on to the flat roof of the coach, which has solid brass rails surrounding it to keep the made-to-fit boxes from falling off. These boxes, which have canvas covers (like those of 'cello cases) to protect them from damage and which can be easily replaced when they become scuffed, are strapped down, and further receive an oilskin cover to protect them from London soot and possible rain.

These boxes contain a precious cargo – new and altered clothes to be delivered to the Prince of Wales. The modestly-wigged and soberly-dressed Louis Bazalgette, his plain brown coat somewhat relieved by a flash of embroidered waistcoat, after a breakfast just sufficient to sustain him until a late lunch at 2 or 3 p.m., takes affectionate leave of his wife and children and passes through the first-floor offices at the rear of the house and through the manufactory, where he is greeted by his chief cutter and foreman tailor. He passes a few words with them on the order of the day, collects his bags of swatches and tailor's bits-and-bobs and then descends the stairs, through the shop, and thence to the mews, where he satisfies himself that the carriage and its load are presentable, and climbs into the carriage, followed by Thomas and another assistant.

The route taken to Carlton House depends on the traffic and on whether Louis has any errands, such as a visit to Coutts Bank at 59, Strand. The intention is to arrive at the mews at the back of Carlton House at about 9.30. The assistants carry the boxes into the Pages' Room, where they wait to be summoned into the royal chambers. The customary wait is about half an hour, but may be longer. Sounds of conviviality may often be heard as the Prince entertains various breakfast guests, as is his wont. Eventually they depart, and the sartorial trio is ushered by a page into the Prince's apartments, where their employer, clad in a pink- and green-striped cassimere robe de chambre, is polishing off his breakfast.

Firstly, they will unpack, for inspection and fitting, the finished clothes, which were ordered a few days ago and have been finished with the customary dispatch. These consist of a bordered check satin vest (short waistcoat), two brown cloth hunting frocks (made from the Prince's own cloth), one 'mixt' cloth ditto, two pairs of drab corduroy breeches, four pairs of drawers (made by a trusted local seamstress to avoid discomfort to the royal person), five espagnolette waistcoats which have been altered from double to single-breasted, a 'corbeau-coloured' frock with an orange silk lining and 24 striped ribbon buttons, a striped beaver frock with a scarlet silk lining, a re-buttoned striped frock, a pair of Saxon-green silk breeches and two pairs of fine flannel drawers.

After these clothes have been tried on and any required changes noted, a business that is not on any account to be hurried, Louis produces his latest swatches for inspection, and there follows a further long discussion of what clothes His Royal Highness wishes to order today. Louis pencils the orders into his notebook, and today they will consist of: a frock coat made from 5½ yards of striped blue beaver, lined with 6½ yards of orange silk and with 24 ribbon buttons, another frock of brown striped beaver with pink silk edging and fancy stone buttons, a striped espagnolette vest and a scarlet ditto, both with pearl buttons, eight further vests in various coloured satins – orange (with embroidered foreparts), scarlet ditto, purple silk with a velvet border, blue ditto with pink & green ditto, white satin with pink & white ditto (the last six to have silk fringes), nine further vests of a variety of materials and colours and six espagnolette morning gowns of the Prince's own material. The cost of this order is £96/12/9, which at 2008 values represents £10,100 using the retail price index and £122,000 using average earnings.

After several hours it is possible for Louis and his retinue to take their leave, allowing those unfortunates with pressing state business belatedly to gain access to the Prince, after he has had time to be dressed of course. This is by no means an untypical morning at Carlton House.

Chapter 1: A Cévenol Family

The Cévennes is a mountainous region at the south-eastern end of the French *Massif Central*, characterized by high grasslands or *causses*, which lie upon limestone pavements. The rain that falls upon the *causses* permeates through the limestone and feeds rivers of sparkling clarity, which over the centuries have carved spectacular gorges through the rock, famous among these being the Gorges du Tarn. The River Tarn, although it rises in the granite of Mont Lozère, benefits from the limestone, which reduces the acidity of the water so that it supports small crustaceans and therefore plentiful trout, chub, carp, pike and other fish. Where differing rock types like the local limestone, schist and granite occur beside each other, there are usually metal ores to be found; in this area it is lead with a moderate silver content. The *causses* are not very productive land, and support little in the way of livestock except sheep, which accounts for the general poverty of the region. The inhospitability of the Cévennes made it one of the last refuges of the more fiercely resistant remnants of the ancient Gallic tribes of southern France, which goes some way to accounting for the Cévenol's toughness, independence and peculiar language.

The Cévenol tongue, from which the Languedoc region gets its name, and which is fast disappearing as the area is invaded by northern migrants, is the *Langue d'Oc*, or Occitàn, which is related to Catalan and has 'the ability to express the finest shades of meaning', as demonstrated by Heather Willings in her very readable book *A Village in the Cévennes*. She writes:

> There are twenty-four tenses in the indicative and eight in the subjunctive. And a great deal can be said in one word, thanks to a comprehensive system of suffixes.
> For example:
>
> oustal = a house
> oustalet = a small house
> oustaloun = a little house

oustalounet = a tiny house
oustalàs = a large, ugly house
oustalaras = a high-rise building
oustalassoun = a small, square, ugly house
oustalettas/oustalounas = a large-sized/small house

Verbs are given the same treatment:

estornudar = to sneeze
estornudejar = to keep on sneezing
estornudounar = to give a little sneeze
estronudounejar = to give a series of little sneezes

The Cévenols were more or less successful over the centuries in repelling waves of potential invaders, some of the most persistent of whom were sent by order of the Church of Rome. Even though from 496 AD Roman Catholicism was the only official religion in France, the Cévenols accepted it only superficially, while in their hearts and minds following their faith as they always had, which was of course not according to the Roman way. So although they were baptised and married in the Catholic Church, they remained closet Protestants, or rather non-Catholics. There was no such thing as atheism. Not to adhere to some sort of religious belief was unthinkable. In the Cévenols' case it was probably a form of the ancient but semi-extinct creed of Catharism.

The river valleys of the Cévennes provide a contrast to the bleakness of the high grassland, and naturally this is where the more prosperous villages are to be found. The village of Ispagnac lies on a fertile alluvial plain, protected to the north by the steep mountain slopes and half surrounded on the southern side by the River Tarn, which turns quite sharply at this point before entering the gorges. This area, now referred to as the 'Jardin de la Lozère', was relatively prosperous, and in the eighteenth century the local peasants, while still very poor, were able to grow some crops, vegetables, fruit and vines, and maybe keep a few chickens and even a pig. In hard times there were always the nuts (*châtaignes*) from the many sweet chestnut trees, which could be milled and made into a form of bread. There were many who were destitute; the poor even had their own 'union', and begging, though illegal, was commonplace. Any but the better houses in the village were little more than hovels.

Standing in the old part of Ispagnac, you would see that it is entirely rimmed by wooded mountains which reach heights of between 1,000 to 1,200 metres. The plain is not large, and extends south-east along the river to Quezac and beyond. Being hemmed in in this way could surely feel oppressive at times, and could well have encouraged a young man to wish to escape.

To the north-east of Ispagnac lies a range of mountains which are collectively named Mont Lozère, the highest point of which is the *Sommet de Finiels* (1,699 metres, 5,612 feet). To the east are the Bougès and to the south the Causse de Méjean. To the north and west rises the Causse de Sauveterre, and the river Tarn has over the centuries carved its deep gorges between these two causses. The steep zig-zag road up to this latter causse gives a spectacular view of the whole valley and of Ispagnac, its neighbouring hamlet of Molines and of Quezac to the south-east. The causse is at a height of about 1,000 metres, and has fine grasslands dotted with stunted pines, although at the higher points it is rocky and more barren. There are post-volcanic depressions (*dolines*) of various sizes which are moister and more fertile and which are used to grow cereals or hay. When the author was there in July 2012 it was lush and green, but usually by that time of year it is more parched. The seed heads of the ripe grasses give a shimmering silver cast to the land which is very beautiful. Wild flowers grow there in great profusion and butterflies are numerous and varied.

There were a few dozen families who managed to prosper and acquire a measure of wealth and property in Ispagnac, and these formed a small bourgeoisie consisting of landowners, merchants and artisans. Amongst these families were the Roberts, the St. Pierres, the Salansons, the Lagets, the Deleuzes and the Bazalgettes. They kept a firm grasp on the money and property that they accumulated, and marrying outside the group was frowned upon. They adopted the Roman law, at least as far as the *dot*, or dower, was concerned, which meant that a bride would be provided with a marriage settlement by her family, a proportion of which formed a jointure exclusively for her own use. A family of tailors such as the Bazalgettes earned a reasonable living by making clothes for the local *Seigneurs* (mainly the Grégoire and Châteauneuf-Randon families) and for the bourgeois families of Ispagnac and the surrounding villages.

The origins of the Bazalgette name and family are, to use a well-worn phrase, the stuff of legend. The stories have been often told in the family but they are included here for the sake of completeness.

The Moors occupied the Gard region in Southern France during the first half of the 8th Century A.D., at which time they were based at Nîmes. They made frequent incursions into the Cévennes, covering an area a day's ride from Nîmes, which took them as far as the River Tarn, and therefore to Ispagnac. The story goes that one of Charlemagne's generals, a Spaniard by the name of Miralles, achieved some success in repelling the invaders. Miralles' prowess apparently prompted the Moors to dub their adversary 'Baz-al-Get' which meant something like 'Hawk of the Field' in their Moorish dialect. In return for his efforts, Miralles was granted lands in the area, and made his home at the place which is still called La Bazalgette, which lies in the Causse de Sauveterre about midway between Mende and Ispagnac.

There may be some truth in this story, but whether it accounts for the origin of the Bazalgette name seems now to be doubted by many Cévenol scholars. Most etymologists seem to be of the opinion that it derives from the local word for a basilica. A basilica was in Roman times a large building with colonnades which served as a commodity exchange or covered market. With the arrival of Christianity the name was then, as today, much used for a chapel or other religious building. In the Gallic regions the word may have either a religious or a secular meaning, and has various dialect forms, for instance: *Bazoches* (in the Aisne), *Bazoque* (Calvados), *Bazougues* (Mayenne) *Bazugues* (Gers) and in the south of France *Bazalgue* (Lot) and *Bazalgette* (Lozère). [Astor, Jacques:

Dictionnaire des noms de famille et des noms de lieu du midi de la France, Editions du Beffroi, January 2002]

If the etymological explanation of the origin of the word Bazalgette is correct it tends to give the lie to the 'Baz-al-Get' theory and therefore to much of the Miralles story.

The name Ispagnac, formally Espagnac and also previously spelt Yspagnac or Hispagnac, suggests a Spanish connection, although these '-ac' endings are reputed to come from the Latin '-acum', much like 'Eboracum', the Roman name for York. The name may therefore date from Roman times.

There is recorded by the French genealogist Nicolas Viton de St. Allais a noble family, Bazalgette de Charnève, extinct by 1880, whose seventeenth-century château still stands on the right bank of the River Rhône at Bourg St. Andéol in the Ardèche. The arms of this family are:

> *Parti: au 1., d'argent, à la fasce de gueules, chargée de trois croissants montants de champ, accompagnée d'un étendard de gueules, semé de croisettes d'or, mis en bande et en pointe, de trois merlettes de sable, et d'une moucheture d'hermine du même, en abîme; au chef d'azur, chargé de deux croix, trefflées d'or: au 2., d'or, au lion de gueules, armé et lampassé de sinople, couronné d'argent, tenant de sa patte dextre un sabre du même, garni d'or. Couronne de comte.*

The 'croissants' bring to mind an image of those buttery pastries that the French like with their morning coffee, but as 'crescents' they would support the Moorish story, were it not for the fact that crescents on a coat of arms usually signify that a family member went on one of the crusades. The simpler arms granted later to Louis's son Evelyn and his grandson Sir Joseph Bazalgette by the British College of Arms were:

> *Argent, on a fess gules three crescents of the field, on a chief azure two crosses fleury or*

There is no known connection in the last four hundred years between the Charnève Bazalgettes and the Ispagnac

Bazalgettes, although it may exist. That there is a connection seems to be universally accepted, and variations of the Charnève arms were granted to Jean Louis, and later to Sir Joseph Bazalgette when he was knighted. The view held by most researchers in the Cévennes is that the source of all of the Bazalgette families is the hamlet of La Bazalgette, and this may well be so.

Following the more westerly road north from Ispagnac to Balsièges, zig-zagging endlessly up the mountainside, you will eventually arrive on the plateau and will see a sign to the right which points to La Bazalgette. This hamlet is made up of about a dozen houses and farm buildings. If there was originally a chapel here, no trace of it has been found. The largest of the houses, now known as *La Cazelle*, was, according to the present owner, M. Paradis, occupied by a Bazalgette family until quite recent times.

The earliest proven ancestor of Jean Louis Bazalgette was Claude Bazalgette of Ispagnac, whose marriage has not been found in the registers. It appears that there were several Bazalgette families in Ispagnac and neighbouring villages at this time, but because of gaps in the registers, no line can be traced further back with certainty at present. An unsubstantiated anecdote from a French researcher has it that there were two Claudes, who were cousins and lived in adjoining houses. One was a tailor and the other a bootmaker. One died and the other married his widow and knocked the two houses into one. Claude (presumably the tailor) and his wife Marie Rainal had three known children between November 1682 and October 1685. These were Jeanne, baptized on 22 December 1682, Etienne, baptized on 22 November 1683 and Pierre, baptized on 24 October 1685. Pierre we know became a *tailleur d'habits*, although the family tradition of tailoring probably goes further back than this. He married Louise Grignard, the daughter of Jacques Grignard and Marie Privat, on 21 May 1707. Their son Etienne, Jean Louis' father, was baptized on 13 July 1709.

Jean Louis' mother Jeanne Deleuze's grandparents were Antoine Deleuze and Antoinette Salanson and their son

Georges married Anne Carcasson, daughter of Gabriel Carcasson and Louise Amat, on 20 July 1713. Their daughter Jeanne was baptized on 26 May 1715, and at the age of 16 she married Etienne Bazalgette on 5 February 1732. Both families must have been well set up, and judging by the size of Jeanne's dowry, the Deleuzes were quite comfortably off. The marriage contract was drawn up by *Maître* Grégoire, notary of Ispagnac, on 14 January, 1732, twenty-two days before the wedding. Jeanne's dowry amounted to 350 *livres*, of which 80 *livres* was provided by her father and 40 *livres* by her deceased mother, as specified in her will. Jeanne's dowry, according to Roman Law, was to be managed by her husband during his lifetime but returned to her on his death. The remaining sum of 230 *livres* was to be paid thus: 30 *livres* the first year after the marriage and 20 *livres* per annum for the next eleven years, without interest. This sum of 350 *livres* was equivalent to about a year's earnings for a weaver in Picardy at that time.

The Bazalgette family's long lineage, self-sufficiency and non-conformist tradition tended to produce scions of great determination and inner strength. Jean Louis was a supreme example as we will see.

Chapter 2: 1750-75

Jean Louis, the youngest son of Etienne Bazalgette and his wife Jeanne Deleuze, was born in Ispagnac, a village of about three hundred 'hearths', on 5 October 1750. A hearth or *feu* approximates to five inhabitants. In the Cévenol tradition, the family was almost certainly protestant, although of the closet sort, since Roman Catholicism was the only legal religion at the time. The baby was christened in the thirteenth-century Roman Catholic Church of St. Pierre, although after leaving France Jean Louis always adhered to the Protestant religion. The register entry reads:

> *Jean Louis Bazalgette fils legitime et naturel á Etienne Bazalgette et Jeanne Deleuze mariés a Ispagnac est né le 5 octobre 1750 et a été baptisé le 6 meme mois et an, son parrain Sr Privat Salançon procureur de Me Jean Louis Robert de St Philip clerc tonsuré, sa marraine demoiselle Marianne Robert epouse de Sr Lacombe marchand presents.*

In other words, Jean Louis was baptized the day after his birth, and his godfather was *Seigneur* Privat Salançon (Salançon was a local name, also that of Jeanne Deleuze's grandmother), who acted as a representative of the priest *Messire* Jean Louis Robert of St. Philip. *Procureur* usually means an attorney, but it seems to have been used here in the non-legal sense. Perhaps our Jean Louis was named after the priest. His godmother was also a Robert, so possibly related to the priest, and was the wife of the merchant *Seigneur* Lacombe.

Etienne Bazalgette was described in records as a *tailleur d'habits* or a tailor of clothes, which in modern times is just shortened to *tailleur*. He was also a *tisserand* or *texier* which means he wove at least some of the cloth for the clothes he made. Prominent among these cloths was apparently one called *cadiz*, a lightly milled wool fabric peculiar to Languedoc.

Jean Louis (or Louis, as he always later called himself) was the youngest of four known children: Pierre (born 11 April

1739), Marie (born 23 March 1743), Georges (born 1746) and Louis (born 6 October 1750). Louis was thus eleven years younger than his eldest sibling. His father Etienne had been born on 13 July 1709 but died, aged only forty-eight, on 22 September 1757, a week before Louis' seventh birthday. Louis' father and his grandfather were both tailors so the family had a well-established business in Ispagnac. There would have been enough family members to teach the boy the tailoring business, even though his father had died so early. His grandfather Pierre would have been seventy-five at the time of Louis' birth and therefore probably was also not around to help with Louis' education.

The apprenticeship for a general tailor at the time was three to four years, depending on aptitude, so there is no doubt that Louis was well versed in all aspects of the business before he left home. He was no doubt already skilled with a needle and shears as a young child, and could have been apprenticed to one of his elder brothers in his early teens. When ready, he would have had to make a suit - his *chef d'oeuvre* - and if it was approved he could be admitted to the local guild as a journeyman tailor or *compagnon*. He would then have aspired to be a master tailor, but in a small town and with two older brothers his chances of achieving this were slim because of the competition. Whoever was the master in the family firm, Pierre or Georges, or possibly both of them, would want their journeymen to stay that way. It was therefore almost always necessary for a journeyman to leave home and to travel to a large town in search of work and advancement. Although, for the reasons stated, journeymen often had to travel, the apparent connection with the word 'journeyman' is coincidental, since it derives from the French word *'journée'*, and originally meant a man who was hired by the day.

A portrait of Louis shows a dark-haired and dark-complexioned man, probably quite short and wiry, which is typical of the natives of the Cévennes. His son Joseph William was described in later life as 'small, about five feet five inches high, and firmly, though lightly, made. His complexion is very dark, his hair thick, and of an iron-grey colour; his eyes are black and expressive, and his nose aquiline.' We can see the same thick wiry hair and other features in Louis. Shortness ran in the family. Joseph William's son Joseph William, the civil engineer, was no more than five feet tall and also lightly built. In turn, his son Edward was also a very small man, according to the author's father.

There was a definite advantage to being apprenticed to a family member. Those apprenticed to masters outside their family could be overworked, harshly-treated or poorly-fed, had no real protection from exploitation and would often have to sleep on a bag of straw under the bench. Louis, as the youngest, probably had his own little truckle-bed and would have been much better fed and looked after. But, like all apprentices, he would still have had to get up an hour earlier than the other members of the household and perform chores like tidying the workshop and lighting the fires in winter. Louis can be imagined, stopping in mid-sweep and leaning on his broom as he dreamed of exchanging his 'rags' for riches.

Family stories tell us that Louis left Ispagnac sometime between 1769 and 1770, at the age of nineteen or twenty. The source of the story that Louis left at that age is a letter written to Sir Joseph Bazalgette's son Edward by Léon Bazalgette, a noted French author and critic, whose best known work was the translation of Walt Whitman's writings into French. Léon was the great-grandson of Louis' elder brother Georges. The letter says that Léon's uncle Albert had a copy of Louis' *acte de naissance*, which he had received from his father Maurice Antoine Bazalgette *dit* Bonaparte. Léon said that his grandfather had often related to him the story that his father Jean Bazalgette (son of Georges) had told him - that Georges' brother, born in 1750, went abroad about the age of nineteen or twenty. He never returned to his home, but in 1830 the mayor of Chambonnet informed Jean that a Bazalgette had recently died abroad leaving a large fortune. Léon was convinced that this story must refer to Louis, and the known facts certainly seem to agree with this opinion. A copy of this letter is in the possession of the author.

Did Louis leave home purely because of his ambition to plough his own furrow, or because he fell out with his family? He certainly seems to have gone forth and never looked back.

Léon said that he never returned to Ispagnac, and that his relatives never heard of his activities until informed later of his death 'leaving a large fortune', from which his birth family presumably received no benefit. Louis, on arriving in London, soon dropped the 'Jean' in his name, pronounced it 'Lewis Bazalgate' (which was how it was often written in a rate book), wrote his personal notes in English and not French, as many another emigrant would have done, spelt French words in an anglicised way and did his best to become an English gentleman. It is perhaps not surprising that he eschewed 'Frenchness', since he was a Cévenol, and would have felt as French as a Scotsman feels British or a Basque feels Spanish. But he seems to have denied his own roots as well. He consciously avoided the conventional filial duty of naming his children after family members. Amongst his children there is not an Etienne, a Jeanne, a Georges, a Pierre or a Marie, or even their English equivalents. Only versions of his own names were passed on - Louis, Louisa and John (Jean). Furthermore, his children were all given typically British names. This deliberate act, in not adopting his family names, is the most telling sign that Louis wanted nothing to do with his family or his homeland once he had left them.

What Louis did after leaving home has been construed in a variety of fanciful accounts. It has been suggested that he left Ispagnac to escape military service in the *milice*, or local militia, but this is very unlikely. France was not at war at this time, nor had there been any notable civil insurrections in the region, such as those of the *Camisards*, for fifty years. If he had been selected for the *milice*, he would have been allowed to stay at home and his duties would have been no more arduous than to attend the odd parade. Of course, there was always the risk, in the event of war, that the members of the *milice* could be sent to fight in some foreign land.

A different Jean Bazalgette from Léon's grandfather, a French relative who was a journalist and used the pen-name 'Jean Bazal', wrote what he called a *roman*, (*Mon Ancêtre Jean Louis: Compagnon De La Fayette*) which purports to be Louis' life story. While entertaining and full of action it bears little relation to fact.

In those days, Ispagnac was charged with providing eight young men annually for the *milice* and it is true that they were chosen by drawing lots. According to Bazal, Louis drew a 'black number', meaning that he had been selected to serve, so to escape this he sneaked off and lived in a cave in the mountains for seven years or so before emerging in 1777 to accompany the Marquis de Lafayette on his first voyage to America. Apart from the lack of necessity to avoid the draft, already referred to, Lafayette's memoirs tell us that he was accompanied on the *Victoire* by the Marquis de Kalb and some twelve hand-picked young French officers; it does not look as if there would have been a place for a draft-dodger. As these officers were carefully chosen it is unlikely that Louis could have been posing as one of them, and the manifests of the port of Bordeaux record no Bazalgettes embarking there during that period, although we cannot rule out the possibility that he embarked under a false name. However, the idea that Louis was prepared to become an outlaw to avoid being sent to fight abroad, and then, after a few years, actually did this very thing makes little sense.

For a young man with the lofty ambitions which we know Louis possessed, his small and shabby home town with its stifling *petit bourgeoisie* would have had absolutely nothing to offer. He therefore had to leave it to seek his fortune in the world.

Louis has been described as a Huguenot, but this is not strictly speaking correct. The Edict of Nantes afforded to French Protestants some protection from Roman Catholic persecution, but when it was revoked in 1685, at least one hundred thousand of them, i.e., the Huguenots, fled France for the protestant countries of northern Europe. Louis, as he was not fleeing from religious persecution, was not one of them. Of course, the Huguenots who had migrated to London a century before Louis had established their own communities and churches, for instance in Spitalfields, and had brought their skills with them, such as silk weaving. Therefore, Louis would later deal with Huguenots on a daily basis and would have moved easily in their circles.

Although it is possible that Louis travelled to the Americas as a young man, no evidence has been found that he did so, or that he fought at the battle of Brandywine in 1777 (when we can show that he was in London) or that he set up a string of fur-trading posts, as Jean Bazal relates. In order to have established himself as a London tailor and a silk merchant by 1775, Louis could not have been gallivanting about the Caribbean or North America for five years. He had to have been learning his trade, building up clientele and connections and getting his business firmly established. It was Jean Bazal who wrote that 'he exchanged wool for silk', and this was obviously the case. He is very likely to have entered a firm of silk merchants or high-class tailors. Although Ispagnac was more 'wool' country, the Cévennes at that time was still a silk producing area of France, so Louis would have had no difficulty in learning about the silk business.

It is possible that Louis first found his way to Lyon, which was the silk production capital of France and was not very far away from Ispagnac. His family probably had contacts there. Perhaps after a year or so in Lyon he graduated to Paris and began exporting silks, embroidered waistcoat shapes and maybe finished garments to England. Or maybe he headed straight to Paris. Indeed, the archives at Lyon have no record of anyone of this name being registered as a journeyman there during that time. He must have had great flair as a clothes designer, and to have been very familiar with all of the different materials available. Most of the silks which found their way to England were smuggled across the Channel, since avoidance of customs duty was extremely prevalent at the time. Louis probably travelled to England as a merchant several times before deciding to settle there. He may have managed to become a master tailor in Paris, but it seems he did not do so on arriving in London, at least according to the records of the Company of Merchant Taylors. If he started there more as a merchant, he would probably have made enough money to open his first shop. As a business proprietor, he did not need to be a guild-registered master tailor. In any case, his business was outside the City of London and therefore was not under the Company's jurisdiction.

Louis may have seen revolution or war on the horizon and decided that London was a better place to achieve his ambitions. There is certainly evidence that he had trading connections with Paris, and his daughter Louisa was placed in a convent there later. He also had dealings with the Swiss bankers Perregaux in Paris, who later became the famous house of Lafitte.

Louis Bazalgette's down-to-earth origin in a rugged but beautiful part of France, and the religious, ethnic and cultural values which he would take with him into the outside world would give him the single-mindedness, enterprise and drive to take him to the very top of his chosen profession. His Cévenol tenacity and the long family tradition in his business meant that he was better-equipped than most to achieve his ambitions.

France before the revolution was a mainly feudal country, with a massive divide between the nobility and the peasants. Louis must have recognized that England was a relatively more equable society, and that the opportunities for advancement there were much better than in his homeland.

Chapter 3: 1775-78

Although Britain and her American colonies had traditionally been on good terms, the disparity between what the average Briton paid in taxes at home (twenty-six shillings per year) and what the colonists paid (about one shilling) caused the British prime minister George Grenville to raise taxes in America. This he did by imposing the Stamp Act in 1765. The colonists resented this imposition on many grounds, not least of which was their lack of representation in the Mother of Parliaments. Following their protests and a boycott of British goods the Stamp Act was repealed the following year. In 1767 Britain used another tactic, which was to impose duties on many imports into the colonies. The main opposition to this was in Boston, where protests and rioting occurred. The British government backed off again and in 1770 repealed all duties except for that on tea, for the main reason that the East India Company was in financial trouble and needed the revenue. This became a symbol of the colonists' resistance to British rule, and in 1773, the Bostonians dumped 342 chests of tea, worth about £4,000, into the harbour. From then on, parliament imposed yet more punitive measures including in 1774 placing Massachusetts under military rule. Relations between the two countries could never recover from these moves on both sides, and by 1775 a state of war existed. The colonists' war effort was supported by loans from France, which were not all repaid. In London, the merchants petitioned parliament for a reconciliation in January 1775 because their trade was hurt and more seriously they were now unable to recover the large debts owed to them by the colonists, particularly by wealthy plantation owners.

The London in which Louis Bazalgette arrived was therefore a city preoccupied with how to deal with the colonists, and although politicians such as Burke and Wilkes supported them the overwhelming attitude of the King and his parliament was that the uprising must be put down at all costs. The result of this policy was a bloody war into which other countries of Europe would soon be drawn, and which created the circumstances leading towards the French Revolution and the Napoleonic wars. It is unlikely that many saw this coming.

What follows is strong evidence that Louis Bazalgette arrived in London and set up shop in 1775. When interviewed by the Parliamentary Commission looking into the Prince of Wales' debts in 1795, Louis said he had been in England for twenty years and had worked for the Prince for seventeen years, which would mean that he arrived in 1775 and started to work for the Prince in 1778, when the latter was about sixteen. Louis himself said later that he served the Prince of Wales for over thirty-two years, which would cover the years 1778-1810 or at the latest 1780-1812.

In order to be recommended to the Prince of Wales, Louis must have been well connected. He certainly seems to have been the Prince's principal tailor, at least in the earlier years. In a court case reported in *The Times* in 1794, characteristically to recover a debt, he described himself as 'Taylor to the Prince of Wales'. No other accounts mention him at all, although Christopher Hibbert in his *George IV, Prince of Wales* gives his name in passing, as does Arthur Aspinall, in his *Correspondence of George, Prince of Wales, 1770-1812*, when listing the Prince's creditors. Some authors have stated that John Weston was the Prince's favourite tailor, but this seems not to have been the case until later when, by 1795, the Prince had fallen more under the influence of his young friend George Bryan 'Beau' Brummell. The men who were then known as dandies favoured the English look and used English-style tailors. Before Brummell appeared on the scene, the Prince mostly preferred the very gaudy clothes affected by the fops, which were more of the French style and which Louis naturally was well qualified to supply. Although the Prince later started to dress more like a dandy, he always retained a great love for rich and colourful outfits, particularly uniforms of his own design.

Louis would have had an efficient operation importing the finest silks and other cloth from France, and possibly also linens from Amsterdam. British cloth was usually cheaper and was ordered if it was of the required quality. He would have designed the outfits himself, with considerable assistance from the Prince of course, and had them made up in his own workshop by a staff of journeyman tailors and finishers. He stated himself that he always delivered the clothes personally to the Prince at Carlton House. One theory the author holds is that Louis may have initially been supplying costumes to the London theatres. While in earlier times actors had been content with costumes handed down from the nobility, they were by now demanding exotic custom-made outfits in order to make a splash on stage. On 24 April 1781, Prince George wrote to his brother Frederick in Hanover, in response to the latter's requests for some special suits of clothes, which he could not obtain locally.

> Ye hair in ye chain is mine. Yr Vandyke dress is compleat and beautiful; ye hat for it I have ordered of Cater; it was made by ye tailor of Covent Garden Theatre. Ye ruff belonging to it is separate from ye whole and ties with two little white strings and tassels. I do not mean it is a ruff but lace; it is an imitation only, but very beautiful and in ye shape of our shirt collars, only deeper. Remember yr shirt collar or stock must not appear in this dress; you had therefore best not wear any stock at all & tuck your collar down or under.
> [Aspinall; Correspondence of the Prince of Wales, Vol I]

He added in a later letter that the Vandyke dress was sent and also one of lilac 'with pale buff puffs and knots' because 'we considered yt if there was to be a masquerade in ye summer season you could not well wear yt dress.'

We have not so far been able to discover if Louis was 'ye tailor of Covent Garden Theatre'. His name does not appear in the theatre's account books for 1780-1. If he was, it would certainly have brought him to the attention of the Prince, who was an avid theatregoer. Louis was also often later required to make masquerade costumes for the Prince and his friends, and a knowledge of theatrical costume would have helped him with this. Louis had another theatrical connection in that he later lent money to (and made suits for) Richard Brinsley Sheridan, the politician, playwright and co-owner of the Drury Lane Theatre.

There is an anecdote which appears to tell us how Louis found his way into the Prince's favour. This story first appeared in *Chambers' Journal*, published in 1874 by Robert and William Chambers. Where Chambers got the story from is unfortunately unknown.

A FORTUNE MADE BY A WAISTCOAT. Some people have a fancy for fine waistcoats. This taste was more common in my young days than it is now. Stirring public events were apt to be celebrated by patterns on waistcoats to meet the popular fancy. I remember that the capture of Mauritius, at the close of 1810, was followed by a fashion for wearing waistcoats speckled over with small figures shaped like that island, and called Isle of France waistcoats. It was a galling thing for the French prisoners of war on parole to be confronted with these demonstrations. At court highly ornamented waistcoats have been the fashion for generations. George, Prince of Wales, while Regent, was noted for his affection for this rich variety of waistcoats, and thereby hangs a tale. His Royal Highness had an immense desire for a waistcoat of a particular kind, for which he could discover only a small piece of stuff insufficient in dimensions. It was a French material, and could not be matched in England. The war was raging, and to procure the requisite quantity of stuff from Paris was declared to be impracticable.

At this juncture one of the Prince's attendants interposed. He said he knew a Frenchman, M. Bazalgette, carrying on business in one of the obscure streets of London, who, he was certain, would undertake to proceed to Paris and bring away what was wanted. This obliging tailor was forthwith commissioned to do his best to procure the requisite material. Finding that a chance had occurred for distinguishing himself and laying the foundation of his fortune, the Frenchman resolved to make the attempt. It was a hazardous affair, for there was no regular communication with the coast of France, unless for letters

under a cartel. Yet, Bazalgette was not daunted. If only he could land safely in a boat, all would be right. This, with some difficulty and manoeuvring, he effected. As a pretended refugee back to his own country, he was allowed to land and proceed to Paris. Joyfully he was able to procure the quantity of material required for the Prince Regent's waistcoat; and not less joyfully did he manage to return to London with the precious piece of stuff wrapped round his person. The waistcoat was made, and so was the tailor's fortune and that of his family.
[Chambers' Journal, Volume 51; Robert Chambers, William Chambers - 1874]

This is a variant of the above story, which is probably just a rewrite:

When George, Prince of Wales, was Regent, fashion prevailed for gaily decorated waistcoats. A particular pattern was wanted for his Royal Highness, but it was not in any leading tailor's stock. It did not seem possible to obtain it. The stuff was of French manufacture, and the two countries were at war. But "The First Gentleman in Europe" was determined to have his whim gratified, and a member of his suite suggested the means. He said that he knew a Frenchman in London, poor and obscure, but enterprising. If the order were given, M. Bazalgette would almost certainly fulfill it. Accordingly the Court commands were sent to the struggling tailor, and he saw the promise of fortune in the stray commission. All ordinary communication with France was cut off, but Bazalgette formed his own plans. One day he appeared in a boat off the coast of his native land in the assumed character of a refugee. He was kindly received, and sent on his way to Paris. Once there he soon procured the material he required. Shaping it into a makeshift garment for himself, he brought it off without creating suspicion; and, making his way as cleverly back, the waistcoat was speedily produced. The deed set the man on his feet, and ultimately ensured him a competence.

[Manchester Courier and Lancashire General Advertiser, Saturday 11 July 1891, reprinted from Cassell's Saturday Journal]

This story is fascinating for several reasons. Not only is it the only anecdote so far seen which names Louis, but it is believable, although probably somewhat dramatized, and it conforms very well with Louis's character and motivation. It would presumably have happened in 1778-9, since after that Louis was established as the Prince's tailor and would not have had to be pointed out by 'an attendant'. The story also reinforces the view that Louis was seen as a merchant as well as a tailor.

The American War of Independence having begun in 1775, France and Spain seized the opportunity also to declare war on England in 1778. It therefore fits that the 'war was raging' at the time this incident took place. A *cartel* is defined as 'an unarmed ship employed in the exchange of prisoners, or in carrying propositions to an enemy: a ship bearing a flag of truce and privileged from capture'. So Louis' use of such a vessel for this purpose would have been dangerous and too open to scrutiny. Therefore the need to use a small boat and to travel clandestinely was essential.

It is unknown in which 'obscure street of London' Louis had his premises before 1778-9, but South Molton Street (where we know he was in residence by 1779) would probably not have been regarded as 'obscure'. If Louis had become a master tailor in France, which it seems likely he would have aspired to be, he could have started in London with a firm of tailors, although there is no record of him becoming a partner in such a firm, which would have given him the wherewithal to branch out and open his own shop. If this was in an 'obscure street' it would have been harder for him to become an eminent tailor in a couple of years. Therefore, the most likely course he would have taken was to build up his capital as a merchant first.

There is a shadier side to the waistcoat story; if Louis was known to be the sort of cove who would be willing to undertake such a mission it implies that he knew the ropes of the smuggling business. At the time, smuggling was a national industry, and it has been estimated that only a small proportion of goods imported actually had duty paid on them. Smuggling was connived at by all classes, and even if Louis was not himself actively a smuggler it is likely that he was well aware that most of the silks and lace he sold were contraband. He had two partners, Thomas Smith and Peter De Nedonsel, of whom more later, who might have been much more deeply involved. The latter was born in the Pas de Calais and could therefore have handled the French side.

Eighteenth century smugglers were known for the ingenious stratagems that they used to avoid detection of their contraband goods. These included towing waterproof containers up rivers beneath the surface, and of course wrapping yards of silk round their bodies. The following story illustrates the lengths to which they would go.

> A most remarkabe seizure was lately made by Mr. Tankard, of Dartford. The captain of a ship, whose wife died abroad, brought home a coffin, in which was supposed to be the remains of his once beloved wife. It was suffered to be taken on shore without searching, and the *lady* lay in state for several days before she was interred; however, at last, a hearse was prepared and two mourning coaches attended with the relations of the deceased, and the procession moved on slowly towards Stepney, where the coffin was deposited. About twelve o'clock at night, Mr. Tankard and his man coming by the church-yard, observed some men a-digging, and a cart standing by; they watched the motions of those *resurrection*-men, and presently saw them open the coffin and take out the *body*, which consisted of upwards of 500 pieces of muslin and various other contraband articles. Mr. Tankard suffered them to proceed to with their *corpse* till they came to Ratcliff-Cross, where he got assistance and seized the whole. [*The Times* 27 June 1786]

French silks were in hot demand for two main reasons. Firstly, the designs were desired by a rich clientele hungry for all things French. Secondly, the quality of the fabric and the advances in broadloom weaving technology in France (such as the Jacquard loom and its precursors) meant in most cases a far superior product. The best designers and embroiderers were in Lyon. The Lyonnais weavers, or *canuts*, were miserably paid and suffered from poor working conditions. The Huguenots who had since the late seventeenth century made their home in Spitalfields mostly arrived there with very little, having been driven from their own country, with their possessions being forfeited. They therefore owned fewer of the large and complicated looms necessary for the most intricate broadcloth weaving of satins and velvets. In Lyon the looms and the skilled men to operate them continued to exist in profusion, without the disruption which the Spitalfields weavers had experienced.

We should now have enough evidence to pinpoint the year when Louis first began to supply clothes to the Prince of Wales. The Prince's letters talking about clothes he had ordered in 1781, together with the 'waistcoat' story tend to indicate a date of 1780 or thereabouts. It is unlikely that it was much earlier than that because the Prince, although he was already obsessed with clothes, must have had less freedom to buy them before his eighteenth birthday. Following that he had a little more licence, since he was no longer confined in Kew or Windsor, and now had his own establishment, but he still had to live in his apartments in Buckingham House, where his father could keep an eye on him. The King attempted to maintain some control over him, but privately expressed misgivings that should he lay down the law the Prince would simply refuse to obey him. The Prince recognized however that he was to an extent still under the King's thumb, because soon after he became eighteen he said to his uncle, the Duke of Cumberland, that in three years he would have his majority and would be able to do whatever he liked.

The accounts prepared by Louis which still exist show that in the second half of 1786 the Prince ordered clothes from him to the value of £1,628/10/1. In the whole of 1787 his bill came to £4,369/10/2. Since 1787 was the peak spending year that we have seen in these accounts we can extrapolate that the total for 1786 was about £4,000 or a little less. We have no way of knowing whether the Prince's bills started lower and steadily climbed every year, or whether in fact they were previously the same, or even higher, but if we assume an average of £3,000 per year for these earlier years this would take us back to approximately 1780 as the first year. When the Prince's first major debt crisis occurred in 1785-6, the amount he owed Louis was £16,774/3/2. Using the average yearly sum above, this could be the total of about five years of debts. Presumably the Prince must have paid at least some of Louis' bills out of his allowance during this time, otherwise it is hard to imagine how Louis could have stayed in business, considering his very considerable outgoings. If this is the case, it does tend to point to a commencement year closer to 1778.

The list below shows the Prince's total quarterly and annual expenditure on clothes supplied by Louis between July 1786 and April 1795:-

    1786 (second half only).....£1628/10/1
    1787...............................£4369/10/2
    1788...............................£3967/4/1
    1789...............................£3528/16/5
    1790...............................£2451/15/5
    1791...............................£1771/2/11
    1792...............................£1582/18/6
    1793...............................£723/4/9
    1794...............................£1053/6/10 plus £442/8/6 in Livery Account
    1795 (first half only).............£659/18/5 plus £47/14/9 in Livery Account

It can be seen that having apparently peaked in 1787 the annual totals slowly fell as time went on. In 1787 the Prince's debts had been paid, so any brakes on spending were off again. The slow annual decline in the amounts Prinny spent with Louis is probably owing to the fact that his debts to Louis had been notified to Parliament, and the amounts were secured as debenture bonds, which legally had to be repaid on a regular basis. The Prince would therefore have begun to patronize as many other tailors as he could run up bills with, because these debts would *not* have been known to Parliament.

There are of course many anecdotes about the Prince and his self-indulgence, particularly in the matter of dress.

> ... If any doubt survived as to whether the Prince was worthy to be enrolled amongst that select body of dandies which arrogated to itself the direction of the fashionable world this was soon dispelled by the costume he donned at the first Court ball he attended. His coat was pink silk with white cuffs, we are told his waistcoat was white silk embroidered with various coloured foil and adorned with a profusion of French paste, his hat was ornamented with two rows of steel beads five thousand in number with a button and loop of the same metal and cocked in a new military style. Could anything have been more elaborate? One would think not until descriptions are found of his attire on subsequent occasions. Thus we learn when he took his seat in the House of Lords he wore a black velvet suit richly embroidered with gold and pink spangles and lined with pink satin, and shoes with pink heels a la Macaroni of an earlier era while to give appropriate finish to the costume his hair was pressed much at the side and very full frizzed with two small curls at the bottom. But Prince Florizel was not yet at the end of his resource and to prove that in this matter he could out-Herod Herod he devised a costume for a Brighton ball that dazzled all beholders. He made his appearance in a velvet suit of a dark colour with green stripes embroidered down the front and seams with silver flowers, a waistcoat of white and silver tissue similarly ornamented, the ribbon of the Garter fastened with a shoulder knot of brilliants and the usual accessories of the stars of various other Orders. Even the imagination of the heir apparent could go no further and he rested content the most over dressed man of his day! Expense being no object to George since for what he could not pay he was content to owe...
> [Benjamin, Louis Saul; The Beaux of the Regency]

The Regent was singularly imbued with petty royal pride. He would rather be amiable and familiar with his tailor than agreeable and friendly with the most illustrious of the aristocracy of Great Britain...
[Gronow, Rees Howell; Reminiscences of Captain Gronow]

When I was presented to (him), HRH the Prince Regent (was) in the uniform of the Hussars, viz. a yellow jacket, pink pantaloons and silver lace morocco boots and a light blue pelisse lined with ermine. The Prince himself (was) the model of grace and elegance in his time, in a coat of which the waist buttons were placed between his shoulder blades and which if worn by a man now would cause boys to hoot him in Pall Mall...
[W. M. Thackeray; Sketches and travels in London]

In this the last year of his life the country will be gratified in knowing that his tailor's bill was between £4,000 and £5,000 and he was employed in devising new dresses for the guards. The subject of a dress for the guards evidently grew upon his Majesty's mind, for a month later we find a record to effect that no council had been held as the King was occupied in altering the uniforms of the guards and has coats with various colors submitted to him every day. The Duke of Cumberland assists him and this is his occupation. He sees much more of his tailor than he does of his ministers...
[Banvard, John; The Private Life of a King Embodying the Suppressed Memoirs of the Prince of Wales]

His morning levees were not attended by men of science and of genius who could have instilled into his mind some wholesome notions of practical economy, but the tailor, the upholsterer, the jeweller and the shoemaker were the regular attendants on a royal Prince's morning recreations. ...The cut of a coat became of greater consequence than the amelioration of the condition of Ireland; and the tie of a neckcloth, an object of greater importance than parliamentary reform, or the adjustment of our disputes

with America. The morning hours which a patriotic prince would have employed in devising measures for the good of the country, were idled away with a favourite tailor, taking measures of the royal person, and receiving his valuable information on the decided superiority of loose trousers to tight pantaloons. The different uniforms of the army became also, at this time, the peculiar objects of the gracious attention of the Prince Regent; and our brothers of York and Cumberland were called in to describe the trappings and fopperies of the German soldiery, the introduction of which into the British army (setting aside the expense to the nation) has rendered some of the men the laughing-stock of the public.
[Huish, Robert; Memoirs of George the Fourth, 1830]

There is even a story that the Prince's tailor (surely Louis) was summoned from his bed one night to bail his employer out:

In the month of April 1784 his royal Highness and three of his gay companions, elated with the bottle, were interrupted by the watch in a midnight frolic and after a scuffle overpowered and taken to the watch house in Mount-street. The party were obliged to send for one of their tradesmen, who on entering started at the sight of the Prince. The constable and watchmen, on discovering the rank of their prisoner, pressed round him and hoped his royal highness would not be offended at their having detained him. The Prince, who was only elevated with wine exclaimed:- "Offended! My good fellows! - By no means. - Thank God, the laws of this country are superior to rank; and when men of high station forget the decorum of the community it is fit that no distinction should be made with respect to them. It should make an Englishman proud to see the Prince of Wales obliged to send for a tailor to bail him."
[B. C. Walpole, Richard Brinsley Sheridan; Recollections of the life of the late Right Honorable Charles James Fox]

The above anecdote reinforces the Prince's trust of Louis. The watch-house stood at the west end of the large workhouse between Nos 101 and 102 Mount Street, close to the southern end of Charles Street. From Louis' house in Lower Grosvenor Street it was no more than a five-minute ride. Louis would have come by coach, not only for security's sake, since he was carrying bail-money, but because he would also be able to ferry the miscreants to their homes if necessary. No doubt Louis was his usual discreet self and said nothing about the incident, but to the 'charlies' - the members of the watch - it was too good a story not to be told later in the alehouse.

Chapter 4: 18th Century Tailoring and its Ancillary Trades

There were many ancillary trades upon which the Georgian tailor depended. A fascinating book on the subject of London tradesmen, though written thirty years before Louis's time, nevertheless provides us with a succinct and witty insight into the trades practised during the Georgian period. This book is: *The London Tradesman, being a Compendious view of All the Trades, Professions, Arts both Liberal and Mechanic, now practised in the Cities of London and Westminster*, by Robert Campbell, Esq. Such books are quite uncommon, since authors on the subject usually did not state the obvious or direct their remarks to the people who really needed to know the facts, such as the parents of prospective apprentices, and us of course. His puff on the title page, declaiming: 'THE WHOLE Delivered in an Easy, Familiar Style, suitable to the meanest Capacity, and containing RULES worthy the Knowledge and Observation of PERSONS OF ALL RANKS who are Entrusted with the Settlement of YOUTH' sums up his target audience precisely. The author was not burdened by what we now term *Political Correctness*, particularly when speaking of *Women* and *Frenchmen*, but his remarks about them seem intended more to amuse than to be unkind.

Firstly amongst the trades related to tailoring, as described by Campbell, was the pattern drawer who drew patterns for 'the Callico Printers, the Embroiderers, Quilters, Lace Workers and several little branches belonging to Women's Apparel'. Our interest is mainly that they designed patterns which were used for embroidered shapes, which were then made into the foreparts of coats and waistcoats. The next trade listed was that of the lace-man. Without referring to this book one might assume, as the author did, that by 'lace' was meant the point, pillow or bobbin lace made from fine linen or cotton yarns by women in various places in Europe such as Brussels, a famous trade in England being that centred round Honiton, in Devonshire. However, Prinny did not much wear this kind of lace, but his obsession with military uniforms should give us a clue. This lace was that made of gold and silver threads, as used for either cloth-of-gold or tissue, which nowadays we would call *lamé*, or the elaborate decorations applied to military dress uniforms.

As Campbell described it:

> The Lace Shop is furnished with all sorts of Gold and Silver Lace, Gold and Silver Buttons, Shapes for Waistcoats, Lace and Network for Robeings and Women's Petticoats, Fringes, Bugles, Spangles, Plates for Embroidery and Orrice, and Bone Lace Weavers, Gold and Silver Wire, Purle, Sleysy, Twist &c. A Lace-Man must have a well-lined Pocket to furnish his shop; but his Garrets may be as meanly equipped as he pleases. His chief Talent ought to lie in a nice Taste in Patterns of Lace, &c. He ought to speak fluently, though not elegantly, to entertain the Ladies; and to be Master of a handsome Bow and Cringe; should be able to hand a Lady to and from her Coach politely, without being seized with the Palpitation of the Heart at the Touch of a delicate Hand, a well-turned and much exposed Limb or a handsome Face: But, above all, he must have Confidence to refuse his goods in a handsome Manner to the extravagant Beau who never pays, and Patience as well as Stock to bear the Delays of the sharping Peer, who pays but seldom. With these natural Qualifications, five Thousand Pounds in his Pocket, and a Set of good Customers in View, a young man may commence Lace-Man. If he trusts moderately, and with Discretion, lives with Oeconomy, and minds his Business more than his Mistress, he may live to increase his Stock; but otherwise I know no readier Road to a Jail, and Destruction, than a Lace-Man's Business.

Campbell's allusions to the 'extravagant Beau who never pays' and the 'sharping Peer, who pays but seldom' are most perceptive as we know. His remark that the lace-man should be immune to feminine charms surely applied to all such tradesmen, though the high value of the lace-man's stock seems to make this more important to him in Campbell's view.

The main tradesman who served the lace-man was the wire-drawer. Silver wire was drawn as it was, but to make gold wire the silver wire was double-gilded. Even though it was drawn out to the finest thread, the gold plating was so ductile that it remained on the silver wire. The metal was obtained as a rod, and forced through continually smaller dies until it became wire. When thin enough, the wire could be wound on to a spindle and drawn through the die. To make gold or silver thread (sleysy), the wire was passed through rollers to flatten it and a silk thread would then have the wire twisted round it, a similar process to making gimp or the bass strings of a guitar. Purle was made by twisting the wire together and was much used for button-making and embroidery. 'A moist Hand cannot be employed in this work; and it requires much Care to preserve it from tarnishing, and much Experience to complete the Workman... Women are employed in this as well as Men, and may earn Twelve or Fifteen Shillings a Week honestly; but they are much given to pilfering the Stuff, and have a Trick of moistening the Silk to make up the Deficiency in Weight.'

The next trade described was the orrice-weaver, who appears to have made on a loom much of the patterned decoration applied to military uniforms. The bone-lace maker used the traditional hand pillow lace-making techniques, often to augment the work of the orrice-weaver. Campbell's opinion was that the French were much better at both of these types of lace then the British.

The next employee of the lace-man was the silver and gold button-maker, to whom the lace-man supplied all the materials except the moulds, and who would buy back the resulting buttons.

Campbell's book is liberally laced with warnings against the evils of *Women*, *Drink* and *Gambling*, with which pleasures of course the average provincial apprentice would want to lose no time in becoming acquainted on his arrival in London.

The lace-man additionally used the services of the spangle, bugle and button-ring maker. Spangles were made from gold and silver, previously beaten almost as thin as gold-leaf. Striking the leaf with a hammer on a round hollow stake produced a disc. Modern spangles and sequins are very cheap by comparison, being made of plastic. The same technique as was used to make spangles was used to strike button rings. The fringe, frog and tassel-maker was also employed by the lace-man. 'Some of the Button-Makers perform the Work; but it is chiefly done by Women, upon the Hand, who make a very handsome Livelihood of it, if they are not initiated into the Mystery of Gin-Drinking'.

Campbell next described the craft of embroidery, which was used to an enormous extent in Prinny's clothes. He merely stated that it was usually performed by women, and that they mostly did not have the skill to create their own designs, relying chiefly on those produced by the pattern-drawers. Finally there was the livery-lace-weaver, who specialized in coats of arms and other such emblems for the uniforms of pages and other servants, being made on a similar loom to that used by the orrice-weaver. The embroiderer whom Louis mainly used was Peter (Pierre) Chomel, for whom he held a separate bond with the Prince of Wales.

The lace-man therefore had to make use of a varied workforce to produce all of the articles he was expected to supply. According to the accounts in the Royal Archives, Louis' lace-man was probably Louis de St. Farre, for whom he held a separate bond with the Prince, like Peter Chomel's, which would ensure that he would be paid. At that time the Abbé de St. Farre, a cousin of the Duc d'Orleans, was in London as an émigré, accompanied by his brother, and it seems they and their friends so hogged the gaming tables at Almack's that the regular punters could scarcely get a look-in. *The Times* of 14 March 1793 complained bitterly that 'the Banking Ladies of St. James's-square, do not feel themselves much obliged to the Abbé de St. Farre, and his brother, for introducing so many noble Emigrants to their houses. These people come with their crown pieces and half guineas, and absolutely form a circle round the Faro tables, to the total exclusion of our English Lords and Ladies, who can scarcely go one *punt* during a whole evening.' The St. Farre name is unusual enough that Louis de St Farre may have been that brother. If so, his love of gaming boded ill for his business.

Taking Campbell's trades in the order in which they appeared, we now come to his descriptions of the tailor proper, stating that

> Mr. Fashioner is not such a despicable Animal as the World imagines; that he is really a useful Member in Society, and consequently that, though according to the vulgar saying, it takes nine Taylors to make one Man, yet you may pick up nine men out of ten who cannot make a compleat Taylor. A Master-tailor ought to have a quick Eye to steal the Cut of a Sleeve, the Pattern of a Flap, or the Shape of a good Trimming, at a glance : any Bungler may cut out a Shape when he has a Pattern before him; but a good Workman takes it by his Eye in the passing of a Chariot, or in the Space between the Door and a Coach: he must be able not only to cut for the Handsome and Well-shaped, but bestow a good Shape where Nature has not granted it: he must make the Clothes sit easy in spite of a stiff Gait or awkward Air : his Hand and Head must go together: he must be a nice Cutter, and finish his Work with Elegance.

This vivid and poetic description is heart-warming in the way that he champions the tailor in general, even deftly defining those qualities which distinguish a great tailor, such as Louis, from the common herd of the merely competent.

Under the master tailor there were the senior journeymen appointed as foremen, who stood in for the master when he was absent, measuring the customers, doing the cutting and ensuring that the finished work was delivered. They enjoyed the best wages, tips and 'cabbage' - the scraps of material which could not be used but which they could nevertheless sell.

> The next Class, is the mere working Taylor; not one in ten of them knows how to cut out a Pair of Breeches: They are employed only to sew the Seam, to cast the Button Holes, and prepare the Work for the Finisher. Their Wages, by Act of Parliament, is twenty pence in one Season of the

> Year, and Half a Crown the other; however, a good Hand has Half a Crown and three Shillings: They are as numerous as Locusts, are out of Business about three or four Months in the Year, and generally as poor as Rats: The House of Call runs away with their Earnings, and keeps them constantly in Debt and Want. The House of Call is an Ale-house, where they generally use, and the Landlord knows where to find them, and Masters go there to enquire when they want Hands. Custom has established it into a Kind of Law, that The House of Call gives them Credit for Victuals and Drink, while they are unemployed; this obliges the Journeyman on the other Hand, to spend all the Money they earn at this House alone. The Landlord, when once he has got them into his Debt, is sure to keep them so, and by that Means binds the poor Wretch to his House, who slaves only to enrich the Publican.

This is a biased view of the 'house of call' which was used as a meeting place by the 'combinations' or trades unions, and therefore helped them to organize and retain solidarity. There is probably however some truth in Campbell's remark.

> But enough of the Taylor, let us treat a little of those Branches who are employed by him, or with whom he deals. The Woollen-Draper is the first; he furnishes him with Broad Cloths, Linings &c. This Tradesman buys his goods from *Blackwell-Hall* Factory, or from the Clothiers in the West of *England*. They buy their Cloths of one Colour, white from the Hall, in long and short Pieces, and have them dressed and dyed in Town; but mixed Colours, or such Blues as are dyed in the Wool, they buy ready dressed. They not only serve the Taylor here in *London*, by Retail, but the Country Shops Wholesale.

The 'dressing' that Campbell refers to no doubt included 'fulling'. This was a two-stage process, during the first stage of which the cloth was soaked in a weak lye or soapy bath, which de-greased the wool, shrank it and caused the fibres to be more receptive to 'felling'. In this second process the cloth was beaten with wooden mallets, either by hand or in a mill, which consolidated the cloth. The result was that the cloth was thicker, denser and more weather-resistant, and was therefore suitable for use as heavy coating. In Roman times fulling was a single-stage process, in which the cloth was put into baths of urine and trampled by slaves.

> The Mercer is the Twin Brother of the Woollen-Draper, they are as like one another as two Eggs, only the Woollen-Draper deals chiefly with the Men, and is the graver Animal of the two, and the Mercer traficks most with the Ladies, and has a small Dash of their Effeminacy in his Constitution. The Mercer deals in Silks, Velvets, Brocades and an innumerable Train of expensive Trifles, for the Ornament of the Fair Sex; he must be a very polite Man, and skilled in all the Punctilio's of City-good-breeding; he ought, by no means, to be an awkward clumsy Fellow, such a Creature would turn a Lady's Stomach, when they go their Rounds, to tumble Silks that they have no mind to buy. He must dress neatly, and affect a Court Air, however far distant he may live from St. *James's*. I know of none so fit for that Branch of Business, as that nimble, dancing, talkative Nation the *French*. Our Mercer must have a great deal of the *Frenchman* in his Manners, as well as a large Parcel of *French* Goods in his Shop; he ought to keep close Intelligence with the Fashion-Office at *Paris*, and supply himself with the newest Patterns from that changeable People. Nothing that is mere *English* goes down with our modern Ladies; from their Shift to their Topknots they must be equipped from Dear *Paris*.

Campbell's opinion of Frenchmen was very typical at the time. It goes without saying that Louis was not only *French*, but also a woollen-draper and a mercer, as well as a tailor. Campbell's disparaging view of the fashionable Fair Sex is stereotypical but still appears affectionately meant.

The haberdasher supplied the tailor with buckram, wadding, plying, hair-cloths, buttons, mohair, silk, thread, stay-tape, binding and every other article used for trimming, except gold and silver lace. Louis presumably dealt with his father-in-law Philipe Métivier for haberdashery. Campbell completed his descriptions of the tailoring and ancillary trades with:

> The Silk Weaver is mostly employed in *London*; Stuffs, Broad Cloths are chiefly made in the Cloathing Counties of *England*, and the Linnen is the Manufacture of *Scotland, Ireland, France and Germany*. The *Spittlefield* Weavers are a numerous Body. The plain Silk weaver requires but little Ingenuity, but the Weavers of flowered Silks, Damasks, Brocades and Velvets are very ingenious Tradesmen; these ought to learn Drawing to design their own Patterns, the Want of which gives the *French* Workmen the greatest Advantage over us. Were our Weavers as expert in designing as their Rivals, the Weavers in *Spittlefields* need not be obliged to send out to *Paris* for new Patterns.

These inter-relationships between the different trades show us that tailoring at the time was a complex business, requiring considerable acumen in the co-ordination of supplies and services.

Chapter 5: 1779-84

Louis Bazalgette was well established in London by 1779. As already mentioned, he took a house and shop at 18, South Molton Street, Mayfair, which remained his premises until 1784. On Saturday, 14 August 1779, Louis was married to Catherine Métivier at the Anglican church of St. George's Hanover Square, which was already regarded as the most fashionable church in Westminster. The parish register entry reads: 'John Louis Bazalgette and Catherine Métivier, a Minor, both of this Parish were married in this Church by Licence by and with the consent of Philip Métivier the natural and lawful father of the said Minor this fourteenth day of August in the year 1779.' The register was signed by John Louis Bazalgette, Catherine Métivier, Philip Métivier, G. Gaubert, Joseph (or John) Mead and Francis Bagne. Catherine was a minor, i.e., under twenty-one, but although we have not found a record of her birth it is likely that she was twenty or less, based on her parents' marriage date.

Philip (or Philipe) Métivier may have been related to Paul Métivier, a merchant in London, who dealt in furs, cloth, wool, hat making materials, etc., between about 1760 and 1783. He figures in the Hudson's Bay Company's list of buyers at their London fur auctions. Paul was naturalised in 1762. Philipe was initially described as a wool merchant and spinner, later as a haberdasher and hosier, living and doing business at 29, New Bond Street, which was at that time the most fashionable street patronised by the fops and dandies. Today, No 29, re-numbered to No 31 in the early nineteenth century, is occupied by Hublot, the manufacturer of luxury Swiss watches. Tallis' *London Street Views* of 1839 shows No 31 as substantially the same as it looks today - a handsome Georgian house of four storeys, with two windows in each of the upper three floors.

Catherine's mother was Françoise (or the anglicised 'Frances') Reine Daugis, and she and Philipe had been married on 24 September 1759, at St. George's, Hanover Square.

Louis must have come to know the Métiviers through his own business as a tailor. It is also possible that Métivier was

Louis's first contact in London and helped him get started there. No confirmable records have yet been found for the Métivier or Daugis families. Possible siblings for Catherine are Philip, who married Ann Frances Hopkins by licence on 28 May 1791 at St. James, Westminster, and Ann, who married Benjamin Smith at St. Anne, Soho on 28 December 1805. Neither of these marriage register entries mentions who their parents were. There seem to be no records extant to show what happened to Philipe or Françoise Métivier. Rate-books show No 29, New Bond Street as occupied by Samuel Priest in 1761, but his name is crossed out and Philipe Métivier's substituted, so it looks as if this was when Philipe took over the house. The last such record with Philipe's name is from 1796. Occasional entries during these years show 'Peter' instead of 'Philip' but these are probably errors. By 1798 the house was occupied by a Mr. Lane and in 1801 by Lavinia Lavineau.

The *Morning Post and Daily Advertiser* printed on Tuesday, 17 August 1779 this charming announcement:

> Last Saturday was married at St. George's, Hanover-square, Mr. Louis Bazalgette of South Molton-street, an eminent taylor and habit-maker, to Miss Metivier of New Bond-street, an amiable young lady.

This makes the point that Louis was already 'eminent' by then, so he must have already built up a good business. Unfortunately we know little about his clientele in these early years. The word 'amiable', as applied to Catherine, meant 'lovely' rather then the modern meaning which is more like 'good-natured'.

All the witnesses at Louis and Catherine's wedding were involved in the clothing or furnishing trades, the most notable being Guillaume Gaubert, who lived just up the street from Louis at No. 12, South Molton Street. Gaubert rented this house, the owner being Mr. John Daniels, a mason of Camberwell. After Daniels died, his property was offered for sale by Mr. Skinner & Co. on 16 July 1783. The auction particulars in the *Gazetteer and New Daily Advertiser* describe

No. 12 as a 'substantial well-built brick dwelling house, lett to Mr. Gaubert, at 50l. per annum'.

Among the papers of William Henry Cavendish Bentinck, 3rd Duke of Portland, there is a letter from Monsieur Gaubert of which a summary follows:

> The letter is dated 23 August 1776 and is written in French. The letter is from Monsieur Gaubert, 12 South Moulton Street, London, to W.H. Cavendish-Bentinck. It refers to difficulties receiving 'le frac de drap de Silisie brodé' ; says the [assureurs?] could not get through as ships arriving from the Indies had led customs officers to watch the mouth of the Thames and surrounding areas; says the outfit arrived on Friday and the tailor refused it; says he is sending a sample of 'drap de Silesie'. It says the tailor turned the outfit down with regret, finding it [in] good [condition] and new; urges the Duke, when he sees it, to forget the unintentional wrong and not to turn it down; asks him to look at it and if it is not as he has said or does not please him, undertakes to keep it himself; asks, if it is returned to him, that care be taken not to crease it and to maintain its freshness; asks for it be left at the hotel until his return from France on 15 Oct. Asks that he send his instructions to Paris and gives his address there.

It is interesting to conjecture that the 'tailor' mentioned may have been Louis. Gaubert later became the Prince's upholsterer and decorator for Carlton House, and it is possible that Louis supplied him with silk for the purpose. Gaubert and Louis were obviously friends, and shared a connection with the Prince, although whether one introduced the other is open to question. It is very likely that they both had powerful patronage, which was the only way to get on in those days. Such a patron may have been the Duc d'Orleans, who had considerable influence in matters of fashion. Dorothy Stroud, in her book *Henry Holland, His Life and Architecture*, gives us this illuminating passage about Gaubert:

Between them, the Prince and the Duc (d'Orleans) had a marked effect on trade between their respective countries. Mme Campan attributed to the latter the *Anglomania* which, by his frequent visits, the Duc had brought about in his own capital, while the Prince was entranced with Parisian goods of every kind, and his accounts show an extensive patronage of French purveyors of ribbons and lace, embroidery, scent, pomatum, fancy paper, waistcoats and underclothing, apart from the more substantial wares that were soon to decorate Carlton House.

In view of this it is hardly surprising to find that one of the earliest appointments in connection with work on the building was that of a Frenchman, Guillaume Gaubert, who was taken on as Clerk of the Works at £200 a year from 1783 while Chambers was still in charge. Horace Walpole refers to him as 'Gobert who was a cook', but goes on to say that he had previously been employed at Chatsworth as a decorator, and had 'painted the old pilasters of the court there pea-green' and 'was going to play the devil' if he had not moved on. As the Duke of Devonshire was one of the Prince's cronies, this indicates the probable course of Gaubert's progress from the one household to the other. He seems from this time always to have spelt his name thus, but if Walpole was right in giving its original version as Gobert, he may have descended from the celebrated family of artists and craftsmen who worked for the French court in the 17th and 18th centuries, particularly at Fontainbleau and Versailles. If there was any truth in the assertion that he had once been a cook, this was probably to tide him over some difficult period, perhaps in his first months as an *emigré*. By the 1790s he was describing himself as William Gaubert of Panton Street, Maker of Ornamental Furniture. As Clerk of the Works on the site his signature appears jointly with Holland's on some of the early bills. It is significant of the revised ideas for the decorating and furnishing of Carlton House, which developed in the course of 1786, that Guillaume Gaubert was given his *congé* in the following spring.

South Molton Street is a narrow lane which now mainly contains smart fashion boutiques. No 18 is still in the same position, but the original building was at some time during the 19th century demolished and rebuilt, or re-faced, so the building looks very different today. The ground floor is at present occupied by a branch of Dune, a shoe-shop. In Louis' day the street was more down-market, and was inhabited by a mix of shopkeepers, artisans and tradesmen, with the odd writer and professional resident. The poet and artist William Blake rented rooms on the first or second floor of the house next to Louis', No 17, nineteen years after Louis left. Also trading in the street were John Richardson, a grocer and Kenneth Callander, an apothecary. At the bottom of the street was a coal merchant, Benezet's, whom we know Louis patronized. Amongst other residents were Mr. Howarth, a moneylender (No 25), John Moore MD, secretary of the London Lying-in and Inoculating Charity (No 27), John Pool, a wine and brandy merchant (No 64), John Higginbothom, a hosier (No 47), Mrs. Simon, a mantua maker (No 11), Mrs. Fontes, a milliner (No 13), Mr. Saxon, an auctioneer, (No 12), George Bruckner, a ladies' shoe maker (No 54) and Mr. Cottrell, a glazier (No 41).

Louis and Catherine's first known child was Louis, born on 31 May 1781, followed by Louisa on 27 October 1782 and Joseph William on 17 December 1783. There may have been earlier miscarriages or stillbirths of course, bearing in mind the later frequency of children. These three children were not christened until 8 February 1784, when they were all baptised together at St. George's, Hanover Square. There are theories that the family were abroad during the intervening period, but as the business continued to be at South Molton Street this is quite unlikely.

Meanwhile, the sixteen-year-old Prince of Wales began his brief affair with Mrs. Mary Robinson. On 3 December 1779 Garrick's adaptation of Shakespeare's *Winter's Tale* was produced by royal command and Mrs. Robinson appeared in the role of Perdita. It was then that she was first seen by the

Prince. During this liaison, styling himself as her 'Florizel', George was wont, it is said, to send her swatches of cloth and patterns for clothes, presumably for her approval of what he proposed to have made. On terminating the affair in 1781 he paid her off with a bond for £20,000, payable on his coming of age. This bond was later retrieved by Charles James Fox in return for promising her an annuity of £500 a year for life.

The Prince had a brief affair in 1782 with the elegant courtesan Grace Dalrymple Elliott and it may be that he introduced her to Louis' services. She probably ordered riding habits from him because among the papers of one of her other lovers, the Earl of Cholmondeley, was later found an unpaid bill from 'Louis Bazalgette, taylor, for £52 11s 6d'. Grace presumably had 'forgotten' to settle this account.

The Prince came of age on 12 August 1783, and was thus able to indulge himself fully. He was now Colonel of the 10th Light Dragoons, had £50,000 per annum allowed him by Parliament, plus the revenues of the Duchy of Cornwall, which made about £13,000 more. He had been given Carlton House, which was badly in need of repairs, though the King thought he could make it habitable with a lick of paint and some nice furniture. The Prince had other ideas though and immediately set about remodelling it at great expense. He also lost little time in going to Brighton in September to stay with his disreputable uncle, the Duke of Cumberland, of whom the King violently disapproved as a corrupting influence.

Louis having now 'arrived' as a society tailor, a little shop in South Molton Street would no longer suffice for him. The rich and famous might browse in Bond Street for hats and fripperies, but if they wanted a bespoke outfit made by a fashionable tailor they would usually not visit his premises - he and his assistants would come to them. It was therefore unnecessary to have a prominent shop-front, and a grander house in a residential street was what Louis now required. In 1784, the family moved to 22, Lower Grosvenor Street, and they were certainly in residence by 3 June, as the rate-book shows. The shop in South Molton Street was taken over by Francis Tucker, who was a wax, tallow and soap merchant. The

Grosvenor Street premises were insured against fire to the value of £1,000. Of course, Louis still had a shop, but it was tucked away discreetly in 22, Brooks Mews, at the rear of the house. Since he had to visit Carlton House at least every other day, and had to transport clothes and cash in safety, he would have to have had his own coach, so all houses that Louis owned thereafter had their own mews or stables. Brooks Mews was also home to the builders and carpenters whom the residents of the Grosvenor Estates needed to keep their houses in good repair.

Lower Grosvenor Street's residents were all in the upper echelons of society. Next to Louis, No 23 was at various times the home of Viscount Wallingford, son of the 4th Earl of Banbury, Edward Lascelles (latterly Viscount Lascelles), Sir Humphry Davy and Sir Thomas Stamford Raffles, founder of Singapore. The house on the other side was occupied by John Lawson, MP and then the surgeon James Moore. No 20 was the home of the Dowager Countess of Essex, and No 19 belonged to Sir Frank Standish of Duxbury, a successful racehorse owner. In No 18 lived John Crewe, MP for Cheshire, at whose house was held a splendid gathering to celebrate Charles James Fox's election to the parliamentary seat of Westminster in 1784, at which the Prince of Wales was present, dressed like the rest in his Fox uniform. On this occasion the ladies as well as the men wore blue and buff. After supper, Prinny gave a toast to Crewe's wife: "True blue and Mrs. Crewe". The contemporary anecdote relates that 'the lady rose and proposed another health, expressive of her gratitude, and not less laconic, namely, "True blue, and all of you." '

Further Grosvenor Street residents included at No 17, Baron Sandys, and before him Samuel Whitbread, MP, son of the founder of the brewery of that name (who later, like Louis, moved to Dover Street). At No 16 lived the Marquess of Hertford and at No 15, Henry Reginald Courtenay, the rector of St. George's Hanover Square and Bishop of Bristol, who was made Bishop of Exeter in March 1797, and who may have officiated at the wedding and christening ceremonies for Louis and his family. Dr Matthew Baillie, the eminent surgeon who later tried to treat the paralysed arm of Louis' son Evelyn, lived at No 73. There was scarcely a house not occupied by a titled family, an eminent surgeon or a rich merchant.

It appears that having moved Louis and Catherine then decided to have the three children christened at St. George's, Hanover Square on 8 February 1784, but we cannot be sure why there was a delay. On 15 December 1784, Catherine's last son, John, was born, and christened at St. George's Church on 5 May 1785. Four children in three-and-a-half years no doubt took a toll on Catherine's health. She died in the middle of May, 1785 and was buried at St. Marylebone Parish Church on 16 May. This was the old parish church, which was later demolished to make way for the new church, which still stands today on Marylebone Road. A list of monumental inscriptions from the inside of the old church does not mention Catherine, so it seems she was buried outside in the churchyard. Some token tombstones survive, but not hers. The lack of complete records is hardly surprising when we consider that in the church's small acre there had been close to one hundred thousand burials over the centuries. Catherine's son Louis died in infancy (also in 1785, according to one account) and was reputedly buried in the same place, although no record has been found.

Poor Catherine at her premature death was possibly as young as twenty-three and she left three babies behind. It is impossible to know how Louis coped with his loss and with caring for the motherless infants. No doubt he was working long hours and travelling too, building up his business. He would have had to employ staff to look after the children, but we know nothing about what arrangements were made.

Louis' house at No 22, Lower Grosvenor Street consisted of five storeys and a basement, with a large four-storey extension behind, which accommodated an office, a shop and tailoring workshops. The property also included the mews house at the back (No. 22, Brooks Mews) and business access was from the rear, which preserved the residential quality of the house.

> There was another workshop at No. 22. Here a tailor, Louis Bazalgette, who occupied No. 22 Grosvenor Street from 1784 to 1800, had a two-storey workshop over the coach-

house and stables. It was lit principally from the side where a large window overlooked a passage leading off the mews, which was shared with No. 21. Behind the workshop were a counting-house and a 'shop', also entered from the passage. Both 'shop' and workshop communicated with the house in Grosvenor Street, which was able to retain its domestic appearance because the main access to the business premises was from the mews. Part of the passage remains but the mews buildings were rebuilt in 1898-9 at the same time as Nos. 21 and 22 Grosvenor Street. [Survey of London, Vol 40].

A copy of a plan of the house and mews, from the archives of the Grosvenor Estates, prepared for 'Mr Shepherd' (Thomas Sheppard) in 1803, i.e., two years after Louis sold the property to him, shows a tailor's workshop in the mews at the back, over a horse stall, with a passage leading to a shop, presumably occupying what used to be the garden, behind the house itself. A small yard is beside it and a covered passage leads to the rear entrance of the house itself. The house frontage measured 20'2" and extended backwards 37'5", with a small extension. This would have afforded the family at least 4,000 square feet of living space. The yard behind was about twenty feet square, but much of that space was taken up by sheds and the covered passage. The shop itself was on the first floor, over coal and other storage rooms, and was 15'9" by 47' in length – thus about 750 square feet in area. Behind this, and connected to it, was the mews building with horse stalls and a carriage house below and a large tailor's workshop above, measuring 17'2" x 46' – about 785 square feet.

A visitor to London, Hermann Pückler-Muskau, described a tailor's shop which may have been in the style of Louis':

> Everything here is in colossal dimensions, even the workshop of my tailor, which is like a manufactory. You go to ask about the fate of a coat you have ordered; you find yourself surrounded by hundreds of bales of cloth, and as many workmen; a secretary appears with great formality, and politely asks the day on which it was ordered. As soon

as you have told him he makes a sign for two folios to be brought, in which he pores for a short time. "Sir," is at last the answer, "tomorrow at twenty minutes past eleven the 'frac' will be so far advanced that you can try it on in the dressing room." There are several of these rooms, decorated with large looking glasses and 'Psyches', continually occupied by fitters, where the wealthy tailor in person makes a dozen alterations without ever betraying the least impatience or ill humour.
[Pückler-Muskau, Hermann Fürst von; Tour in England, Ireland, and France: in the years 1826, 1827, 1828 and 1829; with remarks on the manners and customs of the inhabitants, and anecdotes of distinguished public characters. In a series of letters (1833)]

The Prince of Wales in 1784 became besotted with Mrs. Maria Fitzherbert and pursued her with great passion, including a melodramatic and probably exaggerated stabbing of himself to gain her sympathy, so that she felt the need to take refuge in Aix-la-Chapelle and then in Holland, France and Switzerland, being eventually persuaded to return to England by the Duc D'Orleans in the following year.

The Prince decided to convalesce, from what some say were trifling injuries, although he was also suffering from swollen glands in this throat, in Brighton (also known at the time as Brighthelmstone), so his chief cook and *major domo* Louis Weltje was despatched thither to arrange his accommodation. Prinny arrived in Brighton on 22 July 1784, and remained there for the rest of the season apart from occasional trips to London.

On 17 July 1784, *The Lady's Magazine or Entertaining Companion for the Fair Sex, Appropriated Solely to Their Use and Amusement* reported:

His Royal Highness the Prince of Wales having been advised by his physicians to sea bathing we are informed that his Royal Highness will set out on Monday next for Brighthelmstone: Mr Weltje the clerk of the kitchen and Mr Gill the purveyor of the stables are now at

Brighthelmstone preparing every thing for his royal highness's reception.

Meanwhile, the Prince's debts were mounting. His treasurer and secretary, Colonel George Hotham, wrote to the Prince on 27 October 1784 because the latter had asked him to give him an estimate of his debts (about £100,000 at that point). Hotham said he would do

> '...the utmost in my power to retrieve your Royal Highness's finances from the wretched and disgraceful state in which they stand at present... It is with equal grief and vexation that I now see your Royal Highness (in matters of expense, I mean) totally in the hands and at the mercy of your builder, your upholsterer, your jeweller and your tailor. I say totally because these people act from your Royal Highness's pretended commands and from their charges there is no appeal. I leave Mr. Lyte to to account to your Royal Highness concerning his own feelings about the two latter...'
> [Aspinall; Correspondence of the Prince of Wales, Vol I]

The tailor in question was obviously Louis, since he was the only tailor mentioned in the later detailed list of George's debts, and he was owed far more than anyone else on the list. It is not known unfortunately what Mr. Lyte thought of him. The builder was Henry Holland and the upholsterer our friend Guillaume Gaubert. The report implies that these people often overcharged the Prince, although Louis stated later that he only charged him what he would have charged anybody. Even if this is true, probably not everybody was ordering clothes of such magnificence and in such quantity, so comparisons are hard to make. In fact, in Louis' accounts with the Prince, when clothes were made for people other than the Prince, the charges *were* slightly less, though this may reflect the Prince's size. Hotham's letter continued in even more exasperated tones:

'For my own part, I deliver in M. Gaubert's (bill), amounting to £35,000, merely because he sends it to me and I have no right and still less inclination to make the smallest addition, but from my own experience of what has passed, I have little doubt but that the expense to you will, at last, be greatly *beyond* that sum, if measures are not taken very different from what have hitherto been made use of; if Mr. Gaubert is allowed carte blanche, as he has been, and if your Royal Highness's orders, so constantly alleged to be given to *him,* are to supersede every direction and care that those much higher in office than himself think proper to make use of for your interest and service, your Royal Highness will find your self involved in fresh distresses, the very moment after you are extricated from the present ones.' [Aspinall; ibid.]

These dire warnings were largely ignored by the Prince, and his financial situation would become critical within the year.

Chapter 6: 18th Century Tailoring Techniques and Apprenticeship

Although there were attempts at the time to produce a workable sewing-machine, they were not in common use until the 1850's, so tailoring in the 1770's meant that everything was hand-sewn. After measurements had been made of the client, the master tailor or cutter drafted the paper patterns or 'gods', which is probably the most skilled job in the trade. These patterns were then used by the cutters to cut out all of the pieces of cloth, which were then 'basted' or 'tacked' together. The loose basting stitches were then snipped and the remnants of threads ('outlets') used as markers for sewing the seams. The term 'basting' was also used to describe the rough tacking together of the pieces of a garment for fitting. The journeyman tailors and their assistants would sit cross-legged on 'boards', i.e., large tables, close to as much natural light as was available. Louis' workshops in Lower Grosvenor Street were equipped with large windows for this purpose. The boards supported not only the tailors but also the large pieces of material, which helped to keep them clean. There are many tailors even today who sit in this time-honoured way if they have hand sewing to do. This working position is used in many crafts where detailed work is required. It is said that it reduces blood-flow to the legs which means more goes to the brain and that this also aids concentration.

Forty years ago the author knew a young watchmaker who would place his lathe-box on a chair in front of the bench and sit on it tailor-wise in order to carry out such exacting tasks as hand-turning a balance-staff for an antique verge watch. The watchmaker's working position was not ideal though, because he had to lean forward over the bench, but at least he did not have to hold that posture all day. The tailor can hold the work close to his body and thus keep his back mostly straight, which helps to reduce neck-aches. The strain on the tailors' eyes meant failing sight for many by their forties. The sewing of military uniforms or indeed any brightly-coloured garments (such as those favoured by the Prince of Wales) was especially hard on the eyes. In contrast, black or very dark fabrics were also a strain to sew, unless the light was very good. Tailors also suffered from other ailments that go with a sedentary occupation, and additionally the so-called 'tailor's bunion', an inflammation of the toe-joints caused by pressure on them from their cross-legged working position. Lung disease was also common, from breathing in the lint particles. Charles Dickens in *All The Year Round* observed that:

> As to the unhealthy conduct of indoor work, not in itself injurious, by the overcrowding and bad ventilation, that breeds lung disease, by working without necessary rest or otherwise - three branches of industry noted for frequent sins of this sort are investigated: the occupations of the dressmakers and needlewomen, tailors and the printers. Dressmakers suffer by overcrowding and deficient ventilation less than printers, printers less than tailors. Tailors work in their close rooms for twelve and thirteen hours a day, sometimes for fifteen or sixteen hours a day; printers have lighter work upon a weekly average, though there may be great strain at one part of the week, especially in the printing offices of weekly newspapers. In printers and tailors, consumption and other lung diseases are in vast excess, and form two thirds of all causes of death.
> [Charles Dickens: All The Year Round, Vol XII, 1864]

The 18th century tailor did not use a tape measure marked in inches, although this was apparently invented by George Atkinson in 1799. He used a 'measure' – a long strip of paper or parchment – to measure his client, marking each dimension on the measure with a small snip of the scissors. He would presumably write by each snip what the dimension was. Although tailors used a yardstick, and could by checking the measure against it record the number of inches in each dimension, the measure was often just placed straight upon the paper pattern in order to mark it, without the use of inches at all.

To make a frock coat the tailor noted as many as fourteen measurements. Each tailor had his own particular way of marking his measure, and thus one tailor would have found it difficult to understand another tailor's marks. Since he himself may not have always done the cutting, it is possible that Louis did record measurements as well, or used a system that his cutter would understand.

The cutter kept master paper patterns (or 'gods') which suited the dimensions of the customer. Although tailors' dummies were not apparently in common use at the time, they did exist, and the author feels it is quite likely that Louis used one or more for the Prince, not least because he had to produce so many garments at such short notice that many personal fittings would have been impracticable. Existing eighteenth century dummies were made usually from wood, with padding added to give the precise size and shape. When preparing to cut a garment for a customer the tailor selected a pattern of the right size, laid it on the doubled fabric on the cutting table and traced around it lightly with chalk. Next, using the customer's measure, he checked the dimensions of the outline, marking the necessary corrections in chalk and redrawing the draft accordingly. The master tailor or cutter then cut the material.

A frock coat in the traditional French style, as Diderot and d'Alembert tell us in their *Encyclopédie, ou Dictionnaire Raisonné des Sciences, des Arts et des Métiers,* was made in this manner: Once all the pieces had been cut out the first task was to stiffen the foreparts of the coat with buckram, which was linen treated with gum arabic or a thick glue size and then dried. The buckram was cut about four inches wide at the shoulders, reducing to about two inches near the armholes and then running all the way down the fronts to the bottom, only a little wider than the space needed for the buttonholes. This layer of buckram was tacked to the back of the coat material. Then the buttonholes were marked out, about two inches apart for a coat and an inch and a half for a waistcoat. A second piece of buckram was then added, not extending so far down as the first, and then the edges were strengthened with a further strip of buckram, whereupon the three layers of stiffening were whip-stitched to the edges of the coat.

The pocket holes were then cut, the pockets attached inside and the pocket flaps stitched on. The back pieces were joined together by back-stitching on the wrong side and fine-drawing on the right side, working from the skirt-opening upwards. 'Fine drawing' is a technique similar to darning, also used in invisible mending. This combination of back-stitch and fine-drawing was known in England at the time as 'rantering'. Before joining the foreparts to the back, they were pinned together and the fit was checked on the customer if possible. The seams from the armholes (also known as armscyes) to the start of the pleats, and the shoulder seams, were then sewn using the same stitches as were used for joining the back. Then the neck-edging was sewn in. The side-pleats of the frock were then made, and firmly secured at the top. The sleeves were fashioned and set into the armholes. The coat would then be pressed to ensure that the shoulders in particular were correct and the seams flat. The heat of the iron would soften the size in the buckram so that it could be moulded, stiffening again as it cooled. With the main tailoring completed, the silk lining would be made and sewn in and then the coat would be passed to the finishers, who would sew the buttonholes, add the buttons and collar and apply any edgings or other decorations.

"The Taylor's Complete Guide, or A Comprehensive Analysis of Beauty and Elegance in Dress, 1796" was the seminal English publication on tailoring, and it here describes how to make a pair of stocking breeches. 'Stocking' (now known as stockinet) could be made of any type of yarn and was made on a stocking frame, a form of knitting machine which looped the yarn rather than weaving it, so of course the cloth would stretch and cling much more than a woven cloth.

> When at your cutting-board and having your stocking-piece before you, observe the following maxim, which entirely results from the stretch or elasticity that there is in all frame-work of this nature, and requires that the breeches must be three inches longer than the measure.

Lay your measure upon the piece within one inch and a half at the top, then extend it to the intended place for the knee, and mark it and cut it longer an inch and a half below at the knee; then for the width, lay on the measure at the bottom of the knee, and mark for cutting one inch narrower than the measure upon the stuff in the double, and one inch less in gradation all the way up the thigh, and be sure to abide by the following example for the stride:-- First make a deep fall down, and having laid your finger upon the measure at the bottom of the knee, with the other hand extend the measure to the fork, and make the stride within three inches of the length of the measure, this will give proper room for the elasticity of the materials, and ease and freedom to the wearer.

Next cut your leg seam very straight, and not hollow as is the common practice, and let your side seams be likewise straight from the knee up to within four inches of the hip; and observe that you put in a gusset piece from that place on the outside of the hip, two inches and a half wide at the top, and cut taper or bevelled to a point five inches long both of the outside and the inside. When this done and your breeches are put on, you will find that the ribs go straight down the thighs, which will avoid and provide against an abominable error in the trade, of twisting the ribs across the thighs, making them appear crooked, inwardly inclining, which seems to the spectator (according to the old vulgar adage) as if people were ill shap'd or knap knee'd. When you have got so far, cut your seat at the joining of the waistband, less by two inches double; and in making, let your knee-band be cut one inch longer than your measure, and back it on lining, and set it with the knee-band to the breeches; this will keep them to the full size at the bottom, and make them lie agreeably, and rise to the springing of the calf of the leg if required. Let both the knee-band and the waist-band be beared on according to your length of them (both) and not the breeches, which though diametrically opposite to the common practice in use, we do affirm is positively right, and the true justified by and proved by long experience, and which will convince every practitioner on his first essay, if he does but adhere to the rule.

Charles Booth's description of the tailor's work in *Life and Labour of the People in London* was written towards the end of the nineteenth century, but traditions in such crafts being what they were, it is unlikely that much had changed since Louis' time:-

> Few workpeople in what are termed the organized trades of the West End spend more time in their workshops than the journeyman tailor. He ordinarily begins work at 8 AM, although many start at 5 and 6 o'clock, and scarcely leaves the workroom until 8 PM, thus usually putting in fully 12 hours continuous work in the day which is often stretched to 14 and 15 hours in busy times. His food, which is generally partaken of in the workroom, may be put down as follows: Breakfast at 8 or half past, consisting of tea or coffee, bread and butter with an occasional rasher of bacon, bloater, haddock or couple of eggs. Luncheon at 11 AM: beer bread and cheese. Dinner at 1 o'clock: beef or mutton, vegetables, pudding and beer. Tea at 4 o'clock with bun or bread and butter. This, with an occasional glass or two of beer, constitutes his day's food and is nearly always taken by the tailor sitting on the board with his work lying at his side and the newspaper in front of him...
> Coatmaking, which is considered to be the principal branch of the trade, is usually carried on by two men working together as partners; one makes the left and the other the right fore part. The left man is the captain of the job; he is responsible for seeing the work put fairly together; he marks with cotton thread all the outlets left on the job by the cutter, cuts all the pockets and linings, makes the left side of the coat, makes and puts on the collar and gives the work the final press off. The right man makes the right side of the coat, both sleeves, and joins the halves together. Partners generally take rights and lefts alternately. Vests and trousers are made by separate and single individual workmen. The foreman who cuts and

gives out the work has a great deal to do with making a shop good or bad for the workers. Some are petty tyrants who never get on well with their workmen; others the reverse but in nearly all instances where the employer is himself the cutter the men are better treated and more considered. In all firms the garments are fitted on at least once, but some cutters require their work fitted on the customer three or four times, while in other cases the customer himself insists on having his clothes tried on again and again, and when finished is never pleased until they have been altered and re-altered times out of number.

A large and busy tailoring establishment like that owned by Louis Bazalgette in Mayfair would have had to take on at least two or three apprentices a year. This was not only to train them in the trade but also to ensure a steady supply of lads who would perform the essential but menial tasks which were required to keep the shop running smoothly. This work would also acquaint them with the proper functioning of the shop and business. The apprentices would be indentured at about fifteen years of age and would probably have to do general work for at least the first year until being 'put to the needle' or allowed to start learning to sew. Tailors started work as early as six a.m., depending on the shop, but the apprentices would have to arrive at least an hour before this to do the jobs which would allow the tailors to work. Their chores would begin with cleaning the grates and bringing up coal for the fires, which were used not only in winter, at least one fire or oven being needed all year round for heating the goose-irons. Then the bench would have to be tidied and any of the work-in-progress hung up on pegs. Bolts of cloth needed to be put away, and then all 'droppings' under the tailors' bench and the cutting table were picked up and put in their places. Any usable pieces of cloth or twist had to be saved for possible re-use. After this tidying the benches were wiped down and the floors sprinkled with water before being carefully swept to reduce dust and lint. This cleaning might have to be repeated during the day.

New garments should be put upon the clothes-horse, or wherever else it may be the master's custom to have them placed, and great care should be taken to fold them so that they be not creased, or otherwise be made to look rough and un-finished. They should, moreover, before the room is swept, be covered with wrappers, so as to keep them free from dust, or otherwise soiled. Such garments as may have been cut out, and have not yet been given to the journeyman, are commonly tied up and laid on the cutting-board till wanted; care should also be taken of these that they be not untied, so as to become intermingled; and if the master or foreman have left a garment on the board only partly cut out, it should be the care of the apprentice, after having removed it for the purpose of cleaning the board, to replace it in the same position as that in which he found it; and, also, to put the measures-book, measuring-tape, rule, or yard-wand, marking-chalk, and shears, or scissors, in such places as that they may be conveniently ready for use whenever they are wanted.
[The Tailor; Anon, c.1801]

The work that the apprentices had to do during the working day, apart from the usual fetching and carrying, included dividing parcels of thread, silk and twist into separate skeins and then storing them away carefully. Finished clothes usually needed some cleaning and brushing and were then packed, ready to be 'sent home' (i.e., delivered to the client). They would often have to deliver them personally if the client lived close by, or if not, they would have to take them to the packet office and have them booked for dispatch.

Only when the apprentice was judged to be keen and competent enough to be 'put to the needle', i.e., allowed up on to the bench, would he begin his true training. The first thing that he had to learn was how to sit properly in the traditional cross-legged 'tailor-wise' position. This could cause him great pain at first, but with perseverence over the days he would become used to sitting in this way for longer and longer periods. Tailors at this time worked at least a twelve-hour day, so a lad who was unable to sustain this position for long periods would go no further in becoming a tailor. Small cushions would be placed under each ankle-joint to help to prevent them from becoming sore and swollen. The stitches in use at the end of the eighteenth-century, and which the apprentice would have to learn, were the basting-stitch, the back-and-fore-stitch, the back-stitch, the side-stitch, the fore-stitch, the back-pricking stitch, the fore-pricking stitch, the serging-stitch, the cross-stitch and the button-hole stitch. In addition there were special sorts of stitch for hemming, filling, stotting, rantering, fine-drawing, prick-drawing and over-casting. These stitches are described in detail in Appendix 2.

Chapter 7: 1785-86

1785 is the first year in which we can see in detail what clothes Louis was making for the Prince, and in some cases when and where they were worn. The earliest reference in Louis's accounts is to masquerade outfits supplied in February of that year, as described below. *The Times* newspaper had begun publication at the beginning of 1785, and in its Court Circular columns it usually reported what the Prince wore to special events. For instance, it printed on 3 January that 'among the persons more distinguished for their dress on this occasion was His Royal Highness the Prince of Wales, in a light velvet of a fancy colour with yellow buttons and dark cuffs'. Two days later, it described 'the new uniform worn by the suite of His Royal Highness the Prince of Wales forms a very elegant undress; it is a blue coat, and buff waistcoat and breeches, and a gold embossed button containing the cypher G. P. in the centre'. This was Prinny's version of the Fox uniform, of which Louis made a considerable number in the following years.

The Queen's official birthday was celebrated on 18 January. Although her actual birthday was in May, it was felt to be too close to the King's birthday in June, so had been moved to January for that reason. It was however a moveable feast, so to speak, since a few years later it was delayed until April. *The Times*, in its usual sycophantic tones, described in very interesting detail the outfit worn by the Prince on that occasion in 1785.

> The Prince of Wales wore a most elegant suit, of extreme richness, yet so happily chosen that it produced all the effect of the gay and the grand, without being in the least gaudy. The ground of the coat seemed to be gold cloth, but its surface was of purple velvet, with intervening spots for the gold to be seen through, the contrast of which gave the mixture of the lively and the grave that we have attempted to describe, and the sight effect was still more heightened by the gaiety of the richly embroidered sattin cuffs and waistcoat.

Louis's accounts show that Prinny was very fond of purple at this time, usually mixed in stripes and spots with other colours. In fact, for the same event two years later he had Louis make a very similar outfit in 'purple stripe & spot velvet'. A further report at the beginning of June described the Prince as wearing a 'Royal purple velvet, richly embroidered with silver' for the King's birthday celebrations.

'The Prince of Wales has again taken a house at Brighton for the season', wrote the *Morning Post* of 11 June 1785, and he left London for his seaside residence on the twenty-second of that month. He occupied himself during the days with sea-bathing, going to the races, shooting and the occasional game of cricket. On Maria Fitzherbert's return from the continent, as a staunch Catholic she still refused to be the Prince's mistress, and so they were secretly married in December 1785.

The Prince and his friends had a taste for masquerades, or fancy dress balls where masks were worn, and we are aware that Louis often made costumes for them. One such jolly jape occurred in the Spring of 1785.

> One of the most remarkable of these entertainments was given by the late Lord Berwick at his house in Grosvenor Square. The company were selected by tickets to the number of five hundred and the rooms were completely filled by the votaries of fashion. At about half past eleven the Prince and his party arrived from Carlton House. They were thirteen in number, habited as the superior and brothers of a convent of Grey Friars. The superior sang an extremely witty song in character with a chorus by the whole fraternity in a circle, which at the request of the company was repeated. After this the brotherhood unmasked and were discovered to consist of the following group:- Captain Morris, the author of the song, as superior; the Prince of Wales; the Honourable Hugh Conway (afterwards Lord Hugh Seymour); his brother George Conway; the Honourable Mr. Dillon; the Honourable Mr Finch; Captain John Willet Payne; Lord Strathaven; the

Honourable Mr St John; Mr O'Byrne; Mr Braddyll; Colonel Gardiner and Captain Boyle.
[G.N. Wright; The Life and Reign of William the Fourth]

At least some of these costumes were made by Louis's tailors, and the members of the fraternity were billed for them. Three of the 'friars', however, refused to pay, so the bills were re-presented to the Prince, and appeared in the account for 15 April, 1791, as: 'To 3 Friars Masquerade Dresses, caps, masques, beads &c. compleat for Mr. Geo. Conway, Mr. Dillon & Mr. Morris (made 5th Feb 1785, which they say was a present to them) at £6/10/- each: £19/10/-'.

The Lower Grosvenor Street premises were clearly able to accommodate a good number of tailors, cutters and other garment workers as well as a storage area for what was no doubt a comprehensive stock of materials. The workers in Louis' manufactory were kept very busy creating clothes for the Prince and his brothers, judging by the debts to Louis incurred by them. We do not know how large Louis' clientele was in addition to this, but this royal patronage cannot have been bad for business. He never seems to have advertised.

By 1785 the Prince was over £160,000 in debt, and the amount owed to Louis was mounting. When Parliament voted in 1787 to pay this debt, the proportion paid to Louis (in five installments) was £16,774, which was by far the largest sum paid to any of the individual creditors. This sum is equivalent to almost £1.5 million at today's values, and was sufficient to make Louis a very wealthy man even at this point in his career. Not only did the Prince and his brothers continue to incur large debts for tailoring, but Louis also probably lent money to them, and certainly to others, as time went on. Louis was the embodiment of the 'snyder' – a regency cant term for a tailor who was not too insistent on payment and who allowed clients to run up large bills on credit.

As he grew richer, Louis became increasingly a moneylender, a financier and an international merchant. In this way he gained influence and power, not minding the odd debt which went wrong – it must all have been good business in Louis' mind, taking him further towards his goal. However, as we will see later, he was not above going to court to get his money.

> In principle, private loans were simple affairs: a lender granted a borrower the use of a sum of money with the conditions that interest be paid for the period of use and that the principal be returned to the lender by a stipulated date. Between 1713 and 1800, the legal maximum rate of interest a lender could charge in Britain was 5%; in the colonies, 6% to 8%. Loans of cash or credit were debited from the borrower's account in the lender's books; in exchange, the lender received a promise to repay (an oral agreement or a promissory note), a bond, a transferable court judgment, or a mortgage securing repayment with property. The borrower's indebtedness was certified by a deed, and the deed was registered with local officials... First of all, lending was profitable. Such rates compared favorably to the 4% interest that navy and victualling bills paid, the 2% to 7% average rates of return they achieved through speculation in the Funds.... Lending also created or cemented 'power and influence.' One way to exert control over others, Samuel Johnson once instructed James Boswell, was to lend 'sums of money to your neighbours, perhaps at small interest, perhaps at no interest, 'privately'; always having their bonds in your possession.' A lender gained a hold over the livelihood of the borrower by such measures.
> [David Hancock; Citizens of the World]

The tailoring accounts presented by Louis Bazalgette to the Prince of Wales between 26 June 1786 and 3 July 1795 have survived, because they were required to be submitted to Parliament when the Prince's debts came under scrutiny in 1795. They found their way into the files of the Home Office, and thence to the National Archives. They are all neatly written in Louis' hand and consist of 285 pages. The original documents are now in a very fragile state but the author managed to have them digitally photographed. It is doubtful whether their condition would allow this to be done again.

The author transcribed these accounts into tables in odd moments, a page or two at a time, a task that took about seven months. The full transcriptions are available from the author by email. The account for a specimen year (1790) will be found in Appendix 4. [Accounts in TNA ref: HO 73/17; Debentures ref: HO 73/28]

Fortunately, Louis' handwriting is clear, well-balanced and easy to read. He tended to run some words together, and his spelling is unusual, although it is mostly consistent, except where proper names are concerned. Some French words he wrote phonetically: for instance, 'applica' for 'appliqué' and 'spaniolet' for 'espagnolette'. The orders were no doubt first scribbled into Louis' notebook, but the accounts were written in 'fair copy'. There were only two or three words in the whole of the accounts which were illegible, either because of damage or from coinciding with a tight fold. Each year is divided into four quarters - the Spring Quarter (January to March), the Midsummer Quarter (April to June), the Michaelmas Quarter (July to September) and the Winter Quarter (October to December). Louis used double sheets, folded in half and then sewn up the fold. The most pages in a quarter is eleven, in the Spring Quarter of 1786. Each foolscap page has a column for the date (presumably of delivery), a description of each item with a list of materials used, a total and a running total, and consists of about 55 lines, so a quick calculation of the busiest quarter mentioned above gives us about six hundred lines, including materials.

The Prince of Wales in 1786, in order to get his debts paid, first asked for £250,000 from the Prime Minister, William Pitt, who refused the request. It is ironic that at that time the ever-indebted Mr. Pitt had probably not settled his own outstanding tailoring bills with Louis, as was certainly the case in 1790. The Prince then wrote to his father asking for help, and the King replied, requiring the Prince to supply a detailed statement of his debts. On receipt of this the King was quite horrified, and refused to grant him an increase of income. The Prince then wrote back and said he would drastically cut back his household, sell his racehorses and stop building work on

Carlton House, and would put the resultant saving of £40,000 in expenditure towards settlement of his debts. This he did, and then retreated to Mr. Kempe's house in Brighton on 11 July, followed shortly afterwards by Mrs Fitzherbert. The newspapers had a field day satirizing the Prince's new-found frugality – as it said in the *Morning Post* of 13 July 1786: 'A morning paper of yesterday says that the Prince of Wales set off for Brighton in a hired chaise and hack horses, but we are informed by authority which we trust will meet with equal credit that his Royal Highness was an outside passenger by the Brighton Ditty.'

On 18 July *The Times* nobly observed:

> Should it be truth that a great personage has resolved to pay the debts of his son, it will be an act of honour redounding as much to the credit of the father of the people as the new economical plan does honour to the son. The Prince of Wales' reception at Brighthelmstone was indicative of the warmest affection, but his Royal Highness has intimated a wish that no public honours, or notice should be paid to him.

Although the Prince was reported to be living in penury at this time, and trying hard to save money, his orders from Louis belie this. In reality, having had his debts paid, George felt free to start spending as freely as ever. *The Times* on 1 June 1786 described the Prince's suit to be worn on the King's birthday as having a 'deep pearl coloured tabinet cord ground with a light foil embroidery.' However, on 7 June it reported that he wore a coat of 'rose silk, covered with a silver spangled netting, which gave it the appearance of a pink. It was superbly embroidered in the shape and over the seams, and looked remarkably beautiful and grand.' This is probably a description of the same suit.

On 10 June *The Times* reported that the Prince had attended a masquerade two days before, and had worn 'a light brown coat, a shawl waistcoat and nankeen breeches, with white silk strings tying them at the knees. His Royal Highness' buckles are quite round and very large, his hat large with a black feather, and his domino plain black silk.' The newspaper quipped that 'the round buckle is at present the rage, to shew perhaps, that the wearers are determined to act no longer upon the *Square*'. About 20 June, Prinny ordered Louis to make for him 'a Windsor dress uniform coat & all materials as usual' for £11/8/10, and a green cloth frock. Maybe he felt he was being economical in having, in the same order, fifteen pairs of drawers and seven waistcoats cleaned instead of buying them new. However, on 28 June he ordered a frock of orange and lilac silk, a 'mixt cloth' frock, five waistcoats, 'a purple striped rich silk dress coat and white silk vest richly embroid'd (own silk embroidery & lining)' for £31/10/-, which does not exactly look parsimonious, especially when followed on 30 June with a frock of 'claret colour & yellow spot rich silk', a striped silk cloth frock and two pairs of 'drab col'd cotton breeches'. On 3 July the tailor was charged with 'altering a Windsor dress uniform coat and making it less in the body' (maybe the Prince had actually lost weight, unless the coat was for someone else), and making an embroidered dimity vest.

On 4 July Prinny ordered a frock made from '8 yds orange striped silk & cotton' and three more embroidered dimity vests. More orders came in, in the usual unrestrained manner, with, on 7 July, a 'mouse coloured poplin frock lin'd (own) silk', a dimity waistcoat embroidered in black & silver, two Prince's Uniform frocks and a pair of black silk breeches, with another four waistcoats on 8 July. For going to the races he required 'a scarlet & blue sattin jockey waistcoat with sleeves, double breasted with gold braid loops – a cap & all materials compleat' on 10 July, and on 11 July, an 'orange mixt cloth frock', 'a white quilting morning gown', a green Brighton Hunt frock and five richly embroidered waistcoats. Between 13 and 27 July Louis supplied two 10th Dragoons frocks, a general's uniform coat, a light blue striped orlean frock, four pairs of buff striped dimity pantaloon breeches at 36/- each, eight pairs of buff silk & cotton breeches at 31/6 each, two white quilting gowns at £6/13/- each and 'a Brighthelmstone uniform frock for Col. Lake'. There was a 3/6d charge for 'box & booking', meaning that Louis sent many of the clothes by courier, or in one of the royal coaches, to Brighton. In August the Prince wanted to play cricket, so he received '2 fine white dimoty crickett waistcoats with sleeves compleat at 36/- each' and 'a pair white striped muslin & a pair dimoty breeches compleat at 31/6 each' for the purpose. There were several large orders shipped during the Summer, the last sent on 29 September, shortly before Prinny returned to Carlton House.

In order for the Prince's orders to be swiftly placed and the work carried out while he was away from London, at Brighton and other places, there were couriers constantly travelling to and fro. They would either go on horseback, which was fast and was presumably used for the clothes orders, mail and dispatches, or would use a coach for collections and deliveries of the clothes. 'Box and booking' probably refers to this: when a box was ready, Louis would send a messenger round to Carlton House to arrange for it to be collected. In one case, Louis charged a larger amount for 'porterage and carriage', suggesting that on this occasion there was no courier available, so that other transport arrangements had to be made. Louis, or his master tailors (later his partners) Thomas Smith and Peter Denedonsel, occasionally made the trips themselves, mainly to Brighton or Windsor, when their expertise was required, and they charged expenses accordingly.

It is hard to calculate how quickly the orders were filled, because the date the clothes were ordered is not written in Louis' accounts. The date given must surely be the date of delivery. It does seem though that a suit could be made in a day or two, and to achieve this it is likely that some sort of 'production line' methods had to be devised.

It appears that the Prince spent a relatively quiet 1786 season in Brighton, trying to give the impression of being strapped for cash of course, and returned to London on 17 October. He continued to order many clothes from Louis, averaging four or five vests, three frocks and two pairs of breeches per day, plus a large number of alterations.

On 31 October 1786, the King's sister Princess Amelia died, and a state of general mourning existed for three weeks. During this time, the Prince's orders did not diminish, and were certainly not more sober, each order including 'Extra for Making now General Mourning'. This surcharge was ten shillings for a coat and five shillings each for a waistcoat or a pair of breeches. This was to defray the cost of the higher wages that the journeymen were paid during these periods. Amelia left the Prince £50,000 in her will, which must have come in useful to the debt-ridden George. *The Times* commented on her death and burial: 'It is said that a dead taylor collects more debts in a week than a living one can in a year. This idea may in some degree be applied to the deceased Princess: her long life of seventy-four years did not attract so much notice, or occasion so much conversation, as the few days which elapsed between her death and her sepulture'.

Between 3 and 21 October 1786, there were no account lines, and the reason is not clear. The Prince seems mainly to have been in Brighton. Perhaps Louis was ill or away. This period began with Louis' 36th birthday on 5 October and ended with an announcement in *The Times*:

> The Prince of Wales, having appointed Col. George Hotham, Henry Lyte Esq., Col. S. Hulse and Col. G. Lake trustees for the management of his revenues, and having been graciously pleased to execute a deed of trust, authorising them to appropriate 30,000*l*. annually, to the Liquidation of his Debts: Those Gentlemen, therefore, desire the several Creditors of HRH will, as early as possible, transmit an exact state of the Balances, respectively due to them, on the 5th of last July, to Mr Robinson, at Carleton House, that the Whole of His Highness' debts may be regularly arranged.

However, to make up for this lull, on 21 October Prinny was billed for two waistcoats - one 'black, white & pink sattin' and one 'scarlet, blue & white do.' On 23 October we see three swansdown waistcoats, one with sleeves, a 'Yellow, pink & black embroid'd vest', alterations to five frocks and 'a pair drab cassimere riding breeches lin'd with leather'. The following day brought a new 'light mixt cloth frock' and an 'embroid'd sattin vest'. The Prince got fully into his stride the next day, and received personal delivery of five espagnolette vests, three beaver frocks (greenish clouded, brown and blue, blue), a pair of buff cassimere breeches and two pairs of drawers, not to mention several frocks which had been taken out. On the next day Louis brought him eight new waistcoats.

The Prince's continued requirement for gaudy waistcoats and vests (the terms seem to have been used interchangeably in the accounts) does not now surprise us but it is still difficult to see how he could ever have got to wear all of them. It seems that the ordering and acquisition of these gorgeous items may have been enough to satisfy him. Running up to Christmas, the richness and expense of the clothes ordered not unexpectedly increased. In particular, on 21 December he spent £233/10/- on four shapes. A shape was the two foreparts of a waistcoat and its pocket-flaps which were ready embroidered and decorated and sold as one or two pieces of cloth, requiring the tailor to cut them out and make up the waistcoat. Louis seems in this case to have supplied the shapes only, presumably for making up later. Perhaps he had received a new delivery of particularly choice items with which to tempt Prinny. The best embroidered shapes were those made in France and then imported, which accounts for their high price. Charles James Fox, though notoriously scruffy and unwashed in his later years, was a very sharp dresser when young, and according to Horace Walpole he thought nothing of making the journey to Paris, and even to Lyon, to seek out shapes that took his fancy.

These shapes supplied to the Prince comprised: 'a purple & pink velvet shape embroid'd with silver & stones' (£73/10/-), 'a green & pale blue striped velvet shape embroidered with silks' (£55), 'a purple & orange do. in silks' (£52/10/-) and 'a purple & pink stripe do. in do.' (£52/10/-). This year of financial restraint was rounded off on 24 December with 'a spotted lilac silk dress coat lin'd yellow ermine and a rich white sattin embroidered waistcoat' costing £53/5/11, for which the ermine lining alone came to £31/10/-. On the same day he had a striped silk dress coat relined with 'drake neck lining' at a cost of twenty guineas for the material. In the last quarter of 1786 he spent £1,084/13/2 with Louis, which was more than in the same quarter in any other year for which we have the accounts. In the first quarter of 1787 he spent even more - £1,312/18/6, which included a black silk stocking dress coat and waistcoat trimmed with 34 rich silk olivets & loops at 6/- each, for which he was charged £30/2/6, 'a black & pink stripe velvet dress coat & breeches & white sattin vest, both richly embroid'd with silver stones & silk' at £69/4/- and a 'black & orange velvet dress coat & white sattin waistcoat both richly embroidered with gold silver & stones (own lining)' which came to £73/17/5.

This extravagance could not continue forever, and the Prince's next debt crisis was not long in coming.

Chapter 8: Organization and Working Conditions in the 18th Century Tailoring Trade

The tailoring trade was organized in the same way as the other ancient city trade guilds. There were the master tailors, who mostly owned the businesses and therefore made the profits. Against these often large profits had to be offset the high cost of materials, wages and the considerable risk of being paid very late, or not at all. Louis employed several master tailors, since he ran a large and expensive operation, whose function was to act as foremen, cutters etc., while Louis spent most of his time taking and delivering the Prince's orders and attending to the accounts. Under the master tailors were the journeymen, 'table monkeys' and apprentices.

There was a distinction, which still exists today in London, between the West End and the East End tailors. The West End trade was almost certainly more extensive than it is now, and catered to the nobility and gentry. In Louis' time the journeymen were reasonably well paid, and worked mainly 'in-house', while in the East End, which catered to the lower classes, the working conditions were much worse, and much of the work was put out to 'sweaters', who lived in squalor and were hard put to make a living at all. Many of the clothes we now wear are made in Asian sweat shops, so the problem is still there – it just is not so much under our noses.

Following the turn of the nineteenth century, conditions for journeymen grew steadily worse. The Chartist author Charles Kingsley, in his novel 'Alton Locke' (1850) brought these conditions to the public's attention. He describes here the young Alton's first encounter with a tailor's workshop.

> I stumbled after Mr. Jones up a dark, narrow, iron staircase till we emerged through a trap-door into a garret at the top of the house. I recoiled with disgust at the scene before me; and here I was to work - perhaps through life! A low lean-to room, stifling me with the combined odours of human breath and perspiration, stale beer, the sweet sickly

smell of gin, and the sour and hardly less disgusting one of new cloth. On the floor, thick with dust and dirt, scraps of stuff and ends of thread, sat some dozen haggard, untidy, shoeless men, with a mingled look of care and recklessness that made me shudder. The windows were tight closed to keep out the cold winter air; and the condensed breath ran in streams down the panes, chequering the dreary outlook of chimney-tops and smoke.

Kingsley also describes well the way the trade was going in the 1840's, mentioning that 'it appears that there are two distinct tailor trades - the 'honourable' trade, now almost confined to the West End, and rapidly dying out there, and the 'dishonourable' trade of the show-shops and slop-shops - the plate-glass palaces, where gents - and, alas! those who would be indignant at that name - buy their cheap-and-nasty clothes.' At least in Louis' time, in the West End, conditions were much better than this.

What of the men employed by Louis and others who did the actual tailoring work? The journeymen tailors had a history of solidarity dating back at least to the late 17th century. What nowadays would be called trade unions were then in existence, under the names of 'clubs' or 'combinations', although they were organized much more at the local level than trade unions are today. They met in 'houses of call', which were usually public houses. The first evidence of their militancy was in 1721, when the master tailors of London presented a petition to the House of Commons, complaining of the combination and strike of their journeymen. These combinations must have been quietly in existence for some years, perhaps starting as friendly societies, for them to have achieved by this time the power to challenge their employers in this way. On five occasions between 1702 and 1720 the masters had appealed to Parliament, but the journeymen were never mentioned in these appeals. In February 1721 the master tailors of London and Westminster complained that the combination of journeymen numbered 15,000, and that they were striking for better pay and shorter hours. A bill resulted, which received the royal assent on 7th June, 1721, and which supported the masters and made it lawful for refractory journeymen to be fined or imprisoned. The effect of this act was to suppress activity in the combinations for twenty years.

On 25 September 1744, the master tailors again petitioned parliament in a similar vein, that the journeymen had again organized themselves into combinations and were refusing to work for the legally enforced wage levels. The Government response was to target the publicans on whose premises the 'houses of call' met, and to prosecute them for harbouring the members of the combinations. No further action was taken by the Government, but the effect was that much public sympathy was generated for the plight of the journeymen. Eventually, in July 1751, the journeymen secured from the Court of Quarter Sessions in the County of Middlesex an order fixing their wages at '2s.6d. per day from Lady Day till Michaelmas and 2s. per day from Michaelmas to Lady Day, in addition to the allowance of three half-pence for breakfast. The hours of work, however, were not altered and remained at 6 am to 8 pm with an hour off for dinner.'

The journeymen appeared happy with this, but there was soon further agitation, which gained them an hour's reduction in their working day. The masters attempted to undo these reforms on several occasions, but without success. In November 1763 the journeymen secured a further small daily wage increase, but the combinations continued to fight for better wages, bringing their activities more before the public gaze, and even making them subject to ridicule. The masters got round some of the restrictions of the legal rates of pay by moving their manufactories out of Middlesex, and sometimes by secretly paying their best journeymen additional amounts in cash.

The London combination again appealed to the Court in 1772 and received a further wage increase of sixpence per day, and one shilling per day during general mourning. In 1795, after further appeals, the Government fixed the journeymen's pay at twenty-seven shillings per week, with double pay during general mourning. Pitt passed through parliament in 1799 and 1800 the Combination Acts, which prohibited trade unions and collective bargaining. This legislation was finally repealed in

1824. Further disputes over wages and hours ensued during the years following, culminating in the events of August, 1805, described below. 'General mourning' was decreed for persons of importance, and although it became increasingly popular as the nineteenth century progressed (by the 1840's there were several 'Mourning Warehouses', such as Jay's, in Regent Street alone), even in 1786 it could mean a sudden rush of trade for tailors.

The journeyman tailors during mourning times received higher wages although they had to work longer hours, so there was a need for the master tailor to add an additional charge to cover the cost. For example, from 2 until 24 November 1786, most of the frocks, coats etc., ordered from Louis by the Prince were followed in the accounts by a line saying 'Extra for making Now General Mourning', with a surcharge of 10/- on a coat and 5/- on a waistcoat or a pair of breeches. This mourning period was, as already noted, for Princess Amelia, the King's sister, who died on 31 October of that year. If Louis had to employ extra staff to handle the rush orders for mourning dress it suggests that the Prince was not his only customer, though the amount of clothing he himself ordered must have been more than enough to keep the Bazalgette manufactory working at full capacity.

As a result of their militancy, the journeyman tailors were often maligned at the time, and this was also partly because their trade was regarded as 'unmanly'. This was not helped by the publishing of poems and plays satirising tailors. There was scarcely a night when in some London theatre a tailor was not lampooned in some way. He would usually be called 'Snip' or caricatured as a goose (from the goose-iron he used). In hard times the impecunious tailors were reputed to live on cucumbers, so there were cucumber-jokes as well. A 'burlesque' entitled: 'The Tailors: a Tragedy for Warm Weather', written by Samuel Foote, had first been produced in 1767, but was revived in August, 1805, when William Dowton presented it at the Haymarket Theatre. The tailors took exception to this production, even though it was not the author's intention in it to vilify them.

On 15 August, about seven hundred men - 'mostly Tailors, were waiting to gain admittance to the theatre at the opening of the doors. The greater portion went to the galleries while some took their station in the pit and the moment they got in commenced shouting and knocking their sticks in the most turbulent manner.' Dowton attempted to address the mob from the stage but was shouted down, and complete uproar continued until the Bow Street runners appeared and ejected the most riotous. A farce was substituted for the play but its performance was so delayed that it did not finish until one o'clock in the morning. The fracas continued outside the theatre and 'a party of the Horse patrolled up and down the Haymarket and remained until the crowd had dispersed.' [Introduction to 'The Tailors']

Following this incident, a mock-heroic poem entitled 'The Tailor's Revolt' was published under the pseudonym of 'Jeremy Swell, Gent.' Both of these works were in turn attacked in a tract called: 'The Tailor's Answer to the Late Attacks Upon their Profession from the Stage and Press With Critical Remarks on Jeremy Swell's Mock Heroic Poem, by 'A Flint'. (A 'flint', a name coined in the above play, was a term used to describe a tailor working in a union shop, a 'dung' being a non-union tailor). In this work appeared the lines

> Does a man degenerate from his nature by becoming a Tailor? Certainly not! Why then do you laugh at us? Is it because we sit *cross legg'd* at our work? Fools who make themselves merry with this Circumstance do not know perhaps that this is the general posture of sitting adopted by all the Eastern nations as the most graceful and natural; nobody was ever seen to laugh at the Grand Signior and his Haram sitting *cross legg'd* at the Circus, but two Tailors in the same position at the Haymarket were deem'd a fit subject for mirth - *o tempore! o mores!* "But," says some pert witling, "a Tailor is only the ninth part of a man."

The Times was certainly not above presenting tailors in a poor light:

It is both whimsical and diverting, to see the degrees of distinction, which are kept up between tradesman and tradesmen, as if all were not on an equality, with regard to profession. Are not these distinctions excessive absurd? And is it possible, that the gentility of the profession can entitle any individual to the smallest respect. The generality of these *Gentlemen*, however, are of a contrary opinion. A wholesale dealer thinks the retailer infinitely beneath him. The butcher, in his turn, looks down on the poor barber; and the barber has his triumph over the taylor and the keeper of a chandler's shop.

Notice where the tailor is placed in this pecking order, despite his high level of training and skill. When as despised a man as a tailor performed a decent and chivalrous act, *The Times* also thought this newsworthy:

The following instance may possibly contribute its share towards wiping off the obloquy of the old adage, viz, nine taylors make a man. A brewer's servant in St. John's-street, beating a horse with the butt end of his whip upon the head, was reproved for his cruelty by a journeyman taylor who was passing at the time. Being but a small-made man, the offender struck the taylor, which brought on an immediate affray, in which the latter became a victor, after a hard contest for ten minutes. A gentleman that was a spectator rewarded the hero of the bodkin with a crown for his bravery. [*The Times*, 24 September 1787]

The expression: 'it takes nine tailors to make a man' has an interesting and convoluted origin. At this time, although it was often used as a slur on tailors, it was also common parlance indicating that a gentleman could not be well-dressed by patronizing only one tailor. The original saying dates back to medieval times. It had nothing to do with tailors *per se*. A death knell was in common use in English parishes from the earliest days, and consisted of peals of a church bell to 'tell' of the passing of one of the parishioners. The number of 'tellers' or peals varied from place to place, sometimes recording the deceased's age, but the commonest convention was to 'tell', or toll, three sets of one (i.e., three) for a child, three sets of two (six) for a woman and three sets of three (nine) for a man. The old saying was therefore: 'nine tellers make a man'. The word 'teller' in some way became corrupted to 'tailor'.

This contemptuous attitude towards tailors became more painfully obvious when the time came for payment. The regency buck or nobleman was usually heavily in debt, but still needed to dress well. The tailor was a necessary evil in this, and *zounds!* - even wanted to be paid from time to time. This attitude to debt and to tailors was neatly summed up in an anecdote by Charles Dickens some years later, in *Household Words*:

> One day while a dunning tradesman was in the room of a nobleman vainly endeavouring to extract money a letter was brought requesting the payment of a very large sum lost at cards. This debt was settled before the wondering eyes of the tailor who was far from pleased at seeing money to which he considered he had a prior claim going into other hands.
> "That was a debt of honour," calmly remarked the nobleman.
> "And may I ask what you call a debt of honour, My Lord?"
> "A debt of honour is one contracted verbally and one the payment of which cannot be exacted by law."
> "Thank you My Lord, then from henceforth I prefer to have no claim on your lordship" and the wily man tore his bill in two.
> The stroke of diplomacy succeeded and the tailor got his money.

Now we will return to the story.

Chapter 9: 1787

The winter of 1786-7 was a very cold one in London, as were many of the winters in this decade. The Prince's creditors were also undergoing a winter of discontent, made scarcely spring by the following view in *The Times* of 5 January 1787, although it may have provided them with a slight reason to hope for payment:

> The *Prince of Wales* is to be pitied - but are not those tradesmen and artificers who are his creditors, and whom he is unable to pay, in still a more pitiable situation? Those who gave unto Caesar what is Caesar's, should in return have their own, or how can Caesar expect his due?

The Prince did not attend the Queen's official birthday celebrations in January, being apparently ill. Although a birthday suit was not made, there were plenty of other rich dress suits ordered from Louis in that month. On 2 January, he delivered 'a blue & black spot velvet dress coat & waistcoat' made from nine yards of spotted plush velvet, with silver and stone buttons, and another made from nine yards of orange puce & white spot velvet at £2/2/- a yard, with twenty-eight rich silver pierced buttons at 5/- each and eighteen silver breast buttons at 2/6 each. The next day, Louis brought another dress suit made from '9 yards purple stripe & spot velvet at £2/2/- a yard'. Two days later there were three India shawl waistcoats and a 'noiset beaver dress coat and waistcoat', using Prinny's 'Own sattin lining & stone & pearl buttons'. On 9 January: a pink and black striped velvet dress coat & waistcoat and another in purple, pink & white satin with a silk covered fur lining, accompanied by a waistcoat richly embroidered in chenille and silks, followed by another the next day made from 9 yards of pink blue & black spot velvet. So it continued - 'a mulberry col'd ratteen dress coat & waistcoat' and then 'a blue & brown striped silk dress coat lin'd with fur', 'a green & noiset striped silk dress coat lin'd pink fur & a white sattin embroid'd vest' and so on in happy profusion.

At the beginning of February Prinny on the same day ordered five assorted striped satin waistcoats - blue and white, pink black and white, carmelite white and green, pink and white and mulberry. A list of such excess must be ended somewhere, so we can finish for now with the dress suits made between 19 and 22 February - 'a Princes embroidered dress coat & wais't lin'd buff silk serge with extra enriching of the embroidery', 'a black & pink stripe velvet dess coat & breeches & white sattin vest, both richly embroid'd with silver stones & silk', 'a green & blue striped velvet dress coat & white sattin vest both richly embroidered with silks' and finally 'a purple & orange striped velvet dress coat & white sattin vest both richly embroidered with silks, the vest enriched as above'.

The Prince attended a masquerade at the Haymarket on 19 February with Mrs. Fitzherbert but the newspapers did not describe his outfit, except that he wore a domino, which was a hooded silk cloak which was worn with a mask.

It may now be the moment to introduce a 'very prosperous' tailor by the name of Daniel Bergman, who had premises at 9, Charles Street, at the east end of Grosvenor Square. This short street was mostly demolished in 1891, and after rebuilding it became the present-day Carlos Place. Bergman was apparently of Swedish extraction but was a native of 'Hesse Cassel', now known as Hesse-Kassel, which was then a landgrave of the Holy Roman Empire, but closely aligned with Sweden and ruled by a succession of Swedish kings until its incorporation into the German Confederation in 1815.

Bergman had arrived in London some time before 14 August 1758, upon which day he married Mary Middleship at the church of St. George, Hanover Square. We cannot be sure exactly when Louis became friends with Bergman but it was probably before 1785. Evidence of Bergman's business activities can be seen in the newspapers. The *London Daily Advertiser* of 5 May 1777 listed him as requiring 'A number of Journeyman Taylors, who are Compleat in the Business, and willing to conform to the late Order of Sessions, (presumably meaning that these tailors must accept the current pay and hours as decreed by the Middlesex courts) may have Constant Employ, by Application to Mr. Daniel Bergman, Charles Street, Grosvenor Square.' Daniel had a succession of business partners, one of whom was William Simson, who died in November 1777. Simson was originally the senior partner, since the firm up until Simson's death traded as Simson & Bergman. Bergman also rented a 'house, offices, gardens and meadow land' in the area of North End, Hammersmith, which would have served as his country residence. He also owned No. 8, Charles Street, next to his official business premises at No. 9, and on the corner of Bishop's Yard, and used both for his shop, offices, manufactory and warehouse. Any spare living accommodation in both of these houses was rented out, as was another property, 33 Albemarle Street, Mayfair. This house still exists, and is the most southerly house of the row which now comprises the famous Brown's Hotel. Daniel's firm was then, or at least later, known as Bergman & Co., and later partners included John Wethly and his son Daniel Bergman Jr. It is possible that Louis worked for Bergman before starting his own business. They were surely good friends and were both denized (naturalized) on the same day in 1792.

On 7 April 1787, Louis married Frances Bergman, the eighteen-year-old daughter of Daniel Bergman, in the Church of St. George, Hanover Square. The parish register entry reads: 'Louis Bazalgette and Frances Bergman a Minor both of this parish were married in this Church by Licence by and with the consent and Daniel Bergman the natural and lawful father of the said minor this seventh day of April in the year 1787.' The register was signed by Louis Bazalgette, Frances Bergman, Daniel Bergman and Joseph Bonnez. Louis was by now thirty-six, twice his bride's age, and had been a widower for just under two years. Frances was known in the family as Fanny, and her mother was Mary Middleship, whose parents were the London-born Edward and Mary Milleship, though it is not clear who decided to change the family name. Fanny was Daniel and Mary's eldest daughter, and her other known siblings were Daniel, William, Thomas, Louisa Sarah and Theresa Philo. Theresa Philo's name passed into the Bazalgette family later after Louisa Sarah's daughter, also named Theresa Philo, married Louis' son Captain Joseph William Bazalgette,

RN, their only surviving son being the famous civil engineer. This name, usually shortened to 'Tizzie' persisted in the family for several generations afterwards.

It appears that Prinny planned to play some cricket at Brighton in the summer of 1786, since in April he ordered 'a fine flannell crickett waistcoat with sleeves, silk bound holes & edges, & flannell breeches with strings buttons & materials compleat'. Obviously 'flannels' were worn for cricket even in those days.

The Prince's comparative 'penury' continued until the Spring of 1787, when his friends decided to approach parliament for aid, and Mr. Nathaniel Newnham, a merchant Alderman and an MP for the City of London, was chosen to open the matter, which he did on 20 April 1787 by asking William Pitt 'whether it was his intention to bring forward any proposition to rescue the Prince of Wales from his embarrassed and distressed situation'. Pitt replied in the negative, so Newnham gave notice that on Friday 4 May he would bring forward a motion upon that subject for the consideration of the House. The motion was in fact brought on 27 and on 30 April, and Fox referred in his speech to a 'rumour of the marriage of the Prince to Mrs Fitzherbert'. Fox was unaware of the marriage and therefore put himself in an impossible situation by denying it in Parliament. George was non-commital, and Fox had to find out the truth from Lord Errington, who was a witness at the wedding. (One account has it that it was Orlando Bridgeman, also present, who spilled the beans.) Whatever the circumstances, this was extremely damaging to Fox and to the Whig cause, and Sheridan eventually had to address Parliament in a game attempt to retrieve the situation.

There were in fact some behind-the-scenes negotiations between Pitt, his ministers and the Prince. In an interview with Pitt, the Prince gave him a written proposal that:-

    1 - The Prince of Wales to have his debts paid off in part at least.

    2 - To have a sum granted sufficient to finish Carlton House, and

3 - To have such moderate increase made to his annual income as may be sufficient to prevent his running in debt in future.

Pitt then took this proposal to the King. According to *Hansard*:-

> With these propositions Mr Pitt took his leave and on Sunday despatched them by a special messenger to Windsor to the King who on Monday last returned his answer signed in form by his Majesty's own hand. This answer was on the same day delivered by Mr Pitt to the Prince at Carlton House and is nearly to the following effect: 1- That his Majesty was glad to find the Prince of Wales ready to submit his accounts to inspection, 2 - That it would be necessary for the Prince not only to ascertain the whole amount of his debts but also the particulars thereof with an exact account of how each debt was incurred, 3 - That the Prince shall engage not to run in debt in future. 4 - That upon the specifications above required would depend his Majesty's determining upon whether he should agree to the payment of the whole or any part of the Prince of Wales's debts, 5 - That his Majesty cannot think any increase of income necessary so long as the Prince of Wales shall remain unmarried.

The Prince then sent his commissioners (Colonels Lake and Hulse and Mr. Lyte his Treasurer) to Mr Pitt with all his accounts for the inspection and information of his Majesty. The account of the Prince's debts which was furnished to the House is as follows:-

SUMMARY OF DEBTS
Bonds and debts £13,000
Purchase of houses £4,000
Expenses of Carlton House £53,000
Tradesmen's bills £90,804
Total £160,804

Expenditure from July 1783 to July 1786
Household etc. £29,277
Privy purse £16,050
Paym'ts made by Col. Hotham..£37,203
Other extraordinaries £11,406
TOTAL £93,936

Salaries £54,734
Stables £37,919
Mr Robins etc. £7,059
TOTAL £99,712

GRAND TOTAL £193,648

The King directed that an additional £10,000 be paid out of the Civil List, and requested parliament to come up with £20,000 for works on Carlton House and £161,000 for the payment of the Prince's debts, to which the Commons subsequently agreed.

In response to Pitt's request for a more detailed set of accounts explaining the amounts not yet accounted for, the Prince replied by letter to this effect:

> Carlton House, 11 May 1787
> The Prince of Wales begs to observe to Mr. Pitt that there must have been some very great misunderstanding respecting the accounts if it is supposed that there is one hundred & ten thousand pounds of which there is no explanation. In the first place the sum is but one hundred thousand pounds, instead of one hundred & ten thousand pounds, which is a mistake in the addition, & in that sum are included a variety of articles which would have been submitted to Mr. Pitt if he had wish'd to see them, & which the Prince now encloses, consisting of bills to various tradesmen, & which if he chuses now to examine he will be further convinced of. These articles appear to amount to half of the above-mentioned hundred thousand pounds, & in the remaining half are included all Newmarket expences & losses (amounting as far as the Prince can ascertain to little

short of twenty thousand pounds), post horses & travelling expences of all sorts, besides all pocket & other disbursements since the time the Prince's establishment was first form'd, & into which it is professed there is no intention to enquire.

The Prince of Wales flatters himself that this explanation will now appear perfectly satisfactory to the King. It is also undoubtedly the Prince's intention to establish proper regulations to avoid debts in future, but in order to adhere to this resolution, his Royal Highness cannot forbear repeating the *total impossibility* he feels himself under of resuming his establishment upon *his present income*, however natural it must be to his feelings to be desirous of living in a manner *suited to his rank & station*, as well as to restore those servants whom his late arrangement obliged him, with great reluctance, to dismiss & who have ever served him with the utmost fidelity & attachment.

ARREARS DUE ON ACCOUNT OF ROBES & PRIVY PURSE
Jeffries - Jeweller.....................£1,203
Martin - do................................£1,312
Gordon - Lace Draper.............£2,180
Mr. Broadhurst........................£2,200
Kings - Mercer........................£2,588
Davies - do..............................£2,683
Gray - Jeweller.......................£12,849
Bazalgetti (sic) - Taylor.........£16,774
Duvall - Jeweller.......................£939
Shrapnell - do............................£380
Bunnell - Laceman....................£384
Newcomb - Bootmaker............£348
Fermin - Button Maker............£309
White - Breeches Maker...........£380
Egg - Gun Maker......................£548
Cater - Hatter............................£523
Vulliamy - Watchmaker............£392
Lawer - Jeweller........................£439
Bland - Sword Cutler................£222
Rymer - Shoemaker..................£236

Derrit - Perfumer............................£250
Embroyderers.................................£310
Painters, &c., &c..........................£1,018
Bicknell - Hosiers..........................£590
Hodgson - Draper........................£350
Beckett - Bookseller.....................£289
Grigson - Watchmaker...............£205
Le Brun - Perfumer......................£269
Sundry Small bills.........................£822

ARREARS DUE FOR STABLE ACCOUNT
For purchase of horses from different dealers:
£5,302/13/6
For purveyance & other exp-. for horses keep:
£5,905/ 7/ 8
Coachmakers, Sadlers, Taylors, Lacemen & other tradesmen's
bills sent in on account of the stables to Mr. Robinson:
£17,366/4/10

£28,574/6/-

£79,566/3/-
[Aspinall; The Letters of George, Prince of Wales]

It is rather typical that Prinny should have to complain petulantly that the sum quoted by Pitt was £110,000, when it was *only* £100,000.

In the 'General Account of the Ballances Due to His Royal Highness The Prince of Wales's Creditors' in the Royal Archives, dated 5 July 1786, 'Bazalgetti [sic], a Taylor of Brook Street' was said to be owed £16,774/3/2. The author originally thought that 'Brook Street', mentioned in the documents as Bazalgette's address, was an error, since the correct address of Louis' shop was 22, Brooks Mews. However, the debentures issued between 1796-1806 all say 'Lower Brook Street and since they are all signed by Louis himself, this must be correct. Brook Street also backs on to Brooks Mews, so access to the

Brook Street house would have been easy while Louis still had the Grosvenor Street house. The leases of houses at the east end of Brook Street were running short by the end of the eighteenth century, so commercial tenants moved in, taking advantage of the lower rents and short leases. Therefore it is likely that Louis rented additional workshop space in Brook Street, which he retained even after selling the buildings in Grosvenor Street and Brooks Mews. The Brook Street workshop would have been run by a master tailor acting as manager after about 1800, and would have existed purely to make some of the Prince's uniforms and to carry out any required maintenance. Since Louis had always taken the orders and kept the accounts himself, he probably continued to do so.

One estimate of George's yearly expenses was £123,000. In a budget drawn up by the Prince for annual expenses after the debt was paid off, £4,000 per annum was allowed for his tailors, which was obviously only going to be enough for Louis' bill alone. It did not allow for the shirts, hats, boots, neckcloths, canes and numerous other items he bought from others. The other proposed expenses under 'Robes and Wardrobe' were all under £1,000. On 24 April 1787, Louis was paid £1,509/13/2 in the 'First Dividend to H.R.Highnesses Creditors amounting to £15,000.'

The further payments which followed were:

August 21, 1787...............£1,526/9/-
November 21, 1787.........£3,022/7/4
January 29, 1788.............£3,214/13/8
May 27, 1788...................£7,501/-/-.

This cleared the Prince's £16,774 debt to Louis.

On 28 April 1787 *The Times* listed the Prince's expenses in some detail, lamenting that after payment of these 'with a small residue of £14,000 he has to maintain his table, his household, his carriages, horses, stables (for there are none belonging to Carlton House), his dress, his patronage of the arts, and what was the best part of his former expence, his benevolence'.

Fox's denial of the secret marriage, the Prince's equivocality and the subsequent embarrassments enraged Mrs. Fitzherbert, but she eventually allowed herself to be mollified and the couple again repaired to Brighton for the season in July 1787.

Since we will now be dealing with Prince George's household, it may be helpful to list the members as they were in 1787. On 23 May 1787, the London Gazette reported:

Carlton-House, May 23, 1787.
THE Prince of Wales has been pleased to make the following Appointments in His Royal Highness's Household, viz.
Lord Southampton: Groom of the Stole.
Lord Viscount Parker, Lord Viscount Melbourne, Lord Spencer Hamilton, and Lord Viscount St. Asaph: Gentlemen of the Bedchamber.
Henry Lyte, Esq: Treasurer.
Hon. Hugh Conway: Master of the Robes and Privy Purse.
Col. Samuel Hulse: Comptroller of the Household.
J. Kemys Tynte, Esq, Col. Sir John S. Dyer, Bart., Hon. G. Fitzroy, Col. Stevens, Lieut. Col. (John) St. Leger, Hon. Lieut. Col. Stanhope, Warwick Lake, Esq, Lieut. Col. Sloughter and the Hon. Edward Bouverie: Grooms of the Bedchamber.
Lieut. Col. Symes, Capt. Wynyard, and Capt. Birch: Gentlemen Ushers of the Privy-Chamber.
A. Robinson, Esq; Major J. Mackay, and W. Wilson, Esq: Gentlemen Ushers' Daily Waiters.
Rev. Dr. J. Lockman: Clerk of the Closet.
Col. Gerard Lake: First Equerry and Commissioner of the Stables.
Col. Charles Leigh, Edward Scott, Esq., Major Churchill, Hon. Capt. Ludlow, and Anthony St. Leger, Esq.: Equerries.
F . G. Lake, Esq, and Edward J. S. Byng, Esq.: Pages of Honour.

The Prince celebrated his freedom from financial worries by ordering an extra special suit in advance to wear for the King's birthday. On 15 June he was charged for what appears in the accounts as 'a very rich spotted silk dress coat & breeches & silver tissue waistcoat richly trimed with an applica in gold, silver & stones for a Birth Day suit but not made up' at £156/15/- for materials only. The suit was not worn on that occasion because the Prince was taken ill at the beginning of June, so could not attend the celebrations. *The Times* printed this story on 4 June:

> The immediate cause of the illness of his Royal Highness the Prince of Wales appears to be this: The evening preceding his illness, his Royal Highness had a large party to dine with him, in consequence of the reconciliation with his Majesty. The meeting was very convivial, nor did the company leave Carlton House till near five o'clock in the morning. The Prince being to attend at Epsom races early the same day, did not go to bed, but threw himself on a couch for a couple of hours and set off for Epsom. When he arrived there, a beef-steak was ordered to be dressed, of which he ate very plentifully, and drank some cordials. After the races were over, on his return to town, the Prince found himself much chilled, and in the evening went to the Duchess of Gordon's rout, where he danced with unusual exertion to keep himself warm, but without effect, as he was shortly taken so ill as to be obliged to withdraw.

That these excesses made him ill is not too surprising. The Prince convalesced at Kew and was well again by 15 June. At the beginning of July he had arrived at Brighton, shortly, according to *The Times*, to be followed by Mrs. Fitzherbert, 'but is it not generally imagined that she will make an appearance at the Rooms, or assume any sort of dignity, that should by *implication* give the lie to a late expedient, though ungracious declaration'.

Here is an extract from Louis' account with the Prince of Wales for 26 July 1787. It includes a riding habit for Maria Fitzherbert. As usual, there are several alterations.

Altering 3 blue frocks as the others at 5/- each
15/-
Altering 3 pair nankeen col'd cotton stocking breeches & making new garters to do. & for new silk strings – 2/6 each
7/6
To a pair lead col'd silk stocking breeches (cotton)
1/11/6
To a pair olive col'd stocking silk breeches as usual
2/14/-
4 pair drawers – 7/6
1/10/-
To making a Levet for Mrs. FitzHerbert
12/-
4 yds brown cloth – 19/-
3/16/-
Silk sleeve lining
9/-
Blue silk cord for the edges
6/-
18 rich enamel painted butt's
5/5/-
Sewing silk & twist
2/6

For the reader's information: nankeen was a type of heavy cotton, originally from Nanking, of a naturally buff or yellowish hue. A 'levet' was a type of riding habit, possibly of a French pattern, since *Levet* is a French name. In common with Louis' propensity to anglicize French words, it was probably usually spelt 'levette'. An advertisement in *The Times* in January 1785 refers to 'levette cloaks, suitable for riding or walking', but since Maria's levette had sleeves it was not a cloak. Riding habits were the only items of a lady's clothing habitually made by male tailors, although stay-makers were very often male. The price of making up Maria's levette was twelve shillings. This is followed by the amount of brown cloth required at 19/- a yard, silk lining just for the sleeves and a blue piping round the edges, rich enamel painted buttons and a charge for the sewing silk. 'Twist' was twisted or braided silk used mostly for buttonholes and decoration.

In August 1787, Prinny decided that a change in fashion was required, and that his waistcoats should have shorter backs and be laced behind. During that month, Louis' tailors altered thirty-seven of his existing waistcoats in this way, and of course all of the new ones would have been made to this new pattern. The back-lacing was used to make the waistcoat fit tighter, and together with a 'belt' or corset it would have helped to rein in Prinny's expanding belly.

A frequent advertiser in *The Times* during this period was a Mr. Robert Croft, who had been granted a warrant in June 1787 to be 'Taylor and Draper to His Royal Highness the Prince of Wales', and who offered a variety of different types of outfits for sale at his premises at No. 65, Fleet Street, 'at very low terms', such as ladies' riding dresses for £4/10/-, or a pair of gentlemen's tabbinet breeches, 'so much admired for not staining or wearing greasy' for a guinea, assuming that the customer was 'of medium size'. These prices do not seem much lower for an ordinary suit than those charged by Louis, and it is not clear if these were fully made to measure or not. Interestingly, he claimed that 'Ladies or Gentlemen, by sending their measure from any part of the country, may have a habit or a suit of clothes made at six hours notice'. It is unlikely that Prinny ordered very many clothes from Croft, but he probably bought cloth, of which he liked to keep his own large stocks. Croft advertised frequently that tailors' bills were so high at the time that he would undercut any of them by twenty per cent.

Louis made a variety of non-military uniforms for the Prince. Most of these George designed himself, of course. The Windsor uniform had however been designed by his father, George III, demonstrating that the Prince was not the only member of the family with this interest, though naturally he carried it to excess like everything else. This uniform had a blue coat with scarlet collar and cuffs and, in the dress coat form, a heavy gold lace oak-leaf panel on the breast. Despite his frequent fallings-out with this father, Prinny retained an affection for this uniform. It still exists in a modified form as part of the court dress worn by high-ranking government officials on ceremonial occasions.

Windsor uniform frocks and dress coats were supplied by Louis in approximately equal numbers. In the accounts the numbers of uniforms made and altered for each year was: 1786 - made one and altered one, 1787 - made five and altered four, 1788 - made nine, 1789 - made three and altered one, 1790 - made four and altered two, 1791 - made four and altered four, 1792 - made three and altered six, 1793 - made fourteen and altered seventeen, 1794 - made six and altered six, and 1795 - made two and altered four. The cloth for this uniform was always supplied by the Prince.

George also designed his own uniform, known as the Prince's uniform, which had a blue coat lined with buff cassimere and a white waistcoat, each having gilt buttons engraved with the Prince's crown and plumes and the letters 'G.P.' (*Georgius Princeps*). This uniform first appears in the accounts in 1787 and between one and three of these were made annually. There was also a fancier 'dress' version listed as a 'Princes embroidered dress coat & waistcoat, lin'd buff silk serge, black velvet collar, new feather & crown buttons, with extra for enriching the embroidery'. For the time he spent at Brighton, there was inevitably a Brighton uniform, with a dark green cloth coat lined with buff cassimere, engraved 'G.P. & feather' buttons and scarlet cassimere cuffs and collar. There was a plainer version with green or buff cuffs and collar, but it was not much seen in the accounts after 1792. For wear at his hunting lodge at Kempshott from 1790 there was the Kempshott uniform, whose frock was of blue cloth with a blue velvet collar, gold binding and '16 gilt engraved G. P. & feather buttons'. George also had his own Kempshott stag hunt whose uniform sported a scarlet frock. He occasionally had Louis make for him the uniforms of the Duke of York and the Duke of Clarence. The former's coat was made of green cloth with many 'F. & coronet' buttons and a buff cassimere lining. The latter was no doubt similar but since the Prince supplied the cloth for it it is not clear what colour it was, though navy blue seems likely.

The uniform that the Prince and his friends wore most frequently, however, was the Fox uniform, first worn by Charles James Fox and adopted by his followers, including a version that was made for Georgiana, Duchess of Devonshire and other female Whig supporters. It consisted of a blue coat and a buff cassimere waistcoat, both with plain gilt buttons. It first appeared in Louis's accounts when he made one in December 1786. He then made none in 1787, five in 1788, twenty in 1789, twenty in 1790, ten in 1791, nine in 1792, two in 1793 and none in 1794-5. These numbers reflect the waxing and waning of Fox's fortunes.

According to the history of the Royal Kentish Bowmen:

> The Prince of Wales was made president of the Society in January 1789; this encouraged many aristocrats to join the group. The Prince of Wales insisted that every member of the Society should wear a 'dandyish' uniform comprising: 'A grass green coat with buff linings, a buff waistcoat and breeches; a black collar of uncut velvet in winter; tabby silk in summer, with yellow buttons'. A white waistcoat and breeches might be worn at all meetings, but the uniform coat was indispensable, together with a R.K.B. buttons with a gold loop to a black round hat, and small black feather, without which no member was allowed to shoot, besides being fined 7s.6d. Captains and lieutenants of the Society were to wear a gold or silver arrow embroidered on their collars. Standard-bearers were appointed to attend every meeting of the Society dressed in full uniform.'
> [Walrond, Colonel: Some Old Archery Societies (Chapter XII)].

The 1791 accounts describe one such, another in 1794 and one in 1795. The Kentish Bowmen's uniform that Louis made for the Prince was made from of 2½ yards of green cloth at 19/- a yard, 3½ yards of buff cassimere at 10/-, a black uncut velvet collar, fourteen gilt uniform buttons and six breast buttons.

Chapter 10: 1788

Louis and his tailors appear to have been kept fully occupied by the Prince's extraordinarily prolific demands for clothes of all descriptions. A transcription of the first entries in 1788 appears below:-

1788
2 January
8 yds purple & brown Striped velvet	31/6	12/12/-
Making a frock of do. Lin'd silk and rich buttons set in gold & all Materials (own lining and buttons)	1/11/9	14/3/9
8 yds purple and green striped velvet	42/-	16/16/-
28 covered buttons 2/6		
5/10/-Making a dress coat lined orange satin and all materials (own lining)	1/17/9	18/19/7
New buttoning a beaver coat	1/6	
30 covered buttons	2/6	6/3
Altering 5 dress coats and waistcoats as some others 5/- each	1/5	1/12/9
24 covered buttons – 2/6 (doz)	5/-	
Making a striped long hair beaver frock and all materials for Major Hanger		18/6
1 ¾ yds green striped velvet	18/-	1/11/6
Making a vest all materials for ditto [Hanger]	15/-	
1 rich emb'd sattin shape in gold and silk	7/7/-	
2 do do 6/6/-/ each	12/12/-	
1 buff satin do. in silver and silk	4/14/6	
2 doz rich glass buttons to do. 14/-	1/8/-	
1 ¾ yds scarlet and white spot velvet 18/-	1/11/6	
1 ¾ yds satin and velvet stripe 18/-	1/11/6	
Double fringe to both 8/- each	16/-	
2 doz buttons to do. 15d	2/6	
Making 6 waistcoats of the above and all materials 20/6 each	6/3/-	36/6/-
Embroidered white Sattin foreparts in spangles and stones (Lauzan) [Lauzun & Fils, Agen]		10/10/-

Making a dress waistcoat of do. then shirts & breast lined satin & all materials		12/12/-
3 January		
Altering a corderoy breeches making puffs to the knees & for new strings		3/6
Repairing and altering a stocking breeches		1/6
5 January		
Altering 5 frocks to fit	1/6	1/1/6
2 pair white cassimere breeches £2 each		4/-/-
4 pair drawers 4/6		1/10/-
8 yds green and black striped velvet	31/6	12/12/-
26 enamel buttons 3/- each		3/18/-
Making a frock lined buff silk and all materials (own silk lining)	1/11/9	18/1/9

The list includes making a frock (coat), a dress coat, a beaver frock coat and vest for George's crony George Hanger, a 'rich embroidered sattin shape' and seven waistcoats, as well as alterations to five dress coats and waistcoats. Although Louis was accused of overcharging the Prince, the reality was that the sheer volume of orders accounted for the high cost. In January 1788 alone, the Prince ordered seventeen frocks, eight dress coats and waistcoats, fifteen vests, nine pairs of breeches, one Polish coat, one robe de chambre, twenty pairs of drawers, a birthday dress suit and one 'very large silk cloke'. Louis attended the Prince on seventeen days in January 1788. Considering that the first twenty-three items in the list above were all ordered on a single day, Louis and several assistants must have spent much of their time at Carlton House, taking and delivering orders.

It is clear from several accounts that the Prince was more likely to want to spend time with Louis than many a more important person, who would often be kept waiting for hours, so they must have been on terms of great intimacy. Although some accounts say that George 'bought his breeches from one tailor and his coats at another', it appears that, at this time, Louis was supplying most of his needs including drawers. To clarify some of the entries in the above table: the materials are described first, followed by the cost of making up the garment.

The Prince liked to buy and stock quantities of materials himself because there are frequent references to 'own lining' and 'own cloth'. 'Cassimere' was a fine wool fabric used in suiting, usually spelt 'kerseymere', the name being derived from Cashmere (Kashmir). In the accounts there are many entries for 'alterations in body and sleeves', which become more frequent as George grew more portly.

On 16 January 1788, Prince George commissioned a birthday dress suit of unparalleled splendour to wear at his mother's official birthday celebrations.
The accounts show:-

> To making a birthday dress suit coquelico sattin coat & breeches and silver tissue waistcoat all richly embroid'd in silver & colours & an applica on the seams etc - £197/10/-
> Own sattin lining. - no charge
> Silk sleeve lining & pockets -   11/9
> Back body lining & pockets to vest -   12/6
> Waistband lining & pockets -   8/-
> 28 rich embroid'd buttons at 36/- doz -   £4/4/-
> 28 heart do. at 18/- doz. -   £2/2/-
> Sewing silk and twist 10/-
> TOTAL: £207/9/9
> (Coquelico[t] is the colour of the wild red poppy).

The *Ladies' Magazine* reported that on the Queen's official birthday 'The Prince of Wales was arrayed in a superb dress: the coat was a pale ruby ground, covered with rich work of white and silver, and beautifully embroidered down the seams with silver; the star of St. George was formed of brilliantes; the loop also was of diamonds; the waistcoat was of white and silver, highly rich and beautiful. The hat in which his highness appeared in the evening at the ball, had a beautiful brilliancy.'

This looks like an accurate-enough description of the above suit as made by Louis.

Reporting the same occasion, in more detail, the *London Gazette* said that the Prince of Wales 'was decorated in a manner almost beyond the powers of description; he wore a coquelicot satin, wholly covered with Mosaic embroidery of silver, pearls, stones and sky-blue foil; the seams were also embroidered with additional labour, and in a superb manner. The cuffs of the coat were made of silver tissue, and a waistcoat of the same, beautifully ornamented; with a diamond George, button, loop and star'.

The Times described the above outfit as 'a most magnificent suit. The coat and breeches of a *coquelicot*, or poppy-coloured sattin, embroidered all over with silver, and coloured spangles and paste beads, enriched with an *appliqué*. The waistcoat, and the cuffs of the coat, were silver tissue, embroidered in the same manner as the coat. The buckles silver, of the *Orleans* pattern; covered eith large gold spangles in the highest taste of elegance'.

A Hussar's Uniform, ordered on 30 March was even more elaborate, though much less expensive because of the lower cost of the materials:

To making a light blue Hussar jacquet & waistcoat, both with sleeves trim'd in figure with broad and narrow gold braid lace, & edged with fur (own lace & fur)
£10/10/-

3 ½ yds blue cloth at 20/-	£3/10/-
3 ½ yds blue shag to line jacquet at 8/-	£1/8/-
Shaloon sleeve lining and pockets	5/-
Cotton to line vest thro' and sleeves	8/-
2 ½ doz large gilt ball buttons at 6/- doz.	15/-
10 doz breast do at 3/- doz.	£1/12/-
Sewing silk and twist	10/6
Making the cap to do.	5/-
Making the long pocket with the arms	5/-
To making a buff waistcoat for do, trim'd with gold braid in figure (own broad & narrow gold braid)	10/6
1 ½ yds buff cassimere at 10/-	15/-
3 doz gilt breast butt's at 3/- doz.	11/3
Cotton backs body lining & pockets	8/-
Sewing silk and twist	2/6

To making a buff cassimere trousers trim'd with gold

braid in figure	10/6
3 ½ yds buff cassimere at 10/-	£1/15/-
Sewing silk & twist &c	2/6
To a pair flannell drawers to wear with the trousers	7/6
To a pair silk brettels for do.	10/6
TOTAL:	£25/1/9

In February 1788, the Prince ordered three frocks, twelve pairs of stocking breeches, eight pairs of other breeches, two great coats, thirty-six pairs of drawers, twelve vests, two *robes de chambre*, four dress-coat-and-waistcoat suits and two Fox Uniforms. The version of this uniform that Louis made used the Prince's own blue cloth for the frock coat, adorned with a black velvet collar, expensive 'feather and crown' buttons, and a buff cassimere waistcoat.

As far as costs are concerned, the outfits ordered in the previous paragraph come to an astronomical total, which of course would never have been mentioned at Carlton House, and would in any case not have received a single thought by the Prince, who characteristically cared not a whit what things cost or how they would be paid for. Typical materials and their prices were:-

Beaver (not the pure beaver underfur, which was felted and used for hats and heavy overcoats, but a woollen cloth, felled and brushed to have a beaver or 'bearskin' texture) at thirty shillings a yard. Bear in mind that a frock coat for the Prince required 5 yards of cloth.
Plain silk for linings at about 7/- a yard and fancy silk at 25/-. Embroidery was extra of course.
Velvet at 30/- a yard,
'Spaniolet' (actually *'Espagnolette*, a French fabric originally made of Spanish merino wool) at 14/- a yard,
Cassimere - usually spelt 'kerseymere', (a woollen suiting cloth of plain or twill weave, corruption of *Cashmere*) at 10/- a yard.
Buttons, unless of the sort covered with the same material as the coat, were expensive – e.g., plated buttons at 8/- a dozen, 'pearl & stone' buttons at 2/6 each, rising to 'rich fancy buttons' at 5/- each.

Stocking breeches were charged at £2/14/- for silk while ordinary cassimere breeches were half the price.
Drawers were 7/6 a pair.

An example charge for a 'fancy' dress coat and waistcoat, consisting of 9 yards of rich spot velvet at 14/- a yard, embroidered satin foreparts in gold and colours, satin linings, 28 covered buttons to the coat and 18 'rich' buttons to the vest – was £35/2/7, of which 10/- was for 'sewing silk & twist' and only £1/11/6 was for all of the labour in cutting and making it up. Assuming that Louis enjoyed, say, a fifty per-cent mark-up on the labour as well as the materials, that would mean that the cutters, tailors, finishers and 'table-monkeys' received very poor wages, which does not really come as a surprise to us.

On 2 February *The Times* printed details of the previous night's masquerade at the Pantheon, reporting that the Prince of Wales appeared as a 'Jovial Landlord' with the Duke of York dressed as 'half a bishop and half a soldier' (an allusion to his position as Bishop of Osnaburgh and his military profession). 'The Opposition' were clad as a 'Groupe of May day Chimney Sweepers'. This was a popular outfit it seems.

The Times reported on 5 February that 'on Saturday night the Prince of Wales appeared at the Opera rather oddly dressed - His Royal Highness had on a plain dark green coat, with black stripes; a white sattin waistcoat, richly embroidered with gold, and light crimson velvet breeches. We suppose he had been at some dressed party, and changed his coat only.' The coat was probably that delivered on 5 January which is mentioned in the account extract above. The breeches may well have been the 'rose col'd velvet breeches' which Louis had altered for him the previous March.

On 5 May 1788, the Prince of Wales received from Louis Bazalgette some rather comical items of fancy dress to be worn at a masquerade. The items consisted of:

> A dove colour stuff masquerade (Countrymans) dress coat & breeches & silk plaid waistcoat, the wais(coa)'t stuffed & all materials
> P(ai)d. for a wigg

> A mask
> A pair stockings
> To an old womans dress jacquet and petticoat & all materials
> To a scarlet cloke
> A wigg
> A large silk hat, silk gloves &c.
> A pair stockings
> A mask – 6/- and a stick – 4/6
> To 2 chimney sweepers dresses with masks stockings shovells brooms & all materials compleat at £6 each
> A silk mask for a Domino (A domino was a hooded Venetian cloak worn over the costume at a masquerade).

Louis must have thought it unusual for a tailor to be asked to supply shovels and brooms.

The *Morning Post and Daily Advertiser* announced on 7 May that a masquerade had taken place on the previous Monday at the mansion of Lady Berwick in Portman Square. The Prince of Wales attended this event, and the report mentions that 'in particular, a facetious OLD WOMAN contributed much to the entertainment of the company' and that 'MRS FITZHERBERT was in *high character*, as we never saw her more beautiful than in her domino'. The old woman's costume listed above was obviously that worn by the Prince on this occasion.

Louis' tailoring accounts show that the Prince of Wales quite often ordered clothes from Louis for other people. Some of them were well known as his friends (who, it goes without saying, were also granted posts in his household). George liked men who were (a) active in the military (to which he himself also aspired) and (b) of questionable morals. Most writers agree that George Hanger (later Lord Coleraine) was one of the more dissolute. The Prince ordered 'a green cloth Brighton uniform coat engraved butt's & all materials for Major Hanger' in July 1786. On 25 July 1788, there was 'a Princes uniform lapelled frock suit lin'd buff cassimere new feather & crown buttons & all materials for the Honbl Major Hanger'. Entries in January 1788 comprise 'Making a striped long hair beaver frock and all materials for Major Hanger' and 'Making a vest all materials for ditto.'

Hanger was an ugly, coarse and awkward man, who was often the butt of unkind jokes and pranks by Prinny and his other friends. The cruellest was when on some pretext Sheridan challenged him to a duel. This elaborate charade went as far as the discharge of pistols, which Hanger did not know contained only powder. Sheridan feigned death, and Hanger spent what must have been a dreadful night convinced that he had killed his friend, and his misery was only relieved the next morning when the joke was exposed. As he grew ever older, coarser and more debt-ridden (he even had to spend some time in a debtor's prison before recovering his finances by going into business as a coal-merchant), the Prince rejected Hanger, but the latter was always true to him, and in his memoirs he described Prinny as the best and truest friend a man could have. One has to question his judgement, or at least his intelligence.

Another friend who benefited from George's generosity (at the public expense of course) was Colonel Gerard Lake, First Equerry and Commissioner of the Stables. In 1786 the Prince commissioned for him a Brighthelmstone (Brighton) uniform frock, which was made of 'cloth grain cloth' and 'dark colour stripe silk cloth' with a black velvet collar and cuff flaps and '28 engraved Brighthelmstone buttons'. This was followed on 14 December by an order for a 'striped blue velvet dress coat and breeches & white sattin vest both richly embroid'd in silks for Col'l. Lake' for the princely sum of £64/11/9. Another expensive outfit on 2 June 1787 was 'a dress suit for Coll. Lake' at £57/16/9.

Lieutenant Colonel George Leigh of the 10th, or Prince's Own, Dragoons was appointed equerry to the Prince of Wales on 29 January 1800 but was his friend before then. On 12 December 1786 the Prince ordered a 'hunting frock for Mr. Leigh' and on 18 April Louis was charged with 'Altering a domino for Mr. Leigh'.

John Willet Payne was a highly-regarded naval officer, who commanded the squadron of ships sent to collect Princess Caroline of Hanover, the Prince's bride-to-be, in March 1795. The weather was frightful and it took several weeks to deliver her safely, and the strain of this adventure markedly affected Payne's far-from-robust health. In 1796 he returned to sea, taking Louis's twelve-year-old son Joseph William with him as a volunteer on the frigate *Impetueux*, so he helped to start the boy on his career as a naval officer. On 25 January 1788, Louis supplied 'a black and pink striped velvet embroidered shape for Capt Payne' for £30. On the same day he provided 'a black & pink spot rich do. for Do.' at £37/16/-.

These four officers were disciplined and competent in the field or at sea but when they were home their derring-do was often of a less savoury sort.

Other such orders included 'A set of rich enamel buttons for His Royal Highness the Duke of York'. Some clothes were ordered for people whose names are not so familiar, being pages or other servants of the Prince, e.g., '12 white dimity waistcoats with sleeves as usual for Mr. Peck at 31/6 each', 'a blue frock for Mr. Mills', 'blue & yellow striped silk cloth frock & all materials for Mr. Hicks (own cloth)' and 'a rich embroid'd vest shape for Mr. Trevis'.

On 22 April, Louis delivered a 'levet', or riding dress, for Mrs Fitzherbert, made from ten yards of black cassimere, followed by another on 10 May, this time of striped silk cloth with a black velour collar. The good life must however have affected her waistline, because in the same month there is the entry: 'Altering a levet for Mrs. FitzHerbert & putting another breadth in do.' On 31 May she received a blue levette with buff silk edging and feather and crown buttons.

The Times on 3 June reported that: 'The [King's] Birth-Day is expected to be the most brilliant ever seen. The Prince of Wales and Duke of York have each making a Diamond Star, Epaulet and George, the largest and most magnificent ever seen in this or any other country'. The paper described what the Prince wore on this occasion as follows:

> The Prince of Wales was arrayed in a superb dress, the coat was of a pale ruby ground, covered with rich work of white and silver, and beautifully embroidered down the seams with silver, the Star of St. George was formed of brilliants, the loop also which confined the Garter was of

diamonds, and the waistcoat was of white and silver, highly rich and beautiful.

This outfit was delivered by Louis on 31 May and the accounts suggest that it was was not all new: 'To making a Birthday suit (own shape). Cleaning the embroidery & joining the seams'. It sounds very like a re-make of the suit that he had worn to the Queen's birthday in January, enhanced with a new waistcoat.

The Prince and Mrs Fitzherbert were again in Brighton from the beginning of July 1788. Having had his debts paid in May 1787, George was again throwing money around in his customary fashion. As mentioned already, his expenditure on clothes with Louis in 1787 was £4,369/10/2, and in the following years it was not much less, although there was a slow downward trend.

By the beginning of November the King's illness became acute, and discussions were begun about a possible regency. At the end of November the King was moved to Kew Palace. By the beginning of February 1789 he was showing signs of a recovery. *The Times* reported gleefully on 5 February that 'His Majesty has been six days in an almost uninterrupted state of tranquility, and there are now the most pleasing and well-founded hope of a recovery. This news is a death-blow to the patriots'.

Writers about the Regency period and the Prince of Wales credit Beau Brummell with influencing George in the wearing of trousers, and relate that they did not come into general use until about 1800. It has been reported that the Prince was apparently strongly opposed to people wearing the things in his company. Brummell did not meet the Prince until 1794, so it is interesting to see in the accounts that Prinny was in fact wearing trousers in 1788.

He had previously sometimes ordered Louis Bazalgette to supply trousers or pantaloons, but these were only as part of certain military uniforms. Suddenly, in 1788 he began to order many pairs of trousers. It is not suggested that these were for evening wear. It looks as if this was not acceptable in polite society until some years later. The rash of trouser-ordering is mainly confined to July of that year, and then abated for some probably whimsical reason. However, it may be that the Prince was suffering from gout or some leg injury that made the wearing of breeches painful during this period.

The Prince ordered no pairs of trousers in 1786 and a few in 1787, e.g, '2 pair India dimoty trousers & all materials at 36/- each' on 7 July, '2 pair nankeen trousers as usual – 36/- each' on 23 July and a 'a pair nankeen trousers' on 24 August. On 30 March 1788, the Hussar uniform that Prinny ordered (mentioned earlier) naturally included trousers to match. On 19 June he ordered 'a pair nankeen col'd cotton stocking trowsers' and another pair on 21 June. On 27 June 'a pair nankeen trowsers as usual'.

Other orders for trousers in July 1788 are listed below:

5 July:
To a pair slate col'd cotton trowsers
To a pair nankeen do.
2 pair nankeen trowsers – 38/- each
8 July:
Altering 2 pair cotton stocking trowsers
To a pair dark green cotton trowsers
To a pair slate col'd do.
15 July:
Altering 6 pair stocking breeches & 2 pair trowsers at 18d each
16 July:
To a pair nankeen stocking trowsers
18 July:
2 pair nankeen trowsers – 38/-
Altering 10 pair breeches 7 trowsers & bringing the fall downs & for stuff – 2/- each
19 July:
To a pair nankeen cotton trowsers
To a pair olive col'd do.
24 July
To a pair dark brown trowsers
To a pair nankeen do.

To a pair patent do. do.
Altering 9 pair breeches & trowsers - 2/- each

Louis was busily shipping clothes to and from Brighton in the summer of 1788, and there are account entries such as 'Pd. carriage of a parcel from Brighton - 2/-' and 'large box with clothes to do. - 3/6'. On the 9th August Louis records that he was in attendance there himself : 'Expences of going to Brighton - 3 guineas', and again on 26 August: 'Expences going to Brighton & for a Man 3 days - 6 guineas'. On 29 August he charged for 'Expence to Windsor on 19th - £1/17/-'. In October Louis was making riding and hunting outfits and on 23 October noted: 'Large box & booking to Newmarket - 4/6'.

At about this time (1788-9) the Prince and his brothers were so heavily in debt from gambling and other extravagances that they tried to raise loans by any means possible. This led to the 'foreign bonds' scandal. The sum of one million pounds was to be raised by selling bonds to foreign banks and other investors, who thought that they had a safe haven for their money, paying interest at six percent.

> A large portion of the money, to the amount of nearly half a million, had been received by the Princes when the revolution in France, in 1793, presented an opportunity to resist the payment of those bonds which had been circulated, and even the interest due upon them was refused...
> During the revolution, some of the holders of these bonds escaped, and arrived in England; and, as their last resource, they made numerous applications to the Princes for the interest due to them, if it were not quite convenient to discharge the bonds in full. But the law-advisers of the Princes pretended that the present holders were not entitled to the interest, as they presumed the bona-fide holders had perished during the troubles in France and Holland; and that, consequently, other claims were not legal. On the part of the claimants, the bonds were produced which they had bought, and their right asserted to claim interest and principal equally as if they

had been the original subscribers. This evasive attempt to resist the just discharge of loans, raised at such great hazards, must ever be considered as an indelible stain upon the characters of the Princes concerned.
[Lady Anne Hamilton; The Secret History of the Court of England]

Some of the creditors attempted to fight this disgraceful evasion through the courts but they received no justice. Furthermore, many were deported and even denounced to the revolutionary authorities, some perishing by the guillotine, while some others, facing financial ruin, took their own lives. The remaining bonds were finally redeemed at a fraction of their value by Sir William Knighton, who was despatched to Paris for this purpose in 1828.

There were many further attempts to raise money abroad during the next few years, including £300,000 from an Antwerp firm just to cover the outstanding interest and the cost of repaying called-in loans, £60,000 from Thomas Coutts and a similar amount from the Duc d'Orleans. Various emissaries, including the Prince's cook Louis Weltje and private secretary John Willet Payne were sent mainly to Holland and Belgium to try to raise further funds, even offering the Duchy of Cornwall and the Bishopric of Osnaburgh as security, but were never able to borrow enough to cover the burgeoning debts of the Prince and his brothers.

These shameful tales give a very good picture of the risks of lending money to Prinny and his brothers. We know that Louis held joint and single bonds for all of them, but since he was well established and connected by now, and since the bonds were arranged by none other than Thomas Coutts, it was less likely that he would have suffered the cruel fate of other less fortunate foreign bondholders. Some followers of Louis' story, including for a time the author, have assumed that Louis lent money to the Prince and his brothers. It is possible that small cash sums were lent, and we know that the Prince was not above touching his tradesmen for loans, such as in the case of Jeffreys, his jeweller.

Louis lent large sums to people at times, but it was always on the basis that property was mortgaged as security. Even in some of these cases, Louis had difficulty being repaid. The Prince and his brothers had problems in providing such security, since mortgaging Carlton House, for instance, would have attracted immediate attention. Louis was too astute, and knew the Prince too well, to lend him money in a large way. The evidence for the assumption that Louis made these loans is in his bank statements, where repayment of interest and principal on the Prince's and Dukes' bonds is seen. However, since the Prince's debts for tailoring were all converted to debenture bonds, and were still being repaid in 1806, it is more likely that it was these bonds which we are seeing. We do not have accounts for Louis with the Dukes, but it is very probable that he supplied them with clothes as he did the Prince. Their names certainly appear in Prinny's account, when he occasionally bought clothes for his brothers. The Prince's brother, the Duke of York, was still heavily in debt at his death, and some of these debts were stated to have been outstanding for 'over 45 years'.

There have been attempts in several recent books to rehabilitate Prinny, and there is no doubt that if he chose he could be charming and generous, but his debts and overspending branded him as uncaring of others. He knew that, however much he spent, as heir to the throne he would always be bailed out. About the best that can be said about his profligacy was that at least he spent or gambled the money so it was redistributed, though not evenly, most going to London tradesmen or fellow-gamblers.

On 3 October 1788, Louis and Fanny's first child, a daughter, Frances Mary, was born, and was christened on 26 October at St. George's, Hanover Square. Her birthday was just two days before that of Louis, who was then thirty-eight. This child died in June 1790.

On 9 December 1788, Louis supplied a riding dress, presumably for Mrs. Fitzherbert, as he had done previously. It was described as 'a fancy green levet, the belts and sleeves trim'd gold binding, lin'd sable, & covered over with silk'. The sable lining alone cost 18 guineas, and including 18 yards of gold binding and 24 gilt sugar-loaf buttons the dress came to £30/13/-. The next day the Prince received a great coat lined with black fur and covered over with silk, for a similar sum. It appears that fur linings were often covered inside with a layer of silk, presumably to make the coat warmer, so the fur would not actually have been visible, except perhaps at the edges. On 13 December there was 'a green striped velvet dress coat & breeches and white sattin waistcoat all richly embroidered in silks (own lining)' for which Louis charged £52/10/-, and the final extravagance of that year was 'a black beaver dress coat & waistcoat shape richly embroidered in silver &c.' which cost £47/5/-. There was also 'a great coat lin'd fur for Captain Payne (own fur)' and shortly afterwards: 'a green great coat, lin'd fur & covered with white silk serge, plated buttons & all materials compleat for Mr Sheridan, same as Capt. Payne's'.

Chapter 11: 1789

16 January 1789 is the first date in Louis' accounts that mentions freemasonry. Firstly: 'altering a Masons uniform coat, making new cuffs & coller & edging to do.' The coat was blue, the cuffs and collar were rose coloured and the edging buff. The same day a new Mason's uniform was also supplied, including '26 gilt engraved B. L. buttons for the Masons coat above at 31/6 a dozen'. The next day brought further alterations: 'Taking the velvet cuffs & coller off a Masons uniform & putting other ones on do'. In fact, George had been introduced to the craft at a special meeting of the Britannia Lodge at the Star and Garter Tavern in Pall Mall on 6 February 1787, by the Grand Master, who was his uncle the Duke of Cumberland. Although in the same year he established his own 'Prince of Wales' Lodge, he presumably retained an affiliation with the Britannia Lodge, of which the above must have been the uniform, because it had the 'B. L.' buttons. The Prince's own lodge, which received its warrant on 20 August 1787, still exists, but initially the members were a mixture of his friends and household such his dentist Chevalier Ruspini (whose idea it was to form this lodge) and his chief cook Louis Weltje. Other founder members were the architect Henry Holland, the banker Thomas Hammersley, William Addington (3rd Viscount Sidmouth, later prime minister) and Arthur Robinson, a gentleman usher and 'accomptant' in the Prince's household. Louis did not become a member of this lodge. On the Duke of Cumberland's death in 1790, the Prince became Grand Master on 24 November. When George became King, the Duke of Sussex became Grand Master and the King was made Patron. No further mentions of Mason's uniforms appear in the accounts. It is said that George mostly enjoyed the social side of freemasonry.

By 1789 Louis was described in directories as a merchant. The Universal Directory of 1791 lists Louis as: 'BAZOLGETTE, Lewis, Merchant, Lower Grosvenor Street. Incidentally, from the way his name was listed in many directories and rate-books it looks obvious that Louis was busy being as anglicised as he could, almost certainly pronouncing his name as 'Lewis Bazalgate'. The tailoring business was carried on until at least 1802, with Louis probably employing a manager to take increasing charge of the day-to-day running. This may have been Thomas Sheppard, who eventually took over the Grosvenor Street premises and probably most of the tailoring business as well, since he subsequently described himself in that location as a 'merchant tailor'. It is likely that Louis was by this time concentrating on other business interests, including lending money to people to make his capital work. He does not appear as a Shylock or a usurer – the loans which we have records of all seem to have been very much above board. He was more in the line of advancing venture capital. Compared to many other merchants and men of wealth, he did not involve himself in good works, politics or other attention-attracting activities, so he hardly appears at all in *The Times*, where these details would have been published.

Unless he was very secretive about it, which seems to have been in his nature anyway, he appears not to have been a very philanthropic man. He would have continued to import silk while this was profitable, although fashions were changing as the end of the eighteenth century drew closer. Under the influence of 'dandies' such as Beau Brummell a more sober style of dress gained ascendancy, although the Prince of Wales (perhaps with Louis' encouragement) retained his taste for gaudy attire until his death, especially uniforms and livery, which Louis continued to have made for him until he fully retired in about 1810. Ian Kelly, in his otherwise excellent biography of Brummell, states that in 1794 Schweitzer and Davidson were making all of the Prince's uniforms, but this is clearly far from being the case. What this shows us though is that if Schweitzer's and others were making large numbers of uniforms for the Prince, in addition to those supplied by Louis, the total number made for him must far exceed that previously thought.

January, 1789 saw continuing extravagant orders from Prinny, such as two dress coat & waistcoat suits both made from 9 yards of striped and spotted velvet at 42/- a yard –

£22/15/5 each, a 'Corbeau col'd cassimere dress coat & waistcoat richly embroid'd in silks' at £45/17/5, 'a purple & green striped velvet dress coat & white sattin vest shape, all richly embroid'd in silks, with, covered buttons', for which the embroidered shape alone cost £73/10/-. Bulk orders for his household rounded off January, such as: '12 plain dimoty vests with sleeves lin'd with cotton & all materials for Mr. Vick at £1/11/6 each', '12 ditto for Mr. Beckt', '12 ditto for pastry cook' and '6 ditto for second cook' for a total of £66/3/-. February also began well, with, on the 3rd a dress coat and waistcoat made from '9 yds blue & orange striped velvet at 42/- a yard' - £22/15/5, on the 4th a similar one for the same price made from striped and spotted velvet, and on the 5th: 'a blue cassimere dress coat & waistcoat shape richly embroid'd in silks' used for a suit costing £47/5/-. On 12 February there was: 'an orange spotted velvet dress coat & white sattin vest, both richly embroid'd in silks for Capt. Payne (own shape & embroidery)' and '2 more different striped velvet dress coats & white sattin vests, both richly embroidered in silks, lin'd with white sattin & all materials as above for Col'l & Mr. St. Leger at £7/5/8 each'. Anthony and John St Leger, the two brothers who were friends of the Prince and members of his household, were nephews of Major General Anthony St Leger, founder of the horse race of that name, which is still run annually at Doncaster. John, nicknamed 'Handsome Jack', was posted to Trincomalee in 1797, where it was observed that his association with the Prince had seriously debilitated him. He died in Madras of a convulsive fit on 31 January 1800.

An extra fancy outfit on 21 February consisted of 'a white cotton velvet embroidered waistcoat & all materials (own foreparts)' and an 'Embroidered green & blue striped velvet dress coat and white sattin waistcoat in silver, steel & silks' for £72/2/5. On the same day probably the most expensive suit so far was ordered, which was a 'Brown & blue velvet dress coat & breeches & white sattin vest, all very richly embroidered, and all over the seams (to be kept till next winter)' which cost the nation £197/10/-. Later in February, the Prince was busy redesigning uniforms again for there is an entry for 'embroidering several different patterns in gold for Generals,

Admirals & Aide de Camps uniforms'. A masquerade must have been in the offing at the end of February, requiring a 'striped velvet dress coat & white sattin vest both very richly embroidered with lace & silk flowers' for £58/17/5, a domino made from 14 yards of rich black lutestring, three masks and for 'trimming a high crown hat with gilt paper & for paper'.

On 5 March Louis charged £4/6/6 for 'making a scarlet velvet dress coat & breeches, & rich gold tissue vest, all richly embroidered in gold, silver & stones, & all materials as usual (own sattin lining)' but did not charge for the materials until a few days later: 'To the above scarlet velvet embroid'd coat & breeches & gold tissue waistcoat not charged above - £100'. The next day, the Prince's Hussar must have been feeling the cold because Louis supplied 'a pair long flannell drawers for the Hussar'. At the end of March Louis was tasked with 'making a black Hussar coat & a scarlet wais't & black wors'd breeches & cap &c. richly embroidered in silver' and 'embroidering the above very richly with silver braid & spangles (own braid lace, spangles & sable for the edges & cap & coat silk lining)' for a total of £28/3/9 and 'a Hussar suit compleat in every respect as the above for Col'l St. Leger'. These outfits were worn at a masquerade at Mrs. Broadhead's on 30 March, to celebrate the King's recovery.

It cannot be confirmed what occasion the dress suit supplied on 21 April was intended for but it may have been for the King's birthday. It was made from '10½ yds purple striped silk to coat & breeches at 25/- (own tissue vest & coat lining)' and Louis charged £52/10/- for adding 'silver & coloured applica & spangles all over the seams'.

On 23 April there was a royal public thanksgiving for the King's recovery, preceded by a procession to St. Paul's cathedral. The Prince and his brothers all wore full-dress Windsor uniforms, George's having been delivered by Louis on 2 April.

There was a ball at Ranelagh Gardens on 26 May. To attend, the gentlemen had to wear a military or Royal Dress uniform. If they did not possess either, a special uniform had been designed, presumably by the Prince and Louis, which guests were obliged to wear for the occasion:

FETE at RANELAGH,- on the 26th of MAY.

THE BALL will be a Dressed Ball.

Military and Royal Dress Uniforms, and a Uniform for the occasion (a Pattern of which may be seen at Mr. Bajalgette's [sic], Taylor, in Lower Grosvenor-street) will be admitted.

Admittance on the 26th May, in the Evening, at Nine o'clock.

[The World, 22 May 1789 and Morning Post and Daily Advertiser, 25 May 1789]

The Times on the following day criticised the conduct of the Prince and his crony Captain Charles Morris at this fete, under the title 'AN AFFRONT AT RANELAGH':

Personages of the highest rank should ever be most circumspect in their behaviour, whenever they appear in public; thoughtless levity cannot be too much reprobated:- this being mentioned, arises from a very unpardonable insult being offered to a Gentleman of fortune, who when in company with some Ladies at Ranelagh, since the season commenced, happening to have the Constitutional Club uniform on, and passing his R. H. in company with Captain M., the latter apparently with his R. H.'s knowledge, came, and loud enough to be heard, uttered a most gross and vulgar epithet, which coming to the knowledge of his Lady, has occasioned constant alarm for fear of her husband's resentment, and been productive of great family uneasiness. As this may probably reach the eye of the parties who have given offence, they will show some repugnance by admitting their error, which may be done through the Conductor of this Paper, with whom the parties have left their address.

Unfortunately it is not clear from contemporary sources who the injured party was. Maybe he was insulted because he was not wearing the approved uniform, in which case he should not have been admitted to the event. The fact that he left his address with *The Times* suggests that he was not known to the Prince. Since the Constitutional Club was pro-Pitt and anti-Fox, the affront may have been more political than sartorial.

On 30 May, at the French ambassador's gala, Prinny wore 'a damson coloured silk, richly trimmed with embroidered wreaths of flowers', but this outfit does not appear in a recognisable form in Louis' accounts.

The Times reported on 5 June that at the King's birthday celebrations the Prince was clad 'in a *corbeau* and blue striped sik coat and breeches, embroidered in a broad and very superb manner, with silver and spangles down the seams; the waistcoat of silver tissue, with an embroidery all over, to correspond with the coat. His Royal Highness wore a most brilliant star and diamond epaulet'. This appears in Louis' accounts of 2 June as a 'corbeau & blue str. silk dress coat & breeches & silver tissue vest richly embroid'd all over the seams in silver &c. (own buttons & lining)', costing a total of £61/12/9, of which £57/15/- was for the shape and embroidery. Since the waistcoat was made from a pre-embroidered shape, it was the coat that was made to correspond with it, rather than the reverse.

It is well known that George IV visited Edinburgh in August-September 1822 and affected a fanciful highland dress for the occasion. However, Louis made one for him much earlier than that, in June 1789. The accounts show:-

11 June	
To making a Highland dress	2/2/-
9½ yds silk plaid to jacquet @ 8/-	3/16/-
7½ yds do. to line @ 6/-	2/5/-
6½ yds do. to petticoat @ 8/-	2/12/-
12 yds do. to the plaid @ 8/-	4/16/-
Silk sleeve lining & pockets	11/9
Velvet coller lining	5/-
Waistband lining & pockets	5/-
2 embroidered epaulets	1/1/-
White cassimere edging to jacquet	3/6

40 gilt rose & thistle butt's @ 8/-		1/6/8
Sewing silk, cord & c.	10/-	19/13/11
To a suit as above for Col'l St. Leger		19/13/11
To a pair cotton stocking trowsers for do.		

Sure enough there was a newspaper report in the *Caledonian Mercury*, Edinburgh, on 18 June 1789: 'The Prince of Wales, and the Dukes of York and Clarence, have provided themselves with complete Highland Dresses.... The tartan plaid, philebeg, purse, and other appendages, were of the handsomest kind...'. It was also reported that the highland dresses were worn at balls celebrating (genuinely or otherwise) the King's recovery from his first bout of 'madness' in 1789. This had put paid to any hopes of a regency at the time, but the Prince put a brave face on it. It is not clear who made the outfits for the Dukes, but it doesn't seem to have been Louis. One can imagine the long-suffering tailor pursing his lips and exclaiming: "*Nom d'un nom!* Where am I going to find seventy-one yards of *silk* plaid?" Perhaps the Prince designed his own tartan, or as a Jacobite sympathiser he chose the Stuart tartan, and had it specially woven in Spitalfields. Both the Prince and Mrs Fitzherbert later appeared in highland dress at Mrs Thellusson's masquerade in June 1804.

At this time of course the French revolution was brewing, and the storming of the Bastille on 14 July providing the touch-paper which ignited six years of savagery and the seizure of power by a succession of evil and corrupt men, culminating in the rise of Napoleon Bonaparte and the horrific wars that his thirst for world domination made inevitable.

In July 1789, and occasionally thereafter, Louis provided 'a striped silk Housewife filled with coloured silks, thread, needles & thimble for the Pages'. The use of this word, often corrupted to 'hussif' or 'hussive' is quaint, but it was a sewing case for the use of the Prince's pages so that they could make running repairs to the royal clothing.

On 12 August the Prince received '4 striped muslin vests with sleeves for Tennis, compleat, & four pair striped muslin breeches for do. with silk puffs &c. - £3/6/6 each.' This was of course for 'real' or 'royal' tennis, for which there was a court at

Brighton. The Prince also had his own court built there in 1802. Tennis was all the rage at the time, the Duke of York being particularly fond of the game. There was a considerable monetary element involved, and thousands could be wagered on the result. This year, Prinny spent his birthday privately at the Royal Lodge, in the evening of which there was a 'very indifferent display of fireworks', according to *The Oracle*. Further sporting attire was delivered on 22 August: 'a scarlet & blue sattin Jocky vest with sleeves trim'd with gold cord in figure, gilt buttons, a sattin cap with gold fringe'. This shows that it was usual for those attending the races to disport themselves in such outfits. 'Jockey' in those days was a term not confined to the men who rode racehorses. It could also mean a race-goer or owner. The Jockey Club was in existence at that time, having been founded in 1750, but was a club for racehorse owners and gentlemen. The riders whom we now call jockeys were not, and never have been, members. The Prince made minor changes his racing colours over the years. In 1783 they were: 'Crimson waistcoat, purple sleeves, black cap'; in 1790: 'Purple and white striped waistcoat with scarlet and white striped sleeves, black cap'; in 1792: 'Purple waistcoat, scarlet sleeves trimmed with gold, black cap'; in 1801: 'Crimson waistcoat with purple sleeves, black cap'; In 1806: 'Purple waistcoat with scarlet sleeves trimmed with gold, black cap' and later, as George IV, in 1827: 'Crimson body gold lace purple sleeves, black cap'. [from: *The Raciad*, quoted in Sir Theodore Andrea Cook's *Eclipse and O'Kelly*]

The Times of 24 September reported a conversation overheard presumably by one of their reporters, between the Prince and his brother, the Duke of Clarence:

"William, your coat don't fit you – it sits awkward about the shoulders – pray who is your Taylor"?

"I don't know Brother – I think it sits well enough."

To this the Prince said: "Let me send you my Taylor;"

The Duke replied: "Is he an Englishman – for I am ___, Brother, if ever I let a Frenchman draw a thread for me, when I can find a Briton that will do it." The Duke was not as enamoured of all things French as Prinny was, to put it mildly, and this indirect reference to Louis is quite characteristic. The only outfit that Louis' accounts record that he made for the Duke of Clarence was on 27 January 1795 – 'To making a blue cloth lapelled frock, black velvet coller, gilt buttons & all materials for the Duke of Clarence (own cloth)'. This was no doubt a gift from George to wear at the impending royal wedding.

Prinny's fancy in September also briefly turned to animal motifs on his waistcoats, such as 'an embroid'd wais't with men, horses &c', an 'embroid'd quilting vest with men, horses, dogs &c.'. In October the Prince paid sixty guineas for a 'bottle green cloth dress coat & waistcoat shape richly emb'd in gold, silver &c.' and then ordered a 'scarlet (Goblin) cloth riding frock with green velvet coller, gilt G. P. & feather buttons compleat'. Whenever scarlet was required, especially for hunting 'pink' coats, the cloth used was always that from the Gobelin factory in France. The price of this cloth was 42/- a yard in 1786 but this was reduced to 36/- a yard in September 1787. In April 1788 it was 38/- and in September 1789 – 36/-. Thereafter the price Louis charged for it fluctuated between 36/- and 38/-, this variation presumably being dictated by the market. This was just about the most expensive cloth supplied by Louis, and it is quite obvious that he was importing cloth throughout the period. The Gobelin factory in Faubourg Saint Marcel, Paris, on the banks of the River Bièvre, was in recent times most famous for its tapestry, but they began as a dye-works where they produced this superior quality cloth of a very intense scarlet colour, of which the dye was fast, making it better for hunting coats because they so often got wet. The vegetable dye used for most red coats at the time was madder, which would fade to brown within a few months owing to the effects of sun and rain, so the Gobelin was a definite improvement. Louis also supplied a similarly-priced black cloth which he called 'Panion', which was also no doubt imported from France. A permanent jet black was difficult to achieve at that time. The main ingredients in use were logwood or brazilwood combined with fustic and copperas. The best mordant would have been chromic acid but Vauquelin did not discover it until 1797, so it is very questionable whether it was in use at this time. It is most likely that Panion's dye was just a particularly good formula and process using the above ingredients, which was enough to make it superior to the British equivalent.

The Prince took delivery on 3 November of 'a pair light colour Fearnought trowsers'. Fearnought was a heavy hard-wearing woollen cloth used for seamen's trousers and jackets, and one wonders what use the Prince put them to, not being known for wearing such rugged clothes. Maybe he dressed up as a seaman for a masquerade.

On 11 December, Louis brought a 'Birthday Suit very richly embroid'd all over the seams & all materials as usual (own shape, embroidery & lining) (Paid for additional embroidery to the applica & cleaning it all)'.

Sir Penistone (Penystone) Lamb (1745–1828), later the first Viscount Melbourne, was one of Louis' debtors. He married Elizabeth Milbanke, who bore him his eldest son Penistone, who died in 1805 at the age of only thirty-five. Elizabeth was a confidante of the poet Lord Byron and an aunt of Byron's future wife Anne Isabella Milbanke. Elizabeth had a number of affairs, such as with the Earl of Egremont, the Prince of Wales and the Duke of Bedford. It is likely that her remaining children were fathered by these men. Her second son William became the second Viscount Melbourne on the death of his brother and in June 1805 he married Lady Caroline Ponsonby, the gifted and passionate daughter of Frederic Ponsonby, 3rd Earl of Bessborough, who as Lady Caroline Lamb is sadly mainly remembered for a short intense affair with Lord Byron. In fact they maintained a long intellectual relationship until Byron's death. William, Viscount Melbourne, went on to become prime minister and advisor to Queen Victoria. The Lamb country seat, Brocket Hall in Hertfordshire, (later the country home of Lord Palmerston) was designed by the architect James Paine. Building was begun in 1760 by his father Sir Matthew Lamb and finally completed by Sir Penistone in about 1780. Sir Penistone lavishly decorated and furnished this great house with furniture supplied particularly by Thomas Chippendale. The cost of maintaining this lifestyle was enormous, and he fell heavily into debt. Records we have seen of his transactions with Louis start in June 1786, with a bond for £1,787/5/6, witnessed by Thomas Howell. Howell's name appears in all of the bonds and in Louis' bank statements, so he was acting for Penistone, and was therefore probably his solicitor. The second bond, dated 25 September 1789, was for £2,000 and the third, in the sum of £2,971/8/- was dated 16 November 1791. A statement also survives, signed by Louis, covering the years 1790 to 1793, presumably showing receipts and amounts outstanding after repayments:

1790 Nov 13 £1,485/14/-
     Dec 31 £104/8/9
1791 Dec 31 £80/14/3
1792 May 16 £1683/15/9 Balance of Bond Interest
     June 30 £124/15/-
     June 30 £107/15/7
1793 Total due to Louis Bazalgette £1,810/13/10
     July 5 £50 paid on account for Mr Louis Bazalgette by Thomas Howell
[British Library, Manuscripts Collection]

Louis' account with Coutts' Bank only dates from 1793, but following that date several payments to Thomas Howell appear, but no receipts are present, though payments through a bank would not necessarily show the debtor's name:-

1794 Oct 11 £16/16/-
1795 Dec 29 £130/-/-
1797 Oct 6 £200/-/-
     Oct 16 £400/-/-

It is therefore clear that Louis' transactions with Lord Melbourne were substantial and timely. *The Times* in January 1785 bemoaned how few of the noble country houses were being kept up, including the 'once gay and affluent Brocket Hall'. On 13 December it remarked dismally that 'the fall of snow is very unpropitious to the merry Christmas at Brocket Hall. No use can be made of the race grounds, or the dogs; there are, however, three billiard tables, and some musicians'. The standing of Brocket Hall improved, no doubt helped by injections of Louis' money, for on 13 May, 1801 *The Times* announced that 'the Prince of Wales and the Duke of Bedford set off yesterday on a visit to Lord and Lady Melbourne at Brocket Hall, where there are races this week.' No doubt they would both be paying their respects in particular to their ex-lover Lady Melbourne and visiting their putative children. The races became a regular event, and on 28 May 1802 the Prince, Mrs Fitzherbert and 'a large assemblage of the sporting and fashionable world' were present. These lavish gatherings cannot have harmed Penistone's chances of becoming Member of Parliament for Hertford, which he achieved that July.

Chapter 12: 1790-91

On 5 January, 1790, Bazalgette supplied a 'cloth dress coat & waistcoat, laced & looped with gold & all materials as before for Mr. Weltje Junior' and 'embroidering new shirts with fishes, buckles &c. for a sattin waistcoat for Mr. Weltje Sen'r'. Weltje Junior could not have been the cook Louis Weltje's son, since he only had two daughters, but was probably the son of his brother, John Christopher Weltje, who was for a time cook to the Duke of York. So it seems that Louis Weltje's nephew may also have been in the Prince's employ.

A week later, for the occasion of the Queen's birthday, Louis made 'a velvet dress coat & breeches and silver tissue vest & coat cuffs all richly trim'd with a very rich applica, the coat all over the seams and the wais't all over & all materials as usual (own applica & vest & coat cuffs)' for which he charged £71/1/9, of which £50 was for 'embroidering the applica on & making considerable additions to do.' The cloth used for this outfit was '9 yds puce col'd & pink spot velvet' at 42/- per yard. This Prinny wore to the ballroom. For the drawing room beforehand his outfit was probably the 'brown & blue velvet dress coat & breeches & white sattin vest, all very richly embroidered, and all over the seams (to be kept till next winter)' which Louis had supplied at a cost of £197/10/- on 21 February of the preceding year. *The Times* of 19 January described the Prince's outfits in this way:

> The Prince was dressed, at the Drawing Room, in a brown velvet coat, and breeches of the same with small blue spots. His waistcoat and the cuffs of his coat were gold tissue. The whole was richly embroidered with gold and silver stones and foil. All the seams were covered. His Highness' dress at the Ball Room, was a brown and pink spotted velvet coat and breeches, silver tissue waistcoat embroidered with a very rich *applica* of silver stones and coloured foils. The coat cuffs were silver tissue, which as well as the waistcoat was embroidered with silver stones and foils of various colours. The lining white sattin. His

Highness's dress was not the less admired for its being of home manufacture. All the embroidery was the work of Spital Fields.

On 13 April the Prince attended a fete at Mrs. Broadhead's rooms in Portland Place. *The Times* reported that he wore a sable domino (probably that supplied by Louis on 15 February) and that Mrs. Fitzherbert was attended by Mr. St. Leger and her brother Walter Smythe. Among the 'loungers' present was William Brummell, father of the Beau, 'with an innumerable quantity of tonish etceteras'.

Between 21 and 26 April that year the Prince bought three expensive outfits from Louis. First there was a 'cloth dress coat & waistcoat shape, richly embroidered in gold & purl & spangles' which when made up came to £71/6/6, then a blue cassimere dress coat and waistcoat richly embroidered in silks for £57/5/8 and finally a dress coat and waistcoat made with 'a bottle green cassimere dress coat & wais't shape of white silk both richly embroidered in silver & stones' which cost £64/9/6. These were followed on 8 May by another dress coat and waistcoat made from a 'striped black silk cloth dress coat & waistcoat shape, both richly embroidered in silks' at £57/18/11.

On 4 June Prinny took delivery of his birthday dress suit consisting of a 'garter blue striped rich silk coat & breeches, and white silk waistcoat & coat cuffs, all very richly embroidered in silver & stones & silk flowers, the coat on all the seams and the waistcoat all over' which was probably his most extravagant yet, coming to a staggering £199/8/-. He wore this suit to a Brighton ball and a newspaper report described it as 'A most beautiful cut velvet gala suit of a dark colour, with green stripes, and superbly embroidered down the front and seams with a broad embroidery of silver flowers, intermixed with foil stones. Waistcoat, white and silver tissue, embroidered like the coat: the garter fastened with a shoulder-knot of brilliants, star, George, etc.' Not content with that, on 12 June he had to have another dress suit made of a 'black & purple striped velvet coat & breeches & white silk waistcoat shape, all very richly embroidered in silks' for £54/6/6. George was partial to fine white quilting vests and ordered them a dozen at a time.

The Prince wore the above birthday dress suit to the King's birthday on 5 June, as confirmed in *The Times*: 'A garter blue striped rich silk coat and breeches, and white silk waistcoat, the whole very superbly embroidered, with silver, spangles and stones. The coat on all the seams was very beautifully embroidered with silk work, the waistcoat covered all over with similar embroidery'.

The court reporter further enthused:

> It being collar day, his Royal Highness did not appear with his new EPAULETTE till the evening in the Ball Room. This piece of jewellery is the most superb ever seen at Court, and estimated in value at 20,000l. The form of it is a long shaped oval, the outer row - a circle of very large costly brilliants; the inner part - filled with a mosaic of diamonds; the center of each part of the mosaic filled with a fine brilliant.
>
> A brilliant of extraordinary fineness, and the value exceeding four thousand guineas, formed a button at the top, and from the bottom of the Epaulette hung a fringe of two rows of large brilliants, extending three or four inches down the arm - this very costly ornamental appendage was set by *Jeffries* of Piccadilly.
>
> In the evening also his Royal Highness wore a superb diamond George, which as collar day, he did not wear in the morning.
>
> To compleat this very magnificent dress, his Royal Highness wore a most superb and valuable pair of brilliant buckles, consisting of stones of great size and value, cemented to each other by a beautiful knot of diamonds; - the knee buckles to correspond.

On almost every day between 1 and 23 of July, Louis delivered new and altered clothes in quantity, in preparation for the Brighton season. The new clothes included '4 fine callico under vests with sleeves compleat at 31/6 each' which were often ordered, probably for attending the races. There was also a blue riding frock, four mixt cloth lapelled frocks, two Fox uniform frocks, two Brighton uniform frocks and 'a scarlet dress hunt coat lin'd buff cassimere with gold lace loops'. Added to that were eleven vests including four more calico under vests with sleeves, just in case of need. The alterations were extensive, beginning with 'new lining a Brighton frock with buff cassimere & putting new buff cuffs & coller to do.', adding new velvet collars to twenty-five frocks and embroidered collars to fifty-five vests/waistcoats, letting out and adding 'new broad waistbands' to thirty-six pairs of breeches and finally supplying four pairs of black silk drawers.

On 23 July 1790 the Prince travelled to Brighton for the season. The following extract from the *St. James's Chronicle* for 1789 tells us something about the Prince's doings at Brighton.

> August 15th: The Prince of Wales's birthday on Thursday was very splendidly celebrated at Brighthelmstone. St. George, [Chevalier Joseph Bologne de Saint-Georges, who had fought a famous bout in 1787 against the cross-dressing Charles de Beaumont, CHEVALIER D'ÉON] the famous fencing master exhibited several trials of his skill with two French masters before the Prince and a large company in a pavilion and marquees pitched about a mile from the town. An ox was roasted whole and given to the populace. The Duke of Clarence gave prizes to several sailing boats which afforded much diversion. The company dined in the pavilion and the evening concluded with a supper and ball at the Castle Inn given by the Dukes of York and Clarence. The illuminations were universal and elegant.

There are, from 1786, occasional orders for pairs of 'brettels', usually in silk at a guinea a pair, in the Prince's accounts with his tailor. Allowing for Louis' sometimes eccentric spelling, and the fact that he phoneticised many of the words of his native tongue, for instance: 'applica' for 'appliqué', 'epaulet' for 'epaulette', it is likely that 'brettels' are actually 'bretelles', which in French basically means a strap, but the word is applied mainly to braces (US: suspenders) or brassiere straps.

In view of the Prince's expanding waistline, it is not surprising that he would have sometimes favoured braces rather than other means of support for his breeches or trousers. Braces as we know them were certainly being sold in 1820 by Albert Thurston from his emporium at 27 Panton Street, Haymarket, London, and it appears they were in use in 18th century France, which explains why Louis was familiar with them. Napoleon wore *bretelles* as well, it seems.

Confirmation that the brettels had a suspensory function can be seen in an order on the 18th November 1790 for 'a pair of (Vanbutchel) elastic brettels' at six guineas. Martin Van Butchell was an extremely eccentric dentist and professed curer of many ills (including *fistula in ano*), practising at 56, Mount Street. Being a pupil of the anatomist and surgeon John Hunter, he had no difficulty in having his first wife Mary embalmed, and he kept her in a glass case in his living room. He owned a small pony, whose shaggy coat he painted with coloured spots, and was often seen riding it in Hyde Park. Unusual person though he was, he was nonetheless very successful, and apart from dentures he designed various elastic devices which were used for trusses, corsets and garters etc. He is also credited with producing a pamphlet which extolled the virtues of temporary self-strangulation as a means of reviving 'failing powers' in men, and recommended his elastic (rubber) ligatures for the purpose. The only snag about 'temporary' strangulation is that it can very easily become permanent. The occasional discovery of ageing film actors, trussed up and hanging in hotel wardrobes, shows us that little has changed over time. The Prince only bought one pair of elastic brettels from Louis, so either he disliked them, or he liked them well enough to go directly to Van Butchell in future. A look at the good quack's advertisements demonstrates his claims to royal patronage. *The Times* was not above poking fun at him though.

> In this age of licentiousness, when wedded love is becoming a standing joke, the rare example of a man valuing his wives even after death will be read with wonder. John [sic] Van Butchell, the celebrated operator

on the *fistula in ano*, makes it a constant practice to embalm the partners of his domestic felicity. In each corner of his room are boxes so constructed, that they not only serve as receptacles for the bodies of his deceased ladies, but as sophas for the convenience of lounging; this eccentric disposition in Van Butchell is not so unprofitable as it may appear at first sight, - he makes it operate to the destruction of human vanity, for when any of his acquaintances exhibit traits of arrogance, he leads them gently to one of his portable mausoleums, and opening the lid, points with his finger to *what we must all come to*. As Van Butchell is a *great philosopher*, as well as one of the *finest gentlemen* of his time, we hope this example of connubial friendship, may be imitated with avidity by all the husbands in Great Britain.
[*The Times*, 25 August 1787]

The supply of new and altered garments carried on apace through August 1790, with one of Louis's master tailors Thomas Smith being despatched to Brighton in the middle of the month, no doubt in a coach stuffed full of clothes. There were several pairs of trousers, now also with the new broad waistbands, which may have been a fashion statement but were more likely to be to provide more comfort for the Prince's expanding corporation. They also had *bretelles*, reminding us of the expression 'belt and braces', which looks like a necessary precaution in the circumstances. Clothes were being returned to London all the time for further alteration, as the account entry 'Paid carriage & porterage of a large box from Brighton' illustrates. Further racing days were indicated by the supply of '4 pink silk under waistcoats with sleeves' and the alteration of 'two jocky vests'.

There is to be found among the papers of William Pitt the younger, the Prime Minister, a quarterly account dated September 1790 showing that he owed Louis Bazalgette £721/14/6, so Pitt was another of the prominent men of the day dressed by Louis. Pitt normally dressed in a plain but elegant style, but at special occasions such as royal birthday celebrations he dressed very finely. *The Times* reported what he wore on three occasions - on 19 January 1788 he wore a black, green and pink velvet suit, 'embroidered with gold and silver spangles, with wreaths of silk flowers' to the Queen's birthday, on 5 June 1789 'a carmelite coloured striped coat and breeches, white silk waistcoat, all richly embroidered in silver and stones' and on 19 Jan 1790 'a corbeau and blue striped velvet coat and breeches and white satin waistcoat, richly embroidered in silk'. These are typical of the outfits being made by Louis at the time. The quarter's expenditure appears to be very high, but it is probable that the account contains many items brought forward, since Pitt spent the whole of his life deeply in debt. In the collections of the Museum of London there is an embroidered suit which is said to have belonged to Pitt. If so, although it has no label, the chances are good that it was made in the Bazalgette workshops. According to John Ehrman's biography of Pitt, *The Younger Pitt: The Consuming Struggle'*, page 85 (footnote), Pitt wore a succession of brown coats embroidered with silver (once with 'leaves of light green intermixed') and once together with 'stones,' at the royal Birthdays at St James's. The sources given were *The Morning Post*, 19 January 1798, 5 June 1799 and 5 June 1800.

The Prince's mentor and uncle, Prince Henry, Duke of Cumberland, died on 18 September 1790. General mourning was observed (with the usual tailoring surcharges) for a month, during which the Prince ordered mainly black clothes, including a black 'weeper coat' for the funeral. Weepers were bands of white cloth, usually muslin, lawn or cambric, which were sewn on to the ends of the sleeves. The term could also be applied to the broad black satin ribbons that could be attached to the hat as a sign of mourning. The Lord Chamberlain decreed on this occasion that gentlemen's mourning dress must consist of 'black cloth, without buttons on the sleeves or pockets, plain muslin or long lawn cravats and weepers; black swords and buckles.' The Prince showed more signs of observing this mourning by the larger number of black clothes he ordered during this period.

On 21 October Louis supplied 'a 10th Dragoon jacquet & waistcoat, laced & looped with silver lace loops & tassells for Cornet [George] Leigh (your own lace, tassells &c.)' together with a great coat, followed by another the same on the first of November. The Prince sometimes bought uniforms for his young friends if they could not afford to pay for their own.

Towards the end of the year, orders for greatcoats naturally became more numerous, and perhaps the Prince was becoming keener on coach driving, because he needed several 'Shepherds cloth coats for driving in'. He obviously intended to spend some time hunting at his country estate at Kempshott because on 16 December he was charged for 'Making a Kempshot Uniform frock & all materials (own blue cloth)' and on 23 December 'Box & booking to Kempshot'. On 20 December, presumably for Christmas celebrations, the Prince bought a 'Fancy striped silk cloth coat & breeches and white sattin vest all richly embroidered in silks (own lining)' at a cost of £54/6/6, and two days later a 'Fancy striped silk cloth coat & waistcoat shape, both richly emb'd in silks (own sattin lining), which were made into a dress suit for £48/17/5.

On the clothing front, 1791 began with Prinny ordering a sober black velvet dress coat, but relieved it with a waistcoat made from a 'Rich gold tissue vest shape embroid'd with silver & stones &c.'. On 4 January he took delivery of a 'dress waistcoat to wear with any coat' made from an 'Embroid'd white sattin shape in gold, silver & stones'. Previously in the case of dress suits he had almost always ordered the coat and waistcoat together, though not always in matching material, since he often favoured embroidered white waistcoats with a coat of contrasting colours. He also planned to wear with it a pair of velvet breeches, because at the same time he had one altered, adding a new broad waistband. On 10 January Louis delivered 'a Couriers jacquet & vest laced with broad gold lace for Mr. Jouard (own blue cloth & gold lace)'.

We will go into the matter of the livery uniforms that Louis made for the Prince's retinue later, but in passing should mention that the Prince kept at least two couriers, of whom Jouard was one, whose job was to ride or drive frequently back and forth between Carlton House and wherever Prinny happened to be, mostly carrying garment orders or delivering clothes. Another example of livery was the supply on 21 January of 'a Hussar jacquet & trowsers, trim'd with astracan &

scarlet silk cord in figure for Master'. The Prince kept his own riding master, who probably supervised the grooms who looked after his horses. At the same time, Louis made a 'dress suit for col'l Byde' consisting of 'a puce col'd cassimere coat & breeches & white sattin vest all richly embroid'd in silks'. Colonel John Byde of the Coldstream Regiment of Foot-guards was made an equerry to the Duke of Clarence in 1789 and retired from the regiment in 1790.

On 17 January, Louis' accounts show 'Altering a brown emb'd velvet dress coat & breeches & gold tissue vest & making new backs to the vest, cleaning the embroidery and repairing a brown frock'. Since this outfit had been made some years before it is not surprising that it needed letting out. On 19 January *The Times* gushingly described this outfit in minute detail:

> THE PRINCE OF WALES was the best dressed Gentleman at Court. His Royal Highness wore a carmelite coloured coat and breeches; extremely elegant, and very curiously embroidered in siver, spangles and coloured stones and foils, in various devices, enriched with Brandenburg loops, intermixed with different coloured foils and stones of various colours. The seams were all covered with rich and elegant embroidery to correspond with the fronts: The other parts of the coat were embroidered in mosaic all over, with silver spangles and coloured foils – the buttons were of stones, set in gold.
> The waistcoat was of silver tissue, but so enriched with embroidery the same as the coat, that the ground of it was scarcely perceptible. It was trimmed with brilliants, as a fringe. The coat cuffs were the same as the waistcoat, and richly embroidered with brilliants, forming the handsomest dress the ever appeared at Court.
> The whole dress did great credit to the embroiderer for his excellent workmanship, and to the person who selected the pattern, for his taste and judgement.
> His Royal Highness wore diamond shoe and knee buckles; a diamond star, George and Garter, and the diamond epaulette which has been so much admired on former

birth-days for its costliness and elegance. His Royal Highness wore likewise a diamond sword.

We can imagine Louis reading this report over breakfast, like an actor reading a review. It must have felt something like the pinnacle of his tailoring career.

At the Queen's birthday celebrations on 18 January 1791, the Prince, according to the *Oxford Journal*, was decked out in 'the most elegant Dress that was ever displayed at St. James's. His Coat was of a Corbeau Blue striped Silk Velvet, the Breeches the same, embroidered in a broad and superb Manner, with Gold and Silver Spangles down the Seams; the Waistcoat of Silver Tissue; withan elegant Embroidery all over, to correspond with the Coat. His Royal Highness wore a most brilliant Star, Diamond Epaulet, and Diamond-hilted Sword and Tassel.' This suit had been made the previous June, described in the accounts as a 'corbeau & blue str. silk dress coat & breeches & silver tissue vest richly embroid'd all over the seams in silver &c. (own buttons & lining)' which was supplied at a total cost of £61/12/9. This outfit he presumably wore to the ball room.

On 25 January it is clear that Prinny was still helping out the young George Leigh, since the accounts mention 'Altering a striped sattin under vest of Yours to fit Cornet Leigh'. The day after, Louis brought a 'Bolton Hunt uniform lapelled frock' in scarlet cloth with silver buttons and a blue velvet collar, to be worn with an embroidered black cassimere waistcoat. This was for the hunt of William Orde-Powlett, 2nd Baron Bolton (1782–1850) of Bolton Hall in Yorkshire. There was also a scarlet version of the waistcoat 'exactly as above', either for variation or for evening wear. Prinny was quite busy hunting, as on the 1st February he received a 'Hampshire Hunt frock & all materials (own blue cloth & 'H. H.' engraved coat buttons)'. To go with it there was 'a scarlet cassimere waistcoat with flannell sleeves' and 'a white sarsnet under vest with sleeves, lin'd thro with the same & interlin'd with oil'd silk'. Presumably this was to help to keep the rain out. Almost all of his orders, well into March, were for riding or hunting attire.

On 1 June 1791, Louis delivered a birthday suit, which the Prince wore to the King's birthday celebrations on 4th June. In the accounts it is described as 'a bottle green & claret striped silk coat & breeches & silver tissue vest & coat cuffs. Shape, all very richly embroidered with silver stones & silks, the coat all over the seams & the waistcoat all over the body'. The materials for this suit came to £190 and it was embellished with a set of 'rich stone sett buttons' costing £21, the total charged being £214/17/9. The *Lady's Magazine* reported: 'His Royal Highness the Prince of Wales, (was) in a green striped silk coat, embroidered in a most superb manner with gold and silver spangles all over, the waistcoat of white silk, covered over with silver tissue, and a small embroidery to correspond with the coat; breeches the same as the coat. His highness wore a most brilliant star, sword and epaulet, both at the drawing room and ball.' *The Times* of 6 June described the same outfit in these terms:

> The Prince of Wales, as usual wore a very superb dress. A bottle-green and claret coloured striped silk coat and breeches, and silver tissue waistcoat, very richly embroidered in silver and stones, and coloured silks in curious devices and bouquets of flowers. The coat was embroidered down the seams, and spangled all over the body, as well as the waistcoat. The coat cuffs the same as the waistcoat. The breeches were likewise covered with spangles. His Royal Highness wore diamond buttons to his coat, waistcoat and breeches, which, with his brilliant diamond epaulette, and sword, made his whole dress form a most magnificent appearance.

Horace Walpole, writing to the Miss Berrys on 8 June, described the Prince on this occasion as 'gorgeous'.

Shortly afterwards on 13 June Prinny left London to spend the season at Brighton, obviously with a masqued ball in prospect, because a week before he departed Louis brought him a 'Friars Masquerade dress, the cap, mask, beads, cross & all materials for Mrs. FitzHerbert' and a 'Fish Womans dress, scarlet jacquet & petticoat, black sattin cloke, hat, handkerchief, gloves, mask &c. compleat' for himself. Maria usually put up with his foibles with some resignation but this time seems to have been prepared to enter into the spirit of one of his japes.

At Brighton, Prinny's fancy turned to the usual military manoeuvres with his pet regiment, the 10th Dragoons, so uniforms were ordered for him in great numbers. Sometimes his dragoon uniforms were embellished with extra embroidery and buttons for variety. He also ordered general's uniforms, which strictly speaking he was not entitled to wear, but that was obviously of little importance to a man who always wanted to be a general but was never permitted to be one.

It appears that Louis did officiate at some social events, but only one record has been found of his doing so. The *Morning Post and Daily Advertiser* of 8 and 9 August 1791 announced that 'His Royal Highness the Prince of Wales's Birthday will be celebrated at the Star and Garter, Pall Mall, on Friday the 12th August, 1791. Stewards: Mr. Jefferys, Dr. Layton, Mr. Meredith and Mr. Bazalgette. Dinner on Table at Four o'clock.' However, the Prince was treated to a Grand Gala at Windsor, so he would not have attended the above dinner, which was held for his tradesmen. Mr. Jefferys was one of the Prince's jewellers. The *Morning Chronicle* reported that 'His Royal Highness's Birth-Day was also celebrated by a number of Masonic Societies throughout the kingdom, and his tradesmen, to a very considerable number, dined together at the Star and Garter, in Pall-Mall, where many toasts propitious to the Prince, and the Brunswick family in general, were drank.' Presumably the Prince footed the bill, and it may have been a sop to those to whom he owed the most money, who no doubt would rather have been paid.

As reported in *The Times* on the same day, this was followed by a Grand Gala at Vauxhall in the Prince's honour.

> Admission, Two Shillings and Sixpence. The New Gallery erected for the Masquerade, will be open for accommodating the Company with Coffee, Tea and Lemonade; and the Gardens will be illuminated in the most brilliant manner. At the end of the improved

TEMPLE WALK, a spacious BUILDING will be finished on an entire novel Construction, representing a GRAND PORTICO, with MOVEABLE COLUMNS, in the Centre of which will be an ARTIFICIAL FOUNTAIN, decorated with Transparencies and Coloured Lamps in perpetual Motion, to be preceded by a few Pieces of FIREWORKS. Between the ACTS, and after the CONCERT, (By Permission) His ROYAL HIGHNESS the DUKE of YORK'S BAND will perform MARTIAL MUSIC. The Doors open at Seven and the Concert begin at Eight o'clock.

On 21 October 1791, Louis' wife Fanny gave birth to her second daughter Theresa, who was christened in St George's, Hanover Square on 28 November. She was probably named for Fanny's sister Theresa Philo. This little girl sadly died in infancy, surviving only to five months. Then on 13 September 1792 their son Louis was born. He did survive, and in fact lived to the age of eighty-five.

Louis was in partnership with two others while trading as 'Taylors and Drapers' at the Lower Grosvenor Street property, and it appears that this partnership began in the Summer of 1792, when Louis changed the name on his Michaelmas Quarter accounts (July-September) from 'Louis Bazalgette, Taylor' to 'Louis Bazalgette & Co, Taylors'. These partners were Peter Francis De Nedonsel, of James Street and Thomas Smith, of Park Street, Grosvenor Square, both described as 'Taylor, Dealer and Chapman'. Smith and Denedonsel were presumably employees before being made partners. A Pierre François Nedonsel was born in Volckerinckhove, Nord, France in May 1757, to Pierre and Eustasia Nedonsel, but died in infancy. It was not uncommon for the next son to be named for the baby who died, thus bringing the name back to life, as it were. This name is so unusual that it is almost certain to be the man. A Harriot Denedonsel was buried in Westminster on 25 November 1792, who may have been his wife or daughter.

The Times of 25 November 1791 reported that for the drawing room to celebrate the marriage of Frederick Duke of York to Princess Frederica Charlotte of Prussia, Prinny wore:

> A violet (blue) Genoa velvet dress coat and breeches, and white sattin waistcoat; the suit very superbly embroidered on the edges with silver and coloured spangles, foils and silks, and enriched with very handsome Brandenburgh loops to correspond. The waistcoat body embroidered all over. His Royal Highness wore diamond shoe and knee buckles; a diamond star, George and Garter, and a diamond epaulette which has been so much admired on former birth-days for its costliness and elegance. His Royal Highness wore likewise a diamond sword; and, as usual, was the best dressed Gentleman at Court.
> The Prince of Wales appeared in a very elegant new suit of cloaths at the Levee on Wednesday, which was much admired. It was a *corbeau* and lilac striped silk dress coat and breeches, the waistcoat very curiously embroidered in different coloured silks and festoons, and bouquets of flowers. His Royal Highness wore yesterday another new dress.

The above blue suit was probably that delivered by Louis on 15 October and described in the accounts as: 'Blue velvet coat & breeches and white sattin waistcoat, all very richly embroidered in silver & stones' and costing £92/15/9. The corbeau may have been the 'striped black silk cloth dress coat & waistcoat shape, both richly embroidered in silks', supplied the previous May for £57/18/11.

James Gillray, in the famous engraving 'A Voluptuary Under the Horrors of Digestion', showed that by 1792, at the age of twenty-nine, the Prince was already very overweight. Louis had to use 1¼ yards of cloth to make a plain waistcoat for him in 1786, 1½ yards by 1792 and 1¾ yards by 1794. By 1797, his weight had climbed to 17 stone 7 pounds (111 kg. or 245 lb.) and his girth eventually reached at least 54 inches. The Prince's increasing portliness was reflected in the increasingly large number of alterations which Louis' tailors had to make to his clothes. The 'gods' or patterns that were kept for the Prince would have needed to be remade regularly to accommodate the Prince's increasing measurements. This meant that Louis would have had to re-measure the royal personage quite frequently. This recalls a tailoring joke from Charles Dickens' magazine *Household Words*:

> TAILOR to a stout customer: "Have the kindness to put your finger on this bit of tape, sir, just here. I'll be round in a minute."

Chapter 13: 1792-93

An article was printed in the magazine *Archaelogia* on 1 January 1792, entitled: *Extract from the Wardrobe Account of Prince Henry, eldest Son of King James I. Communicated by William Bray, Esq. F. A. S. In a Letter to Mr. Wrighte, Secretary.*

In it the writer described the quite modest cost of Prince Henry's wardrobe, but did not miss the opportunity to contrast it with the wardrobe of a certain contemporary Royal Personage:

> I do not recollect that any one has given us a tailor's bill for any of our Edwards or Henrys, or their courtiers. Will it then be quite improper to produce a bill of this sort for one year's cloaths for prince Henry, son of James the First? To those who have paid the bills of a Regnier, or a Bazalgette, the amount of £4,574 for one year's cloaths, (for such it seems to be, though there are not dates to the several articles) near 200 years ago, may not seem altogether surprising, considering the person for whom they were made; and yet, unless such a bill as this was preserved, the bills of those modern adorners of the person might excite the admiration of future antiquaries, if any of them should by accident be found at the bottom of a chest, or in a corner of a steward's room, especially if there should be receipts at the foot.

The bills certainly do excite our admiration. The Regnier referred to was John Regnier, a ladies' riding habit and staymaker of 28, Conduit Street

For the Queen's birthday celebrations in January of this year, the Prince ordered a dress suit made from 9 yards of 'Carmelite coloured' (i.e., dark brown) velvet for the coat and breeches and two yards of rich silver tissue for the vest. 'Embroidering the whole suit very richly all over & with Brandenburgh loops & all over the seams, with silver and coloured stones & foils & vest shirts & coat cuffs. Edged with rich bullions & fringe (own rich buttons & sattin lining)' alone cost £197/10/- and the whole suit came to £266/17/9 - probably the most splendid suit yet. This suit was very similar to that which he had worn to this occasion in the previous year. It was as usual described enthusiastically on 19 January in *The Times*:

> THE PRINCE OF WALES was as usual the best dressed Gentleman at Court. His Royal Highness wore a carmelite coloured velvet coat and breeches, extremely elegant, and very curiously embroidered in silver spangles and coloured stones and foils, in various devices, enriched with Brandenburg loops, intermixed with different coloured foils and stones of various colours. The seams were all covered with rich and elegant embroidery, to correspond with the fronts; the other parts of the coat were embroidered in mosaic all over, with silver spangles and coloured foils - the buttons were stones set in gold.
> The waistcoat was of silver tissue, but so enriched with embroidery the same as the coat, that the ground of it was scarcely perceptible. It was trimmed with brilliants, as a fringe. The coat cuffs were the same as the waistcoat, and richly embroidered with brilliants, forming the handsomest dress that ever appeared at Court.
> The whole dress did great credit to the embroiderer for his excellent workmanship, and to the person who selected the pattern, for his taste and judgment.
> His Royal Highness wore diamond shoe and knee buckles; a diamond star, George and Garter, and the diamond epaulette which has be so much admired on former birthdays for its costliness and elegance. His Royal Highness wore likewise a diamond sword.

The newspaper also observed that the 'newest and most splendid suits, which were apparently made for the Birth-Day, were all *a la Brandenburg*' and included the Prince's suit amongst these. It then made the following remarks:

> Many of the Nobility were disappointed of their Birth Day Suits, which they had ordered from France, through the vigilance of the officers at Dover, who lodged them safe in

the Custom-House. It is astonishing the Nobility will suffer the anxiety and run the hazard of disappointment, when it is an acknowledged fact, that the *best dresses* that appeared at Court, were *entirely of English Manufacture*. The velvets, &c. made in Spitalfields, and the Embroidery done in Bond-street. [Probably by Gouldsmith & King, 108 New Bond St.]

If Gentlemen would give full encouragement to the English Manufacturer, by giving him every reason to hope and expect a sale for his articles - it would encourage speculation; and there is no doubt, but they would be supplied with a variety of dress cloathes - not only in a *newer* style than they generally receive them from France, but better made, and positively cheaper. But prejudices require the aid of time to limp away.

The Prince continued to order clothes throughout January, although at a reduced volume compared to the year before. This was a steady downward trend, the reasons for which have already been suggested. On 26 January he received what sounds like a handsome outfit, consisting of a striped silk dress coat and swansdown waistcoat, with black silk stocking breeches. Two days later, another solution to the inconvenience of hunting in the rain was tried, which involved 'Covering the pockets of a scarlet hunting frock with oiled silk'. Most of the orders that followed were for making alterations to various hunting and uniform frocks. On 15 February Louis brought a repaired domino and a black silk mask for a masquerade, with 'a dark col'd striped velvet dress coat & breeches & white sattin wais't all richly embroidered in col'd silks'. He had also been 'Altering Masquerade (Spanish) dress for Mr. Poyntz & for new roses'. This was Stephen Poyntz, cousin of Earl Spencer and father of Georgiana Duchess of Devonshire, who held for a time a commission in the Prince's regiment, as well as being in charge of his staghounds at Kempshott. This is where the Prince and his friends were at the time, since we see an accounts entry on 17 February for 'Box & booking to Kempshot'. There were also several new Kempshott uniforms supplied. By April it was manoeuvre season again and most of the orders were for new or altered 10th Dragoons or general's uniforms.

In this year the Prince went down to Brighton earlier than usual, in April, and his regiment was quartered there for the defence of the coast, in anticipation of a war with France and a possible invasion attempt. *The Sussex Weekly Advertiser* of 21 May reported: 'On Friday the 10th Regiment of Light Dragoons had a grand field day in honour of the Prince, after which his Royal Highness honoured the officers with his company to dinner at the Old Ship Tavern, and the next morning set out for town. The Prince is expected at Brighton this day previous to the grand review of his regiment tomorrow by Gen. Lascelles on the Downs near that place. On Friday next the above regiment is to have another field day in review order at which the Duke and Duchess of York are expected to be present'.

At the end of May, Louis delivered some more masquerade kit including two black silk masks and 'a Friars Masquerade dress with beads caps cross & compleat'. The Prince's dress suit for the King's birthday this year was suitably splendid - an 'Olive col'd striped silk coat & white silk waistcoat & coat cuffs all very richly embroidered in silver & stones & curious silk flowers, the seams all covered with a rich applica & the whole body embroidered all over with silver spangles &c.'. The total cost of this suit was £199/8/-.

At the drawing room on the King's birthday, according to *The Times* of 5 June 1792, the Prince was

> ... as usual, the best dressed Gentleman at Court - His Royal Highness wore a carmelite and pale blue striped silk coat and breeches, and white silk waistcoat and coat cuffs, the whole very richly embroidered in silver and stones, and very curious flowers of different colours. The seams were all covered with an *applica* to correspond with the coat border; and the body of the coat was covered with silver spangles, which gave the dress a very splendid and light appearance, notwithstanding it was so richly embroidered. His Royal Highness wore diamond show and knee buckles, a diamond star, George and Garter, and

the diamond sword and epaulette which has been so much admired on former birth-days.

The *The Sussex Weekly Advertiser* printed a story on 3 September, describing a fete given by the Prince on 27 August, in honour of his thirtieth birthday:

> At the Prince's fete on Brighton Level last Monday no fewer than four thousand persons were supposed to have attended, the majority to feast their eyes while the others feasted more substantially on a fine ox with a proportionate quantity of bread and strong beer prepared for the occasion. The ox was taken from the fire about 3 o'clock and very skilfully dissected by Mr Russel at the bottom of a large pit while the spectators and expectants stood in theatric gradation on its sloping sides. The day proved very favourable to this rustic festivity. His Royal Highness's guests were very accommodating and good-humoured to each other until the strong beer began to operate. The Prince and Mrs Fitzherbert looked on for a considerable time with great good humour and had the satisfaction of hearing that no accident nor injury occurred in so large a concourse except a few black eyes and bloody noses at the close of the evening.

Louis himself had to do a little travelling that year, claiming expenses to Bagshot and Brighton in August. There is a curious account entry on 18 September - 'Putting up several cases of Prussian Dresses at Carleton Ho.'. One wonders for whom these were intended and upon what occasion. The rest of the year brought no particularly exotic orders, though on 4th December there was 'a lead col'd quilted robe de chambre, lin'd thro' with the same intirely & interlined with elder down wadding' and on the same day 'a lead col'd silk & mohair great coat quilted as above, intirely lin'd thro' with the same'. Why they should match is interesting to guess at since they must surely not have been worn together, unless Prinny, who keenly felt the cold, was intending to be a guest in a poorly-heated house.

Sometime in 1792 Louis decided that life in the capital was too unhealthy for his wife and family so he bought a house in rural Turnham Green. It appears that Guillaume Gaubert was also renting a property there at this time. According to the records of the Sun Fire Office, the house Louis bought had an attached carriage-house and detached wash-house, with a field beside it and was situated at the 'corner of Chiswick Lane, Turnham Green'. We know that Louis leased several parcels of land from the Prebend Manor of Chiswick, but the records are not too precise about where these were. The Prebend Manor lands were leased to landlords who then sold sub-leases for smaller parcels of land. Alexander Weatherstone held the main lease from 1770 to 1783, followed by his widow Ann until 1795. The Will of Ann Weatherstone appointed her friends Marriott Steward and George Richards to be executors and guardians of her son Henry and bequeathed her 'undivided third part or share of and in the Prebendal Manor of Chiswick' to them in trust for Henry until he should attain the age of 21 years.

The freehold copyhold and leasehold estates on which Louis bought leases were in the possession of Edward Bishopp until his death in 1792, and he left them to William Bownas and William Justin, who in their turn sold them leasehold to Louis. Although the plots are described in the proceedings of the Court Baron their locations are vague, such as '... the said messuage and two pieces of land...situate upon Turnham Green near the High Road heretofore near to the Pond since filled up in the Parish of Chiswick commonly known as the Pond House.' The name 'Pond House' seems not to have been used during Louis' ownership. The location of the house was deduced by checking those who lived nearby, which were listed in the churchwardens' and overseers' accounts and in the 1801 and later censuses. In most lists there are four or five small plots quite close by Louis' house, which look on a parish map to have been those beside the Packhorse and Talbot public house. Other neighbours at various times were Robert Whitlock, coachmaker (on the High Road to the east of Chiswick Lane), William Grimsdale the baker, William

Linguard the victualler, who ran the Roebuck public house nearly opposite the Packhorse and Talbot, and Thomas Adey the grocer. Chiswick life at the time is vividly described in this passage from a memoir written by one of Adey's descendants:

> Most of Chiswick was covered with 'parks, paddocks and private grounds' of the 'truly respectable', including scores of the nobility, Chiswick Park even seeing distinguished visitors from all over Europe as guests of the Duke of Devonshire. Around the splendours of the village grew acres and acres of the 'whitest, most thin skinned and mellowest barley in England', many market gardens sending vegetables and fruit up to Covent Garden, and wide meadows of grazing for cattle, some giving milk and others fattening again for Smithfield Market after having (been) driven, sometimes for days, from distant farms in the west and Wales. The parish church and village centre, pleasant with large trees, looked across the Thames, busy with sailing barges and private boats, to open country where, in winter, snipe and hare were shot.
>
> There was, however, another side to this picture. In winter the village was almost cut off because of the deep muddy, even dangerous, roads while even the river was often iced over as the nineteen narrow arches of London Bridge slowed up the current. Only the well-to-do got fresh water from pumps in the house or yard, and others had to rely on water-butts or on water brought in barrels on horse or donkey back from Hammersmith. Sewerage there was none, and the houses of the city merchants in Turnham Green were separated from the high road by paddocks as protection from dust in dry, and mud in wet weather.
>
> [Quoted by permission of the author, Frank C. Adey, a descendant of Thomas Adey, grocer, who was a neighbour and contemporary of Louis Bazalgette]

On 18 October 1792 Louis Bazalgette was denized (naturalized) on the same day as his old friend Daniel

Bergman. Louis was described as being of Grosvenor Street, Grosvenor Square, gent, and Daniel as being of Charles Street, Grosvenor Square, gent. Some of these denization records give details of the subjects' birthplace, but in their entries it just says 'aliens born.'

For the Queen's birthday in January 1793 Prinny wore a 'general's uniform suit with his diamond star and epaulet, but was only present in the Ballroom' reported *The Times* on 16 January. This was probably the 'Generals uniform frock with gold embroid'd loops' as delivered by Louis that morning.

The year also began with some initial reductions in Prinny's household:

> Yesterday Colonel HULSE held a Board of Treasury at Carlton House, when the long intended reduction in the Prince of WALES'S household took place; the only persons discharged, out of livery, are two Pages of the presence, and three of the Back Stairs; and a Cook.
> [*The Times*, Wednesday, 23 Jan 1793]

On 28 January *The Times* announced that the Prince had been appointed colonel of the 10th Light Dragoons, by a commission bearing the date of November 1782, with the rank of a general in the army.

On 28 February 1793, Louis' wife Frances gave birth to a further son, Daniel, who was christened on 28 March at St. George, Hanover Square.

On 11 April, Louis' accounts show that the Prince was again providing uniforms for his young friends in the 10th Dragoons. This time it was George Quentin, whom the Prince had just appointed a cornet. Entries are: 'Altering a reg'l coat to fit Mr. Quinton', 'making a regimental jacq't & wais't & all materials as usual (own cloth, lace, tassells &c.) for Mr. Quinton' and then making a white cassimere waistcoat and pair of matching breeches, and new buttoning a regimental vest & breeches for him. Another uniform was delivered to him on 10 July. Quentin rose quickly through the ranks and was lieutenant-colonel of the regiment by 1808, commanding them during the

Peninsular War. In 1814 he was court-martialled for neglecting his troops in France but acquitted on three of the four charges. Following Quentin's almost complete exoneration, twenty four officers of the 10th Dragoons sent a 'round robin' to Colonel Palmer asking him to request that the Prince should cashier Quentin. This action by the officers was regarded as a conspiracy, and Quentin had little choice but to challenge Palmer to a duel. Quentin had married in 1811 Georgiana, the younger sister of James Lawrell, whose father previously owned Eastwick Park and then sold it to Louis later. Lawrell was therefore Quentin's brother-in-law and acted as his second. At the duel, which took place on Friday 3 February 1815, Quentin fired first, at 12 paces, and missed (perhaps on purpose). Palmer then fired in the air and both the combatants agreed that honour was satisfied. Quentin then served at Waterloo and was badly wounded but was made a Companion of the Bath as a result. Sir George later became Aide de Camp to George IV, though his wife Georgiana was one of the Regent's mistresses. Quentin died in 1852 at the ripe old age of 91.

Similarly, on 6 May Louis supplied 'a fancy pattern jacquet laced broad gold lace for Capt'n Hammond (own lace & epaulet)' in scarlet with blue cuffs. Thomas Hammond later became a general, and chief equerry when George was King. On the same day there was also 'a Light Dragoon jacq't & waistcoat trim'd with silver braid broad & narrow in figure & loops for Gen'l Harcourt'. Lieutenant-General Harcourt served under the Duke of York in the early campaigns against the French in Flanders, distinguishing himself at the battle of Willems on 10 May 1794.

For the King's birthday in June of that year the Prince appeared in his regimentals, as colonel of the 10th Light Dragoons. In September, both of Louis' master tailors, Smith and Denedonsel, were sent to Brighton to attend the Prince, as their expenses in the accounts show. Louis himself had to go to Windsor in November. On 27 September there was 'a habit & petticoat for Mrs. FitzHerbert (own cloth)'.

In about April 1793, and certainly by July 1793, Louis had become a client of Coutts' Bank at No. 59, The Strand. It is not known with whom Louis banked before 1793. Nor have records been found for all of his business transactions, although many of these appear in his personal account. We can be fairly sure that he kept an account with the Swiss bankers Perregaux in Paris. Perhaps he did all his banking with them before moving to Coutts, but this would not have been very convenient once he had settled in London.

The ledgers of Coutts' Bank are still kept in their archives and it was therefore possible to photograph all of Louis' statements from 1793 until some years after his death in 1830. Coutts' bank ledgers are large leather-bound books which are arranged alphabetically by customer name. The ledger containing the customer's account is known as a nominal ledger, and uses a simple double-entry system as used by all banks at the time, and still of course used today. This means that the balance is shown twice, which makes the debits and credits easy to reconcile. The left hand of the two pages is the debit side, where all outgoing payments are recorded. The facing right-hand page is the credit side or 'contra', where all amounts received into the account appear. During the working day, all transactions were recorded by the tellers in their daybooks, and some amounts could be totalled there. The bank would close about two hours before the employees finished work, to allow the tellers to dictate their daybook entries to the clerk, who wrote them in 'fair copy' copperplate into the nominal ledgers.

There were many opportunities for spelling errors to occur, mainly in names, either in writing them in the daybook or in getting them transcribed into the ledger. Many examples of these errors can be seen in the Coutts' bank ledgers, which often makes it difficult to track the name of the payer or payee. The names are also usually just recorded as 'Mr. Smith', and not so often 'Mr. J. Smith' or 'Mr. John Smith'. On the credit side, payments may be simple or quite complex. For instance, the customer himself could make a cash deposit. In this case, the credit will just show 'cash'. If the payer brought in cash or bank notes, the name would usually be mentioned. In the case of cheques, the payer and his own bank would be recorded, e.g., 'Mr. Smith on Robarts & Co', or if the payment was from a bank or a company it would appear as 'Bell & Co on Esdaile & Co'. Coutts' Bank at this time had a limited clearing system with some other London banks. In modern times, most British banks are part of the 'clearing houses' system, which facilitates transfers of funds between the member banks.

Thomas Coutts on 10 April 1793 drew up a document outlining the debts owed to his clients by the Prince of Wales. Louis Bazalgette was owed sums of £17,000 and £2,735, for which he received £800 and £136/15/- annual interest respectively. The bond was actually for £22,212 jointly held by the Prince and the Duke of York, the £17,000 being the Prince's share. The money owed to Louis Bazalgette was for 'robes'. The joint bond for the Prince and the Duke of York dated 10 January 1792 for £22,212, repayable over four years, was entered by D & G Farrer of Lincoln's Inn Fields on 6 April 1793. A separate bond dated 5 January 1792 was set up for Louis to receive £2,735 in interest. Both were signed by Prince George and John Willet Payne. £67/7/6 interest was paid every six months, ending in February 1795.

Coutts Bank had a close relationship with the Paris Bankers Perregaux, with whom we have seen already that Louis had dealings.

> Coutts & Co. had come to Louis Napoleon's rescue and similarly, in the aftermath of revolution and uncertainty that followed the French defeat, were able to help many of their French customers and banking colleagues. They had had a close connection with the French House of Lafitte since 1788, when it was known as Perregaux.
> [Coutts – The Story of a Private Bank; Edna Healey]

Louis also in 1793 became associated with Coutts Trotter, who was a partner in the business of Coutts & Co, and whom Louis eventually made one of his executors. Trotter was a kinsman of Thomas Coutts, which facilitated his entry into the bank. He was born in Scotland, and after his arrival in London had worked as a clerk in the Navy Pay Office under his brother, Alexander, who was Deputy Paymaster. Between 1802 and 1806, Alexander Trotter and his master, Lord Melville, the

Treasurer of the Navy, came under scrutiny over naval monies. Melville allowed Trotter to transfer navy funds from the Bank of England to his account at Coutts where he invested the money on his own behalf, retaining the interest it earned. The Admiralty Office was located just south of Charing Cross at the time and therefore was conveniently close to Coutts' Bank in the Strand. Both men were acquitted but were 'seen to have acted rashly'. Although Melville had friends in high places and was cleared following his impeachment, the scandal ultimately bought about his political downfall. It is hard to imagine that Coutts Trotter was unaware of his brother's financial dealings, considering how close they were. The three Trotter brothers, the other being John, had lived frugally together after their arrival from Scotland in a modest apartment in the Strand.

Melville's trial took place in the House of Lords in May of 1806.

> Throughout the months of May and June, public attention had been absorbed by the famous trial of Lord Melville. So early as May 6th, Mrs Stanhope had written delightedly:-- "You will be glad to hear that the cross-examination of Mr Trotter went in favour of Lord Melville who looked perfectly composed the whole time." But not till the 12th did the end arrive. Your sisters both attended the trial and had the gratification of hearing Lord Melville acquitted. The Prince had the good sense not to vote. The Court was as full as possible & when the two youngest Peers voted on the first charge & said Guilty, there was something like a hiss from the House of Commons. I am glad it is over & I hope the country will not be put to the expense of any more trials of the same kind for many years. The Princes went and shook Lord Melville by the hand as soon as it was over.
> June 13th, 1806.
> [The Letter-Bag of Lady Elizabeth Spencer-Stanhope v. I., by A. M. W. Stirling (compiler)]

A piece of trivia about Melville: his son Robert, 2nd Viscount Melville, lived between 1785 and 1806 at Warren House on

Wimbledon Common. This house was later renamed Cannizaro House and was bought in the mid-19th century by the author's great-great-grandfather John Boustead, a wealthy coffee planter with estates in what was then known as Ceylon. He was bankrupted by the coffee rust and his daughter Ethel married the author's great-grandfather Charles Norman Bazalgette.

For the King's birthday in June, Prinny for the first time wore the uniform of the 10th Light Dragoons, in contrast to the rich and gaudy outfits he had worn in the previous years. This was the beginning of a trend.

Chapter 14: 1794-95

Put to the needle

Thomas Sheppard, one of the apprentices in Bazalgette's tailoring shop, has been informed by one of the masters, Mr. Smith, that tomorrow, after his chores have been completed, he will be put to the needle. Thomas is pleased at this news, because he has been champing at the bit for some months to be allowed to begin to learn his trade. He does not sleep too well because he is too keyed-up to settle, so is happy when next morning at half past four he can rise, perform some perfunctory ablutions and hurry off at a gangly pace on the twenty-minute walk to Brooks Mews. That morning he cheerily performs his chores in record time and is then told by Mr Smith that he may go and join the workmen.

Thomas's entry into the sewing room, with its long table and large east-facing windows, is greeted with a variety of remarks, loudest of which is: "Here's the squeaker! Come aboard, my lad!" which comes from a muscular fellow who extends a rope-calloused palm to help Thomas on to the table. This is Horace, nicknamed Horatio, a name he bears with pride. Horace was once impressed into the navy, and had to serve two years before managing to absent himself from his ship and return to tailoring. His language is consequently well-salted with nauticisms. As the tailors are making room for him he sees a hand flapping at the other end of the board - he is being beckoned by a serious, even studious-looking young man, and uncertain whether by protocol he should stand or not, he crawls over to him. The man introduces himself as Pierre, though his nickname is Pete, a name he bears with resignation. Thomas will find later that this clouded face can very occasionally and suddenly break into a sunny smile, showing for a moment the true beauty in his heart.

Pierre tells him that before starting to sew he must learn to sit properly.

"The cross-legged position is the only way that you can work, both in sewing and pressing. You will find it painful to sit this way for long, but you must persist or you will never find your way past this obstacle. You will get used to it in time and it will feel very natural. When the pain in your thighs or back becomes too much to bear you may change your position a little to get some relief for a while, but you must return to the correct position as soon as you can bear it. As you become tired, resist the tendency to slouch. You must keep your back straight, otherwise you will have trouble with your neck. Here are two small cushions which you must place under your ankle-joints. If you do not use them your joints could become very sore and swollen. I repeat that you must not give up - otherwise you will have fallen at the first fence, as it were, and will never become a tailor."

"I just couldn't stand it, myself," whispers the man sitting next to Thomas, "so I kept shifting about and never got settled. It wasn't in this shop, but they forced me to sit right by putting a sleeve-board across my knees with a twenty-pound goose-iron on each end. It hurt like the divil I can tell you! After half-an-hour of this I begged to be released, and promised to do better. It was a hard lesson, but I finally made it. Nothing I did could hurt as much as that sleeve-board!"

Pierre touches Thomas on the shoulder and asks if he feels comfortable.

"Not bad - I think I must be quite loose-jointed." He can see how the position could be much more of an ordeal for a short, stocky man.

"In that case, Thomas, we will try some stitching. I am pleased to hear that you have shown interest already by watching, and asking some of the tailors what stitches they were making. Here are two pieces of calico. First, please baste them together. I expect you know how to do that, but make the seam as straight as you can. That is fine. Now let us try the back-stitch. Make the stitches as even as you can and do not let them get longer as you go. The most important point to note is that your seam must follow the line, otherwise the seams will pucker or the clothes will not fit."

Thomas spends the next two hours practicing some basic stitches until his legs are very stiff and his buttocks have long ago gone to sleep. He is then allowed down from the board, and *has to spend some time trying to get his legs to walk. He hopes tomorrow will be a little better.*

Louis' tailoring accounts show little that is of interest in the early part of 1794, and certainly none of the opulent dress suits of previous years. Louis was by now supplying very little of the cloth for these garments, apart from Gobelin red, because the more sober matte cloths by now being used for his client's coats were readily available in England. There were continuing copious alterations, and for new outfits the Prince was increasingly ordering uniforms, breeches and vests. The Prince for the second year running wore a regimental uniform to the Queen's birthday, rather than the splendid suits of previous years. On 29 January Louis supplied 'a blue fancy frock for General Hulse'. Hulse was for many years the Prince's treasurer and receiver-general, and on the accession of the Prince to the throne, General Hulse was nominated treasurer of the household, and governor of Chelsea Hospital. On 21 February there was another masquerade in the offing since Prinny ordered a black silk mask and 'a blue cloth sailor's jacquet lin'd thro' with white cassimere, silk sleeve lining, gilt buttons & all materials (own cloth)'. The following hussar outfit from 19 March is shown in detail below with its materials:

> To making a scarlet cloth Hussar ripper jacquet & looped with white worst'd lace & cord in figure (own cloth, lace & cord)
> 2 yds white shaloon to line body
> Sheep skin cuffs, coller & edging
> 18 large round top plated buttons
> 3 doz. breast do.
> Sewing silk & twist
> To making a light blue do. laced & looped as above (own cloth &c.)
> Cotton body & sleeve lining
> 18 butt's as above & 36 br.
> Sewing silk & twist

Making a pair light blue cloth pantaloons lin'd with linnen & trim'd with cord in figure (own cloth, cord &c.)
Making a pair outside do. to button up all the side seams & straped with leather, 4 doz. metal buttons & all materials
To making a scarlet cap turned up with blue, tassell &c.

For the King's birthday celebrations on 4 June George wore a full dress uniform with a diamond star. On 21 June Louis went to Windsor to wait upon his royal client and also to re-clothe his two couriers - 'To 2 black cloth frocks with velvet collers compleat for Mr. Pacquet & Mr. Jouard - £4/3/4 each'. At the beginning of August Louis was back at Windsor, supplying amongst other items '8 fine white India dimoty vests with sleeves compleat for Mr. Ince, Pastry Cook at £1/11/6'. On 15 August Louis brought 'a New Uniform regimental coat, laced & looped with silver lace Brandenburghs & tassells on both sides & sleeves (own cloth, lace, tassells & epaulets)', so it looks as if the Prince was experimenting with his regimental dress again. Louis adds rather testily: 'Making a pattern for do. & altering *several times*' [author's italics]. On 21 August he was again making alterations to a 'New Uniform dress coat', 'making a 'Hussar jacquet, laced & looped on both sides with narrow & broad lace & at hips & cuffs (own cloth)' and 'Altering & new buttoning 2 Chasseurs coats & putting new epaulets & corners to do. (own epaulets, corners & buttons)'. On the 28th - 'Making the kings Hare Hunt uniform coat & all materials' and two days later, again 'Altering the New Uniform jacquet and new lining do.'.

At the beginning of September there was further work on new uniforms, requiring Louis to make another trip to Brighton. This involved 'making a plain Hussar jacquet (own blue cloth)', 'Making a green cloth waistcoat & breeches for Chasseur, the waistcoat trim'd with gold cord in figure (own cloth, cord & buttons)' and 'Making a green waistcoat & breeches with gold cord & all mat's as above for Chasseur'. Another re-design of the hussar's trousers showed in 'Making a blue cloth outside pantaloons lin'd brown holland, black leather on the seams & bottoms of the legs, regimental butt's & all materials (own cloth)'.

On 8th September, Louis paid £100 to Mr. Leader, the coachmaker, whose premises were in Liquorpond Street, Holborn, and who was also patronized by the Prince.

In early October, Prinny turned his attention to redesigning the 10th Dragoons' regimental uniforms as well, requiring Louis to create several new patterns for various ranks. The list consisted of:

> To making 2 Pattern reg'l jacquets and waistcoats & all materials for a Quarter Master & Serjeant (own cloth & lace) at £5/9/- each
> To a do. trim'd with worstead lace & cord, compleat for a Private Dragoon
> To making 2 pair blue cloth pantaloons laced up the seams & round the fall down flap & all materials – 25/- each (own cloth & lace)
> Making 2 pair more of do. plain & edged with scarlet cassimere – 25/- each
> To a pair white cassimere pantaloons & all materials compleat
> Making 2 pair of outside pantaloons (blue & mixt colour) trim'd with leather & all materials £2/5/- each (own cloth)
> To a blue livery cloth Pattern of a dress reg'l coat, trim'd with tape, lace, cord & tassells, buttons & all materials as Col'l St. Leger's
> To a do. for a jacquet trim'd with tape, lace, cord & butt's compleat.
> To pattern of a Hussar jacquet & waistcoat of green & scarlet stuff, trim'd with tape & cord in figure, tape, cord &c. compleat

The Prince then decided to have new livery made for the pages, starting with 'making a blue cloth dress suit laced with broad silver lace for Mr. Santagne (Page) (own lace & cloth)'. Santagne was probably the longest-serving of his pages and was still in his employ at George's death in 1830. Although at that time his brother William IV lost no time in dismissing all of George's French servants, at least Santagne apparently received a pension in recognition of his long service. The order for the pages' dress suits is of interest as it lists them all by name:-

> To making 14 Pages dress suits and all materials as the above for Mr. Mills, Mr. Pacquet, Mr. McEwen, Mr. Jouard, Mr. Hownam, Mr. Lucas, Mr. Rookby, Mr. Cole, Mr. Beckt, Mr. Ince, Mr. Bidgood, Mr. Sarsfield, Mr. Dalton & Mr. Troop - £8/4/6 each - Total £115/3/-.

December 1794 brought a new surge of activity:

> To making a fancy chintz robe de chambre & waistcoat (own chintz)
> 16 yds blue silk to intirely line do. – 5/6
> Elder down wadding to interline both thro' & sleeves
> Pockets to gown & waistcoat
> Sewing silk & twist, butt's &c.
> To 2 shaded silk robe de chambres & wais'ts with sleeves, lin'd thro' with the same & interlined with elder down wadding & all materials at £12/5/- each
> Making 4 white spaniolet robes de chambre lin'd thro' with flannell & all materials - £1/11/10 each (own spaniolet & flannell)
> To making a blue great coat trim'd with Brandenburghs & fur edges & cuffs (own cloth, fur &c.)
> 10 yds silk to line thro' – 6/6
> Sewing silk & twist
> To making a scarlet Polish Hussar jacquet trim'd with silk lace loops & edges & fur on the edges & cuffs
> 5 yds silk to line – 6/6
> 1 ½ yds scarlet cloth – 25/-
> Silk cord loops & edges
> Elderdown wadding to interline
> 6 dozen 10 round top gilt butt's – 3/6
> Sewing silk & twist &c.
> Making a blue cloth do. exactly as the above & all materials.

It may now be time to note the appearance on the scene of George Bryan 'Beau' Brummell, who upon leaving Oriel College, Oxford, was noticed one day by the Prince, and who on 17 June 1794 was gazetted at the age of sixteen to a cornetcy in the 10th Dragoons. His stylishness is famous of course, and his influence on the way Prinny dressed cannot be understated. However, although he is credited with persuading George to use English-style tailors such as Meyer, Schweitzer & Davidson and John Weston the annual decline in the number of clothes supplied by Louis had been apparent for at least five years, showing that this transition was far from a sudden one.

In 1794, possibly on the advice of the Prince's comptroller, the livery accounts presented by Louis were separated from the main accounts. This gives more details of the members of his establishment and what uniforms they wore. Occasional livery uniforms still appear in the main account. A sample is given below:

> To making 13 full dress suits & all materials compleat for 2 coachmen Pether & Milward (2 coachmen to the Mast'r of the Horse & Ladys of Bedchamber) Fawkener & Wilsmere, footmen Hargrave, Lourie, Stradling, Behr, Lightland, Brockis & Euston – and 2 footmen (to the Mast'r of the Horse & Ladys of Bedchamber) King & Jackson at £5/5/- each (own cloth & lace &c.)
> To making 11 dress frock suits & all materials compleat for for all of the above (except coachman & footman to the Ladys of the Bedchamber) £3/13/6 each (own cloth, lace &c.)
> Blue velvet to each dress frock suit – 15/-
> To making 14 Summer frock suits & all materials compleat for all they who had full dress suits above & also for Smith 2nd coachman to the Mast'r of Horse at £3/13/6 each (own cloth & lace &c.)
> To making 9 scarlet jacquets & blue cloth waistcoats for 7 footmen & King & Jackson footmen to the Mast'r of the Horse & Ladys of the Bedchamber at 36/- each (own cloth, lace &c.)

To making 9 scarlet French great coats & all materials for do. at 18/- each (own cloth)
To 8 mixt cloth jacquets & wais'ts & all materials compleat for do. except Jackson - £4/4/- each
To 8 drab colour kersey drab surtouts compleat for do. at £4/12/- each
To making 16 scarlet cloth frocks & blue cloth waistcoats, plain & all materials for Pether, Milward, Fawkener & Wilsmere, Wheeler, Little and Potter, Hanwell, Leigh, White, Dicks, Crude, Romney, Chapman, Bacon & Oliver at £1/12/6 each (own cloth &c.)
To making 4 plain sca't frocks and blue cloth vests & blue shag breeches & all materials for 2 porters Jeffereys & Dermot at £2/2/- each (2 suits each)
To making a suit as above for Phil'p Krichelar (footman to yr. Princess's woman)

The post 'master of the horse' was a sinecure for the ineffectual Lord Jersey, and his wife Lady Jersey (formerly Frances Twysden, with whose family the Bazalgettes later intermarried) was a lady of the bedchamber - in more ways than one, as she was also Prinny's mistress. There were also uniforms for two chairmen (who must have needed to be well built to carry the portly Prince) and for his Hussar and his Chasseur. These latter two gentlemen probably fulfilled ceremonial escort duties.

According to his bank records, between July 1794 and January 1796, Louis paid seven large 'round' sums to a Mr. Deneufville. The total paid was £8420/-/-, which was a huge sum - about £600,000 in today's money. There were several Deneufvilles in London at the time, as shown in the denization records. They were probably Huguenots, and the best known of them was Jean Deneufville (b. 1729) who was a shipowner and merchant in Amsterdam, and who was abortively approached by John Adams to help to finance the American War of Independence. What these payments were for is a matter for conjecture. Perhaps Deneufvilles were acting as intermediaries in loans to persons unknown. The firm of Deneufville seems to have been still supplying material, particularly linen, at this time – perhaps these payments were for shipments of cloth but if so it is not likely that it was all for Louis' own use, so it looks like very considerable mercantile activity on his part.

On 10 January 1795, the Prince of Wales commissioned Bazalgette to make a dress suit as a gift for his second younger brother the Duke of Clarence to wear at the Prince's forthcoming wedding. The order was listed in a separate account under 'His Royal Highness the Prince of Wales for Wedding Cloathes gave a Present to His Royal Highness the Duke of Clarence'. The suit consisted of velvet, richly embroidered in gold and silver 'all over the body', lined with 10½ yards of rich satin and cost £72/4/-. On 29 January, another suit was ordered for him, also in velvet but this time embroidered in 'silks, nett-work &c' and lined with coquelicot (red poppy-coloured) satin and costing £42/-/9d.

The partnership which Louis had formed in 1792 was dissolved in 1795.

> January 29, 1795
> Notice is hereby given, that the Partnership between Louis Bazalgette, Peter Francis Denedonsel, and Thomas Smith, of Grosvenor Street, Grosvenor Square, in the County of Middlesex, Taylors, in this Day dissolved by mutual Consent; and all Debts owing by the said Partnership will be paid by the said Louis Bazalgette, and all Debts due and owing thereto will be received by him and Mr. Dawson, Solicitor, 37, Warwick Street, Golden Square, who are authorized to receive the same.
> Louis Bazalgette.
> P. F. Denedonsel.
> Tho. Smith.
> [London Gazette]

Smith and Denedonsel were both subsequently declared bankrupt, so the dissolution 'by mutual consent' does not quite ring true. If they had somehow lost or diverted funds, they would have had to make restitution, and then they would either have needed to declare bankruptcy because they had to sell everything, or as a stratagem to avoid having all of their assets seized. Even were it not for these possible irregularities, the dissolution would have still appeared to have been necessary, merely because of the reduction of demand for clothes from Louis on the Prince's part. No record of later partnerships has been found. Louis was associated with Thomas Sheppard later, but probably as an employer rather than as a partner.

On 1 February 1795, Fanny and Louis' daughter Caroline was born, and christened on 5 March at St. George, Hanover Square.

The much delayed royal marriage between the Prince of Wales and Princess Caroline of Brunswick took place on 8 April, and, as reported in *The Times* of the day after, the Prince wore a blue Genoa velvet coat and breeches, with a silver tissue waistcoat and coat cuffs, richly embroidered with silver and spangles. The whole suit was covered with large and small spangles. This suit was made by Louis and was delivered on 24 March, being listed in the accounts as a 'Blue velvet coat & breeches & silver tissue waistcoat and coat cuffs, the suit elegantly embroid'd in silver, stones and the body all over with double spangles', at a cost of £203/12/-. A linen case was also provided for this suit. The Duke of Clarence, who acted as the bride's attendant, wore a blue velvet coat and breeches, spotted with gold, and very richly embroidered with gold lace. This is probably the first of the two suits which had been made for him by Louis that January, as gifts from the Prince.

The accounts gathered from the National Archives come to an end at the beginning of July 1795, because later ones were not required to be presented to Parliament at this time, and therefore may not have survived. The last accounts contain none of the fancy striped and spotted velvet and satin of earlier years. The plainer and darker colours that the Prince was now wearing probably owe perhaps less at this time to Brummell's influence than to the fact that they drew less attention to his bulk. There were several Royal Kentish Bowmen's uniforms and Kempshott frocks, and the only other exception to this more sober style was the delivery of his wedding suit.

According to a schedule presented to Parliament up to April 5, George's debts at the time were as follows:-

> Debts on various securities and bearing interest
> £500,571/19/1
> Amount of tradesmen's bills unpaid
> £86,745/-/-
> Tradesmen's bills & arrears of establishment from Oct 10 1794 to Apr 5 1795
> £52,573/5/ 3
> Total
> £639,890/4/4

On 27 April the King sent a message to his long-suffering Commons respecting an establishment for the Prince and Princess of Wales and in the last paragraph he wrote:

> Anxious as his Majesty must necessarily be particularly under the present circumstances to relieve the Prince of Wales from these difficulties his Majesty entertains no idea of proposing to his Parliament to make any provision for this object otherwise than by the application of a part of the income which may be settled on the Prince but he earnestly recommends it to the House to consider of the propriety of thus providing for the gradual discharge of these incumbrances by appropriating and securing for a given term the revenues arising from the Duchy of Cornwall together with a proportion of the Prince's other annual income and his Majesty will be ready and desirous to concur in any provisions which the wisdom of Parliament may suggest for the purpose of establishing a regular and punctual order of payment in the Prince's future expenditure and of guarding against the possibility of the Prince being again involved in so painful and embarrassing a situation.

On 14 May, according to *Hansard*, when the House went into Committee on the subject, William Pitt pointed out that 'fifty years previously the Prince's grandfather as Prince of Wales had an annual income of £100,000.' He therefore now proposed that the income of his Royal Highness should be £125,000, exclusive of the Duchy of Cornwall, which was only £25,000 a year more than was enjoyed 50 years ago. This being the only vote he had to propose, he should merely state in the nature of a notice those regulations which were intended to be made hereafter. The preparations for the marriage would be stated at £27,000 for jewels and plate and £25,000 for finishing Carlton House. The jointure of the Princess of Wales he proposed to be £50,000 a year, being no more than had been granted on a similar occasion. The addition to the Prince's income was carried by 241 votes to 100. In the course of the debate Pitt proposed that the revenues of the Duchy of Cornwall and part of the income of £125,000 should be applied to the payment of the interest of the debts and to the gradual discharge of the principal and that the sum so taken should be vested in the hands of Commissioners. From the income of £125,000 a year he should propose that £25,000 should be deducted annually for the payment of the debts at 4 per cent and that the revenues of the Duchy of Cornwall should be appropriated as a sinking fund at compound interest to discharge the principal of the debts which they would do in twenty seven years. Finally by an Act which received the royal assent on June 27 1795 (35 Geo III cap. 129) £60,000 per annum was to be set apart and vested with Commissioners from the Prince's income as well as £13,000 per annum from the Duchy of Cornwall to pay the Prince's debts.'

In the continuing saga of the Prince's debts, the Parliamentary Commissioners required all creditors to submit their accounts.

On 5 May 1795, Louis had presented his claim for £24,539/14/10 – about £1.8 million in modern currency. The record in the Royal account book says:

    LOUIS BAZALGETTE - Brook Street, Taylor
    To the Prince's joint bond..................£17000/-/-

 His single bond..£2735/-/-
 Chomel's bond...£435/16/-
 St Farre's bond...£812/-/-
               =======
 TOTAL...£20,982/16/-
               ==========
 2 Year's interest due 5th July...................£524/11/4
               ==========
               £2,150/7/4

 Bills...£3,086/7/6
               ==========
               £24,593/14/10

 Discount 10 Pct..£2,459/-/-
(This 'discount' of 10% was taken off all creditors' final bills by the commissioners.)
[Royal Archives document RA Geo Box 7/34 GIV Accounts]

The Journal of Proceedings explains this in more detail:

> Louis Bazalgette, Tailor, claims £17,000 on a joint bond of the Prince and the Duke of York and £2,735 on a single bond of the Prince and also claimed a bond granted to Peter Chomel of [blank], embroiderer, for £435/16/- and another which had been granted to Louis de St Farre for £812 and both of which had been assigned to him making in all £20,982/16/- and £3,086/7/6 for cloathes made for HRH and for materials found and for which he charged only what he would have done to other persons for like articles, that the cloathes were all delivered at Carlton House by himself and that he gave the orders for such lace as was wanted to the Lacemen.
> [Royal Archives document RA Geo Box 7/32 in GIV Accounts]

During the lengthy deliberations in Parliament over the Prince's debts there were assertions made that Prinny had frequently been overcharged. The reader can see from Louis' accounts that he himself acted fairly, but this was certainly not the case with all tradesmen who were patronised by the Prince. In particular, his jewellers were singled out as offenders. A typical story was told in the House by Mr. Michael Angelo Taylor on 5 May, to support his demands for a public enquiry rather than a secret commission. *The Times* reported:

> He would mention to the House a circumstance which would throw a light on the imposition practiced on the Prince. A gentleman (his friend) went to buy a pair of buckles from a certain shopkeeper, who demanded four guineas and a half for them, which as he did not wish to give it he went away; but as he was struck with their beauty he returned again, and found that they had been in the mean time sold to the Prince of Wales, and valued to him at fifteen guineas! Any gentleman who heard that circumstance could not wonder that the Prince's debts increased. He did not think that the House should permit his Royal Highness to be the victim of extortion; all gentlemen in distress were charged exorbitantly, and above all, a distressed Prince.

Laudable as Taylor's sentiments were, he was naïve in not seeing that the Prince's situation overwhelmingly resulted more from over-consumption than from over-charging.

The forty-three debenture bonds for varying amounts were drawn up by order of the Commissioners of the Prince's Debts, pursuant to the act of 35 Geo. III. Cap. 129 in the total sum of £22,130 bearing interest at 5% payable half-yearly. They were signed by Henry Strachey (Master of the Household), Thomas Walker, John Fordyce and Louis Bazalgette, and witnessed by Henry Hodgson (Secretary to the Commissioners). No doubt the filling in and signing of this number of documents resulted in some writer's cramp. The first indenture was for £134 in order to round up the numbers, followed by three for £1,000 and the remainder for £500 each, the last being paid on 5 July 1806. The total amount for all the creditors was £318,672/1/1 and was signed off by Thomas Coutts on 9 January 1807. These were the last of Prinny's bonds whose payments appear in Louis' bank records.

Louis still held bonds and annuities with the Duke of York for many years which were administered by John Willet Payne until his death. These were for various amounts such as £67/4/-, £72, £304 and several each of £500 and £1,000. The last payment was made on 17 October 1826 and was for £135/13/6. Louis also held a bond for the Duke of Clarence for £400 which was paid off in May 1810. It is likely that these were for long-unpaid tailoring bills.

What effect did the fact that Louis was Prinny's tailor have on subsequent events? The result of Prinny's massive spending was that by 1795 he had no choice but to apply to the King and Parliament to pay his debts. We know that Louis was his largest creditor, so he was certainly instrumental in bringing about this national crisis. Prinny had no alternative but to agree to the King's terms, which were that in exchange for payment of his debts the Prince must marry Princess Caroline of Brunswick. To be fair to King George III, it was not only that he wished for an heir, but also that Prinny would settle down and become a responsible adult. This was a fond hope of course. In the circumstances it is not unreasonable to say that Louis in part brought about this disastrous marriage. The child of this marriage, the intelligent, feisty and caring Princess Charlotte, had she not died in childbirth at the age of twenty, would certainly have become Queen instead of Victoria. Now that would have been an even bigger alteration in the course of history, which would have been partly caused by the Prince's devotion to his tailor.

A final extract from the livery accounts for January-March 1795:

> Putting fur on the edges, cuffs & coller of a jacquet for Mr. Notzel (own fur)
> To a scarlet sup. cloth jacquet & cassimere waistcoat, with blue cloth sleeves laced with gold & gold lace loops, & the wais't with gold cord and all materials for Littler (Postilion) (own lace cord & buttons)

To 7 pair mixt cloth pantaloons lin'd thro' with flannell & the foreparts interlined with oiled silk trim'd with buck skin round the bottom of the legs, and the leg seams trim'd also - plated buttons & all materials for Footmen at £2/12/6 each
To making a plain summer frock suit and all materials for Mr. Barrett of the silver scullery (own cloth shag & buttons)
To making a scarlet cloth frock & blue cloth waistcoat and all materials for Groom Ramsden (own cloth &c.)
Making a scarlet drab great coat & all mat's for do. (own drab)
To 2 striped stable waistcoats as the others for do. - 21/- each
Altering a livery frock & wais't to fit new servant of Lord Jerseys
Preparing 2 Postilions jacquets as patterns
Making a jacquet & waistcoat for Postilion Wheeler, the belt cuffs & coller laced with gold
2 ¼ yds blue (2d) cloth - 14/-
Scarlet cloth belt, cuffs & coller
6 ½ yds gold lace - 9/-
Body & sleeve lining to jacquet
Do. to wais't & shaloon sleeves
Sewing silk & twist (own butt's)
To a plain blue cloth jacquet & waistcoat & all materials as the above (only no lace) for Wheeler.

Although Louis continued to serve as one of the Prince's tailors until about 1812, particularly in making and maintaining uniforms and livery, he himself by this time was far more interested in the merchant life that by his efforts he had carved out for himself, so we see a change of emphasis from now on in his career and in that of his sons.

Chapter 15: 1796-98

Debenture bonds attract interest and can be bought and sold like stocks. In January 1796, a first payment was made to Louis from the Commissioners of £1,134 plus £553/7/- interest, and in July 1796 a further payment was made for £1000 with £525 interest. Thereafter, each year between 1797 and 1806 a sum of £500 was paid in January and another in July with interest which decreased by £25 each time from £525 to £25 in July 1806. [Royal Archives document RA Geo Box 7/5/26]

Other creditors such as Jeffries the jeweller had poorer luck in getting what was owed to them, as the Royal Academician and diarist Joseph Farington relates:

> Jeffries mentioned a change in his own situation. After the trial of his charge to the Prince of Wales, - Mr. Pitt struck off 30 per cent from the whole Sum. - Jeffries applied to Pitt who said He considered that in so doing He had discharged His duty to the Prince & to the Public, & that should Jeffries think Himself ill used, He must again *apply to the Law.* - Jeffries referred His case to Charles Fox, Sheridan & others. They inspected the act of parliament for the payment of the Princes debts & told him they found it so loosely worded that it gave a great latitude to the Commissioners, - & that by going to Law again He would incur a considerable expence & Anxiety and the event be very uncertain, they advised him to accept the terms, - which He has done.
> [Joseph Farington's Diary, 9 March, 1797]

As recorded in O'Byrne's Naval Biographical Dictionary of 1849, Louis' eldest son Joseph William, by his late wife Catherine, 'entered the navy in October 1796, at the age of twelve, as a 'Fst.-cl. Vol' [a 'volunteer, first class'] on board the French-built frigate *Impetueux* (74 guns), attached to the fleet in the Channel, firstly serving under Captain John Willet Payne, then under Sampson Edwards and finally under Sir Edward Pellew, (later Lord Exmouth) who was given command on 1 March 1799.' [*Impetueux* was originally named *America*, was built at Brest in 1788 and was captured at the sea battle known as the Glorious First of June, in 1794. As there was already a ship called *America* in the British fleet (upon which coincidentally Joseph later served), she was renamed *Impetueux* in 1795.] From 1799 until 1805, Joseph served, chiefly as Midshipman and Master's Mate, mainly in the East Indies, in the *Terpsichore* (32) under Captain John Mackellar, *Eurydice* (24) under Captain Chas. Malcolm, *Phaeton* (38) under Captain George Cockburn, and *Trident* (64) bearing the flag of Admiral Peter Rainier'.

It appears that eldest sons did not often enter the navy at this time, since it was a hazardous occupation and the eldest would be the principal heir, and would enter the family business if there were one. The tradition of second and third sons entering the military and the church was very much a reality. Therefore Joseph had either to be extremely keen to serve, or in a more sinister way perhaps Fanny put her foot down and wanted him out of the house. Louis was by this time very influential and surely had connections in the Admiralty, so it is likely that a good 'place' would be found for him on a ship where he would receive proper education and his interests would be looked after. Such a suitable commander was Captain John Willet (or 'Honest Jack') Payne, who, apart from being a most competent naval officer and one of the Prince of Wales' friends, was comptroller of the Prince's household and his private secretary. Since Louis was a frequent visitor to Carlton House he knew Payne well, having made several outfits for him, and when the latter was returning to sea in 1796, after falling out of favour with the Prince, it was easy to arrange that he would take young Joseph along with him.

The Times of Thursday 28 July 1796 gave this explanation of Payne's departure from the royal household:

> Tuesday, THOMAS TYRWHITT, Esq. was sworn Privy Seal at Carlton-House, to the Prince of Wales. Captain PAYNE had an audience of his Royal Highness, when he resigned the Seal into the hands of the PRINCE. Mr. TYRWHITT

now enjoys the auditorship at Carlton-House, which is 800l. per annum; and *Privy Seal*, which is 200l. more.

Captain PAYNE was the officer who had the charge of bringing over the Princess of WALES. Lady JERSEY and he have always been at variance since they set out on that extraordinary expedition in the winter of 1794, to fetch her Royal Highness from Germany. Captain Payne has always shewn great attention to this deserted Lady; and is at length superceded by Mr. THOMAS TYRWHITT, who, with Mr. LEE, were the companions of the PRINCE when he was last at the Grange.

On 21 June 1796, George had written to the Queen citing Payne's 'infamous conduct' the year before in supporting Princess Caroline. On 10 July Payne submitted his resignation of the auditorship and the keepership of the Prince's privy seal, requesting that in the interest of economy he should receive no continuance of salary.

On 25 October *The Times* reported that 'Commodore Payne has also received orders to hoist his broad pennant on board L'Impetueux, of 78 guns, to proceed immediately with a squadron on a cruize'.

Joseph served under Payne on the *Impetueux* until 1798, when Payne resigned his commission through sickness.

It is interesting that Louis' children by his first wife, Catherine, seem to have left the family home - or probably died in Louis junior's case - at early ages. Louisa was sent to a French convent at about the age of thirteen and Joseph joined the navy at age 12. John joined the army on 29 July 1796, so was even younger. The surviving family Bible has no record of Catherine's children, although somebody added them much later. Fanny, quite naturally, wanted her own Bible with her own family recorded in it, but the impression remains that somehow these earlier children were not very welcome in her home. The ages at which boys joined the army or navy were very typical at the time. In the case of the navy, a boy could be assigned to a ship but not actually go to sea for several years, in the meantime gaining seniority.

The Times Law Report of 26 May 1797 reads:

> BAZALGETTE v. CARTWRIGHT
> This was an action in which the Plaintiff, who is taylor to his Royal Highness the Prince of Wales, brought against the Defendant, to recover the sum of 70*l.*, which he had lent him.
> The Defendant said, this money had been lent him on an Usurious Contract, he having engaged to pay interest at the rate of 12 per cent for it, and that consequently it could not be recovered.
> In answer to that Plea, the Plaintiff said, this 12 per cent was not received as interest for the loan of this money, but as a rent-charge, in the nature of an annuity, issuing out of certain Premises belonging to the Defendant, and which it was perfectly lawful for him to receive.
> After all the evidence was heard on both sides, and an excellent summing-up by his Lordship, the Jury gave the Plaintiff a Verdict to the amount of his demand.
> – Verdict for Plaintiff 70*l.*

This confirms that Louis was still 'taylor to his Royal Highness the Prince of Wales' at the time. A more detailed version of the proceedings between Louis and James Lock(e) Cartwright appeared in two parts in the *Evening Mail* of 19 and 21 June 1797:

> It appeared that the Defendant applied to the Plaintiff, and represented he had agreed to purchase Fozard's Riding Stables, in Park Lane, and to enable him to compleat such purchase, it was necessary for him to raise the sum of 70*l.* to pay off a mortgage which the premises were subject to, and to induce the Plaintiff to advance him such 70*l.* proposed to grant a rent-charge issueing out of the premises; but as is was necessary to have the money to pay off the mortgage before the Defendant could make title to the premises, he requested the Plaintiff would advance the same upon his assurance that he would then go and pay the mortgagee, and on the next day deposit the title deeds

in the hands of Mr. Dawson, Plaintiff's Attorney, to prepare the deed for securing the rent-charge, this the Defendant did not do, but the Plaintiff's Attorney prepared the necessary deed, which was approved of by the Defendant's Attorney, and although repeated applications were made, the Defendant evaded executing the deed, and after near three months delay, the Defendant called on the Plaintiff, representing that he had executed the deed, and everything was settled and in the hands of his Attorney; and that as three months rent-charge, amounting to 21*l*. was then due, and having received a quarter's rent from Mr. Fozard, the tenant, he would pay the same; the Plaintiff, believing this statement, and being a foreigner, desired the Defendant to give him the form of a receipt, which the Defendant did, but instead of expressing 21*l*. to be for a quarter's rent-charge, he stated it to be for one quarter's interest on 700*l*. This the Plaintiff copied and gave the Defendant, but the Plaintiff calling on his Attorney, and not finding the deeds in his possession, and executed as so stated, and although the deed was repeatedly tendered to the Defendant, yet he refused to execute it, and in consequence thereof, brought the action against the Defendant to recover back the money so advanced; but the Defendant resisted, upon the grounds of the contract being usurious, and to support such defence, produced the receipts so obtained from the Plaintiff; but the form of the receipt being given in the Defendant's own hand writing, and the circumstances of the case fully proved, and an excellent summing up by his Lordship, the Jury gave the Plaintiff a verdict to the amount of his demand. Verdict for Plaintiff 700*l*. – Counsel for the Plaintiff, Messrs *Garrow and Marryat*; for the defendant, Messrs. *Erskine and Gibbs*.

Whether Louis in fact made some of his loans at illegal interest rates is not clear, but it is unlikely since the top rate that could be charged was 6% at that time. Cartwright agreed when requesting the loan that, as Louis was to hold the title deed as security, he (Louis) should also receive the rent from

James Fozard (who had gone bankrupt the previous year and had had to sell up). Cartwright did not deliver the deed, so effectively had free title to the property, and was in a position to give the deed to another party as security to raise a further loan or mortgage. He was quite crafty in attempting to pass off the rent payment as interest, because £21 per quarter on £700 equates to twice the legally permitted rate. Probably the 6% ceiling applied to secured loans anyway, and this was effectively unsecured. Following judgement against him, Cartwright would have needed to sell the property or raise another loan to pay Louis back. If he could not, he would have had to spend some time in a 'sponging house' or debtor's prison, but he was fortunate not to be charged with deception. The Old Bailey proceedings in 1830 mention a James Lock Cartwright, though as a plaintiff, describing himself as a 'cabriolet proprietor', which is probably the same man, given his connection with the horse trade.

However, despite his apparent propensity for sharp practice, James was from a good family – the Cartwrights of Marnham, Nottinghamshire, which means he was related to Edmund Cartwright, the well-meaning vicar who invented the power loom and unwittingly put many thousands of hand-loom workers (including probably some of the author's maternal ancestors) on parish relief. James married well too - Marianna Elizabeth Strombom, who was the daughter of Isaac Strombom, a merchant of Cape Town and Old Broad Street in London, and his wife Elizabeth (neé Peacock). Strombom (more correctly Strömbom) was of Swedish extraction and was a partner in Strombom, Hudson, Lowrie & Co, becoming bankrupt in 1817. In 1832 he was granted a patent for 'a medicinal composition or embrocation for the cure relief or prevention of external and internal complaints which composition or embrocation may alone or with alterations be beneficially used as internal medicine', which sounds as if it would not be much good for treating anything. How he managed to patent something as generally vague as that is strange indeed.

According to the Brighton newspapers:

'15 May 1797 - On last Thursday evening the Prince of Wales accompanied by a single gentleman arrived at his Pavilion at Brighton. His Royal Highness the next day reviewed the Monmouth and Brecon Militia on the Downs near the above place. To day we hear the Prince leaves Brighton having come there only for a few days by the advice of Dr Warren for the benefit of the sea air. His Royal Highness has lost much of his corpulence since he was last at Brighton. He went again on July 24 to be present at the races and it is recorded that on October 23, the Prince of Wales amused himself with a day's shooting at Petworth, on an invitation from the Earl of Egremont. The next day His Royal Highness being on his way to London with post horses very narrowly escaped being overturned about a mile and a half on the other side of Cuckfield where the horses by some means took the carriage off the main road to the side of a bank and with an inclination that threatened its overturn for the space of many yards, but fortunately and owing to the lowness of the carriage it was kept upon its wheels.'

At about this time, Louis lent money to Dr. William Battine, who was a Fellow of Trinity Hall, Cambridge and a gifted lawyer in Doctors Commons, but who, though always in debt, was very dilatory in repaying, if he paid at all. He was not poor, and held several lucrative sinecures, including Chancellor of the Diocese of Lincoln, Commissary of the Royal Peculiar of St. Catherine's, Gentleman of the Privy Chamber and His Majesty's Advocate-General in His Office of Admiralty. It was possible that in this last capacity that he came into contact with Louis, although it is more likely to have been because he was a confidant of the Prince of Wales, whom he had reputedly met because his father's property was close to Prinny's Kempshott estate. Louis' old friend Guillaume Gaubert was also unwise enough to lend Battine money. Battine was still being dunned, and his pension garnisheed, after Louis' death in 1830, but in 1797 Louis was getting £200 per annum paid directly from Battine's Admiralty salary. Louis' bank records routinely show entries such as: 'received £49/6/6 at the Navy Office 1 quarter salary due to Doct. Wm Battine at Mich's last', which means that by this time Louis had already got judgement against Battine.

Further examples of Louis' transactions at Coutts Bank show that on 6 June 1798, Louis received £100 from 'Wm. Adam & Thos. Coutts on Acct of a debt due from HRH the Duke of York'. This was probably the William Adam who was an MP until 1794; he was also the Prince's of Wales's legal advisor for many years. On 1 August of the same year Louis was paid £164/11/- from the Duke of York's accounts, and £258/19/- in March 1799. [Royal Archives documents RA 43200 and RA 43204].

Louis' great-grandson the Reverend Evelyn Bazalgette recorded in a scribbled note in his Bible that Louis' daughter Louisa (by Catherine) '...was in a French convent all through the French Revolution, and recollects seeing Marie Antoinette in the Tuileries with the young Dauphin. Also relates how their (carriage?) used to stop in front of the guillotine when (an) execution going on...' The only problem with this is that Louisa, having been born in October 1782, would only have been six years old at the outbreak of the Revolution - that she was sent to Paris then is hard to believe. An estimate based on the number of females in Louis' house in the 1801 census suggests that she was home by then. We have other evidence which shows that she was in Paris but which suggests that she was home by 1797. On 6 November 1795, Louis paid his Paris banker Mr. Perregaux £80/-/- for Louisa's use. This sum was returned unused in 1797, implying that she was no longer in Paris. It is therefore unlikely that Louisa was taken to Paris before 1792. By 1795 the revolution was not then raging as it had previously, and the *Directoire* assumed power in that year, meaning that relative stability had returned to the capital. Louis could therefore feel safer in taking Louisa to Paris at that time.

Louis applied for a passport in 1797 for the purpose of going to visit Louisa and he had probably decided that it was wise to bring her home again. This was just as well because Napoleon arranged a *coup d'état* on 18 Fructidor (4 September 1797).

Louis' passport application was in the form of a letter, written in rather stilted French, to James Harris, Lord Malmesbury, that most trusted diplomat, who had in 1794 been despatched to collect Caroline of Brunswick, the Prince's intended bride, and who had tried vainly to instill in her some manners, dress-sense and personal hygiene. Malmesbury is known to have been in Paris in 1796 and in Lille in 1797, so the letter might have been sent to him while he was in France, which may explain why Louis' letter was in French, but it is more likely that Louis was following the protocol of using French because it was the traditional diplomatic language.

My Lord,

I take the liberty of addressing these few lines to you, for you kindly to oblige me with a passport to allow me to go to Paris to look for my daughter whom I put there in lodgings before the war and to return to England with her. Pardon My Lord the liberty I take - and permit me to thank you with all possible respect and consideration.

My Lord,
Your humble and obedient [servant],
Louis Bazalgette

Grosvenor Street, Wednesday morning.

Chapter 16: 1799-1802

On 7 February 1799, Messrs. Sheridan, Grubb and Richardson, the proprietors of the Drury Lane Theatre, wrote Louis a bill of exchange (effectively a post dated cheque) for £60/15/6, to be cashed 10 months after the cheque was written. Two days later they wrote another for the same amount, to be cashed 11 months later. The play *Pizarro* (adapted by Richard Brinsley Sheridan from Kotzebue's *Spaniards in Peru*) was presented at Drury Lane on 24 May 1799, so no doubt these sums were to help finance this lavish production. Years of unpaid debts had put Sheridan in the position of having few people left to borrow from. Louis had previously paid 'Mr Sheridan' £614/-/- in January, 1797. *Pizarro*, despite being a great success and making him a profit of £1,000, was Sheridan's last production, and heralded the theatre's effectively going into receivership. The final disaster was when it burned down on the 24 February 1809. It is most unlikely that Louis was ever repaid, but this was small change to him. On 19 October 1799, Louis received £125/-/- from 'Lord Southampton on Coe & Co'. The first Lord Southampton, who died in 1797, was a go-between in the negotiation between the Prince and his father about his debts. This must be his son, Lt-Gen. George Ferdinand (Fitzroy), 2nd Lord Southampton, who was at this time Colonel of the 34th (the Cumberland) Regiment of Foot. Lord Southampton was a Groom of the Stole in the Prince of Wales' household.

The property that is still known as Oakley Farm, in Mottisfont, Hampshire was bought by Louis from Walter Smythe, of Brambridge, on 4 June 1799 for £5,350. The property was conveyed using the legal procedure known as 'lease and release', which was used to circumvent the ponderous process of admission to a manorial court, which Louis had to follow when buying the Turnham Green house and later Eastwick Park. The 'lease' part was for a year on payment of five shillings, and the rent of a peppercorn. The following day, under an indenture of 'release' the owner then released his rights to the reversion of the property. In fact, this was a very complex transaction because it involved eight parties, all of whom had to approve and 'sign, seal and deliver' the indentures. We can see Louis' faithful solicitor John Dawson and his clerk Ben Parnell traipsing around the country to get all of these signatures. The complexity began when the earlier owner of the property, Henry Wells of Brambridge, who died in 1765, left it in his will to Walter Smythe, the father of the Walter (known as 'Wat') Smythe who sold it to Louis. One of the provisions of Wells' will was that it respected a 'jointure' or endowment made in 1759 to his wife Frances, nee Doughty, who after Walter's death had married Charles Biddulph. Wat's half-uncles Henry Errington and Lord Sefton were appointed trustees of the estate of Walter Smythe senior, whose will also provided an income from the estate for his wife Mary Smythe. Henry Wells devised part of his estate to Henry Penton (MP for Winchester), Edward Gore and Charles Wolfran Cornwall (speaker of the House of Commons), so they appear in the indenture as well. Ambrose Pitman was a poet, whose works included 'The Distress of Integrity and Virtue: A Poem in Three Cantos' and 'Eugenio, or the Man of Sorrow, a Legendary Tale, by a Young Gentleman of Seventeen'.

The Smythes were a very old English Catholic family. Wat's sister Mary Anne, after two marriages, had become very well-known under the name of Maria Fitzherbert. After the death of her second husband Thomas Fitzherbert, Maria went into a period of extended mourning, from which she was eventually persuaded to desist by her half-uncles, Sefton and Errington, who re-launched her into society, where they introduced her, 'still veiled in her widow's weeds', to the Prince of Wales, who had in fact first noticed her some years before when a youth of eighteen. The Prince's pursuit of, and eventual secret marriage with, Maria have already been alluded to.

> It was December 15th, 1785. The Cumberlands and the Devonshires evidently got cold feet and were all 'out of town', but Maria found two witnesses of her own religion who were willing to run the risk of committing a felony. Wat Smythe remained 'much against his sister's marriage with the Prince of Wales', but another brother, Jack, and

her uncle, Henry Errington, bravely accepted to stand by and witness the certificate of marriage.
[Leslie, Anita; Mrs Fitzherbert, a Biography]

Oakley Farm has a further claim to fame, its 366 acres enclosing two arms of the River Test, and is even today one of the choicest trout fisheries on this most celebrated Hampshire chalk stream. F. M. Halford, regarded by many as the father of English dry-fly fishing, fished this stretch so often from the 1890's to the 1920's that he had a fishing-hut built there, which still stands today as a national monument to him.

Louis owned Oakley Farm for thirty years, and after his death it was sold to Sir Charles Mill. The author, a keen trout fisherman in his youth, wishes it were still in the ownership of his family today. Louis employed a gamekeeper for it named James Jackman in 1800, so he presumably valued it as a sporting estate. As the farm was always let to a tenant, we have to wonder why Louis bought it. With Louis's already strong royal connections we can only guess how this all came about. Perhaps Wat Smythe was in debt, and Louis, as was his habit, bought it to help out a man who would have been, without the strictures of the Royal Marriage Act and the Act of Settlement, the brother of the future Queen of England. There is no real evidence that Wat was in debt, but the brothers sound a bit wild, so gambling or extravagance should not be ruled out. The second brother, Jack, according to an anecdote in *The Times*, was apparently so 'remarkably handsome' that he was accosted by some French officers when he was coming out of the Paris Opera, who insisted that he must be a woman. He at once 'drew his sword', (as the *The Times* archly put it) which seems to have persuaded them otherwise.

Meanwhile at home her four younger brothers began to be a worry to her parents. These boys had grown up in the country, handsome, strong, wild and possessed of an energy for which there was no outlet. Because they were Catholic the Penal Laws excluded them from the Bar, the Army and the Navy as well as from all Government appointments of trust. Not being rich, the Smythes

wondered what to do with these exuberant colts, barred from proving their worth in their own land. One of them eventually obtained a commission in the Austrian Army. The others kicked their heels and became subject to challenges and duels.
[Leslie, Anita; Mrs Fitzherbert, a Biography]

Of course, it is possible that Louis was an enthusiastic angler himself. He had been born and raised by the beautiful River Tarn. Chiswick had an extensive fishery when he was living there, and he also later bought South Stoneham House, with its famous salmon pool on the River Itchen.

At the King's sixty-first birthday celebrations, according to *The Times* of Wednesday 5 June 1799, the Prince apparently wore a 'superb suit of blue and silver'. It looks as if Louis may still have been making his special dress suits.

1799 also saw the death of Fanny's father Daniel Bergman. In his will he appointed Thomas Treslove, his brother-in-law Robert Middleship and Joseph Addington to be his executors. Thomas Treslove was a button seller. It appears he banked with Drummonds of Charing Cross. One of his sons was Thomas Crosby Treslove, a lawyer, practising at Old square, Lincoln's Inn. One of his legal clients was Harriett Wilson, the noted courtesan. Thomas Treslove's uncle Thomas was a partner in Treslove, Pulsford & Son, Button-sellers & Haberdashers of 40, St.Martin's-lane, Charing-cross. Joseph Addington was a woollen draper, of 16 St. May's Building, St Martin's Lane. In Daniel's will, his son Daniel was to have an annuity of £300, and each of his daughters, Frances Bazalgette, Louisa Bergman and Theresa Philo Pilton (later to marry Louis' son Joseph William), were left £500 plus a third of the interest from the product of the sale of the estate each, except that Fanny got £3,000 less principal than her sisters because that had been given to her at the time of her marriage. The money was not to be 'subject to the debts or control of any husbands' and was for their own sole and separate use, i.e. a 'jointure' in legal terms. The freehold properties in Charles Street, Albemarle Street and Old Brentford were to be for the benefit of his widow Mary until her death and then sold. In his codicil, he relented and gave his son Daniel a further annuity of £50, but stipulated that if Daniel contested this, or laid claim to any of the freeholds, then 'from thenceforth the said annuity of three hundred and fifty pounds shall cease and be no longer payable.' Daniel did however contest the will, suing the executors and other beneficiaries, and the bill was still being dragged through the courts in 1831.

The Times of 20 August gleefully reported:

> Mrs. FITZHERBERT is at Ramsgate; and the rumour there is, that the Prince of WALES is expected. -- It is very probable.
> Admiral PAYNE, the former companion of the PRINCE, has sold his house, furniture, and wines, at Brompton; and is once more about to live with his Royal Highness. He has been the negociator of a recent reconciliation!

The Times printed sadder news on 19 October:

> Mr. ARTHUR ROBINSON, with his Lady and female servant, were a few days since drowned in the river Trent, by the overturning of the Liverpool coach. He was many years in the Prince of WALES'S family, as one of his Gentleman Ushers and Under Treasurers; and likewise Under Treasurer to the Dukes of YORK and CLARENCE, and the younger Princes. When the Prince's establishment was broken up, his Royal Highness settled a pension of 500l. upon him. The persons of the unfortunate sufferers were identified by the inscription on the collar of a favourite spaniel that accompanied them.

Mr. Robinson was a Gentleman Ushers' Daily Waiter, as well as being the Prince's accountant and sub-treasurer to whom Bazalgette delivered his tailoring accounts, so he must have been very well known to Louis.

In 1800, Fanny's middle sister Louisa Sarah Bergman married the auctioneer James Denew, whose father's auction house (Denew & Dawson) was located at 30, Charles Street, just down the street from the Bergmans.

On 20 February, the *Morning Chronicle* advertised one of Daniel Bergman's houses for sale by auction, although in his will he had specified that they were to be retained until after Mary's death:

> By Mr. Devenish, on the Premises, on Thursday next, by order of the Executors of Daniel Bergman, Esq. deceased,
> A Substantial HOUSE, containing two Rooms on a Floor, with an additional large dining room, kitchen, cellars, and every convenience; a counting office and rooms over, arranged to form a manufactory or warehouse, or with facility convertible into a part of the dwelling, eligibly situated, No. 8, Charles-street, Grosvenor Square. The premises have been recently repaired, and altered to the present taste, in an elegant stile, at a considerable expence, judiciously applied, and are a desirable residence for a genteel family, held at a small ground-rent.
> At the same time will be sold, the fashionable and excellent HOUSEHOLD FURNITURE, comprising large pier glasses, a drawing-room suit, mahogany bookcase, sideboard, card, Pembroke, and set of dining tables, double and single chests of drawers, chairs &c. Wilton carpets, bedsteads with dimity curtains, bedding, kitchen utensils, china, two eight-day clocks, and numerous other effects.
> The House may be viewed on Monday, by tickets; the Furniture on Wednesday, and Particulars and catalogues may be had as above, and of Mr. Devenish, auctioneer, and agent for the letting and sale of houses and estates of every description, Villiers-street, Strand.

Sometime between April 1800 and March 1801, Louis sold his premises in Lower Grosvenor Street to his master tailor Thomas Sheppard, who continued to carry on a merchant tailoring business there. Sheppard was still in occupation as a tailor in 1842, unless it was one of his sons carrying on the business. John Gunning, Esq., Surgeon Extraordinary to the

King, Inspector of Army Hospitals, and Surgeon to St. George's Hospital, was also living there in 1822. A solicitor called F.W. Sheppard, presumably one of Thomas' sons, then lived in the house until the 1850's, when a Mr and Mrs Bennett took it over. They seem to have let the upper floors furnished, as well as advertising other rental property in *The Times*. In 1868 the upper part was advertised as having 'three drawing rooms, four best and servants' bed rooms, dressing room, kitchen, servant's-hall, butler's pantry. A ground floor of four rooms, 76ft. in extent, would be available for the occasional soiree'. It is not clear who owned the house after the Bennetts, but William Johnson MD, Surgeon General of Her Majesty's Indian Army, was living there in 1883. The house, together with no 21, was demolished in the 1890s to make way for a new development. The present Nos 21 and 22 were erected as private houses in 1898-9 to the designs of Eustace Balfour, the estate surveyor, and Thackeray Turner, his partner. Part of the passage remains but the Brooks Mews buildings were rebuilt at the same time as Nos. 21 and 22 Grosvenor Street.

On 3 March 1800, the *Morning Chronicle* featured another advertisement:

> FREEHOLD, DOVER STREET, PICCADILLY.
> To be SOLD by PRIVATE CONTRACT,
> By Messrs. SKINNER and DYKE, with immediate Possession,
> A Very eligible FREEHOLD ESTATE, desirably situate on the West-side of Dover-Street; comprising a substantial Brick DWELLING HOUSE, Office, and Back Court, No. 41, in the occupation of Mrs. H. BRISTOW.
> Also a Messuage in Dover-yard, adjoining, let to Mr. LEWIS, Tenant at Will; the annual value of the whole about ONE HUNDRED POUNDS per annum. - To be viewed by Tickets only, which may be had, with full Particulars, of Messrs. Skinner and Dyke, Aldersgate-street.

Louis bought the house advertised above, 41 Dover Street, Piccadilly, which is now numbered 43, and which was until recently occupied by the Portal Gallery but is now a branch of Jigsaw Fashions. Dover Street was a mixture very common in Mayfair at the time in that it contained smart houses but also several brothels and gaming houses. The house has a smaller floor plan than the Grosvenor Street house, though it has six storeys. There is an alley beside it to the north, still visible through an arch, which leads to Dover Yard, which served as the mews, with carriage access on the west side, between what were then Nos. 7 and 8 Berkeley Street. Even so, it was probably used not as a tailor's shop but more as a 'counting house' by Louis in his mercantile activities. He paid £275/-/- to his solicitor John Dawson a few days later, presumably in connection with this transaction. He was shown to be in possession in the rate-book on 28 March but still also at 22, Lower Grosvenor Street, though replaced there by Thomas Sheppard in the 1801 rate-book. The family home remained in Turnham Green.

The house-buying and selling carried on, as Daniel Bergman's executors continued to advertise the remainder of his property for auction, on this occasion in *The Times* of 26 March 1800:

By Mr. DEVENISH,
At Garraway's on Tuesday. April 1. at 12 o'clock, by Order of the Executors of DANIEL BERGMAN, Esq. deceased,
Lot 1. A Capital substantial FREEHOLD HOUSE, No. 33, Albemarle-street, Piccadilly, comprising 3 large rooms on each floor, the drawing-room 23 feet 6 by 20, and the others of suitable dimensions, 2 staircases, convenient offices, &c. in excellent repair, in the possession of Mrs. Codrington, on Lease for 10½ years, determinable at the end of 3½ years, at the annual rent of 150*l*.
Lot 2. A genteel LEASEHOLD HOUSE, No. 9, Charles-street, Grosvenor-square, containing 3 rooms on a floor, spacious shop, parlour, &c. let to Mr. Lind for 15 years, at 42*l*. per annum. Held for 23¾ years, at 4*l*. per ann.---

To be viewed on Monday and Wednesday prior to the Sale, by leave of the Tenants, with Tickets only, which, with Particulars, may be had of Mr. Devenish, Villiers-street, Strand; Particulars may also be had at the Place of Sale.

According to the 1801 census listing for Pond House in Turnham Green, Louis was the sole occupier and the household consisted of eleven persons: three male and eight female, none of whom was 'engaged in either agriculture or manufacturing'. The three males were Louis and his sons Louis and Daniel. Joseph had already joined the navy and John the army, and the next boy, Evelyn, was not yet born. The eight females were Fanny his wife, Louisa his surviving daughter of the first marriage, Caroline (6) and Cecilia (12) and four others who were presumably domestic staff.

On 20 October 1801 the Bazalgettes' son Evelyn was born. The entry in Jean Louis' Family Bible reads: 'Evelyn Bazalgette son of Louis and Frances Bazalgette was born on Oct 20th 1801 and half baptised and registered in the Parish Church [of St Nicholas], Chiswick, Middlesex and baptised and registered in the Parish of St. George Hanover Square on the [blank] 1802.' It is not clear why, after they left Turnham Green and returned to London, they chose to christen him again.

In 1801, Louis loaned or gave credit, by way of a bond, the sum of £784/18/3 to General William Gardiner, (1748-1806), who was from 1799 colonel in the King's Royal Rifle Corps, and a diplomatist and special envoy at Brussels. He received half-yearly interest payments of £19/12/5 until Gardiner's death. On 27 November, Louis paid £200 to 'Mr. Christie' - probably James Christie the auctioneer, of 91 Pall Mall.

Daniel Bergman junior began the process of contesting his father's will, and sued the executors and beneficiaries in a bill in Chancery named Bergman v. Trestlove [sic] (Thomas Treslove was the first of the executors). James Denew in turn lodged what appears to have been a counter-claim against Daniel. As already stated, these actions dragged on for some years.

Returning to the matter of the Prince's debts:

In our Paper of this day we have continued to give several Items of Expenditure from the Report of the Committee on the CIVIL LIST Establishment. The following is the manner in which the Sums advanced to the three older Princes is to be repaid:-
The 22,500*l.* advanced to the Prince of WALES is to be repaid by a Debenture of the Commissioners for liquidating his royal Highness's Debts on the 10th of October, 1806.
The 54,735*l.* advanced to his Royal Highness the Duke of YORK, is to be repaid by Instalments of 1000l. quarterly, from the 1st of January, 1805.
The 14,316*l.* advanced to his Royal Highness The Duke of CLARENCE is to be repaid by Instalments of 750l. per quarter, the 1st payment commencing the 5th of Jan. 1803.
[*The Times*, Tuesday, 23 Mar 1802]

It is not mentioned in the above newspaper report, but the Prince's advance of £22,500 was all owed to Louis. In July 1806, Louis received the last payment of £1,000 plus £25 interest from the Commissioners for the Prince's debt. 'At that time it was said that Bazalgette had received the principal sum of £22,134 and interest of £6,382/7/- making a total of £28,462/7/-.' [Royal Archives document RA Geo Box 7/5/26]. Louis also held three bonds for the Duke of York which were finally paid off in 1826.

On 25 March 1802, the Treaty of Amiens was signed, and peace, which was to last for under a year, returned to Britain and France. Although the politically sage saw the 'peace' for what it was – a ploy by Napoleon to remove the blockade on the French ports to allow the re-provisioning of his army - the British *Haut Ton* lost no time in returning to their beloved Paris in their thousands.

The Dover and Calais mail packets did not recommence running till the 18th November 1801, but English visitors had begun to arrive as early as September or October. One of the earliest packets brought sixty-three ladies, and the Calais hotels were packed, seven hundred and ninety-eight passengers landing in ten days. In the last decade of Prairial (June 1802) there were ninety-one arrivals, in the last decade of Thermidor (August) ninety-seven, in the last decade of Fructidor (September) one hundred and fifty-six. The cost of a trip to Paris was what in those days seemed moderate. For £4/13s you could get a through ticket by Dover and Calais, starting either from the City at 4.30 a.m. by the old and now revived line of coaches connected with the rue Notre Dame des Victoires establishment in Paris, or morning and night by a new line from Charing Cross. Probably a still cheaper route, though there were no through tickets, was by Brighton and Dieppe, the crossing taking ten or fifteen hours. By Calais it seldom took more than eight hours, but passengers were advised to carry light refreshments with them. The *diligence* from Calais to Paris, going only four miles an hour, took 54 hours for the journey, but a handsome carriage drawn by three horses, in a style somewhat similar to the English post-chaise, could be hired by four or five fellow-travellers, and this made six miles an hour. £30 would cover the expense of a seven weeks' visit, including hotels, sight-seeing, and restaurants.

[Alger, John Goldsworth; Napoleon's British Visitors and Captives, 1801-1815]

Louis was no exception in wishing to return to Paris, though his reasons were more prosaic, as he took the opportunity to sort out his business affairs. These obviously required his attention, because they had been handled by a representative, with a power of attorney, and this arrangement was by now not all it should be. Louis stayed at the Hotel d'Irlande, Rue de la Loi, a very fashionable street which was renamed the Rue de Richelieu in 1806. On 15 October 1802 he appeared before the Notary Public in the Département de la Seine and gave his London address as 41, Dover Street, Piccadilly. He summoned Citizen Barison to give account of his holdings and dealings, as

Barison had been acting as his proxy or agent and was in default. Barison had been summoned to attend at the same hour of 9 a.m., but as he did not show up by noon, judgement was given against him.

Louis then found a replacement agent, for a fortnight later, on 3 November, Louis again appeared before the Notary and this time granted his power of attorney to Joseph Guillon, of 263 Rue Montmartre. This suggests that Louis had kept a representative in Paris throughout the 15 years of war, and that some form of trade, presumably in silks, other cloth and shapes, was carried on during this period. The fact that he continued this arrangement implies that he was still importing materials in 1802, even if his tailoring activities had diminished. To allow judgement to be completed, the magistrate requested confirmation from the mayor of Ispagnac that Citizen Louis Bazalgette was the same Jean Louis Bazalgette who had been born in Ispagnac in 1750. In confirmation, a copy of Louis' *Acte de Naissance* was received by the court on 20 March 1803.

According to the book from which the quotation on the previous page was taken, Louis was on the list of visitors who had an audience with Napoleon. Many of the more important British visitors did so, and although Louis was by this time a British subject there was potentially a risk that he could have been regarded as an emigré and interned, or worse. No doubt his passport and other documents stated his importance to the Prince of Wales. Passports at the time had to be issued by the French government or ambassador.

It would have been interesting to be a fly on the wall at that audience and to know what they talked about, unless it was just a paying of respects. Since he was a royalist it seems unlikely that he would have chosen to visit the Emperor on his own account. It is possible that Louis had been sent to see him on some delicate matter, bearing in mind his very long association with the faithless and fickle Prinny, and his reputation as a discreet, resourceful and trusted servant. Louis returned to London soon after the beginning of November, 1802.

According to his bank records on 4 December Louis paid £150 to William Vale, followed by £264/2/- on 16 December. This may be the clockmaker of this name. On the sale of the family's furniture later there were several longcase and bracket clocks listed. Vale made both kinds of clocks.

Chapter 17: 1803-06

By 1803 the King was better disposed to ask Parliament to grant the Prince further funds, writing a letter to Henry Addington, (1st Viscount Sidmouth) the Chancellor of the Exchequer, in this vein:

> His Majesty having taken into consideration the period which has elapsed since the adoption of those arrangements which were deemed by the wisdom of Parliament to be necessary for the discharge of the incumbrances of the Prince of Wales and having adverted to the progress which has been made in carrying them into effect recommends the present situation of the Prince to the attention of this House.
> Notwithstanding the reluctance and regret which his Majesty must feel in suggesting any addition to the burthens of his people he is induced to resort in this instance to the experienced liberality and attachment of his faithful Commons in the persuasion that they will be disposed to take such measures as may be calculated to promote the comfort and support the dignity of so distinguished a branch of his Royal Family.

On 23 February 1803, according to *Hansard*: 'The House went into Committee to consider the King's message and the Chancellor of the Exchequer Addington pointed out that on the 5th of the previous January £563,895 had been paid off the Prince's debt of £650,000 and that the whole would be discharged in July 1806. He moved 'That his Majesty be enabled to grant a yearly sum or sums of money out of the Consolidated Fund of Great Britain not exceeding in the whole the sum of sixty thousand pounds to take place and be computed from the 5th day of January 1803 and to continue until the 5th day of July 1806 towards providing for the better support of the station and dignity of his Royal Highness the Prince of Wales.' This resolution was agreed to.

In about 1803 Louis started to keep records in the new family Bible. We know that it was Louis because the handwriting matches that in the accounts with the Prince of Wales, and in letters that he wrote in 1797 and 1823. The recorded events start with his marriage to Fanny in 1787, and the handwriting and shade of ink are consistent up to the record of Evelyn's second baptism in 1802. On the back carpet page, written in the same handwriting, is a full page story of Evelyn's tribulations due to his paralyzed arm, with further additions made after January 1804. Subsequent entries are made by the same hand, though the ink and size of writing are not consistent. According to family lore Evelyn's injury resulted from his being dropped by his (possibly drunken) nurse. The children of Louis' first marriage are not mentioned in this Bible at all except in the later pencil additions, probably made by somebody else. Notably, Louis was not sure of the exact dates of the events, for some were added later with a different pen and some were left blank.

> Evelyn Bazalgette, born Oct 20th 1801, lost the use of his left Arm January 1803. Dr. Richard Croft was consulted thereon who was of opinion that it was occasioned by the child's Teething. He lanced his Gums several times and ordered dry frictions with other remedies - in a few months he could use his fingers but the arm continued much the same. In March 1803 Dr. Denman advised Electricity which was tried for near 3 Months without perceiving any benefit.
> In July 1803 Dr. Bailey was consulted and joined with Dr. Denman in advising the child's taking steel [i.e., tincture of iron] by way of strengthening his general habit and the using an artificial Tepid salt water Bath. This plan was persever'd in for some Months without any visible amendment in the arm, but the child's general health improved. Drs Denman and Baillie wished to take the opinion of Dr. Pritcam who advised continuing the same plan as that presented by Drs Baillie and Denman. On Feby 7 1807 the Pere Eliser was consulted who order'd Evelyn to try the Baths of the prepared Barye [barytes]

Waters. This was persevered in for four Weeks and the child's health altered visibly and he became weak and relaxed. Upon this the bath was given up and the child continued until Jan 1808. A Mr. Peyt was recommended as having wrought several cures of lost limbs. This Mr. P--- attended for several months daily and used the feeble arm in a variety of muscular motions from which are Life Benefits but as yet no perception of amendment has been perceived.
[Louis Bazalgette's Family Bible]

Barytes or baryta water, a solution of barium hydroxide, is highly alkaline, corrosive and toxic, so it is unlikely to have been pleasant to be bathed in, even if it were only his arm. Eliser sounds more like a priest than a doctor, so maybe he should have tried exorcism instead.

Dr Thomas Denman of Old Burlington Street is listed in the Universal Directory of 1791 as licentiate in midwifery of the Royal College of Surgeons. He attended George III for a time during his 'malady' as well as a confinement of Georgiana, Duchess of Devonshire. His son-in-law, Dr. Richard Croft, attended, with Dr. Matthew Baillie, the fatal confinement of Princess Charlotte on 6 November 1817, and was blamed by some for negligence following her death. Although he was judged by the royal family not to have been at fault, he was observed by many to be very depressed after this disaster, and on Friday 13 February of the following year, at the house of a patient, Mrs Thackeray, he blew his brains out with two pistols which he had loaded with slug and shot, and which he had presumably been carrying in his doctor's bag. With further reference to Princess Charlotte's death, in his book, *Charlotte & Leopold: The True Story of the Original People's Princess*, James Chambers noted that when Charlotte was expecting, Leopold was advised to have Sir William Knighton attend her, as he was acknowledged as being the best accoucheur in London.

But the Regent mandated that Sir Richard Croft should attend the princess. Croft was a fashionable accoucheur, but he had significantly less real medical training than did

Knighton. Did Prinny, a confirmed hypochondriac, make that decision so he could keep Knighton by his side, unwilling to be without his physician's full-time attention? We can only wonder what the outcome might have been, had Knighton been attending Charlotte.

No 'Dr Pritcam' has been traced but it is very likely that this was Dr David Pitcairn of Lincolns Inn Fields, Physician Extraordinary to the Prince of Wales and also a surgeon at St Bartholomew's Hospital. Perhaps Louis only saw the name written down, and it would have been easy to mistake 'rn' for 'm' in the script of the day, especially if it were written by a doctor. 'Dr Bailey/Baillie' was Dr Matthew Baillie, who was the mentor of Pitcairn.

It is another indication of Louis' good connections, as well as his wealth, that he was able to procure the services of four of the most eminent surgeons practising in London at the time. Apart from Croft they were all Scots, and the families intermarried, further strengthening their pre-eminence in the profession. For example, in 1791 Dr Baillie married Sophia Denman, daughter of Thomas Denman and Elizabeth Brodie. His other daughter married Dr Richard Croft. Baillie was also the nephew of probably the most famous anatomists of the time, John and William Hunter. Pitcairn married Elizabeth, the daughter of William Almack, who founded the famous assembly rooms of that name. We have found no trace of 'Pere Eliser' or 'Mr Peyt' – they were probably practitioners of what we would now call 'alternative medicine'. It is somewhat sad, but not too surprising, that despite the best efforts of current medical science no cure could be found for Evelyn's paralysis, which probably resulted from neurological damage. According to the Reverend Evelyn Bazalgette's Bible, the arm remained useless for all of Evelyn's long life. To prevent the limp arm from dangling he used a strap which he wore round his neck, under the collar and lapels of his coat. The clawed fingers were then hooked over this. Despite this disability, although he never married, it did not prevent him from pursuing a distinguished career as a barrister, Queen's Counsel and bencher, and becoming treasurer of Lincoln's Inn.

An extract from Louis' statement at Coutts' Bank in the summer of 1803:

Jun 24: Rec'd £19/12/5 Cash of Gen Wm Gardiner's account for interest to this day on his bond of £784/18/3
Jul 9: Rec'd £255 as Midsummer Divd on £17,000 Cons'd 3%
Jul 9: Rec'd £44/18/11 from the midsm'er dividend on £2996/12/7 on the names of Thos Treslove, Jos Bunnell and Jno Williams
Jul 9: Rec'd £250 as 6 mos paymt to 1st May on £500 Imperial Annuities
Jul 9: Rec'd £512 as Principal of int of a Prince of Wales debenture - £500
Jul 9: Ditto [total £1,025]
Jul 11: Withdrew £2050 in cash
Jul 12: Rec'd £150 as 6 mos int to 5th Inst P.O.W. [Prince of Wales] debenture
Jul 15: Rec'd £19/12/6 of the D of Kent 6 mos int to 5th inst on bond of £785
Jul 15: Rec'd £37/10/- of the D of York 6 mos do to do on 3 bonds of £500 each to J Payne, and £110/16/- of Do 3 mos payment to 10th ult on H.R.H's 2 annuity bonds of £304/7/2 p. ann and for 3 mos Do to 5th
Jul 15: Paid Mr Masters £4/-/-
Jul 22: Paid Mr Comp [Cowp?] £36/15/-
Jul 23: Paid Mr Thomas £200
[Ledgers of Coutts Bank]

It can be seen how many debentures and bonds he was still receiving interest on from the Prince of Wales and his brothers. Prinny's interest adds up to £1,325 during this period alone, which at today's values is over £90,000. One such entry is marked 'J. Payne', who is no doubt the John Willet Payne mentioned earlier. He had by now returned to the Prince's favour and was again comptroller of the royal household, but he had not long to live, dying on 17 November of that year. This extract also gives a taste of Louis' typical investments, such as a large holding of Consols and Imperial Funds. He also invested heavily in other government stocks such as Navy Bonds.

On 21 December 1803 Louis paid £120 to Francis Goold, who lived at 16, Dover Street, near to Louis' 'compting-house'. Goold was a musically-inclined Irish gentleman of considerable means who was attempting to gain control of the King's Theatre, Haymarket. William Taylor owned the theatre but was perilously in debt, and had previously got himself elected MP for Leominster to render himself immune from prosecution. Before Parliament was dissolved in 1802 Taylor fled to France to avoid his creditors, but in the subsequent general election he lost his seat. He was therefore forced to sell one-third of his interest in the theatre to Francis Goold in 1803 for £13,335, on the understanding that Goold would be the sole manager and conductor at the theatre. Goold raised the money by various means including borrowing from Louis. Goold's brother Thomas may have repaid this loan with interest, because on 27 February 1804, Louis received £200 'on Thomas Goold's note'. On 2 March 1804, Louis paid Francis Goold another sum of £207/18/-, presumably to help finance Goold's further purchase of shares in the theatre for £4,165, which increased his holding to seven-sixteenths, and then to nine-sixteenths for an additional £1,535. Goold seems to have run the theatre successfully, but died on 17 January 1807. He was still a man of wealth at his death, as the auction of his effects shows. As well as his house in Dover Street he had some very fine furniture and five hundred dozen bottles of wine in his cellars. Since the contract with Taylor was only valid until the death of one of the parties, Taylor took back the management of the theatre and refused to let Goold's executor, Edmund Waters, have any part in the running of it. There was much litigation but eventually Waters was able to take over the whole theatre.

By 1804, life at Turnham Green seems to have palled. The rapid development taking place along the Chiswick High Road meant that many new business premises and smaller houses were springing up, as the large houses were sold off and the land divided up and in-filled. Louis's family had also grown, and he could certainly afford to pay cash for a 'real' country estate without feeling it. So when the following advertisement appeared in *The Times* on Wednesday, 13 June 1804 it must have taken his fancy.

HAMPSHIRE.— TO be SOLD by AUCTION, some time in September next, if not previously disposed of by private Contract, the MANSION HOUSE and PREMISES, of HANS SLOANE, Esq. Situate at South Stoneham, in Hampshire, 3 miles from the town of Southampton (that Gentleman being about to remove to Paultons, in the said county); consisting of and eligible Freehold Residence, with every suitable accommodation for a family of respectability, with lawn pleasure-ground, and sheets of water, laid out by the late Mr. Brown; an excellent kitchen garden, with walls covered with choice fruit trees. 2 hot houses, sheds, gardener's tool house &c. and an ice-house. The Mansion house contains 2 handsome drawing-rooms, a commodious eating-parlour, gentlemen's library and closet, a large entrance-hall and staircase, 7 family bed-chambers, 5 dressing-rooms, and in the attic 2 good Gentlemen's bed-chambers, besides various servants' rooms, a lofty kitchen, with suitable commodious domestic offices, and remarkable good cellaring, the house being built on arches: also contiguous, sundry enclosures of very rich arable, water meadow, pasture and wood-land, lying perfectly compact, in a ring fence, with a quantity of remarkably fine timber growing thereon; a capital farm house, two large brick and tiled barns, a cart, stable for 8 horses, cow house, large piggeries, 2 large waggon and cart sheds, a pigeon house, well stocked with pigeons, sheds for ploughs, harrows &c. and a very good farm-yard, walled in; the whole containing 177 acres or thereabouts, in the most perfect order, and in the highest state of cultivation; being freehold, and a Manor within itself, together with the Royalty of the river Itchin, held under the Bishop of Winchester for three lives, in which there is a valuable salmon fishery. Also the two Mills, called Wood Mills, let out on lease to Mr.Taylor; one a capital block mill, for supplying the navy with blocks; the other a very considerable corn mill, to which vessels can come up; held under the same lease, for the same lives; the land-tax redeemed. May be viewed during the month of June, on Mondays, Wednesdays, and Fridays, between the hours of 12 and 4, with tickets only, which, with particulars, may be had of Mr. Peter Watts, above Bar, at Southampton; and of Mr. Thomas Richardson, Durham Place, Chelsea.

The house was built as manor house for the Dummer family in 1708, almost certainly by Nicholas Hawksmoor. Louis either bought South Stoneham freehold or on a short lease. On 3 November 1804, Louis paid £9,768/2/1 to Hans Sloane (Stanley), and on 17 December, he paid him £989/11/9, with a further £300 the following May. He also purchased two additional properties - Wood Mills and a close called Horseleaze. He paid duties for game certificates in 1805 and 1806 for South Stoneham, and in 1804 for both South Stoneham and Oakley Farm, employing a gamekeeper called Robert Stephens to take care of both estates. His last payment to Sloane was 15 guineas in 1809 (perhaps remaining ground rent), which implies he stayed there until that time.

It seems a strange decision for Louis to buy an estate so far from London, and it may be that he spent little time there, especially as he was about to buy another house in London. As the River Itchen was navigable right up to the estate it occurred to the author that it might have been used for shipping, or rather smuggling, goods such as silk and lace. It was also perhaps a useful base for Joseph William whenever he returned from sea. It was certainly an idyllic spot at the time, and would have been much enjoyed by the family in the summer holidays.

In January 1805 Louis did his bit for the war effort (and/or for his finances) in advertising a great number of the trees at South Stoneham for auction:

SOUTH STONEHAM, HANTS.
Capital Oak, Elm, and Ash Timber,
FOR SALE BY AUCTION,

By Mr. WATTS,
At the Dolphin Inn, Southampton, on Monday the 7th day of January, 1805, at two o'clock in the afternoon, Dinner on table precisely at one o'clock.
NINE Hundred and Thirty-four capital OAK TIMBER TREES, fit for the Navy.
191 Ditto Ash ditto
125 Ditto Elm ditto
Now standing and growing on the Estate of L. Bazelgette, Esq. at South Stoneham, three miles from Southampton, adjoining and contiguous to the Winchester Navigation, and about one mile distant from Northam, from whence it may be shipped to any port in the kingdom. For a view of the Timber, apply to Mr. W. Lee, on the Premises; of whom particulars may be had; also at the George Inn, Winchester; Crown, Portsmouth; Dolphin, Gosport; Red Lion, Fareham; Bugle, Titchfield; White Horse, Romsey; Angel, Lymington; Crown, Ringwood; of Mr. William Collins, Twyford, near Winchester; and at the Office of the Auctioneer, Southampton.
[*Hampshire Telegraph, and Sussex Chronicle; or, Portsmouth and Chichester Advertiser*, 24 December 1804]

Bazalgette did not sell Pond House in Turnham Green, and it appeared in the records of the Sun Fire Office as his property until about 1825. Earlier records show it was let to a Mr. Morrell, (probably a descendant of the Reverend Thomas Morell, who died in 1784) but for most of this time it was rented to a spinster lady named Mary Stevenson, who may have enjoyed rattling around in a large residence, but is more likely to have used it as a school or boarding house. Pond House was later renamed Grosvenor House, and it still exists, now being just called No 2, Chiswick Lane. It is a now owned by the Missionary Sisters of Verona (Comboni Sisters) and is a home for retired and novice nuns.

The new London house that Louis purchased in 1805-6 was 45 Gloucester Street, Portman Square He bought it from William Petrie, who was probably the builder, as the Portman estates were growing rapidly at that time. It would still have had a rural outlook to the north and west, but this was not to last for long. Louis argued about the rates and had them lowered from £230 to £170. At the time it was the last house going north on the west side of the street. Fairly soon afterwards when the street became wholly built up the house became No. 86, Gloucester Place, which it remained throughout the Bazalgette tenure. In Louis' will it is described as a 'town house together with yard, gardens, stables, and coach house buildings'.

The house still exists, as No. 73, although it was almost gutted by a German bomb during the Second World War. The façade on the ground floor probably looks much as it did, but the rest was rebuilt in a much plainer style, though with what appear to be its old window surrounds, and it has lost its original top floor. It now serves as the rectory for the Parish. One incumbent was the instigator of a scheme to open up and reuse the crypt of St Mary's Church, Marylebone, about which more later. Amongst later known occupants of the house were Frances Ann (Fanny) Kemble, who, died there on 15 Jan 1893, aged 83. She was an actress and was the daughter of Charles Kemble, and niece of John Kemble and Mrs. Siddons. At that time it was the residence of her son-in-law, the Reverend Canon Leigh.

In July 1806, Louis received the last payment of £1,000 plus £25 interest from the Commissioners for the Prince's debt. At that time it was said that Bazalgette had received the principal sum of £22,134 and interest of £6,382/7/- making a total of £28,462/7/-. At 2006 values, this sum represents £1,708,272/7/7, using the retail price index.

Louis continued lending money to people, using mortgaged property as security. There is a record of one such joint transaction dated 13 May 1807:

> No: 487 Dawson & Lavie
> An Indenture of Assignment of 7 parts dated the 13th May 1807 between
> <u>John Dawson</u> of Warwick Street Golden Square in the County of Middx, Gent of the first part

Thomas Sheppard of Lower Grosvenor Street, Grosvenor Sq in the same County, Gent, of the 2nd part
Louis Bazalgette of Dover Street in the parish of St George Hanover Sq, Esq of the 3rd part
Andrew Dennis O'Kelly of Cannons (Whitchurch) in the Co of Middx, Esq of the 4th part
Michael Atkinson of Harley Street, Middx, Esq of the 5th part
John Richards of Red Lion Square, Middx, Gent of the 6th part
Germain Lavie of Fredericks Place, [Old Jewry, City of] London, Gent of the 7th part

Concerning All and Singly the Capital and said Messuages tenements pieces or parcels of land and ground and heredits mentioned and comprised in certain Indenture of Mortgage of ... bearing even date with the said Indenture of Assignment a memorandum whereof was registered on 24 Nov 1807 BC No 197 which is Indenture of Assignment as to the Execution thereof by the said John Dawson Louis Bazalgette and Andrew Dennis O'Kelly is witnessed by Samuel Parkinson of Symonds Inn London Gent and John Wrigley of Fredericks Place, London, Gent as to the execution thereof by the said Thomas Sheppard is witnessed by Fred Lewis Lacy of Fredericks Place aforesaid Gent is hereby required to be registered by the said Thomas Sheppard witness his hand signed and sealed in the presence of Thomas Sheppard Jr, - F L Lacy of Fredericks Place
[O'Kelly papers; Archives, University of Hull]

The property covered by the mortgage comprised Clay Hill, Epsom and Little Round Wood and Furze Fields on Epsom Downs. Andrew Dennis O'Kelly was an Irish racing man, and was the nephew and heir of the once famous Colonel, ironically styled 'Count' Dennis O'Kelly, owner of Eclipse, the most famous racehorse of the English turf. On Dennis' death, Andrew was his main beneficiary and Eclipse was already at stud at Clay Hill. Of the remaining parties, John Dawson was Louis' solicitor. Thomas Sheppard was Louis' old master tailor, who had bought his house and business in Lower Grosvenor Street. John Richards was probably the same man who was a partner in Armstrong & Co, West India Merchants, of whom we shall see much more later in the story. Germain Lavie, who presumably acted for O'Kelly, was a solicitor of Huguenot extraction, who is known to have acted also for Emma, Lady Hamilton.

The loan to O'Kelly was the subject of an earlier case in chancery – Jones v. Bazalgette, in November 1803. Henry Thomas Jones of Gower St and William Inigo Jones of Turnham Green (a descendant of the architect) were owed money by Dennis O'Kelly and Andrew Dennis O'Kelly so they sued Louis. Canons (the O'Kelly estate) had been bequeathed to Thomas Birch, William Atkinson and Charlotte Hayes (the famous madam and Dennis' mistress), with leases to William Hallett, John Harris, Philip O'Kelly and Andrew Dennis O'Kelly. Many other debtors were listed including Francis Const and Michael Hodgson. It seems that although Louis had lent £8,000 against O'Kelly's estates he was not permitted by this bill to sell them to recover this debt. This illustrates the common problem that the man who takes the estates as security gets sued by the other creditors when he receives them, even though the value of these estates is not even enough to satisfy the debt to him, let alone the others. And because the estate is left to beneficiaries, they get sued as well.

Chapter 18: 1807-12

Louis was still in occupation at 41, Dover Street in March 1807 but had left it by March of the following year. Since he now had another London house he no longer needed it, so he leased it to a tenant, since he did not sell it, and he still owned it as late as 1823, when it was shown in the Sun Fire Office records as No 44. This is certainly the house, since it had a mews and stables, which other houses in Dover Street did not.

> DOVER-STREET, Piccadilly.-- To be LET, for any term not less than 6 months, a good FAMILY HOUSE, 3 rooms on a floor, in complete repair, and furnished in the first style of elegance; it may be had on lease, and the Furniture purchased. A double coach-house and 7-stall stable. Enquire of Seddon and Blease, Dover-street, Piccadilly.
> [*The Times*, Wednesday, Dec 30, 1807]

Just six doors up from Louis' house, at 35, Dover Street, lived Samuel Whitbread the younger, who was the son of the founder of the brewery of that name and an MP. He maintained a majority shareholding in the brewery, but was financially embarrassed because of his association with Richard Sheridan and his investment in building the new Drury Lane Theatre. These burdens are thought to have contributed to a depressive illness, which culminated in his taking his life by cutting his throat with a razor on the morning of 10 July 1815, at his Dover Street house.

For some years, Louis Bazalgette had been doing business with Joseph Dowson, who appears to have been a ship-broker, as well as a member of a firm of ship-builders and shippers, probably of general merchandise but also of sugar. Identifying precisely which transactions were with Joseph Dowson the broker and which were with John Dawson the solicitor is difficult because the handwriting in the ledgers of Coutts Bank does not always clearly differentiate between an 'o' and an 'a'. Transcription errors were common in bank ledgers of the time because the teller would record the transaction in a daybook and it was later copied 'fair' into the ledger by a clerk. As a further complication, there was also a ship-owner named John Dawson who, with Joseph Dowson, was a member of the Society of Ship-Owners of Great Britain.

Louis paid large sums to Dowson so it is fairly obvious that by this time he was investing in the 'West India', and maybe also the 'East India' trade. As confirmation of the latter, his name appears in *A List of the Members of the United Company of Merchants of England Trading with the East Indies who appear by the Company's Books Qualified to Vote at the General Election, 12th of April, 1815*, and on the same date in 1825 and 1826 as having one vote. The members were allotted one vote per £1,000 of stock that they held in the company. In August 1830 his son Daniel was elected to the Committee of West India Planters, and in the same month attended a meeting at which the committee passed a motion to request the government to reduce duties on sugar and rum.

There is an anecdote in the Rev. Evelyn Bazalgette's Bible in connection with the West India trade, which tells us that Frances had a streak of flamboyance:

> The second Mrs. Louis Bazalgette used to drive in Hyde Park in a scarlet Flamingo Boa and Muff. Her husband's ship had made a voyage to the West Indies, which had taken 3 years to accomplish and brought the trophy back. Daphne W[ickham] possesses these now.

A Caribbean newspaper has the following announcement concerning Joseph Dowson:

> Whereas Fifty Casks of Oats were shipped by Joseph Dowson & Son, (brokers,) on board the Brig Trafalgar, John Gibb, master, marked TMK, for which no Bill of Lading were signed, and for which no owner appears in Surinam; the Subscriber as Supercargo makes known through the medium of this Advertisement, that he has landed and warehoused the before-mentioned 50 casks of Oats, and shall keep the same for the space of eight days, at the disposal of whoever can shew claim thereof, upon

condition of such person or persons paying freight, warehouse rent, and costs of advertising, &c. and after the expiration of the said eight days, he intends to dispose of the said fifty casks of Oats by public Sale,, for account of whosoever may be concerned.

The Undersigned besides advertises, that the Brig Trafalgar will sail with the first Fleet for London, and has commenced taking in her cargo, consisting of Coffee.

A. De Boer.

Supercargo of the Brig Trafalgar.

Demerary, 28th Novr. 1807.

[The *Essequebo & Demerary Royal Gazette*, Saturday, 28 November 1807]

Louis' eleven-year-old son John had entered the army as an ensign or cornet, by purchase of a commission in the 80th Foot Regiment, on 29 July 1796. He was promoted to lieutenant on 26 April 1799 and to captain (now in the 98th Foot) on 11 September 1805. In the summer of 1807, he was transferred with the 49th Regiment of Foot from the Bahamas to Bermuda. There he met and married Sarah Crawford Magdalen Van Norden. Sarah's father, John Van Norden, was Mayor of St. George's, Bermuda for nineteen years. John's father Gabriel Van Norden had served with the New Jersey Volunteers during the American Revolution, arriving in Shelburne, Nova Scotia as an Empire Loyalist in 1783. John became one of the first instructors at Kings College in Windsor, Nova Scotia and 'later removed to Bermuda'. John and Sarah Bazalgette remained in Bermuda until at least 1823, when John, by now a Lieutenant Colonel, was transferred to Halifax, Nova Scotia, where they settled and raised a large family, and most of their sons in turn entered the military, with the exception of George, who joined the Royal Marine Light Infantry and later became commander of the British garrison on San Juan Island during the so-called Pig War.

In February 1807, Louis employed a Miss Agassiz, at a salary of £64/13/6 half-yearly, with an initial payment of £80/9/5. These payments continued until 1809. Perhaps she was a governess, though this would have been a rather large salary for such a post. She may perhaps have been an expensive music-teacher. She may have been related to the Swiss merchants of the same name. It is possible that the following advertisement from *The Times* is relevant, although it appeared somewhat later. Perhaps it referred to a younger sister?

> A Young Lady, a native of Switzerland, a Protestant, wishes for a SITUATION in a family as GOVERNESS; she undertakes teaching French grammatically, history, geography, and music, also English and Italian sufficiently to keep her pupils in practice in the absence of masters. Address, post paid, to C. R., at J. G. Agassiz's, at 223, Piccadilly.
> [*The Times*, Tuesday, 21 Nov 1820]

Louis' bank records show that on 26 March he paid £11 'for a Lottery Share'. On this day the sale was announced in *The Times* (notice the encouraging name of one of the sellers):

> GOVERNMENT STATE LOTTERY begins drawing 14th April, 1807. - RICHARDSON, GOODLUCK and Co. respectfully acquaint the Public, that the NEW STATE LOTTERY TICKETS and SHARES, are now on Sale, in variety of numbers, at their Licensed Lottery Offices, corner of Bank Buildings, Cornhill, and facing the Gate of the King's Mews, Charing Cross.
> Scheme contains
> 4 Prizes of 20,000l.   4 of 10,000l.
> 4 of 5,000l.   10 of 1,000l.
> 10 of 500l. &c. &c. &c.

In 18 October 1807, Frances was delivered of a further son, Augustus, who was christened on 7 April 1808. On 25 February 1808, Louis Jr. 'the third son of Louis Bazalgette, of South Stoneham, Esq.' was admitted into the Middle Temple. He never graduated as a lawyer. In those days, you could be a member of one of the Inns of Court by paying a membership fee and 'eating your terms' (equivalent to dining 'in hall' in a university) once or twice a week. It was more like a gentlemen's club, but no doubt was useful for making contacts. Louis Jr. then joined a firm of West India merchants, Armstrong & Scott, of 11 Clement's Lane, Lombard Street. This partnership became Armstrongs and Co., the then partners being the brothers Charles and William Armstrong. Members of the firm were Louis Jr. and also his brother Daniel, who later travelled for the firm to New York. Louis and Daniel eventually became partners in the firm, which was then known as Armstrongs and Bazalgettes, until the Bazalgettes left it in 1827. The partnership between Charles and William Armstrong and Daniel Bazalgette, under the name of Charles Armstrong & Co., was mutually dissolved on 30 April 1827. That between Charles and William Armstrong and both Daniel and Louis was dissolved in July of the same year.

We know that two of Louis's sons were actively involved with West India merchants, but how much Louis senior carried on this business is unknown. That he was in partnership with the Armstrongs seems to be proved by an entry in a Post Office Directory in 1800 listing Armstrong and Bazalgette, West India merchants, at Louis' house, 22 Lower Grosvenor Street. The anecdote about Fanny's red boa having been brought back from a voyage of one of Louis's ships to the West Indies is a further clue. Another is the fact that Louis had dealings with shipbrokers like Joseph Dowson, as well as the Armstrong brothers.

We are not talking about the triangular slave trade at this time; slavery was declining and was not far from abolition. There was a regular back-and-forth trade between Britain and the Caribbean, in order to satisfy the resident Europeans' requirement for all manner of goods which could not be obtained from America, especially during times of war or blockade. Although sugar prices fluctuated from year to year it was still a valuable cargo. It not likely that Louis actually owned any ships himself. He would have used the shipbroker to find a suitable ship. The broker would also employ the captain and probably find much of the outgoing cargo. If Louis had cargo to export it would be included, and he would finance all or part of the venture, perhaps sharing the cost with one or more other merchants. There were many risks in this trade.

Ships could be lost or held up on the perilous outward or return voyages, bad weather being the most likely cause, although the depredations of pirates, privateers or enemy navies were significant. Some of the ships used were old, rotten and poorly fitted out. Having reached the West Indies, it was the responsibility of the captain to deliver the cargo to the required ports, of which there might be several. The cargo might be paid for in cash or promissory notes or in exchange for cargo of equivalent value. There were often lengthy waits for payment, or for the outgoing cargoes to be ready for embarkation. During these delays, disease was likely to strike down the crew, particularly if they were allowed ashore. With all of these difficulties taken into account, it was still regarded as a worthwhile venture, so the profits must have been considerable to justify the risk.

Louis' country house was attacked, either as an act of vandalism or of someone with a grudge, in November 1808. He offered a reward for information but it is not known if the miscreant was caught as a result:

> A REWARD OF TWELVE GUINEAS.
> Whereas on the night of the 15th of November, 1808, some person or persons did maliciously BREAK the WINDOWS the Dwelling-house of LOUIS BAZALGETTE Esq. of South Stoneham, by throwing a thick Stick, three feet nine inches in length, against the Windows of the said L. Bazalgette, which broke the glass, and scattered it several yards within his house, to the danger of wounding himself and family: This is to give Notice, that will give information thereof, so that the offender or offenders may be convicted, shall receive a Reward of TWELVE GUINEAS.
> LOUIS BAZALGETTE.
> Stoneham House, Nov. 16, 1808.
> [Salisbury and Winchester Journal – 26 November 1808]

On 27 February 1809, Louis's son Joseph William

'... while cruizing near Bilbao, on the North coast of Spain, was detached in charge of a single boat in pursuit of a French man-of-war schooner, *La Mouche*, which he gallantly boarded and captured, after an action in which her commander, a *lieutenant-de-vaisseau*, was killed. A night or two afterwards he was again successfully engaged in the boats in cutting out from under the batteries in a neighbouring port three armed luggers, laden with stores and provisions for the French army in Spain; and while in the act of boarding one of the vessels, was severely wounded by a musket-ball in the left thigh which placed him for some months under surgical treatment, and eventually rendered him lame for life. On being sufficiently recovered, Lieut. Bazalgette was appointed [to his next command] in Feb 1810.'
[W.R. O'Byrne, *Naval Biographical Dictionary*, 1849, p.59]

Joseph's injury was described officially as a 'severe wound in the left thigh and hip'. On returning home he received treatment at the Haslar Hospital in Gosport. He returned to service twelve months later, and at the end of the war was retired with a gratuity of £50 and a pension of £150 on account of his wound, which according to one account gave him a limp 'like Long John Silver's' for the remainder of his life.

Louis may have decided to demolish one of the cottages he owned on the South Stoneham estate. Perhaps it was derelict, or it spoiled his view.

SOUTHAMPTON, HANTS.
To be SOLD by AUCTION, on the Premises, on Wednesday the 18th day of March inst. at three o'clock in the afternoon, by Mr. Watts,—The MATERIALS of a brick-built Farm-house; consisting of a large quantity of brick work, some stone pavement, oak in floors, partitions, roof, lintels and bend timber; oak and deal floor boards, skirtings, linings, stair cases, doors, and cupboards; transom windows, with square glass and casements, &c. &c.; the same being situated north of the mansion-house of Lewis Bazalgette, Esq. and near the road leading to

South-Stoneham Church. Also, a small quantity of Round Oak and Timber, lying near the above premises.
Particulars may be known by application to the Auctioneers, Southampton.
[Salisbury and Winchester Journal - March 1809]

1809 was the year when Louis decided to give up South Stoneham House, which he sold to the merchant John Lane for £16,986/2/3. Lane was bankrupt by 1815, whereupon the house was purchased by John Willis Fleming, M.P, whose family then owned it for the next 150 years. South Stoneham is a fine large house with an impressive staircase, and is now a student residence on the campus of Southampton University, dwarfed by a hideous pre-fabricated tower block.

Louis decided to buy a more conveniently-situated country estate: Eastwick Park, Great Bookham in Surrey. James Lawrell had owned the house since 1801, when he had bought it from Richard Howard, the last Earl of Effingham. James Lawrell the elder and his wife Catherine lived in Lower Grosvenor Street (possibly how he came to know Louis) and also owned Frimley Park in Surrey. James Lawrell the younger, of Frimley Park, was a famous amateur first class cricketer, as well as a gambler. He apparently lost the greater part of Frimley Park to John Tekell in a card game, at which the Prince of Wales was present, which is why part of it is called Tekel's Park today. The Lawrells were good friends with Prinny, and part of his Brighton set. Perhaps Lawrell mentioned to the Prince that he was looking for a buyer, and received a reply such as: "My little tailor Jean Louis is looking for a country seat, so I will ask him if it interests him. He has plenty of cabbage, ha ha!"

Eastwick Park House was built by the French Huguenot architect Nicholas Dubois (c.1665-1735) in 1726-8 for Elizabeth, daughter of John Rotherham, and recent widow of Thomas Howard, 6th Baron Howard and her new husband Sir Conyers Darcy. Dubois was a leader of the Palladian revival and built or altered many houses in London, but it appears that he built only two country houses from scratch – Eastwick Park, and Stanmer Park near Brighton. Stanmer still survives, and the two houses are almost identical in many features. Eastwick was the seat of the Howards for some seventy years, but Lawrell gave it a coat of stucco, so no trace of its original red brick remained by the time Louis bought it. In the archives of the Royal Institute of British Architects is a sketch by the Newcastle-born architect William Newton (1735-98) which is described as being of Eastwick Park. The sketch, dated 1735, is very crudely drawn in charcoal and appears to show a row of windows, but they are not recognisably part of the house. This suggests however that Newton may earlier have done some work there.

> The interior is very elegantly decorated, and the apartments are well arranged. In the breakfast-room, are ornamental panels resembling sienna marble, with imitative bronze relievos of classical subjects.
> [Brayley, Edward W: A topographical history of Surrey; 1854]

Louis may well have enlarged and embellished the house further while he owned it, but there is no detailed description of the house at the time he purchased it so we do not know for sure. All that the June 1809 advertisements in *The Times* said was that: 'The Manor house is a capital edifice, of handsome elevation, and has been recently modernised and improved under the direction of an eminent and skilful architect, at the expence of many thousand pounds, and contains a handsome suite of principal apartments, elegantly fitted up, and elegantly decorated by distinguished artists; numerous bed chambers and dressing rooms, and proper apartments for servants, suitable to the establishment of a family of distinction'.

Despite selling the estate and house to Louis, Lawrell retained the lordship of the manor of Great Bookham. Either he wanted to keep it or (perhaps more likely) Louis was not interested at that time. In 1811-12 James Lawrell and his wife jointly conveyed the manor to the solicitor John Harrison Loveridge, who was acting for George Holme Sumner, who then became lord of the manor and who offered it for sale at auction in 1822-3. Louis then decided to buy it, and had set aside £14,000 for the purpose, but because of a dispute over forestry rights he refused to complete the sale. Sumner then sued him but the case was not resolved until 1828, when Louis finally became lord of the manor. The case of Sumner v. Bazalgette is described in more detail later.

A watercolour by John Hassell was painted in 1822 and shows the house as quite plain. J.T. Allom's picture from 1833 makes it look much more Italianate, with dentils under the cornices. Photographs taken about 1912 show it as more plain again. One of the later sale advertisements describes the house as 'an Italian mansion' so it rather looks as if Louis did make these changes. After his death, when it was sold in 1833, the property was described as:

> A Capital and highly important Freehold Property, the greater portion tithe-free; comprising the Eastwick-park estate, situate in the parishes of Bookham and Fetcham, 2 miles only from Leatherhead, and 21 from London, in a neighbourhood of the very first respectability, and most picturesque and delightful part of the county of Surrey. The mansion is a substantial and uniformly-constructed building, of chaste and simple elevation, standing on a moderately elevated site, combining every comfort and accommodation for a family of distinction, viz. a saloon or billiard room about 27 feet square, a morning room 25 by 20, a library, eating room 31 feet by 20, a noble drawing room 70 feet by 20, intersected by two screens of Ionic Scagliola columns, 6 capital bed chambers, a lady's boudoir, 4 dressing rooms, 10 secondary and servants' sleeping rooms, with domestic offices of every denomination, and extensive cellaring, stabling and coach houses, large walled kitchen garden, with grapery, ornamental dairy &c. The park includes about 150 acres of grass land, ornamented by fine grown forest timber, with several enclosures of arable and meadow land, terminated by fine woods forming an excellent preserve for game; the whole comprising 390 acres, and lying within a ring fence, and nearly surrounded by a high park paling. The farm buildings are numerous, complete, and in perfect order.

This desirable property is most enviable as a family residence, particularly to any person desirous of an extensive command of field sports, the Union fox hounds being kept on the skirts of the estate.

Very little can now be seen of the house, which was demolished in the 1960's to make way for housing and a junior school. Part of the wall of the farmyard is still there, as are the main gates, which can be seen in front of 102a, Lower Road, and according to S.E.D. Fortescue in his book *Great and Little Bookham*, 'the remains of the dairy building, allowed to fall to ruin, still exist in a dell to the west of Eastwick Drive and nearby were the ice-house and a well with the unusually large diameter of 6 feet 3 inches.' Water in Louis' time which supplied, amongst other things, upstairs and downstairs water closets, was raised to a storage tank in the attic by a horse-driven pump situated in the basement. The horse must have been led round and round, tethered to a beam. The horizontal circular motion would have been geared to an upright flywheel with a crank that drove the piston of the pump.

There are no reports in the local newspapers that the Bazalgettes ever entertained in style at Eastwick Park, though to maintain their status in local society, even though by many of the upper crust Louis would still have been regarded as 'trade', Fanny must surely have done so, if on a more modest scale than the lavish ball held by her predecessor, Mrs. Maria Anne Lawrell, in January 1808, probably to mark their impending departure. The following description shows us what it could have been like if Fanny had pushed the boat out.

MRS. LAWRELL'S BALL,

Given at Eastwick Park, near Leatherhead, in Surrey, was of the most spendid description. The company exceeded 250 persons of rank and fortune. Every apartment in that noble mansion was illuminated in the most splendid style possible. At about half-past 10 o'clock THE BALL was opened by MR. LAWRELL and MRS. HANKEY; LORD FREDERICK BEAUCLERK followed with Miss SUMNER. In the second dance, *"Lady Montgomery"* three sets were

formed; they mustered nearly a hundred couple. The novelty of seeing so many persons dancing at one time together, and in one direct line, had a singular effect. To account for this apparent impossibility, it is necessary to state that the Ballroom is upwards of 200 feet in length; it is really the most extensive room, for a modern dwelling-house, that we have ever seen. The most magnificent display of Grecian lamps and chandeliers was made, and those were of singular beauty. It was not until three o'clock that the supper took place; it was a banquet of the most sumptuous description. The dancing re-commenced at four in the morning; it was past the dawn of day (half past seven o'clock), when the music ceased, and not till then the company separated. This was one of the finest Balls the season has produced. Mrs. LAWRELL, the elegant hostess, was highly complimented on the occasion. Mr. GUNTER superintended the tables at supper; the most costly wines were introduced. Mr. GOW was the leader of the band.
[Morning Post; 21 Jan 1808]

The Miss Sumner mentioned in the above extract was probably Sophia, the surviving daughter of George Holme Sumner, M.P. Sumner's sister Catherine had married James Lawrell the elder so there was a close connection between the two families. Gunter no doubt refers to the famous teahouse in Berkeley Square, which was known to provide the catering for such events. A two-hundred-foot ballroom seems an exaggeration since the largest room in the house was about seventy feet by twenty.

It seems certain that Louis had already by now also acquired property in Ireland. His will mentions that he did so, worth an annual rent of £500, and this matches what we now know. On 9 December 1809 he received the first recorded payment of £150 'from Josh Pike on John Pimpem by M.H.Becher by order of Mr French'. Other intermediaries shown later in Louis' bank records include Delacour & Co, e.g., '£250 by cash of DelaCour & Co on Johnston & Co rem by M.H. Becher by order of Mr French'. Michael Henry Becher of Creagh, Co Cork, who died in August 1778, married Catherine French of Marino, Co Cork. Their third child was the Reverend Michael Henry Becher who was born in 1773 in Cork. He attended Dublin University & then Oxford, graduating in 1799. He was ordained a priest at Cloyne in 1799, Prebend of Cooline in 1825, & Rector & Prebend of Cooline, Cloyne in 1825-1847, Bridgetown 1836-47 & 1836-47 Rector of Kilshannig, near Mallow. He was also a keen horseman and rode regularly to hounds. He lived in a fine Georgian house called Clyda, by the River Mallow. The Delacour family were also connected to the Bechers by marriage, in that a Mr James Delacour married Henrietta Georgina Lombard, who was the daughter of Anne Becher, a cousin of Michael Henry Becher, the father. The Reverend Becher therefore had relatives who were French's. It looks as if Rev. Becher rented a property, presumably somewhere in Co. Cork, for his uncle, named Richard Temple French, and collected the rent from him, which was then remitted by his bankers to Louis. Temple French leased several properties as well as apparently residing at Thornhill, Co. Cork. Other properties he leased were in Cove Lane in Cork city, Lakenshoneene, Lisnacon, Kildeynake, Currycrowly and Knockaneady (all in Co. Cork) and a house in Limerick City, where his wife originated. We do not know which of these estates (if any) was the one owned by Louis.

According to the surviving records of Broadwood & Son, Louis Bazalgette on 28 November 1809 bought a 6-octave 4-legged grand piano (Serial No. 4626) for which he paid £94/10/-. This instrument was noted as being for Mrs. Simmy, who was perhaps the family's music teacher. On 6 April 1810 another 6-octave grand piano was delivered to Louis, and carriage of £1/16/- was paid for it to be moved to the country estate - Eastwick Park, Great Bookham. However, the porter's book says that this piano was returned on 12 April by Miss Bazalgette for a full credit refund. Quite what the confusion was is hard to see. Perhaps Miss Bazalgette decided that she did not like the second piano, or decided that one was enough. Louis did not pay for the piano which they kept until 7 March 1811, which either means he was a slow payer or that Broadwood's were slow to invoice. 'Miss Bazalgette' was probably Louis' eldest daughter Louisa, who was nineteen at the time, or perhaps Caroline, who was fifteen, or Cecilia, aged ten. The other children were probably too young to play such an instrument.

The Broadwood ledgers, addressed in earlier years to 'Mr. Bazalgette' and later to 'Mrs. Bazalgette', show that on 3 January 1811 the piano was moved from Eastwick back to the London house at 86, Gloucester Place, where it probably got a lot of use, being tuned on 17 January, 26 February, 13 April and 17 May. On 27 May it was carried back to Eastwick again. It was brought back yet again on 1 January 1812 and was tuned monthly until 30 April, when it went back to Eastwick. These movements carried on from year to year, in approximately May and December, reflecting the fact that the children, at any rate, spent their summer seasons in the country and their winter seasons in Town.

This piano was comparatively easy to move, since it could be detached from its four-legged undercarriage and placed in its own wooden case for transport. It was also lighter than the modern pianos because it had a wooden frame, not an iron one. On 15 December 1816 the piano was moved from Eastwick Park to London, at a cost of £1/16/-, was tuned in January and May and was then taken back to Eastwick Park on 22 May 1817. Broadwood's charged 5/- for tuning it in London and a guinea in Great Bookham, because of the extra travelling involved. The piano was tuned on 8 August and then brought back to London on 18 December, being tuned a few days afterwards. Further tunings were done in March, May and June 1819, the last tuning being before it was moved back to Eastwick on 9 June. It seems odd that they would tune it before shifting it, because any journey tends to make a piano go out of tune, especially a wooden-framed one, which is why they are usually tuned after arrival at the new location. It was in fact retuned, but not until 21 June. On 15 December the piano was on its travels again back to London, where it was tuned on 30 December, and again in March and May 1820. The porter's book has an entry for May 1820 for 'moving G.P. in the House (3/6)', tuning it, and moving it back again on the following day. Presumably the family held a special concert so the piano was shifted downstairs for this purpose. Finally on 23 July 1820 the piano was moved back to Eastwick.

The comings and goings of the hapless instrument continued until at least 1831. By then Louis was dead. His widow Frances lived on until 1847, and the last mention of the piano that the author has found was when it was offered at auction in London following her death. It is to be hoped that the purchaser got it for a good price, considering its mileage.

By 20 February 1810, after almost a year of treatment, Louis' son Lieutenant Joseph William was sufficiently recovered from his thigh wound to return to naval service.

> Lieut. Bazalgette was appointed First [Officer] of the LEONIDAS(38) under Capt. Anselm John Griffiths, and until superseded on the 21 Sept following, saw much active service in the Adriatic, where on different occasions, in command of the boats, he succeeded in capturing and destroying, together with the vessels under their protection, the towers of Badisco, Trecase and Emiliano, on the coast of Italy, each mounted with cannon; and for his exertions received the thanks of the senior officer, Capt. Geo. Eyre. He next served for nearly two years on board the WARSPITE(74) under Captain Hon Henry Blackwood, also on the Mediterranean station...
>
> [W.R. O'Byrne, Naval Biographical Dictionary, 1849, p.59]

In March 1811, Louis further enlarged his Eastwick Park estate by purchasing Millfield (at that time known as Woodwards) and Northend Farm, both on the northern side of Bookham Common. In the same month he paid £98 to Broadwood & Son, finally settling accounts for the pianoforte which he had taken delivery of eighteen months earlier. He also started to make payments (e.g., £165/18/-) to 'Mr Ravizotti's'. Gaetano Ravizzotti was an Italian tutor, and according to advertisements in *The Times*, he was a teacher of Italian, French, Latin and Spanish who published 'A new Italian Grammar in English and Italian on a Plan different from any hitherto published, pointing out in a clear and concise Manner the best Rules and easiest Method for the Attainment of that elegant and harmonious Language, equally calculated for the use of Schools and private Instruction, By Gaetano Ravizzotti, late Teacher of Languages at Naples, Dedicated to the Honourable Henry Temple (i.e., his pupil Palmerston)'. The first edition was printed in 1797, the second in 1799, and a new improved edition in 1817.

Ravizzotti also published a collection of Castilian Spanish poetry (*Coleccion de poesias castellanas extrahidas de los mas celebres escritores*) in 1800. He tutored the young Palmerston during his family's grand European tour before the latter went to Harrow. He returned with the Palmerstons to England in 1794. Although 'M. Gaetano', as that family called him, was no doubt a gifted teacher, he was not such a good businessman, and Palmerston had to bail him out on several occasions when he got into difficulties with overspending on the girls' school which he had established in Kensington. He and his growing family remained a financial burden on Palmerston all of his life. Ravizzotti may have tutored Louis' children at home, or perhaps one or two of the girls attended his school. It looks as if Louis's growing family, of whom the newest was Emmeline, born on 29 January 1813, was now being provided with every opportunity to become accomplished and cultured.

Chapter 19: 1813-16

The naval career of Joseph William, despite his lameness, continued to flourish:

... in 1813-14, [Joseph], having joined the AMERICA(74), [under] Capt Sir Josias Rowley, participated in the attacks on Leghorn and Spezia, as also on Genoa, where he commanded a division of boats belonging to the squadron, and where for his conduct, both at the capture, and in the after direction of the enemy's batteries, the guns and mortars of which were effectively employed against the city, he obtained the high commendations of his Captain, and was rewarded, the day after the surrender, in being promoted by Sir Edw. Pellew to the command of the COUREUR, a captured sloop-of-war.
[W.R. O'Byrne, Naval Biographical Dictionary, 1849, p.59]

It was good of Pellew to award Joseph command of his own ship, though it was no less than he deserved, because as a 'master and commander' he could be addressed as 'Captain' and would be also able to draw a pension. He brought home the *Coureur* brig, which was armed with sixteen twenty-four pounders and two long nine-pounders, and paid her off in July 1814.

It appears that during his service in Asian waters Joseph had acquired a trophy – a Chinese dagger, which he later presented to the King at a 'drawing room' in January 1807. It is catalogued in the royal armoury as a 'Chinese Dagger, with one edge, damascened steel blade, handle of dark coloured horn, weighted with lead. Presented by Mr. Bazalgette, in January, 1807, who Wrested it from a Chinaman, in a Murderous Struggle. [Item 142. Windsor Castle Catalogue of Articles in the Collection Museum and Grand Staircase. 1900. (RCIN 1046413)].

It is just as well that Joseph managed to survive these dangerous exploits, since otherwise a whole line of descendants, including the author, would never have seen the light of day.

It was also in 1814 that what we might term Louis' 'Jamaican period' began in earnest. We have already seen that he was investing in the West India trade via the merchants Charles and William Armstrong, by whom Louis Jr. was already employed. One of the major Jamaica planters for whom Armstrongs acted was Anthony Gilbert Storer, of Purley Park, Berkshire, who with his wife Ann Katherine Storer owned the Jamaican sugar estates of Belleisle, Frome, Fontabelle, Carysfort Pen, Camp Savannah, Haddo Pen and others.

> During the late 18th century many fortunes had been made from sugar and rum but by 1809 sugar planters in the West Indies were going through hard times. The early 19th century saw a fall in sugar prices after the Battle of Trafalgar in 1805, and an increase in plantation costs followed the abolition of the slave trade in 1807. By the time that slavery was ended in the sugar plantations in 1833 many West Indian estates were abandoned and worthless. Anthony Gilbert's letters indicate that by 1809 he was in a state of near bankruptcy. Many letters contain plausible excuses as to why he cannot pay off his debts just at the moment, but that he will do so very soon. There are no figures to show by how much the income from Jamaica had fallen but there are indications that by 1809 the Storer estates were already heavily mortgaged. In a letter to Messrs C & Wm Armstrong of Clements Lane, London, he appears to be in debt to them for £6,000, which was said to be the total value of his Jamaica estates. As result, they controlled the income available for his living expenses. The income from his uncle's estate was also slow in reaching him, possibly because the Executor, Lord Carysfort, (his mother's brother) was in Ireland at the time, serving as Lord Lieutenant.
> [Fullerton, Peter; The Storers of Purley Park]

So it was that what would nowadays be termed a 'massive bail-out package' was needed to rescue the Storer fortunes. A loan of £10,000 was arranged in January 1814 by Louis Jr. and the Armstrongs, and Louis Sr. put up the money. In return the Storer estates in Jamaica, and certain lands at Tilehurst, Berkshire, were mortgaged to Louis as security.

Storer owned property in England as well as in Jamaica including his seat Purley Park and (supposedly) 90 acres of farmland at Tilehurst, so despite the fact that his Jamaica estates may have been worth less than the amount of the loan, it looks as if Louis was prepared to accept the risk. He had also invested considerable sums in Armstrongs' and did not want to see them go under, especially as two of his sons were involved in the firm. Louis' bank records show that he paid large sums to Armstrongs', presumably towards the cost of cargo they were exporting. This came to £6,000 in 1812, £2,000 in 1815, £2,000 in 1817, £8,000 in 1818, £5,000 in 1819 and £4,000 in 1820. As already mentioned, the Armstrongs kept a tight grip on Storer's sugar earnings, so they also must have felt reasonably secure that they could recoup any losses. However, the way events unfolded showed that the lenders were over-confident.

The story of what happened next is well documented in a bill of Chancery filed by one John Sherwood of Purley, Berkshire in 1825. It appears that Sherwood, having purchased certain common lands comprising 93½ acres in Tilehurst, Berkshire, following one of the Acts of Enclosure, had an agreement with Anthony Gilbert Storer that Storer would buy these properties and rent them back to Sherwood. Sherwood kept possession and sowed the land with wheat. Payment was to be made in four parts. Storer returned to Jamaica, died in New Providence, Bahamas in July 1818 and thus never returned to England. After Storer's death his wife Ann Katherine Storer proved his will in the Proper Court of the Island of Jamaica but it was not proved in England until later. The payments to Sherwood ceased at Storer's death. Sherwood sued his estate for the remainder.

Ann Storer must have been a very strong-minded woman. She was joint executor with the Reverend William Gorden and William Armstrong, but because she managed to prove the will in Jamaica rather than in England, and additionally, and very unusually, had gained sole administration of the estate there, she was able to put off settling some of her debts in England.

In one very unusual case, the Jamaican Court of Chancery appointed a widow, Katherine Ann Storer, as joint receiver of her husband's plantations. The six estates were the center of several lawsuits among members of the Storer family, and between the Storers and Armstrong and Bazalgetto [sic], their London consignees. At no other time in the twenty-year period from 1823 to 1843 did the court appoint more than one receiver at a time, and certainly never a woman. [Kathleen Mary Butler; The Economics of Emancipation: Jamaica & Barbados, 1823-1843]

William Gorden was an interesting man. We have not discovered how he was connected with the Storer family. An extract from his obituary in 1837 reads:

He was a native of Islip, was matriculated as a Bible Clerk of All Souls' college, Oxford, in 1788; was afterwards a Jackson's Scholar and Bible Clerk of Merton College; and graduated B.A. 1792, M.A. 1795. In 1794 he was presented to the vicarage of Dun's Tew, by the late Sir Henry Dashwood, Bart, to whose son he afterwards became tutor. He accompanied his pupil to France during the short peace of 1802-3, and in 1803 they were both detained prisoners of war, and sent to Verdun. During a period of eleven years' detention in France Mr. Gorden's prudence and discretion, and his influence with the French authorities, founded solely on esteem for his character, enabled him to render important services to many of his countrymen, prisoners like himself— while his talents for business, his readiness to oblige, his unremitting labour in the committee of management for the relief of the distressed English in France, as well as the manner in which he discharged his duty as a clergyman, won the respect and regard of all.

[*Gentleman's Magazine, 1837*]

Sherwood's action was against all of Storer's executors and beneficiaries, namely 'Ann Katherine Storer, Reverend Wm. Gorden, Anthony Morris Storer, Elizabeth Storer, Ann Storer, Charlotte Storer, Margaret Storer, George Reynolds & Margaret his Wife, Charles Armstrong, William Armstrong, Louis Bazalgette and The Provost, Fellows & Scholars of Eton College and His Majesty's Attorney General'. Eton College was a beneficiary because they had been promised a valuable collection of books by Storer's uncle, Anthony Morris Storer, from whom the younger Storer had inherited the Storer fortunes (and debts). The Attorney General was involved because Eton College was a registered charity.

Sherwood and Storer entered into an agreement on 5 February 1813 for the purchase of the 93 acres, and Storer made an initial payment of £1,000, to be followed by further sums of £2,000 in November 1814 and November 1815 with a final payment of £1,154 in November 1816 '& also such further sum as the said John Sherwood hath already paid for the fencing ploughing & harrowing of the said Land & for the seed wheat with which the same has been sown, the ploughing to be calculated at the rate of 30/- per acre the harrowing at 4/- per acre & the seed wheat at the rate of two bushels & a half to an acre at the price of £7/10/- per quarter together with the lawful interest for the said sums of £2,000 £2,000 £1,154 & the sum at which the said fencing ploughing harrowing & seed wheat shall be calculated as aforesaid from the day of the date hereof to the respective times of payment thereof'. Some payments were made by Storer but upon his death, his agents Armstrong and Bazalgette refused to pay any more. The reason for this was that when they lent Storer £10,000, the property in question was also used as part security for the loan.

... the Defts Charles Armstrong William Armstrong & Louis Bazalgette the younger of St Clements Lane in the City of London Merchants who acted as the Agents of the said Anthony Gilbert Storer allege that they some time in the month of January 1814 borrowed for the use of the said

Anthony Gilbert Storer the sum of £10,000 of Louis Bazalgette the elder of Portman Square in the County of Middlesex Esquire & that for securing the payment thereof with Interest the said Anthony Gilbert Storer agreed to grant them the said Charles Armstrong William Armstrong or to Louis Bazalgette a mortgage of the said estate & premises so purchased by him of Plt as aforesaid and that Plt declined to convey the said Estate to the said Charles Armstrong & Louis Bazalgette without the directions of the said Anthony Gilbert Storer but Plt offered to receive the said sum of £2000 & give credit for the same on account but the said Messrs Armstrong declined to pay the same...

After much exchange of solicitors' letters, Ann Storer tried to mollify the vexatious Sherwood by leasing back to him most of the land in question, plus a part of the Purley Park estate, but Sherwood, although he was in possession of the land, complained that no lease had been drawn up. The judgement in this case was that Storer's estates were to be sold and the proceeds used to complete the transaction. However, it did not turn out to be as simple as that because there were many other claims on the estate, including much larger ones such as those by Louis and the Armstrongs, so litigation over the Storer estate dragged on for many years after this.

There were many other players in this business, and extracts from later bills in Chancery give us some of the names of the people involved, some of whom we shall meet again later. For instance, in January 1812, George Hanbury Mitchell, late of Titchfield, Hants, was seized of a plantation/sugarworks (Camp Savannah, in the parish of Westmoreland, County Cornwall – part of the Frome Estate) mortgaged at £4,000, with interest to be paid to the London Merchants Barham Plummer (the partners being Joseph Foster Barham, Thomas William Plummer, John Plummer and Mathew Combe). The balance was paid to C. & W. Armstrong. These premia were then used as security in an indenture (i.e., lease) of 31 March 1814 with assignment made between the Armstrongs and Louis Bazalgette. £10,000 was paid by Louis Bazalgette to

Armstrongs at 5% pa. This was the sum which was lent to Anthony Gilbert Storer, owner of the Frome estate. Payments to Louis were later found to be in default.

Mitchell died intestate in 1816. George Kirlew of Jamaica was appointed his attorney to act on his behalf regarding Camp Savannah. Kirlew also represented the Armstrongs. Mitchell's firm of merchants in Fenchurch Street, which was originally composed of George Hanbury Mitchell and James Cockburn, was formed in January 1800, and was dissolved in September 1802, by the death of Cockburn. Mitchell then continued in business under a new firm, composed of George Hanbury Mitchell, Hugh Ellis, Hugh Lindsey and Thomas Fleming, under the style of Mitchell, Lindsey, &, Co. On 5 May 1826, in a bill in Chancery Louis sued for repayment of the debt of the late John Simpson and Thomas Fleming in the sum of £25,120/9/6.

An incident recorded in the *Morning Post* of 30 October 1814 told of the loss of some bills of exchange:

BILLS LOST—. LOST, in a PARCEL sent on Tuesday the 18th instant, from the Post Office, Ledbury, and forwarded by the Worcester Mail, directed to James White, Esq. 9, Old-square, Lincoln's-lnn, London, TWO BlLLS of EXCHANGE, the one being the second of Exchange, dated Kingston, Jamaica, 2d of July, 1814, for £246 12s. 4d. sterling, drawn by Messrs. Fox and Steele, at ninety days sight, and payable to the order of Mrs. Jane Stock, executrix of William Stock, deceased, addressed to Messrs. Armstrongs and Bazelgetts, London, and accepted by them 24th September last, payable at Messrs. Masterman and Co.'s. The other being the first of Exchange, dated Jamaica, 20th July, 1814, for £232 6s. 11d. sterling, drawn by George Gordon, at ninety days after sight, and payable to the order of William Appleton, Esq. If the said Bills, or either of them, should be offered to be paid away, or discounted, stop them; or if taken to Messrs. White and Son, 9, Old-square, Lincoln's-inn, London, a REWARD of TWENTY GUINEAS will be paid. Payment of both Bills is stopped.

This gives more information about the Armstrongs' clients, including William Appleton, one of whose estates is still famous today for the production of rum.

Storer's Jamaica estates continued to be worked, more or less, under a succession of attorneys and overseers, and sugar and rum were shipped to Armstrongs and Bazalgettes, who presumably kept any profits to put towards the discharge of Storer's debts. The cargoes shipped had considerable value. For instance, according to the crop books in the National Archives of Jamaica, in 1819 the Belleisle estate shipped 404,546 pounds of sugar and 8,346 gallons of rum, in 1820 250½ hogsheads (524,356 gross pounds) of sugar and 75 puncheons of rum and in 1822 336 hogsheads of sugar and 9,413 gallons of rum. By 1824 its output had fallen to 178 hogsheads of sugar and 56 puncheons of rum. In 1817 the Fontabelle estate shipped 248 hogsheads of sugar and 143 puncheons of rum, in 1819 261 hogsheads of sugar and 71 puncheons of rum, while by 1820 its output of sugar had dropped to 180 hogsheads. The Frome estate, under the direction of Joseph Stone Williams, in 1823 shipped 52 hogsheads of sugar and 11 puncheons of rum. The largest barrel in use at the time was a tun, which usually held 256 imperial gallons. A puncheon held a third of a tun (about 85 gallons) and a hogshead a quarter of a tun (about 64 gallons). All of these cargoes went to Armstrongs and Bazalgettes in London.

The titles of the mortgaged Jamaican estates themselves should also have devolved to Louis but it is unclear whether, or how much, this was made to happen. The *Jamaica Almanac* for 1838 lists Fontabelle and Belleisle as in the possession of 'descs of A.G Storer', while Frome and Carysfort Pen were owned by Storer's son Anthony Morris Storer. This is probably because the ownership of these estates was still in dispute. One property of which we have the final sale details is Haddo Pen. A 'pen', as the name implies, was mainly used for raising cattle for local consumption, though not by the slaves. It was generally felt that red meat would make them aggressive, so they traditionally lived on salt fish and ackee, and whatever else they could grow themselves. Coffee, cocoa and pimento were also frequently grown in pens. In the National Library of Jamaica there are four detailed maps of Westmoreland, prepared from surveyors' maps in about 1880. One shows Haddo Pen, 'transferred by Evelyn Bazalgette to Benjamin Vickers on July 30, 1856, Lib 925 Vol 13'. It consisted of 1,580 acres, near the Hanover border. Many of these estates, including also Belleisle, Frome and Fontabelle, were sold to Vickers, who was part of a consortium called The West Indies Sugar Company Ltd., which later became a subsidiary of Tate & Lyle. As we have got somewhat ahead of time we must leave the Storer saga for a time and go back a few years, since other things were happening which need to be recounted.

In the first restoration of Bourbon rule in France in April 1814, Louis XVIII was in power until Napoleon decided to return from Elba, arriving back in Paris on 20 March 1815. During this brief period of monarchy, the new French King rewarded supporters of the royalist cause with medals such as the *Decoration du Lys*, which was at first awarded to the National Guard for gallantry in defence of Paris, but was later extended to others. Louis was the 5,046th recipient of the decoration on 1 August 1814, the citation being signed by the Duc d'Aumont, the *Premier Gentilhomme de la Chambre du Roi*. On Napoleon's return to France at the end of the '100 days', he officially banned the decoration and made it clear that to wear it was not a wise thing to do.

Louis's citation is much stained and hard to read, but says: 'I have the honour to inform you, Monsieur, that the King has deigned to accord to you the Fleur de Lys; you are in consequence authorised to wear this decoration. Please accept, Monsieur, the assurance of my distinguished consideration.'

In May 1815 there was a minor family scandal. Louis Junior, who seems to have remained in London with Charles Armstrong, had a dalliance with a young woman named Ann Moxom. On 25 February 1816, Julia Augusta, the daughter of Louis Bazalgette & Ann Moxom was born and baptised the next day in St. Mary's, Marylebone. The Register entry lists her as Julia Augusta, daughter of Ann Moxom and Lewis Bazalgette.

Beside the fact that it is highly unusual for the mother's maiden name to be given at all, her name is hardly ever given first, as it was in this case. There are several records of Ann Moxoms marrying later on, though it is not clear which, if any of them, is her. We also know nothing else about her, or what happened to Julia Augusta. Perhaps she died in infancy, or was adopted and quietly and rather shabbily forgotten; Louis Jr.'s will makes no mention of her either.

In 1815, John Lane, who had bought South Stoneham House from Louis, became bankrupt and the estate was again offered for sale as a result. The advertisement in *The Times* of 21 June 1815 gives a more detailed description than when Louis bought it:

> Valuable Freehold Estate, exonerated from Land-Tax; Manor, Mansion, Fishery, Water-Mill, Farms and Lands, at South Stoneham, near Southampton – by Mr Hermon, at the Auction Mart, on Wednesday June 28, at 12 o'clock, in 5 lots, by direction of the Commissioners named in a Commission of Bankruptcy against Mr. J. Lane, with consent of the Mortgagees, A HIGHLY valuable and very compact FREEHOLD ESTATE, comprising the Manor or reputed Manor of South Stoneham, and the capital Mansion, called South Stoneham House, most delightfully situate on the banks of the Itchen river, distant only two miles and a half from Southampton, with offices of every description for a family of respectability, gardens, pleasure grounds, hot houses, ice house, sheets of water, fish ponds and 360 customary acres of arable, meadow and wood land, about 40 acres of which form a beautiful Paddock, in which the Mansion stands, the remainder divided into a farm, with farm house and buildings; and a capital farm, called Town Hill Farm; the exclusive and important rights of the salmon fishery, and right of other fishery, in the River Itchen, extending from Alresford ponds to Itchen ferry, a distance of nearly 30 miles, with capital water corn and block mills, store house, mill house and cottages; and a desirable Farm, called Shamblehurst Farm, containing

about 20 1/2 customary acres, situate on the turnpike road, about a mile from Botley.

South Stoneham was then bought by the M.P. John Barton Willis Fleming, whose family owned the estate for the next 150 years.

By 1816, after the end of hostilities in Europe, and between Great Britain and the United States, Armstrongs and Bazalgettes concluded that the business required that an office be set up in New York. It was decided that William Armstrong and Daniel Bazalgette would run the American side of the business. Calling themselves Armstrong, Bazalgette & Co., they had already set up an office at the Liverpool Docks, first at 5, Paradise Street, moving in 1821-2 to 15, Exchange Buildings.

Charles and William Armstrong, who were born in Chunarghur, India in 1776 and 1778 respectively, were sons of the surgeon John Armstrong and his wife Margaret. Charles married the widow Jane Man at St. Pancras on 16 March 1827. Their known children were John, born 1827, Mary Ann, born 1828 and Charles, born 1831. Charles' brother William married his Dominican-born wife Elizabeth around 1810. Their earlier children were Emily, (christened 21 August 1811), Elizabeth, (christened 5 February 1813), Mary, (christened 1 January 1816) and Charles, (christened 6 March 1816). These children were all christened at Camberwell, Surrey. One daughter that we know of, Julia, was born in New York in about 1820, so this shows that Elizabeth joined William some time before then.

Louis' family Bible contains the significant entry: 'On March 21st 1816, Daniel Bazalgette took leave of his family to go to New York'. It is not clear if this means that was when he actually left the family home to undertake the uncomfortable two or three day coach journey to Liverpool, or whether he sailed on that date for New York. So far we have not found a likely ship that he would have sailed on, and no manifests have been seen which show his passage, either alone or accompanied by William.

The voyage from Liverpool to New York at that time took a minimum of forty days, and sometimes a week longer, depending on the weather. The return trip took between twenty-two and twenty-seven days. This also depended on the type of ship of course. These travel times were steadily decreased, especially by 1818 when the fast packets of the American Black Ball Line began to run as a regular service.

Daniel would have travelled on one of the cargo ships chartered by Armstrongs, but as he was a partner his accommodation would no doubt have been as luxurious as it was on the packets. On these ships, passengers would pay a fare of about £25, which would include all food and drink. A typical day at sea, assuming that the weather was moderate, would begin for the passengers with a seven o'clock bell, and breakfast would be available at any time between then and nine o'clock and consist typically of coffee, chocolate and tea, veal cutlets or beef-steaks, sausages and hot toast and butter. A cow was kept on board to provide fresh milk, cream and butter and other livestock such as chickens, ducks and sheep would be kept for meat. After breakfast, if the weather allowed, the passengers could stretch their legs on deck, suitably wrapped up. Apart from reading and conversation, much of the rest of the time would be taken up by eating and drinking and napping in one's berth.

At about eleven o'clock, appetizer drinks such as wine and bitters would be served, followed by lunch at twelve consisting of cold meat, cheese, biscuits, seed-cake, port and Madeira wine, cider, ale and porter. This would be followed either by a nap or by reading or conversation until the next meal was announced, which was dinner at four o'clock with soup, roast turkey, ducks and fowls, poultry pies, and beef, or mutton, with hot tarts, or puddings (which on Sundays were always plum-puddings), followed by a dessert of apples, almonds and raisins, hickory-nuts, figs and other preserves. As unlimited wines were provided, some diehards would stay drinking until almost tea-time at eight p.m., punctuated by the occasional cigar on deck. The rest of the evening would be taken up with card games, backgammon or reading, until after copious nightcaps of whisky punch the exhausted passengers would finally turn in and sleep like the dead. [Description based upon

Letters from North America, written during a tour in the United States and Canada; Hodgson, Adam, 1824]

The young Daniel must have cut quite a dash in the New World, impeccably tailored of course, and sporting expensive cigars, and seems to have made an immediate impression, because a year had scarcely passed before he married Margaret MacCrea at the First Presbyterian Church in Philadelphia on 19 June 1817. The marriage was performed by the pastor, the famous Reverend James Patriot Wilson. The MacCreas were an influential merchant family in Philadelphia, originating from Ballyheather, Co. Tyrone, and had been established in Pennsylvania and Virginia since the early eighteenth century.

Daniel took his new bride from the comparative gentility of the larger city of Philadelphia to the bustle and clangour of commercial New York, where they moved into a brick-built two-storey house, No. 45, Franklin Street, in a fashionable part of Manhattan, which afforded an easy twenty-block ride, or a brisk walk, down Broadway to the offices of Armstrong, Bazalgette & Co. at 2, Marketfield Street, 'on the north side of the Battery, next to No. 1, Broadway'. No. 2, Marketfield Street was owned by Robert Fulton, the steamboat and submarine builder, until his death in 1815. It was probably then rented by his widow to Armstrong and Bazalgette. No. 1, Broadway was at that time the residence of Nathaniel Prime, the first president of the New York Stock and Exchange Board.

The following extracts from *Reminiscences of an Octogenarian of the city of New York (1816-1860)* by Charles Haynes Haswell give a striking picture of what life was like in the city during the period:

> The street dress of gentlemen consisted of a blue coat with gilt buttons, white or buff waistcoat with gold buttons, knee breeches of buckskin, buckles and top boots. 'Spencers' or cloth jackets in cold weather were often worn over coats and for outer wear box coats, as they were termed - that is great coats with from one to seven or more capes buttoned on. Wellington boots introduced and so termed after the Battle of Waterloo cut high with tassels at the tops prevailed; they were worn outside of the

pantaloons. Shirt collars were very full; false collars and wristbands or cuffs were unimagined; black or white cravats, none other - not the ribbons etc of this day but stiffened with a pudding of wool horse hair or hog's bristles; to the bosoms of the shirts were attached low down pleated frills. Black clothing was never worn except for mourning or by clergymen. The full dress of gentlemen was dark dress coat with rolling collar running down low in front, short waisted white waistcoat, frilled bosom to shirt, knee breeches with gold buckles, black silk stockings and pumps, watch chain and seal displayed pendent from a fob in the breeches....

There were several gentlemen residing in the lower part of the city who were frequently seen walking up Broadway Greenwich Street or the Bowery shouldering a gun and followed by their dogs on the way to the suburbs for the shooting of woodcock, English snipe and rabbits...

The average of the passages in 1817 hence to Liverpool was twenty-three days and from Liverpool to this port forty-five days....

There were not in this year ten private carriages proper (1819)....

An ocean steamship company with Cadwallader D. Colden, John Whettin and Henry Eckford as trustees was organized with a capital of three hundred thousand dollars with power to increase to five hundred thousand. In March of this year (1819) was built the steamer *Savannah* of 380 tons old measurement, said to have had folding water wheels which were taken out and laid on deck when not in use, presumably when she was under sail alone. She sailed to Savannah and thence to Liverpool where she arrived on June 20, the first steam vessel to cross the Atlantic Ocean....

In August 1819 a case of yellow fever occurred in the vicinity of Old Slip and soon after the disease became so much so as to render necessary the removal of contiguous inhabitants and the closing of the infected area by a fence....

In 1822 Franklin Market at the foot of William Street (Old Slip) was erected and opened. Hogs were permitted still to run at large in the streets although the practice was objected to by most of the citizens and the frequent mortifying references thereto of Boston and Philadelphia editors added to the opposition; yet the common opinion was that the hogs were the best scavengers was supported for many years after the indifference to the practice shown by the Common Council. In support of this inaction it is to be considered that at this period all garbage and refuse matter from dwellings was thrown into the street. Some years after 1825 an ordinance of the Common Council authorized the furnishing and equipment of a cart and operators to arrest swine in the streets. The advent of the cart and the endeavor to arrest the swine were attended with such forcible opposition by men and boys that the ordinance necessarily became a dead letter until the amour propre of our citizens despite the unpopularity of the cart was aroused; the enormity of the practice was realized and swine were removed from the streets.

Charles Dickens visited New York in 1842 and amusingly refers to the swine as well, so they were still at large at that time. An extract from his description is:

> Here is a solitary swine lounging homeward by himself. He has only one ear; having parted with the other to vagrant-dogs in the course of his city rambles. But he gets on very well without it; and leads a roving, gentlemanly, vagabond kind of life, somewhat answering to that of our club-men at home.
> [Dickens, Charles; American Notes, 1842]

Back home in England, Louis' son Joseph William, after seventeen years at sea, punctuated by the occasional shore leave and his year-long convalescence from his wound, became attached to Theresa Philo 'Tizzie' Pilton. Theresa was Fanny (Bergman's) niece, daughter of her sister Louisa, who had married James Pilton of Chelsea. It is likely that Joseph and

Theresa had known each other since childhood, given the close family connection, but since Joseph had gone away to sea at the tender age of twelve, there would have been little chance for the romance to blossom until he returned.

The Pilton family were wireworkers, producing all manner of garden furniture and fences for the gentry. In 1809 James Pilton's Manufactory in King's Road advertised its fences, verandahs, and other ornamental metalwork. James Pilton invented what he called his Invisible Fence, which was a 'fence made of tort elastic wire, which becomes invisible at a comparatively short distance, calculated for pleasure-grounds'. Presumably if used across a vista on a country estate in conjunction with thin metal posts it would keep the stock out of the gardens and not spoil the view, as it could hardly be seen at a distance, and would be cheaper and less permanent than a ha-ha. James Faulkner, in his *An Historical and Topographical Account of Chelsea and its Environs*, published in 1810, says:

PILTON'S MENAGERIE.
In the King's Road is a grand menagerie for foreign and English birds, the property of Mr. James Pilton; as also his manufactory of light fences for inclosing lawns, shrubberies, and ornamented walks; which is, very properly, called *Invisible Fence:* as at a comparatively small distance they vanish from the eye, and leave the prospect free and uninterrupted. We understand that this manufactory has been established under the distinguished patronage of their Majesties and Royal Family, who have been graciously pleased to honour the proprietor with their presence to view the works and grounds. The manufactory also extends, generally, to various other and ornamental works, which are particularly adapted to country residences. Indeed, the novelty of this establishment, altogether, and the judicious manner in which the various specimens are displayed for public inspection, render it highly interesting, and worthy of attention.

In 1812, Pilton leased 20, New Bond Street from Richard Platt, but as Pilton had been made bankrupt in 1811 he had to abandon the property. It does appear that Pilton, although a man of considerable enterprise, overextended himself and the business eventually had to be sold.

Theresa Philo was therefore probably happy to escape from her father's financial troubles, and she and Joseph decided to marry. A property was bought, perhaps by Louis as a wedding present, at Clay Hill in Enfield. There is no known family connection with Enfield before this time, so it may just have been chosen as an attractive area, not too far from London. The property, which was, at least by 1836, known as Hill Lodge, seems to have had a small house on it in 1803, according to the enclosure map of that date, but the large and handsome Georgian house which was there in 1816 had either been already built by a previous owner, or was built for the Bazalgettes. It stood next to the Fallow Buck public house, which still exists, but Hill Lodge was demolished in 1965, although parts of the original garden wall can still be seen.

Banns were published at St Mary, Battersea, on 4, 11 and 18 February 1816. Both parties were said to be 'of this parish', which is probably untrue. They therefore planned to marry on 25 February. Maybe they did not have the permission of Tizzie's father James, which would have been needed since she was under twenty-one. It is possible that he disapproved of Joseph as a son-in-law for any number of reasons, such as for being French, a naval officer, an evangelist or even for walking with a bad limp. If so, they might have decided quietly to marry on the other side of the river. In fact, the couple were married on 16 February 1816 by licence at St Luke's, Chelsea, two days before the banns were read for the final time at Battersea. This time Joseph was said to be 'of this parish', i.e. St Luke's, and Theresa was of the parish of 'Endfield' [sic]. Perhaps therefore, James had got wind of what they were planning, but relented and allowed them to marry at once, as long as it was in his home parish. At some point there was another change of plan, because banns were also read for them at St. Andrew's Church, Enfield, describing them as 'both of this parish', on 11, 18 and 25 February.

The marriage in Chelsea may have been declared invalid for some reason, maybe because James had not in fact given his consent, or perhaps because they wished to be married by banns rather than by licence. Whatever the reason, Joseph and his Tizzie were married for the second time at St. Andrew's Church, Enfield on 5 March 1816, this time with James' consent. The witnesses were James Pilton Jr., (Tizzie's brother), Alex Young the verger, and Sarah Rosen. The newlyweds lost no time in starting a family, for on 15 May 1817 their daughter Theresa was born at Enfield. She was baptised at home at Hill Lodge on 18 June 1817, suggesting that she was a frail child.

Chapter 20: 1817-19

Back in New York City, Armstrong, Bazalgette & Co. were shipping and receiving goods of great variety, and used the *New York Gazette* to advertise ship arrivals and departures as well as cargo wanted and merchandise for sale. The first advertisement found, on 10 May 1817, reads:

> FOR LONDON – The Fine fast-sailing British brig PETER ELLIS, R. Johnston, master, 260 tons, coppered and copper fastened; has half her cargo engaged, and will meet immediate dispatch. For freight or passage, apply to the captain on board, west side Old Slip, or to
> ARMSTRONG, BAZALGETTE & CO.
> 2 Marketfield-st. next door to 1 Broadway

A further *Gazette* announcement on 7 August 1817 reads:

> COALS, BOTTLES &c. – 200 chaldrons Newcastle Coals.
> 300 gross wine bottles, 12ops. Cot. Bagging, 20 grindstones, 50 crates Window Glass, 170 Patent Blocks, with brass cogs, from 6 to 16 inches – in the ship HORNBY from Newcastle, lying east side Flymarket wharf, and for sale by
> ARMSTRONG, BAZALGETTE & CO.
> 2 Marketfield-street, north side of the Battery.

This is interesting as the cargo, or at least the coals, originated in Newcastle. The coal frequently acted as ballast, so was very cheap to ship. A chaldron was 25½ hundredweight, so this was 255 tons of coal. In view of the mixed cargo it is possible that the ship stopped at another port on the way. Armstrongs usually shipped from Liverpool or London. There seems to have been a shortage of glass and bottles in the USA at the time.

LONDON HATS, &c. – 5 cases, cont'g 4 dozen each, Gentlemen's supf. fashionable black Hats, will be landed in a few days from the ship Radius.
2 do. Ladies' and Children's fancy hats, calculated for the southward
38 groce Wine Bottles in bulk
1 Grand Piano, by Kirkman, London, which will be sold low to close a consignment

WANTED TO CHARTER
A British vessel, of 300 tons; or two, of about 150 tons each, to load here with lumber for the North side of Jamaica. Apply to
ARMSTRONG, BAZALGETTE & CO.
2 Marketfield-street, north side of the Battery.
[*New York Gazette*, 23 September 1817]

The above advertisement shows much about the workings of the partnership. Not only did they receive a cargo which looks to be from London, but they were already planning a ship to Jamaica, since they were of course still plying the West India trade. The ship they were seeking, when chartered, would unload timber in Jamaica and then come back, to New York or to a British port, with a cargo of sugar, rum, pimento etc. The next advertisement shows that the ship *Hornby*, under its master John Walker, had been secured for the voyage and was due to sail on Sunday 5 October, also offering 'good accommodation' for passengers.

DEMARARA SUGAR & RUM.
TWENTY seven hhds Sugar, 29 puns Rum, will be landed this day, at pier No. 4, N. R. from the brig British Tar, and for sale by
ARMSTRONG, BAZALGETTE & CO.
2 Marketfield-street, north side of the Battery.
Who have, 143 casks London Brown Stout, and 2 casks Ale, landing from brig Unison, at Market-slip – for sale as above.
[*New York Gazette*, 4 October 1817]

So business was brisk enough that, in the space of a couple of days, the partners handled at least three ships and their cargoes. The above advertisement announces the arrival of a ship from Jamaica, and it is interesting that the hogsheads of sugar and puncheons of rum could now be sold in New York instead of being shipped to England. The savings of time and reduction of risk in this arrangement must have been considerable, and the turnaround of cargoes much faster. At the same time, they offered a consignment of British ale and stout. One wonders how good it tasted after six weeks at sea.

On 24 October 1817, Armstrong and Bazalgette announced two further consignments for sale, namely ten cases of Gentlemen's London Hats, and sundry Woollens, from the *William*, and 30 bales of 'Cloths of different qualities' from the *Venus*. The schooner *Mary and Elizabeth* brought from the West Indies in mid-November of the same year a cargo 20 puncheons of 'Montserat Rum, said to be 4th Proof and of Superior Flavor', which must have helped to keep the cold out. And cold it certainly was, following the 'year without a summer', which had been caused by much volcanic activity in the previous years, culminating in the massive eruption of Mount Tambora in Indonesia. That winter in New York the temperature dropped as low as minus 32° Celsius and Upper Bay froze over.

In the autumn of 1817, Louis presumably sought to improve his image as a nobleman, rather than just a man of property, by applying for a coat of arms to Nicolas Viton de St. Allais (1773-1842), the noted French genealogist and author of *Nobiliaire Universel de France, ou Recueil Général des Généalogies Historiques des Maisons Nobles de ce Royaume*. This was supplied by St. Allais, and was based upon the Bazalgette de Charnéve arms. An expert at the *Société Française d'Héraldique et de Sigillographie* responded to the author's enquiry about this with the remark that St. Allais was most accommodating to such requests as long as the price was right. Since no recent connection between the noble Bazalgette family and Louis' has been found there is no reason to disbelieve him, but the document St. Allais supplied is attractive enough.

The Times of 30 December 1817 listed all subscribers to a public monument to Princess Charlotte. Louis gave one guinea, which does not seem very much considering his past royal connections.

Louis and Fanny's third son Evelyn, he of the withered arm, was admitted to Balliol College, Oxford in 1818, when he was seventeen years old. In January 1822 he achieved his B.A., Second Class, in Mathematics and Physics, became a student of Lincoln's Inn on 29 January 1823 (then aged 21) and on 2 June 1825, he was awarded his M.A. He was called to the bar on 25 May 1827, rose to Queen's Counsel on 9 January 1858, and was made a bencher at Lincoln's Inn on 11 January 1858. It was just as well he was a legal eagle, because, as will be seen, the family was to have great need of his expertise in the ensuing years. The first mention of Evelyn in *The Times'* law reports was in the Rolls Court in January 1842, where in the case of Clarke v. Tipping he represented the plaintiff. Coincidentally, he acted for the Storer family in the case of Storer v. The Great Western Railway Company in November of that year. The company had built a line overlooked by the Storer mansion (Purley Park) and the Storers were pressing for it to be placed in a tunnel. The Bazalgettes were still in dispute with the Storers at the time over the sale of their Jamaican estates. Evelyn also appeared for the plaintiff in March 1843 in Clayton v. Swainson and for the trustees in Kearsley v. Woodcock in July of that year. His was kept very busy and his career continued to flourish for many years.

In May 1818 the Bank of Scotland offered a share issue, and *The Times* listed those who subscribed, while expressing some concern about the number of 'foreign' investors, though these were all London-based merchants who had foreign names. Louis bought one share for a total of £223/1/-. He also around this time made several payments to a 'Madame Marian Bazalgette', who must have been a French relative, and to a Monsieur Roux Amphoux, whose name is so distinctive that it must surely be Jean Pierre Roux Amphoux, a merchant and banker whose property in Nîmes was destroyed in 1818 by

Catholic ultra-royalists because he was a protestant. He had previously served as the vice-president of a revolutionary tribunal and was also a member of the Nîmes chamber of commerce. He must have fled to England, and may therefore be one of the émigrés whom Louis is reputed to have helped.

> The premises of M. Roux Amphoux were besieged and entirely pillaged; all the property that could not be carried off was broken and thrown into the street; and this notwithstanding the known fact that the proprietor had subscribed towards the equipment of the troops of the Duke d'Angoulême.
> [Wilks, Mark; History of the Persecutions endured by the Protestants of the South of France, and more especially of the Department of the Gard, during the years 1814, 1815, 1816, &c. including a Defence of their Conduct, from the Revolution to the Present Period; Longman, 1821]

On 26 February 1819, Louis lent £5,000 to Sir Godfrey Vassall Webster, the 5th baronet, of Battle Abbey, Sussex. This loan was as usual secured by property, and a mortgage deed for £6,000 was drawn up covering land up to a total of about 500 acres in Sussex, including Bodiam Castle. £5,103/8/5 (presumably including some interest) was paid back to Louis by Webster on 26 June, possibly because he had managed to borrow most of the money elsewhere without having to mortgage all of his property. This repayment was fortunate for Louis, because Webster promptly skipped to the continent to avoid his debts. Sir Godfrey's father, the 4th baronet, had himself inherited vast debts, but married Elizabeth, daughter of Richard Vassall of Jamaica, which improved his finances considerably. The couple were not together for long however, as Elizabeth eloped with Lord Holland, and while in Spain acquired some dahlia tubers, which she brought home with her, thus being credited with the introduction of this species to England. Webster's father succeeded in getting a divorce, but committed suicide soon afterwards, leaving his son Godfrey to succeed at the age of only ten. He did little to decrease the family's debt, and in fact spent large sums restoring the neglected family seat, Battle Abbey. Webster's loans were arranged by John Dawson, who was of course also Louis' solicitor. In the period from 1814 to 1817 he borrowed £3,400 from George Rutherford of Dean Street, St Anne's Soho, £10,000 from Edward Millward of Hastings, £20,000 from George Saltwell of Keppel Street, Russell Square and £10,000 from Francis Charles Conway, Earl of Yarmouth.

28 March 1819 saw the birth of a son to Joseph and Tizzie. He was named Joseph William after his father, and was christened at home like his sister. Joseph was very small and sickly and suffered from asthma, an ailment which later caused the premature death of his own eldest son Charles Norman Bazalgette, the author's great grandfather. As history shows us, young Joseph developed a precocious talent for civil engineering, and despite his frailty he was possessed of enormous energy, perseverance and attention to detail.

Sir William Knighton was physician to Prince George, and the Regent was becoming increasingly dependent upon him. When Princess Charlotte became pregnant, Knighton, who was acknowledged as the best *accoucheur* in London, was the obvious choice to have attended her, but it has been suggested that the hypochondriac Prince did not wish to lose Knighton's services, even for a while. Sir Richard Croft, although perhaps less experienced than Knighton, was therefore appointed to take care of the royal confinement. Croft was, however, physician to George III and had written a treatise on childbirth, so was not by any means incompetent. The reader may recall that Croft was one of the physicians called in to attempt to cure Louis' son Evelyn's paralysed arm. It is not clear whether his treatment of Charlotte made her death on 6 November 1817 any more certain, but this tragic event caused Croft great anguish. Dr. Franco Crainz, professor of obstetrics and gynaecology at the University of Rome, in his book *An Obstetric Tragedy*, makes it clear that Croft acted properly according to contemporary medicine, and prints letters from Croft's colleagues which also supported his conduct.

On the night of 12-13 February 1818, Croft was called to attend a patient about to give birth, a Mrs Thackeray, at the home of her sister, Miss Cotton, at 86, Wimpole Street. He was offered a bed so that he could rest while on call, and reluctantly accepted. At about two o'clock in the morning, the lady's husband, the Rev Dr Thackeray, heard a noise 'like a chair falling' but went back to sleep. The lady went into labour about an hour later, and when a servant informed Dr Thackeray of this he went down and knocked on Croft's door, which was ajar. Receiving no answer he entered the room and found him dead. In the words of the report on the inquest in *The Times* on 16 February:

> At the conclusion of the evidence, the Coroner and Jury retired to take a view of the body of the deceased, which lay in an upper apartment, and was in a dreadful condition, the head being blown to pieces, and the deceased's bed and bed-clothes being covered with blood; each hand grasped a pistol, which had been loaded with a slug and small shot; the contents entered at the temples. On a chair by the side of the bedstead on which the deceased lay were several of Shakespeare's plays. The room was very small, and it appeared as if the deceased had been reading. One of the play-books lay inside the fender, and was entitled "Love's Labour Lost." One of the jury took up the book and noticed to his brother jury-men that one of the characters used the following expressions in the page which lay open on the hearth: "Good God! Where's the Princess?" The jury remarked this as a singular coincidence, and returned to the jury-room, where the Coroner (Mr. Stirling) summed up the evidence, and the jury, after a short consultation, returned a verdict of - "Died by his own act, being at the time he committed it in a state of mental derangement."

There were several accounts published which told a different story - that Croft had happened upon a loaded pistol in the living room and decided on impulse to end it all there and then. This version was perhaps circulated by his family to suggest that his suicide was not premeditated, but since he used two pistols 'loaded with slug and small shot' he must have been carrying them around in his doctor's bag for some time.

To return to Daniel's adventures in New York, he had by now joined St. George's Society, a charitable society of Englishmen. In the spring of 1818 the partnership of Armstrong, Bazalgette & Co. had moved their premises to 102, Greenwich Street. On 19 May 1818 they advertised, that for 'Freight or Charter, to England or the West Indies', the British brig *Bacchus*, 'coppered and copper fastened, about 18 months old and 140 tons' was ready to take on cargoes. As an afterthought they mention that remaining for sale on the ship was '600lb wt of English Cheese'. Since ice was not in use at the time for keeping food cool it is to be hoped that they sold this before summer arrived, or the air around the already malodorous Old Slip would have become scarcely breathable.

> JAMAICA RUM, MOLASSES &c. – 50 hhds molasses, said to be of a most excellent quality
> 11 bags Pimento – will commence landing this day at Gouverneur's-wharf, from ship Urania, for sale by
> ARMSTRONG, BAZALGETTE & CO.
> 102 Greenwich-street.
> [*New York Gazette*, 21 August 1818]
>
> ST. CROIX RUM, HATS & PORTER.–
> 20 puns, choice St. Croix Rum, will be landed this day from brig Rapid, west side of Old-slip, and for sale by
> ARMSTRONG, BAZALGETTE & CO.
> 132 Front-street – up stairs.
> Who have on hand,
> A few cases best superfine men's London Hats, which they will sell very low to close sales, and 208 casks light London bottled Porter.
> [*New York Gazette*, 4 & 8 June 1819]

St Croix rum is still made today, in what is now the US Virgin Islands. The advertisement above shows that cargoes continued to be received from the West Indies and London, though William Armstrong had again moved his office to 132 Front Street – upstairs, and was doing his best to clear what must have been a glut of London Hats. Perhaps they were no longer regarded as fashionable headwear. The sultry New York summer had come round again, so the storage and disposal of 208 casks of light London Porter may well have taxed Armstrong's ingenuity.

Chapter 21: 1820-28

No more advertisements by Armstrong, Bazalgette & Co. have been found in the *New York Gazette*. It is not known what decision was made about the New York office. William must have agreed to stay on there for a while, since his wife Elizabeth gave birth to a daughter in New York in 1820. There may have been a need for Daniel to return to run the Liverpool office, especially as it appears the partners were getting into the cotton-shipping business, and Liverpool was a major receiving port for cotton, for onward carriage to the insatiable mills of Cheshire, Lancashire and Scotland. Daniel advertised his house at 45, Franklin Street to let in the *New York Evening Post* in March 1819, including all or part of the furniture, stating that he was leaving the country. Daniel and Margaret were in Liverpool by 1820, where their only child, Frances Elizabeth was born, according to the 1871 census, though she was christened in Middlesex. Frances, or Fanny, as were all so-named members of the family called, grew up to become an academic whose main interests appear to have been in theology and German, talents which equipped her to perform her *magnum opus* – the translation from the German edition of the two-volume 'Meditations on the Life and Doctrine of Jesus Christ' (*Vita Et Doctrina Jesu Christi*), by the Austrian Jesuit Nicolaus Avancinus (Nicola Avancini (1612–1686)), published in London in 1875, shortly after her death. It seems somewhat of a waste of time to translate it from German when the original was in Latin; all the more so because in the same year a translation from the Latin by Dr John Tauler was also published.

By 1824 Daniel and the family had returned to London and were living at 1, Nottingham Terrace, Regents Park, a house owned and insured by Daniel's father Louis, and they were still living there in 1828. By 1825 Daniel decided to buy or build a country house at Little Hampton, on the west side of Evesham, in Worcestershire. This house he called Eastwick, after his father's house in Great Bookham. This house is now no longer in existence, though the name remains, e.g., as Eastwick Drive.

In July 1825 he and Margaret were well-established there, and keen gardeners to boot, since *Berrow's Worcester Journal* reported that Daniel in that year won a first prize for 'panzies' at a meeting of the Vale of Evesham Horticultural and Floral Society, and an extra prize for a melon in September 1836. Margaret later won an extra prize for her carrots in May, 1839, and for both cabbages *and* carrots in the following year. No. 1, Nottingham Terrace was still in the family's ownership in 1842, listed in Robson's Directory as the home of 'Miss C. Bazalgette', probably Louis and Frances' daughter Caroline, who never married, and who died in 1851.

There were periodic announcements in the *Liverpool Mercury* of the arrivals and departures of ships brokered by William and Daniel, but the few examples found probably mean that they only advertised when they were actively looking for cargo, and that most of the time they had no problem in filling the ships.

> To sail about the 1st of August.
> FOR PHILADELPHIA,
> The fine Philadelphia-built Ship BINGHAM, WM. FLEMING, Master;
> Copper-fastened, and newly coppered this voyage; having good accommodations both in cabin and steerage. – For freight or passage, apply to the Captain, King's Dock, or to
> WM. ARMSTRONG & DAN. BAZALGETTE
> 5, Paradise-street.
> [*Liverpool Mercury*, Friday, 21 July 1820]
>
> PASSAGE FOR BALTIMORE.
> The brig FABIUS,
> Captain MYERS;
> Having a full cargo engaged, will sail on Friday, 19th October. She has good accommodations both in the cabin and steerage for passengers, who will be taken low. – For terms apply to the Captain, on board, in Prince's-dock, or to
> ARMSTRONG, BAZALGETTE & Co.
> 5, Paradise-street.

[*Liverpool Mercury*, Friday, 12 October 1821]

FOR PHILADELPHIA,
The well-known Philadelphia-built Ship
BAINBRIDGE,
JOSEPH BERRY, MASTER;
Burthen 370 tons; having the chief part of her cargo engaged, will sail positively on the 24th March; for remainder of freight or passage, apply to the Captain, on board, east side Prince's Dock, or to
ARMSTRONG, BAZALGETTE & Co.
15, Exchange-buildings.
[*Liverpool Mercury*, Friday, 15 March 1822]

Examples of arrivals show part cargoes to be delivered to the firm are 'November 2, 1821, The *Jones*, H. Davies, from New York, with 187 bales cotton for Armstrong & Bazalgette – Prince's Dock', 'May 31, 1822, The *Endeavour*, G. Duncan, from Jamaica, 3 brl 26 bg pimento Armstrong, Bazalgette & Co – Prince's Dock'.

Although their main office in the Northern USA was in New York, they also shipped to and from Philadelphia, New York and Baltimore. They possibly also shipped directly from Mobile, Alabama, which was a fast-growing city because of the cotton trade. On 1 December 1820, the *Mobile Gazette & General Advertiser* printed this letter, previously printed in the *New York Gazette*:

The following interesting letter is given with much pleasure, as well on account of its merit, as a desire to introduce to the notice of our mercantile friends, the respectable house of Wm. Armstrong and Dan. Bazalgette:

Liverpool, Sept 9^{th,} 1820
Messrs. Lang, Turner & Co ...
[Owners of the *New York Gazette*]
GENTLEMEN – As old subscribers to your newspaper during our residence in your city, we take the liberty of annexing a Circular, which we have sent to some of our

friends in America by this conveyance. As it relates to a subject which is generally interesting in the United States, we think its insertion in your newspaper cannot fail to be generally acceptable. We are, your most obed't servants,
WM. ARMSTRONG and
DAN. BAZALGETTE

(CIRCULAR)
Liverpool, Sept 9 --- Our Cotton Market has continued in a state of stagnation for such a length of time, that it becomes a subject of curiosity as well as of interest to inquire into its causes. We think the solution is very simple, and is to be found in the unprecedented, import particularly of the United States, and Brazil cotton which has taken place during the present year. The quantity of these descriptions imported into this country during the first eight months of the present year, amounts to 398,000 bags, while the import for the corresponding period last year was only 268,000 bags. The growth of cotton both in the Brazils and the United States appears to have increased very considerably. For the last three years the import from the United States into this port, has not varied very materially: in 1817, 164,000 bags - 1818, 173,000 - 1819, 175,000; but for the eight months of the present year, 251,000. From Brazil, the quantity imported into this country the first eight months of the last year was 85,000 bags; for the eight months of this year it is 118,000 bags. It is very certain that the quantity of cotton raised is much more than adequate to the consumption, or in other words, that the supply is greater than the demand. The annual consumption of the country is computed at 430,000 bags, and the quantity that has been imported during the eight months of this year amounts to 473,000. From this comparison of the supply with the consumption, we can be at no loss to account for the present stagnation. At the end of the present year, the stock will have greatly accumulated, and there is no doubt that it will be larger at that time than it ever was in the same period of any former year. When we take into account the heavy stock that will

be lying over till next crop, and the large quantities that must be imported from the United States and the Brazils, while their productions continues on its present extended scale, it is very evident that the whole cannot be consumed, unless the prices are reduced. It is possible that the consumption of Uplands and Orleans, at reduced prices, may be so much extended as to displace the use of East India descriptions altogether. In that case the consumption may become equal to the supply, but until process are materially reduced below the present currency, we see no probability of the present stock being diminished. Upon the whole we calculate upon very low prices for the ensuing season.

This glut of cotton was mainly due to increased production and growing mechanization – the Eli Whitney cotton gin, invented in 1793, could do the work of ten men, and as its use increased in the southern states the average price of upland cotton sank from 18.9¢ in 1810 to 16.8¢ in 1820 and 12.2¢ in 1830.

Louis's bank ledger for 29 May 1820 shows the receipt of '£1,000 from Gibbons & Co on Ourselves (i.e., Coutts Bank) rem'd by order of Sir W McMahon stated to be in satisfaction of the late Sir J. McMahon's moiety (i.e., portion) of an Annuity granted by him and Geo Leigh Esq'. Lieutenant Colonel George Leigh of the 10th, or Prince's Own, Dragoons was appointed equerry to the Prince of Wales on 29 January 1800, the same day that the notorious Colonel John M'Mahon (late lieutenant-colonel in the 87th foot) was made vice-treasurer and commissioner of accounts to the Prince. George Leigh in 1811 married Augusta, Lord Byron's half-sister, with whom the latter reputedly had an incestuous relationship during the summer of 1813. On 15 April 1814, Augusta gave birth to Elizabeth Medora Leigh, whom Byron nicknamed 'Libby'. While the child bore the name Leigh, Augusta had been separated from Colonel George Leigh since 1811. In 1813, Leigh was in serious financial difficulties, as he had fallen from grace when it came to light that he had cheated the Prince over the sale of a horse and fiddled regimental accounts to fund his gambling habit. It appears therefore that Louis also lent him money, jointly with McMahon.

The Times of Saturday, 20 January 1821, recorded a

> General Meeting of Merchants, Shipowners and Traders of the Port of London - His Majesty's Ministers having under their consideration the renewal of the charter of the West India Dock Company, we, the undersigned, request a meeting of the Merchants, Shipowners and Traders of this metropolis, at the City of London Tavern, on Thursday next, the 25th Inst., at 12 for 1 o'clock precisely, for the purpose of taking such steps as may be considered best calculated to avert a measure so injurious to the commercial prosperity of the Port of London, and to secure those advantages which the public are entitled to expect (as the expiration of the existing Charters of the several Dock Companies) from the establishment of a principle of fair and open competition, instead of the present system of monopoly and exclusive privilege. London Jan. 19th 1821.

Among the firms whose representatives were listed as attending were Armstrong & Bazalgettes, Joseph Dowson & Sons (Louis's ship-brokers) and Agassiz, Son & Co., who may have been connected with the Miss Agassiz whom Louis previously employed. Many of the merchant bankers of the day were there, though probably not all as West India merchants - more as interested investors. William Pitcairn, one of the surgeons who attended young Evelyn, was also present, as was the firm of D.H. & J.A.Rucker & Co, one of the founding partners of which was Johann Anton Rücker, a merchant from Hamburg, born about 1718, who came to London and anglicised his name in the typical fashion to John Anthony Rucker. He has a connection with the Bazalgette family, as the following story shows.

Rucker bought the West Hill Estate on Wimbledon Common in 1789, demolished the mansion house and replaced it with a hunting lodge and hothouses for the cultivation of grapes and pineapples, and had a fine neo-classical mausoleum built in St. Mary's Church Yard, Wimbledon. Lyson's *Environs of London*, 1792, says: 'A very handsome villa has been lately built by Mr. Gibson of Hackney, for John Anthony Rucker, Esq. It stands near Lord Spencer's park, on the site of a house which was built for the present Lady Rivers, and lately occupied by Lord Stormont. Its elevated situation renders it a conspicuous object in the neighbourhood, and gives it the advantage of a beautiful prospect.'

This architect was Jesse Gibson, and he may also have designed his tomb. Rucker died in 1804 and was interred in one of the nine vaults of the mausoleum, but since he had no children he languished alone in his tomb for over seventy years. His wastrel nephew, Daniel Henry Rucker, his main beneficiary, sold the estate in 1825, and at some point presumably the mausoleum as well. It was eventually bought by Sir Joseph Bazalgette, who still lies therein with six members of his family, as belated company for their strange bedfellow Rucker. The mausoleum was described by W.A. Bartlett in *The History and Antiquities of the Parish of Wimbledon, Surrey*, 1865, as a 'pyramid with an iron railing, vault underneath', so it possible, judging from the present style, that the whole thing was rebuilt and/or enlarged by Bazalgette.

Emma Smith, who later married James Edward Austen, Jane Austen's only brother, wrote a letter, probably to her mother, on 25 October 1821 in the following vein:

"... Since Augusta [her older sister] wrote to you we paid a very agreeable visit at Mr Curries (Horsely). The country about his place is particularly pretty indeed altogether I should think Surrey a most delightful county to live in ... a Mr Basilgate has still got Eastwicke he is not a person much known there...". This rather odd statement serves to support the evidence that Louis did not spend much time at Eastwick, and that the Bazalgettes largely chose to keep themselves out of the local social whirl.

The Prince of Wales had now become King, but even this did not put an end to his financial difficulties. He signed a document dated 16 October 1822, surrendering control of his financial affairs to Sir William Knighton, his unofficial private secretary and keeper of his privy purse, authorising Knighton to give notice 'to our several Tradesmen that they are not to take orders or to furnish any articles of furniture or to incur any expense whatsoever without receiving a specifick Order in writing for that purpose from the said S[i]r Will[ia]m Knighton Bart and directing him during Our Will & Pleasure, to undertake the entire management of my Private Affairs with a view to the observance of the most strict & rigid Oeconomy that We may have the opportunity of relieving Ourselves, from certain embarrassments.'

This surrender of authority over his own financial affairs by a ruling monarch was surely without precedent in English history. Knighton (1776-1836) became one of George's physicians in 1810 and after the death of Lieut Col Sir John McMahon and the fall of Sir Benjamin Bloomfield, he was appointed as the King's private secretary, although this post had been abolished. He exercised greater control over the King than any of his predecessors. His strictures proved effective, however, and George Canning recorded that Knighton was able to claim in 1825 that 'the King was now free of debt, and in a state of ease as to his finances that he had never been before.'

This new appointment must have reminded Louis that when his bills had been previously paid in 1795, ten percent had been withheld by Parliament. He had been led to believe by the Prince's then private secretary, Sir Thomas Tyrwhitt, (a Devonshire M.P., well-known for causing the construction of Princeton Prison on Dartmoor) that the Prince had promised that he would in fact receive the remaining money, so he tried a letter to Knighton on 5 May 1823.

> 86 Gloucester Place, Portman Square:
> To Sir William Knighton, Bart.
>
> Sir, It is necessary for me to apologise to you for the liberty I take in writing the following statement to you. When the Commissioners under the direction of Parliament (in the year 1795) took arrangements for paying the Debts of his

present Majesty the Prince of Wales, My Bill amounting to £24,069 was examined and found to be a just one, but I was told that Ten per cent must be reduced from every creditors Bill - and that I must submit to share the same fate with the other Creditors. A few days after this intimation I was at Carlton House in attendance on his present Majesty; Sir Thos Tyrwhitt came to me in the Pages room; and told me, that by the desire of His Royal Highness the Prince of Wales he came to assure me, that H.R. Highness would pay me the Ten per cent reduced by the Commissioners from my Bill; as soon as it should be in his Power. I felt extremely grateful for the condescension of his Royal Highness - and waited several years before I made an application to Col McMahon on the subject; he always gave me hope of my receiving the sum of Two Thousand Four Hundred Pounds (the sum reduced by the Commissioners) - but unfortunately for me, Sir J McMahon died before this promise was fulfilled. During more than thirty-two years that I served his present Majesty, I never made application to His Majesty for the debt he owed me. I do therefore solicit you Sir, to represent to His Majesty the facts above stated - and I humbly hope that he will take my case into consideration, and give orders that I may be paid.

I have the honour to remain, Sir,
Your Obdt Humble Sert,
Louis Bazalgette.
[Royal Archives; Doc no. RA 317236]

There is no banking evidence to suggest that this money was actually repaid to Louis. Since Knighton was trying to get the royal finances back into credit he would have found this letter easy to ignore.

The Armstrongs and other creditors filed a bill in Chancery (Armstrong v. Storer) in 1823, in an attempt to recover their debts from the Storer estate. Eventually, a decree was made by the judge that a 'master' be appointed, whose job was to track down all of the defendants, even travelling to Jamaica to interview them, but this achieved nothing so the bill lapsed.

The lord of the manor of Great Bookham, George Holme Sumner, offered the manor at auction, the transaction to be handled by Christie's and by his solicitor John Harrison Loveridge. The following advertisement appeared in The Times on 24 May 1823:

> Manor and Freehold Estate, Great Bookham, Surrey.- By Mr. Christie, at the Auction-mart, on Wednesday, June 25, at 1 precisely, in several lots, The valuable Manor of Great Bookham, near Leatherhead, Surrey, together with the rights, members, and appurtenances, courts leet and baron, quit rents, fines, and heriots, the royalties extending over the whole parish, consisting of about [blank] acres of cultivated land, and 785 acres of highly picturesque commons and wastes, viz. Bookham-common, containing 349, and Ranmore-common, 436 acres of land, with the lord's right of growing timber on the same, the former bearing a quantity of fine thriving oak timber, for the growth of which the soil is particularly favourable; the latter covered with ornamental beech woods, of considerable extent and beauty, both of them presenting an object for investment of great accumulating value; the whole abounding with pheasants and other game, and the country excellent for fox hunting and field sports in general. Also, in several lots, Sole Farm Freehold, with a substantial brick-built farm-house, capital barns, farmyard &c. and 384 acres of arable, meadow, pasture, and wood land, contiguous to the village of Bookham, or adjoining to Feltham [sic - means Fetcham], Bookham Grove, Eastwick Park, and other distinguished properties, in a country scarcely to be surpassed for beauty of scenery, respectability of inhabitants, and for game. The distance 2 miles from Leatherhead, 5 from Dorking, 9 from Guildford, and 21 from London. Particulars are preparing, and may be forthwith had at the office of Mr. Loveridge, solicitor, Charlotte-street, Bloomsbury; of Mr. Christie, Pall-mall; and of Mr. Thos. La Coste, banker, at Chertsey,

who has for several years been steward of the estate, and is intimately acquainted with all the details of the property.

Louis was successful in bidding for the manor, but its transfer to him was delayed for five years, as we shall now see.

On 10 May 1824, a bill in Chancery was brought against Louis by George Holme Sumner, from whom Louis had bought the lordship of the manor of Great Bookham in 1823. Sumner owned the nearby estate of Hatchlands Park, and was Member of Parliament for Guildford. Sumner's statement was that he was seized in fee simple and well entitled to the manor of Great Bookham, and agreed to sell it to Louis Bazalgette for £4,000. It was agreed that Louis would not touch the trees on Ranmore Common but that Sumner could cut and remove them as long as he did so by 24 June 1825. The trees were supposed to be valued as part of the sale.

After the sale went through, Louis and Sumner appointed Thomas Crawter and William Eager respectively to decide which trees were measurable and to value them, with John Stable arbitrating. Values agreed were £2,160/11/1 for the trees on Ranmore Common and £8,065/2/- for those on Great Bookham Common. Adding on the £4,000 for the lordship of the manor, the total was £14,225/13/1, which Louis was supposed to pay him on completion. Sumner applied to Louis several times for payment of this sum. 'But now the said Louis Bazalgette combining and confederating with diverse persons unknown to Sumner contriving how to injure and oppress your orator in the premises' refused to pay. '...and he pretends that Mr. Kenrick is entitled to cut trees on Ranmore Common and hath exercised such rights by cutting down trees'. Louis knew that Sumner had the rights to the title because he had bought Eastwick Park in 1809, and in 1823 their lawyers sent copies of the title back to both parties. Sumner charged that Kenrick never had any rights to the trees. Kenrick cut the trees, Sumner seized them, and Kenrick brought an action against Sumner. A court in 1820 stipulated that Kenrick was not to cut bushes on Ranmore Common and the court sent a copy of the proceedings to Louis.

Louis' answer to this charge was that he agreed that Sumner held the lands in fee simple and that the valuation was a condition of the sale, but at the time of the auction, when commons rights were published, no satisfactory bids had come in. During the lengthy correspondence between Louis' and Sumner's solicitors concerning the sale of the manor, according to Sumner's lawyers: '...in the course of such correspondence the said complainant repeatedly attempted to impress upon the defendant the great value of the right of growing timber on the commons...' but never alluded to any rights of copyholders or other tenants to cut down trees. Louis' understanding was that upon purchase of the property 'he would become entitled to the sole and exclusive right to the timber and other trees without any interference whatsoever', so he entered into the agreement to purchase and prepared to complete his part by 30 November 1823. He also set £14,000 aside with his bankers for this purpose. He stated that treaties sent by Sumner's solicitors to his solicitors contained information about the rights and royalties belonging to the manor, and that before signing the final papers they appointed Crawter and Eager to value the trees. Louis said that Sumner showed nowhere that he had title to them, and admitted that he therefore withheld the £14,000 and was justified in doing so. Louis was aware of the action brought by Sumner against Kenrick, in which the magistrate wanted a trial to establish whether Kenrick could – by custom – cut down those trees, but Sumner had so far not pursued this in the courts. And that since this matter was still outstanding, Louis's lawyers advised him not to pay any of the £14,000 because it could involve him in endless litigation.

Furthermore, Evelyn (acting as Louis' counsel of course) had discussed the matter with Kenrick, who said that Sumner knew full well that he and other tenants had the right to cut wood for firewood, but not to sell it. Kenrick said he had cut down trees to exercise his right, hoping that Sumner would take it to court so he could provide the proof of it. The case for the defence was that Sumner had attempted to sell to Louis the exclusive rights to the commons, which he did not possess. Therefore Louis was justified in withholding the £14,000 and refusing to complete the sale until Sumner provided proof of exclusive rights.

The manor did not actually become Louis' property until 1828, when presumably all of the above proceedings had been satisfactorily wound up.

In November 1824 there was a burglary at Daniel and Margaret's house, No 1, Nottingham Terrace (on the north side of Marylebone Road, close to where Madame Tussaud's now stands). The *British Press* of 29 November told the story:

> A young man named *William Lilly*, who has been detained under a charge of having stolen plate in his possession, was brought up for final examination on Saturday, in consequence of an owner having been discovered for the property, through the instrumentality of a report of his last examination, which appeared in the public print.
> William Lee, one of the officers of this establishment who took the prisoner into custody, stated, that on the day of his apprehension, which was nearly a month since, witness, and Limbrick, his brother officer, were going through Wilderness-row, and observing the prisoner and another fellow lurking about a pawnbroker's shop they suspected them to be about to make away with some article improperly obtained, and after having dogged them some distance the fellows, perceiving they were observed, took to their heels but being closely pursued, witness overtook the prisoner Lilly, in Great Sutton-street, Clerkenwell, and having remarked his frequently putting his hand to his hat, as if to prevent its falling of, while running, witness took it off his head; prisoner strove hard to prevent him, but on searching the hat, it was found to contain (wrapped up in a silk handkerchief) six tea, four dessert, and two tablespoons, all marked 'M M C' in a cypher on the front, and the figure of a shell engraved on the reverse, but having no Hall-mark. The prisoner, on his first examination, did not endeavour to account for the possession, and was accordingly remanded. The property was then advertised, but no owner could be found until on

the publication of the police report, it chanced to meet the eyes the gentleman from whose house it was stolen, Daniel Bazalgette Esq. of Nottingham Terrace, Regent's Park, who immediately sent his butler to examine the spoons, and the property being satisfactorily identified, the prisoner was fully committed for trial. The difference of initials, and the absence of the hall mark were thus accounted for by Mr. Bazalgette's servant in his examination: Mrs. Bazalgette is an American lady, and the spoons belonged to the lady's family, the name of which corresponds to the M.M.C.; and being made in America, are not marked in the same way as British plate. The prisoner is presumed to be one of that numerous fraternity, called *sneaks*, or sometimes *divers*, who watch opportunities of darting into the areas of houses, and carrying off any thing they can lay hold of.

At the Old Bailey trial on 2 December 1825, William Lilley was indicted for the theft of twelve silver spoons. Here is the transcript of the trial:

Before Mr. Sergeant Arabin.

WILLIAM LILLEY was indicted for stealing, on the 8th of November, at St. Mary-le-bone, twelve silver spoons, value 4l., the goods of Daniel Bazalgette , in his dwelling-house .

SARAH EMMETT. I am cook to Mr. Daniel Bazalgette, who lives in Nottingham-terrace, Regent's-park, in the parish of St. Mary-le-bone. On the 8th of November I put a dozen spoons into the kitchen cupboard, and saw them there at eleven o'clock in the morning, and missed them at half-past one - I was at home all the time - the area gate was not locked; a person could come down there to the kitchen. I found them at Hatton-garden on the Saturday week following; they were four table, two dessert, and six tea spoons.

Cross-examined by MR. LAW. Q. Does your master keep the house? A. Yes. I cannot exactly spell his name.

WILLIAM LEE. I am an officer. On the 8th of November, about two o'clock in the afternoon, I met the prisoner in

Wilderness-row, Clerkenwell, in company with another person; I suspected him - I followed them, and took the prisoner; he ran away, leaving his hat in my hands, and in it were these twelve spoons. I followed him two hundred yards, and he was stopped. I asked him where they came from - he said I should soon find out.
Cross-examined. Q. You met him a great way from Mary-le-bone? A. Yes, three miles - another person was with him.
SARAH EMMETT. I know these spoons to be my master's, by the initials M. M. C., which are on all his plate; I do not know why. I have lived five months with him.
THOMAS LEWIS STILES. I am a silversmith and jeweller. These spoons appear to be silver, but I would not swear that they are so - (*breaking one*) - Yes, they are silver, but of a very inferior sort. I suppose them to be made abroad; we dare not sell such; they have not got the hall mark. I should think them worth 4s an ounce; the largest weighs about two ounces; the dessert spoons about half an ounce, and the tea spoons about a quarter of an ounce.
Cross-examined. Q. Which is there most of, silver or alloy? A. Silver. I must assay it to tell the exact quantity of it.
Prisoner's Defence. I picked them up - the officer immediately came and laid hold of me.
GUILTY - DEATH. Aged 21.
[Old Bailey Proceedings, t18241202-116]

In practice, by this time, death sentences for larceny were commuted in about ninety percent of cases. The initials 'MMC' on the spoons were of course those of Daniel's wife, Margaret MacCrae. These 'inferior' spoons were presumably made for her in Philadelphia or New York.

Lilley's sentence was indeed commuted to transportation for life (usually fourteen years), and he was sent to New South Wales with 151 others aboard the convict-ship *Marquis of Hastings*, departing on 19 August 1825 and arriving on 15 September 1826. The ship was ill fated, and William and his fellow prisoners were lucky to arrive safely. As *The Sydney Gazette and New South Wales Advertiser* reported:

Arrived in Table Bay, Sept. 15, the ship *Marquis of Hastings*, Mr. Martin, second officer in command, in consequence of Captain Ostler being missing since the 8th of the same month.

On the morning of the 9th of September, when Captain Ostler of the *Marquis of Hastings* was missing, a note was found on the desk in his cabin to this effect:- 'A bad crew and bad first officer, have been the destruction of W. Ostler.' At two o'clock on the previous day, fire was discovered, but soon extinguished, in the store-room of the ship. It must have been put into the scuttle by some person maliciously inclined. Captain Ostler struck his forehead, replying to Mr Martin that it was a very strange thing, and then retired to his cabin. The vessel put into the Cape of Good Hope by desire of the crew (so says the *South African Commercial Advertiser* of the 19th of September) for refreshment. The fore and spring stays were found burned by vitriol. She had put into Mossel Bay in distress on the 1st of the same month. The whole affair appears to us involved in mystery. Row, the chief officer, had been suspended from duty by Captain Ostler on the 19th of August.

It appears that the unhappy Ostler had a death-wish, sabotaging the ship several times, but fortunately (at least for the ship's company) he decided to end it all on an individual basis and jumped overboard. Or perhaps somebody pushed him. The ship had further tribulations on the way home:-

The ship Marquis of Hastings, late a transport ship to Sydney, bound to England from China with a full cargo, struck a rock in the Java seas and had put into Batavia with considerable damage. One thousand chests of tea were sold at Batavia to defray the expenses of repairing the damage sustained in the Java Sea, and coffee taken in to supply the deficiency.
[*The Sydney Gazette and New South Wales Advertiser*]

In the 1828 census Lilley was listed as a 'messenger'. In 1830 he was at the Port Stephens Establishment of the Australian Agricultural Company, whose Commissioner at the time was Sir William Edward Parry. Among Parry's letters there is one of 26 May 1830 which mentions Lilley in his role of messenger: '...that an Office-Messenger, upon the footing detailed in Mr. Barton's Communication as established by the late Committee at Sydney (of which I was not before aware), is an entirely useless expense to the Company, as all the business required from such a person upon the Port Stephens Establishment, can be performed by a boy, or a convalescent, or some other person already supported by the Company. William Lilly is, for the present, to go backwards and forwards twice a day for this purpose...'

William married Catherine Holden in 1834 at the Sydney Scots Church. Catherine travelled free to Australia as a bounty immigrant on the *Renown* in 1832, listed as Catherine *Holding*. It is noted on their application to marry that William's master Mr Shepherd had agreed to engage both of them after William obtained his ticket-of-leave. He was granted a conditional pardon in 1840 and moved to Sydney. He and Catherine had several children, and later moved to Melbourne, where they lived at 12, Vere Street. William died there in February 1869, and Catherine in 1885. This story had tragic beginnings but ultimately altered the history of William's family – hopefully for the better.

Joseph William's baby daughter Emily died on 25 January 1825, and his daughter Julia was born three days later. Louis and Fanny's son Sidney was admitted to Bailliol College, Oxford, in this year, gaining his B.A. in 1827, and being admitted to the Inner Temple in 1828. His brother Augustus entered Pembroke College, Cambridge in 1827, migrating to Emmanuel College the year after. There is no record of Augustus' graduation but that was probably because he seems to have been more interested in horse-racing.

The ledgers of Coutts' Bank, showing Louis' financial dealings, tell us that by 1825 he had become less active. He was after all seventy-five years old, and presumably less able to get about. The transactions changed from very frequent to much less so, and he drew larger amounts of cash but less often. Louis' property was still insured with the Sun Fire Office. The entry for Michaelmas 1828 reads as follows:

Policy No: 1065574
Premium: £13/11/-
Duty: £24/12/-
Louis Bazalgette No. 86 Gloucester Place Portman Square Esq:
On his now Dwelling house & Offices communicating situate as aforesaid Three thousand pounds.
Household goods Wearing Apparel printed books and plate therein only Eleven hundred pounds.
China and Glass therein only Two hundred pounds.
Mansion house & Offices adjoining situate at Eastwick Park Surry in his own occupation Five thousand pounds.
Household goods Wearing Apparel printed books and plate therein only Three thousand eight hundred pounds.
China and Glass therein only Two hundred pounds.
Barn Stables and other Farm Offices all adjoining near timber One thousand pounds.
Farming Stock & Utensils in said Farm only Six hundred pounds.
Cottage only situate in Eastwick Lane near late in tenure of Wells a farmer Five hundred pounds.
House only No. 1 Nottingham Terrace New Road Marylebone in tenure of Daniel Bazalgette private One thousand pounds.
All Brick or Stone except mentioned tiles and slated with the usual Farming Clause.

The total insurance value of Louis' property was therefore given as £16,400/-/-

Joseph William was by now the honorary secretary of the Naval and Military Bible Society. He was also active in such benevolent societies as the Sailor's Home and Asylum, the Seaman's Floating Church, the Royal Naval Female School, the London Society for the Promotion of Christianity Amongst the

Jews and the Association for the Discouragement of Duelling, his brother John also being a member of the last-named society.

Chapter 22: 1829-32

In 1829 there was some talk of selling Eastwick Park.

Viscount Downe, who purchased Bookham Grove in 1775, may have contemplated acquiring the Eastwick Park Estate, as amongst his papers are particulars of the proposed sale of the property by the Auctioneer, Mr. James Christie on Thursday 1st July 1829.
[S.E.D Fortescue]

On 16 February 1830, Jean Louis Bazalgette died in London, at the age of seventy-nine, and was buried in the crypt of St. Mary's, Marylebone on 22 February in the family vault (No. 11), on which it was inscribed:

> The Family Vault
> of
> Louis Bazalgette
> of
> 86 Gloucester Place

The Times of Wednesday 17 February contained the short announcement: 'On the 16th Inst., at his residence in Glocester-place, Louis Bazalgette, Esq.'

A memorial for him in Great Bookham church reads:

> This tablet is erected as a tribute of affection by his surviving children: his other children died in early infancy. His material remains are deposited in a private vault under the rectory church of the parish of St. Mary le Bone in the county of Middlesex.

There must have been a memorial service at Bookham, because on 27 April Louis' executor Evelyn paid £13/18/- to the Rev. William Heberden, who was the vicar. Heberden's father, Dr. William Heberden, was a noted physician who had attended George III.

Louis was a man with a burning desire to better himself, in which he succeeded in a spectacular way. He must have been very talented and personable in order to become a royal tailor, and yet it is clear that he shunned publicity. His name almost never appeared in the newspapers, not even in advertisements, and certainly not as a contributor to worthy causes, except a donation of one guinea to the erection of a memorial to Princess Charlotte and £10 to the organ fund of St. Nicholas' Church in Chiswick. We find him not apparently generous in a public way, but he did lend money to people on what looks like rather weak security, so he must have had some wish to help his fellow man, and there is some evidence that he helped refugees from his own country. He was awarded the *Decoration du Lys* when the French monarchy was restored, although this was awarded to many royalists. He appears to have been a family man and a loving father. He was very hard-working, a shrewd businessman and a very successful investor, though mainly in 'gilts' or government stocks and bonds rather than in more speculative shares. This was just as well as it helped to counteract his somewhat ill-advised lendings.

On 5 May 1830, Evelyn, one of Louis' executors (the other being Sir Coutts Trotter), wrote the following letter to John Smallpiece, a local solicitor and factor of the Eastwick Park estate, who also presided over the manorial court sessions if the lord of the manor was absent. Smallpiece was also solicitor to Princess Charlotte until her untimely death in 1817. The references to the 'court' and to 'admittance' are concerned with the manorial court of Great Bookham, and Evelyn had taken over as lord of the manor after Louis' death. It is obvious that Evelyn was exasperated with the behaviour of Coutts Trotter, who, despite being generously provided for in the will, refused to play his part in executing it.

> Dear Sir,
> My father devised his property to Sir Coutts Trotter, Bart., and to myself, but Sir Coutts Trotter has carefully avoided in any manner acting in the business, and would have executed a Deed of Renunciation and a Conveyance of the legal Estate had it not been postponed at my request until

I could make arrangements, as I have now done, to prevent any question of merger with reference to some property in which I have interests distinct from those which I take under my Father's will – under these circumstances he would probably prefer that his name should not be used even in holding a Court, which perhaps you may think the parties to be admitted would not be exposed to risk by our dispensing with, especially after the doubts raised upon the necessity of a Deed of Conveyance by the recent cases in B&A and B&C.

With respect to the annual value of the Premises of which the late Mr Waterer died seized, I am at present unable to give you any information, and, if it will not be giving you too much trouble, perhaps you will favour me by ascertaining it yourself, as I doubt whether I shall be able to get to Bookham in time for the purpose, and you are more competent to form a correct opinion on the subject. Should I be able to acquire any knowledge respecting it, I will communicate the same to you.

A Copyhold property consisting of a house, garden &c. held by Mr Leach and now or lately occupied by the Rev'd Mr Farley was advertised for sale by Auction in the first week of April last; I am not aware whether it was then sold, but if so, the purchaser might like to avail himself of this opportunity to be admitted.

Mr Nicholson sometime ago applied to me for an order, and afterwards went to view our Estate at Eastwick. As I conceived him, from what he said, to be the Gentleman of whom you spoke when last I had the pleasure of seeing you, and as I have not since heard from him, I have not troubled you any further respecting the Matter. The property will in a few days be advertised for sale, and I am now ready to treat with any one who will make an offer for it.

The Old Map and Terrier of the Manor of Great Bookham I will take an early opportunity to forward to you

I am, Dear Sir,
Very truly yours,

Evelyn Bazalgette
5 New Square, Lincoln's Inn
[Surrey Archives]

Evelyn had started to try to recover Louis' loans some time before his father's death, and afterwards, being responsible for winding up the estate, he redoubled his efforts, though without great success it seems, judging by the long list of bills in Chancery that he brought against the descendants of the borrowers. Although Louis' will was proved in March, it was many years before all of the properties could be disposed of and his father's affairs brought into some sort of order.

Eastwick Park was first advertised for sale by auction in *The Times* on 10 June 1830:

> Manor, capital Mansion, and Park, with Farm, and Woods abounding with game, at Bookham near Leatherhead, Surrey. - By Mr. CHRISTIE, at the Auction Mart, on Thursday, July 1, at 1 precisely, THE very admired and distinguished Freehold mansion and Estate, called Eastwick Park, situated in the parishes of Bookham and Fetcham, 2 miles from Leatherhead, and 21 from London, in a highly fashionable neighbourhood, and in the most picturesque and delightful part of the county of Surrey; consisting of the manor of Great Bookham, with courts leet and baron, rights and royalties, together with the lord's right of the soil, and the growing timber on Bookham and Ranmore commons, comprising nearly 800 acres, and affording extensive shelter for game, independently of the closed woods and covers of the estate. Eastwick Mansion is substantial, square, and uniformly constructed edifice, upon a compact scale, but containing the fullest accommodation for a family of fashion or distinction, and commanding from its moderately elevated site, a wooded landscape of great extent and beauty, numerous offices and stabling, capital large walled kitchen garden with graperies, ornamental dairy, ice-house, farm yard, and capital farm buildings.

The park contains about 150 acres of grass land, with ornamental timber, and sundry enclosured of meadow and arable, terminated by a semi-circle of noble woods, ahout 60 acres, and affording cover for pheasants, and game of every description; the whole upwards fo 390 acres. The mansion comprises, on the ground floor, a hall or billiard room, 27 feet square, a morning room, 25 feet by 20, library and water-closet, dining room of singularly beautiful proportions, 31 by 21, and a noble saloon or drawing room, 70 feet by 20, supported by a double screen of Ionic Scagliola columns in imitation of purple brecchia, the different apartments warmed by concealed stoves, besides the ordinary provision of fire places, the doors of mahogany or fine wainscot, six principal bed chambers, with dressing rooms and water closet, and secondary bed rooms in proportion; offices in the basement and in a wing for every domestic purpose. This truly valuable property is most enviable as a family residence, particularly of anyone desirous of an extensive command of field sports, the Union fox hounds being kept on the skirts of the estate, and 2 other packs frequently hunting in the neighbourhood; it deserves the attention of any monied purchaser, as the lands are highly improvable, and the extensive commons and wastes promise at a future day considerable profits and advantages to the lord of the manor. The mansion may be viewed with cards only: printed particulars may be had at the office of Messrs Adlington, Gregory, and Faulkner, 1, Bedford-row; at the Spread Eagle, Epsom; Swan, Leatherhead; Grayhound, Dorking; Castle, Kingston; White Hart, Guildford; Star and Garter, Richmond; at the Auction Mart; and of Mr Christie, 3, King-street, St James-square.

Although Louis was some twelve years older than King George IV, the latter did not outlive him by more than four months, breathing his last on 26 June 1830. What happened to all of the clothes made for him by Louis and others?

When his affairs came to be looked into, a curious condition of things was revealed. He seemed to have had a mania for misplaced hoarding. All the coats, boots, and pantaloons of fifty years were in his wardrobe, and to the end he carried the catalogue of them all in his head, and could call for any one of them at any moment. He had five hundred pocket-books, and all contained small sums of money laid by and forgotten; £10,000 in all was thus collected. There were countless bundles of women's love letters, of women's gloves, of locks of women's hair. These were destroyed. In 1823 Lord Eldon had made the King's will, and the executors were Lord Gifford and Sir W. Knighton, but his private effects were of comparatively small value.
[Dictionary of National Biography: George IV; John Andrew Hamilton, 1889]

We know of at least two auctions of his wardrobe, but there must have been more. In his memoirs, the diarist Charles Greville recounted attending one such auction on 2 August 1830:

August 3: I went yesterday to the sale of the late King's wardrobe which was numerous enough to fill Monmouth Street and sufficiently various and splendid for the wardrobe of Drury Lane. He hardly ever gave away anything except his linen which was distributed every year. These clothes are the perquisite of his pages and will fetch a pretty sum. There are all the coats he has ever had for fifty years, 300 whips, canes without number, every sort of uniform, the costumes of all the orders in Europe, splendid furs, pelisses, hunting coats and breeches, and among other things a dozen pair of corduroy breeches he had made to hunt in when Don Miguel was here. His profusion in these articles was unbounded because he never paid for them and his memory was so accurate that one of his pages told me he recollected every article of dress, no matter how old, and that they were always liable to be called on to produce some particular coat or other

article of apparel of years gone by. It is difficult to say whether in great or little things that the man was most odious and contemptible.
[The Greville memoirs: a journal of the reigns of King George IV and King William IV; R.H Stoddard, Ed.]

Monmouth Street, Covent Garden was famous for its second-hand clothing shops.

However, there is no mention in *The Times* or any other available newspaper of an auction around this date, although later auctions were so announced, being handled by Phillips & Co. Perhaps earlier auctions were held by other auctioneers and advertised elsewhere but it seems strange that they were not advertised in *The Times*. The first auction that the author has found there was in December, 1830:

> A Portion of the Wardrobe of King George the Fourth.
> MR. PHILLIPS respectfully announces, that THIS DAY, at 1, he will SELL by AUCTION, at his great Rooms, Bond-street, an ASSEMBLAGE of splendid FANCY DRESSES and UNIFORMS of the 10th Hussars, the Windsor, and Artillery, superbly embroidered velvet and satin robes, two Highland dresses, velvet and beaver hats and caps, sword belts, plumes of ostrich and military feathers, 30 dozens of silk hose and shirts, of the finest texture, partly new, handkerchiefs, stocks, neckcloths, pieces of new superfine scarlet and other broad cloths, a sable fur coat, about 100 dress, undress and hunting coats, the dress worn by His Majesty on his visit to Scotland, 50 pairs of silk, cotton and leather pantaloons and trousers, masquerade dresses, racing caps and jackets, gloves, 130 pairs of military and dress boots, shoes, and slippers; part of the costume of the late coronation, dressing case, escritoire, Meersham pipes, Chinese negligees, opera glass, pistols, chessmen, 70 pairs of silver shoe buckles, various boxes, epaulettes, silver and steel spurs, whips and sticks, and miscellaneous items. May be viewed 2 days preceding the sale, and catalogues had at 1s. each at Mr. Phillips's, 73. New Bond-street.
> [*The Times*, Friday, 16 and 17 December 1830]

The above no doubt contained many items made by Louis, particularly the hussar uniforms and some of the large number of Windsor uniforms. A subsequent auction of special articles in the late King's wardrobe which had been held back was held on 9 June 1831:

> The select and splendid portion of his late Majesty's Wardrobe.
> MR. PHILLIPS will have the honour to SELL by AUCTION, at his great Rooms, Bond-street, on Thursday, June 9, at 1, the reserved and splendid PORTION of the WARDROBE of his late Majesty King George IV, including the sumptuously embroidered Costumes of his Coronation, a Mantle presented by the later Emperor of Russia, a superb Point Lace Scarf, &c. May be viewed 2 days preceding the sale, and catalogues then had at 72, Bond-street.
> [*The Times*, Saturday, 4 June 1831]

The *Caledonian Mercury* subsequently remarked that 'there was very slight competition for any of the articles, and we did not observe that they were knocked down to persons of distinction. The proceeds of the sale could not have amounted to any considerable sum. Most of the costumes were superbly embroidered in gold, from original drawings and designs by artists of celebrity'. Some of the prices that were paid for items in this sale were described and these were also later also listed in *The Annual Register*:

> Sale Of His Late Majesty's Coronation Robes.— A portion of his late Majesty's costly and splendid wardrobe destined for public sale, including the magnificent coronation robes and other costumes, was sold by auction, by Mr. Phillips, at his rooms in New Bond Street. There were 120 lots disposed of, out of which we subjoin the principal in the order in which they were put up:
> Lot 13. An elegant yellow and silver sash of the Royal Hanoverian Guelphic Order, £3/8/-.

Lot 17. A pair of fine kid-trousers, of ample dimensions, and lined with white satin, was sold for 12/-.
Lot 35. The coronation ruff, formed of superb Mechlin-lace, £2.
Lot 50. The costly Highland costume worn by our late Sovereign at Dalkeith Palace, the seat of his Grace the Duke of Buccleugh, in the summer of 1822, was knocked down at £40.
Lot 52. The sumptuous crimson-velvet coronation mantle, with silver star, embroidered with gold, on appropriate devices, and which cost originally, according to the statement of the auctioneer, upwards of £500, was knocked down at 47 guineas.
Lot 53. A crimson coat to suit with the above, £14.
Lot 55. A magnificent gold body-dress and trousers, 26 guineas.
Lot 67. An extraordinary large white aigrette plume, brought from Paris by the Earl of Fife, in April, 1815, and presented by his lordship to the late King, was sold for £15.
Lot 87. A richly embroidered silver tissue coronation waistcoat and trunk hose, £13.
Lot 95. The splendid purple velvet coronation mantle, sumptuously embroidered with gold, of which it was said to contain 200 ounces. It was knocked down at £55, although it was stated to have cost his late Majesty £300.
Lot 96. An elegant and costly green velvet mantle, lined with ermine of the finest quality; presented by the Emperor Alexander to his late Majesty, which cost upwards of 1,000 guineas, was knocked down at £125.
[*Annual Register of 1831*]

It is curious how little of Prinny's wardrobe is known to have survived, considering the vast number of articles of clothing that were made for him. His coronation robes were eventually bought by Madame Tussaud's waxworks and they still have them. Enquiries at the Royal Collections, the Victoria and Albert Museum, the Museum of London and the Brighton and Hove Museum, to mention but four, have produced disappointingly little. This paucity makes it even less likely that a garment will be found that is directly attributable to Louis, though there must be some surviving examples out there somewhere. The author even approached a specialist dealer to ask if she had ever sold such an item during the last thirty years and she could not recall one. Hopefully something will turn up one day.

The despised late monarch's mostly outmoded clothes would have been bought cheaply by dealers or tailors. The latter would often remake them, and it is likely that many would have undergone this treatment several times until they ceased to be of any use. The theatre was a voracious consumer of course, and the garments would have been put to hard use until they became so tatty that they were discarded. In Victorian times they would have been used for fancy dress, and by then they would have been valued so little that the owners would have had no compunction in disposing of them.

The relationship of a gentleman (or, of course, a Prince) with his tailor is a unique one. The tailor knows his client intimately, and instinctively knows how to make him look his best. The Prince of Wales was very knowledgeable about cloth, clothes and tailoring, as his discarded wife Caroline is famous for having pointed out. He was also narcissistic and self-obsessed. The fact that he kept Louis as his personal tailor for 32 years suggests an extraordinary mutual trust and closeness that George must have had with very few men apart perhaps from his own brothers.

Joseph Farington in his diary records this anecdote of his friend Rossi, the sculptor:

> July 2, 1796. Smirke told me that Rossi was with the Prince of Wales to-day modelling a small head of him in the Uniform of the 10th regt. of Dragoons. Rossi waited 3 hours to-day before He was admitted, during which time the Prince was entirely engaged by a Shoe-maker, and two Taylors who succeeded each other. The Shoemaker carried in at least 40 pair of Boots, and was with the Prince an Hour while He was trying them. The first Taylor that was admitted, after many trials of patterns & cuttings was

dismissed, not having given satisfaction. The other was then sent for. Rossi, yesterday waited 5 hours in vain.

This event took place after the Prince had met Beau Brummell, and was exploring the new English style of dress, as made by English tailors. Louis continued to make his uniforms and other costumes for fifteen years after that. The story demonstrates how demanding, and how fickle, the Prince could be. That makes it all the more unusual that he should have stuck with Louis for so long. It suggests a loyalty, understanding and respect almost without equal, and great strength of personality on Louis' part in being able to fulfill the Prince's constant and exacting requirements over such a long period.

Louis's property Oakley Farm, which he had originally bought from Wat Smythe in 1799, was advertised after his death.

OAKLEY FARM - To be SOLD by AUCTION, by Mr. Danton, at the White Hart Inn, Winchester, on Wednesday, July 13th, at 3 o'clock, a very desirable and compact FREEHOLD FARM; consisting of an excellent-planned substantial farm-house, garden, warm farm yard, cowhouses, cart lodges, and other suitable husbandry buildings, with a detached cottage, garden, barn, and yard, and 336 acres of rich meadow, pasture, arable and wood land, in a ring fence; most eligibly situate at Mottesfont, in the vicinity of the New Forest. In the neighbourhood are fox hounds, and a plenitude of field sports. The estate is intersected by the River Test, esteemed for its trout fishery. The country around is beautiful, and the estate presents several delightful situations for the erection of a villa. Oakley Farm is 4 miles from Romsey, 4 from Stockbridge, 11 from Southampton, 12 from Winchester, 14 from Salisbury, and 70 from London. May be viewed by leave of Mr. John Bradley, the tenant, any time before the sale, and particulars may be had on the premises; at the White Hart, Winchester; the White Horse, Romsey; Hotel,

Stockbridge; Dolphin, Southampton; White Hart, Salisbury; and of Messrs. Adlington, Gregory, and Faulkner, 1, Bedford Row, London, where a plan of the estate may be seen.
[*The Times*, Wednesday, 15 June 1831]

When Louis bought the farm in 1799 it consisted of 180 acres. Louis had purchased more land, enlarging the farm to 336 acres in August 1802 by buying Oakley Meadow from William Steele Wakeford of Andover. Oakley Farm was then bought by the local landowner Sir Charles Mill, who had probably had his eye on it for some time.

There were numerous court cases following Louis' death. Some of these proceedings have been transcribed and added to those legal books which lawyers love to consult when trying to establish precedent. The other cases were summarised, by the author and his wife, from the Chancery rolls which the National Archives stores in an abandoned salt mine in Cheshire, where conditions are ideal for such storage. The rolls really are that – usually about thirty large parchment documents rolled up together in a heavy bundle – and are extremely dirty. The author recommends a day of this activity to any dedicated researcher looking for a truly 'hands-on' experience. The summaries of the cases in these rolls are mercifully short for obvious reasons. Reading early nineteenth century legalese (and the sometimes impenetrable script) is an acquired taste.

Evelyn's attempts to wind up his father's complicated estate were, as we can see, beset with many headaches, not least of which was the case of Bazalgette v. Bazalgette, which began to be heard on Tuesday 21 December 1831. The whole family (in other words the beneficiaries of the will) took Evelyn to court. It is very likely that Evelyn was in full agreement with this action, because he probably hoped that it would help to resolve some of his difficulties. There was certainly no animosity involved, and Evelyn continued to represent the family for many years afterwards.

Not much had happened for over a year after Louis' death, and the family became impatient. Sir Coutts Trotter then renounced probate of the will, and issued a disclaimer saying that he and his heirs would no longer have anything to do with it. Then Evelyn took the will to the Prerogative Court of Canterbury and was granted probate but, according to the plaintiffs, he withheld far more money than was necessary for the payment of Louis' debts, legal fees and funerary expenses. Fanny had not been paid the money that she was supposed to have received immediately after Louis' death, and the estates which were to be sold, so that the profits could be divided, had not been sold; moreover, they had been undervalued. Evelyn claimed that he had not taken more than was necessary and he was working on the sale of the estates. The court ruled that he had to provide accounts of the debts and fees, a third party would have the estate evaluated, the properties had to be sold, and that Fanny was to start receiving her money forthwith.

In other words, the family got a court order enforcing the execution of the will. References were again made in the transcript to estates in Ireland and Jamaica, as usual without them being specifically named. [Bazalgette v. Bazalgette, 1831. PRO C33/824]

According to the court's ruling, Eastwick Park was again offered for sale:

> To be peremptorily SOLD, pursuant to an order of the High Court of Chancery, made in a cause wherein Frances Bazalgette, widow, and others, are plaintiffs, and Evelyn Bazalgette is defendant, with the approbation of James Trower, Esq., one of the Masters of the said Court, on Tuesday, the 20th day of August next, at one o'clock in the afternoon, in 2 lots, all that FREEHOLD ESTATE, called Eastwick-park, situate in the parishes of Bookham and Fetcham, in the county of Surrey; together with the manors of Great Bookham, with Courts Leet and Baron, Rights and Royalties, and Rights of Timber growing on the wastes of Bookham and Ranmore-common. The Estate is situate about 2 miles from Leatherhead, 7 from Epsom, and 21 from London. Printed particulars may be had (gratis) at the said Master's chambers, in Southampton-buildings, Chancery Lane, London; of Messrs, Adlington,

Gregory and Faulkner, 1, Bedford Row, London; the Spread Eagle, Epsom; the Swan, Leatherhead; Greyhound, Dorking; Star and Garter, and Talbot, Richmond; Castle, Kingston; White Hart, Guildford. The mansion may be viewed with cards only, by application at the office of the said Messrs, Adlington, Gregory, and Faulkner. [*The Times* Saturday, 20 Jul 1833]

Eastwick Park was then sold by Louis' executors to the brewer and banker Hedworth David Barclay.

Although, as previously related, we do not know precisely if any of the estates in Jamaica actually became Louis' property during his lifetime, but mostly their ownerships were still in dispute at his death. Slavery was officially abolished on 1 August 1834. There was a transitional period when most of the former slaves were termed 'apprentices' and continued to work on their estates, while the long procedure of unravelling the slavery system was going on. The last of these 'apprentices' was finally fully released by 1840. Part of the Emancipation Act allowed for the former slave-owners to be compensated by the British government for the loss of the services of their former slaves. All estate proprietors had to make a return of their slaves for the purpose of submitting these claims for compensation. Since by this time very few proprietors were actually living in Jamaica, most estates were under the control of attorneys or overseers, and it was these men who entered the returns of slaves. The return made by Edward Bond, the executor of Evelyn's attorney William Lambie in 1832 for Elysium estate in the Parish of St George listed the number of slaves in Lambie's possession on 28 June 1832 as two hundred and ninety four. Evelyn's claim under the Emancipation Act was eventually settled on 12 October 1835. Compensation was awarded for 265 slaves, valued at £17/7/- each, giving a total of £4,596/15/11. The Elysium sugar estate in St George had previously been mortgaged to Evelyn, presumably as security for a loan to George H. Cosens, who also owned Sherwood Forest, Beau Desert and Devon Pen until his death in 1816. It was then administered by the attorney William Lambie. Since Evelyn was effectively the sole owner, he was able to collect the compensation on it. By 1850 the estate seems to have been abandoned:

> And the receiver-general is hereby authorized to relieve Moses Mendes Sodas, collecting constable for the parish of Saint George, to the amount of sixty-nine pounds four shillings, being duty surcharged to Elysium Estate, in the said parish, on six hundred and ninety-two gallons of rum, at two shillings per gallon, which he was unable to realize, in consequence of that estate having been totally abandoned, and there being nothing whatever to levy on for the same.
> [The Acts of Jamaica passed in the year 1851-52]

Having passed through the hands of the Hannaford and Campbell families. Elysium had become a banana plantation by 1910, in the ownership of the United Fruit Company.

The amount awarded to Evelyn on 12 December 1836 for Camp Savannah was £2,756/ 3/7 for 155 slaves.

The reader can be forgiven for not remembering that in 1823 an attempt was made by the Armstrongs to recover the Storer debts by forcing full administration of his estate. This Bill eventually lapsed, but Evelyn filed a 'Bill of Revivor' following his father's death, and so the case of Armstrong v. Storer was then brought back to the Chancery Court. The case before the Master of the Rolls was summarised in *The English Reports*. Very little was achieved in recovering the debts, further delaying the full execution of Louis' will.

Chapter 23: 1833-36

After Eastwick Park had been bought by Hedworth David Barclay, the residue of Louis' furniture and effects was offered for auction by Winstanley & Sons:-

The Furniture and other Effects at Eastwick Park Mansion, Great Bookham; comprising upwards of 30 bedsteads, with suitable bedding, chairs, carpets, curtains, sofas, wardrobes, drawers, dressing stands, lounging and other chairs, an excellent set of dining tables, card, sofa, loo and pembroke ditto, sideboards and sideboard tables, dumb waiters, cellarets and wine coolers, bookcases, several pier and chimney glasses of large dimensions, a full size billiard table with lamps, cues etc. complete, 8-day and other clocks, some linen, china, glass and books, a patent mangle, brewing utensils and casks, kitchen and dairy requisites, the fixtures of the mansion and offices, and other valuable effects. Also about 150 dozen of choice wine, a few pictures and prints, and the live and dead stock belonging to the farm, including 20 cows, 10 horses, 3 waggons, 4 carts, 7 ploughs, 2 land rollers, harness, harrows, ladders, racks, hay, seed and winnowing machines, rick cloth, some poultry etc.
[*The Times*, Saturday, 26 October 1833]

On 24 January 1833, the bill of Bazalgette v. Simpson was heard in the Court of Chancery. In summary, the plaintiff, Evelyn Bazalgette, stated that Louis had in a previous bill on 5 May 1826 sued, for repayment of a debt, the late John Simpson and Thomas ffleming, merchants, in the sum of £25,120/9/6. They had been already ordered to repay this sum to Louis in 1829. Premises were mortgaged to Charles Leak who was to execute the will of Simpson, who had no issue but had a brother with descendants. It was these beneficiaries whom Evelyn was attempting to pursue: Fred Harding, Mildred Courlam, Lucy Edman, Vincent Simpson and John Francis

Simpson. The defendants did not appear at the hearing and judgement was deferred. [TNA: 1006/37]

The other cases involved in these proceedings were heard together later and were mainly concerned with taxation – the legal term for allotting and limiting costs. They were: Armstrong v. Storer (No. 2), Bazalgette v. Armstrong and Armstrong v. Jeffreys.

On 18 May 1835, a cushion was stolen from a carriage that had been lent to a Mr. Bazalgette, of Gloucester Place – perhaps Evelyn. The perpetrator was brought to trial at the Old Bailey on 15 June 1835.

> WILLIAM BUCKINGHAM was indicted for stealing, on the 18th of May, 1 cushion, value 10s., the goods of Joseph Coatsworth.
>
> DAVID COOPER (*police-constable D81*) On the night of the 18th of May, I was on duty in Bulstrode-street—I saw the prisoner coming up the street with this cushion under his arm, between ten and eleven o'clock, in a hurried manner—I asked what he had got—he made no answer—I then took him to the station-house—he then said he found it.
>
> HENRY SMITH I am coachman to Mr. Bazalgette, of Gloucester-place—we hired a carriage that day, which was waiting at the door of our stable, in Gloucester-mews—the driving-cushion was on the box, and it was stolen.
>
> JOHN SLY I am ostler to Mr. Joseph Coatsworth, who lives in Clay-street—we lent the carriage, with this cushion on the seat, to the master of the last witness.
>
> Prisoner's Defence. I found it.
>
> GUILTY . Aged 28.— Transported for Seven Years.
> [Old Bailey Proceedings, t18350615-1475]

William was transported, with 279 others, on the convict-ship *Recovery*, with Captain Johnson and Superintendent Dr. Neill in charge, which left London on 26 Oct 1835 and arrived in New South Wales four months later on Thursday 25 February 1836. He was granted a ticket-of-leave on 18 Feb 1839 and his certificate of freedom in June 1843.

On 23 April 1835, Louis' son Sidney married Caroline Montague. 'Sidney Bazalgette of the Parish of Banstead in the County of Surrey, Esq., widower, and Caroline Sarah Montague, Spinster, of this parish (Caversham, Berks), a minor at the time of granting the licence but now of age, were married in this Church by licence with consent of the father, this 23rd day of April 1835.' All of the witnesses were Montagues. [BRK CRO D/P 162/1/9 (MF 91071, fiche 7, page 71)]

On 11 August 1835, the bill of Armstrong v. Storer had another airing. The complainants were 'Chas Armstrong of Fenchurch St Merchant & William do., Louis Bazalgette Jr, Gent, of Ewell and Daniel Bazalgette of Hampton Worcs'. On 23 August 1823, when they filed complaints against Ann Katherine Storer, it was ordered that account to be taken of interest on estates including several plantations, lands and premises at Purley and Tilehurst. Money was supposed to come from sales and rents, an attorney was appointed and produce was shipped to the complainants. The defendants were still abroad and outside the court's jurisdiction. The plaintiffs were allowed to appoint commissioners to go to Jamaica to question the defendants. These commissioners were empowered to inspect everything necessary for them to work out the value of the estate and to use the proceeds to pay debts. The original bill was 'abated by Louis Sr's death'. A 'Bill of Revivor' was then filed, to resurrect the claim previously made by Louis Sr. Complaint was made against Evelyn by the Armstrongs, Louis Jr and Daniel. There was £9,500 left to pay back out of the original £10,000 loaned to Storer. Louis Jr was pressing for payment, but there had been no response from the commissioner. The Armstrongs were urged by Louis Jr to complete the winding up of the estate after Louis Sr's death. [TNA: 1867/18]

Evelyn's suit (Bazalgette v. Kirlew) was heard on 19 November 1836 before Charles Christopher, Baron Cottenham. The claim for compensation for the estate of Camp Savannah in Westmoreland was made jointly by Evelyn Bazalgette and George Kirlew, and they would have each received a proportionate amount of the award. The estate and sugarworks at Camp Savannah had been mortgaged to Louis for £16,957 on 23 January 1812 by George Hanbury Mitchell, who died intestate. George Kirlew took over the estate as attorney and spent 'considerable sums' on it, which is why in the case of Bazalgette v. Kirlew he was judged to be entitled to a portion of the compensation as a result. The total sum awarded was £2,756/3/7 for 155 slaves valued at £17/15/6 each.

Compensations claims for the slave-owners were recorded in the Parliamentary Paper entitled: *1837-38 (215) Accounts of slave compensation claims; for the colonies of Jamaica, Antigua, Honduras, St. Christopher's, Grenada, Dominica, Nevis, Virgin Islands, St. Lucia, British Guiana, Montserrat, Bermuda, Bahamas, Tobago, St. Vincent's, Trinidad, Barbadoes, Mauritius and Cape of Good Hope: 16th March 1838.*

Since all of the Storer estates were still under litigation these claims all appeared under *Parish of Westmoreland, County of Cornwall, Litigated Claims, List D*. These figures show that in the matter of Armstrong v. Storer the total sum claimed was £9,828/2/6 for a total of 526 slaves. In the case of Evelyn Bazalgette v. Kirlew the sum was £2,756/3/7 for a total of 133 slaves.

As bald statistics these are somewhat shocking to us at the present time, since they show to what extent slavery was regarded as acceptable amongst the moneyed classes of Great Britain. Sadly, the attitude towards what is now referred to as human trafficking was no different then to what it is today in many parts of the world. There is little point in trying to apologise for the actions of our ancestors, uncomfortable though it makes us feel. At least in those days there was a strong enough ground-swell of opinion in Britain that slavery should be abolished, so we can feel a little better about it that something was being done to redress these wrongs. Life for most people in those times was very tough, and in many parts of the so-called civilized world, conditions for the poor were little better than they were for slaves, and sometimes much worse. In modern society most people give little thought to the reason why we enjoy the cheap prices of goods produced in the third world. They accept it as normal, and turn a blind eye, just as their forebears did.

The abolition of slavery in the British Empire was achieved at a very heavy financial cost: approximately twenty million pounds, which was about forty percent of the national budget. This sum was mostly raised from bankers such as Rothschilds. If a deal had not been struck to recompense the slave-owners for every slave whose services they would lose, abolition would never have happened when it did. However, this was not a case of 'the government versus the slave-owners'. Those who profited from the labours of the enslaved were spread throughout moneyed society. Estates in the West Indies and elsewhere were owned or part-owned by businessmen, lawyers, doctors, clerics (even bishops) and of course the members of both houses of parliament. There were many of these who were 'absentees', so they never went to the Caribbean or even saw a slave. Of approximately 30,000 claimants, only about a fifth were domiciled in Britain, with the rest mostly living in the colony for which the claim was made. However, these British-based claimants made disproportionately large claims and were awarded around fifty percent of the total compensation. In the circumstances it was therefore not a difficult deal to make, since almost all of the great and the good in Britain would profit handsomely from it. The timing was also rather apt, since estates in the West Indies had suffered from the fall in the price of sugar and many had been abandoned and were therefore next to worthless. In the case of estates which formerly belonged to estate owners of whom Armstrongs were the agents, such as the Storers, the compensation turned out to be virtually the only return that the lenders, such as the estate of Louis Bazalgette, were able finally to reap.

In the earlier cases in Chancery such as Bazalgette v. Storer, Evelyn acted for the family, but it was easy for the defendants to argue that he was acting on his own behalf. It therefore appears likely that, to avoid this perceived conflict of interest, Evelyn entered into a private agreement with the Armstrongs that the main case they would pursue would be Armstrong v. Storer. No doubt, following judgement, they then divided the resultant awards between them.

The final judgement in the case of Armstrong v. Storer was made on 22 August 1836, and affected most of the Storer estates, principally Bellisle, Frome, Haddo Pen and Fontabelle. This paved the way for the Compensation Board to make its decisions. In each case the first claimant was Charles Armstrong and the second Ann Katherine Storer, so they each received a proportionate share. The compensatory amounts paid out for these estates were:

Belleisle, 88 slaves at £19/16/4, total £1,744//7
Frome, 100 slaves at £18/14/6, total £1,877/4/5
Haddo Pen, 184 slaves at £19/12/2, total £3,608/5/3
Fontabelle, 187 slaves at £13/15/-, total £2,567/12/5.

As shown in Armstrong v. Storer, there was a further complication in the case of Fontabelle. Ann Storer was the original receiver of this estate, to be succeeded by Joseph Stone Williams, who asked to be relieved in 1831, claiming a balance owed to him of £3,654/2/-. On Williams' death his executor James Grant petitioned to be paid the above sum from the compensation, but this claim was disputed by Ann Storer. Evelyn arranged with Grant to purchase this debt, and Ann Storer's counter-claim was still unresolved at her death on 9 April 1854.

There was one estate of which Charles Armstrong was owner-in-fee and was therefore the only claimant - Geneva in Westmoreland. For this he received £1,855/10/8 on 21 December 1835 for 96 slaves. Geneva was previously owned by George Marcy, who also owned the Kepp estate, but it was under Armstrong's control by 1831. If Armstrongs were Marcy's agents, it is likely that Geneva was mortgaged to them as security for a loan, and as there was no other claimant to the estate, such as was the case with the Storer properties, it was easy for them to get possession of it. Another estate for which Charles Armstrong was the first claimant was Windsor Forest, also in Westmoreland. Its owner was James McIntosh, succeeded by Joseph Foster Barham (a partner in the London merchant firm of Barham Plummer, to whom was also mortgaged the Camp Savannah estate) and then Samuel Jeffries, of Pickstone, East Grinstead in Sussex, who died in December 1819. His executors, apart from Armstrong, were Jesse Curling of Bermondsey, a shipbuilder, and William Barth of Great Yarmouth, a merchant, which is why Curling and Barth were also claimants. The sum awarded on 18 January 1836 for this claim was £4,059/11/3.

It appears that it was not until after Ann Katherine Storer's death that some of these disputed estates were finally able to be sold, meaning that it had taken Evelyn over twenty-five years to wind up his father's estate. Had he known this, he might have baulked at the job of executor, as had Sir Coutts Trotter many years before.

Were Louis and his family slave-owners? This is somewhat doubtful, though Armstrongs and Bazalgettes were of course West India traders, so they actively supported the planters by shipping goods to them in Jamaica, and sugar and rum back to England, and thereby profited from the labour of slaves. They also held mortgages on the estates in security for the large loans that they made to Storer and others, but they mostly did not acquire title to them. Charles Armstrong did personally own the Geneva plantation, but the ownership of the other estates listed above was in dispute until well after slavery was abolished. William Armstrong also received awards for claims on two estates in Jamaica and six in Barbados. Ann Katherine Storer seems to have hung on until the bitter end in using the courts to deny recompense to her creditors. By the time Evelyn secured title to whichever estates he ended up with, it was the 1850's. The only estate whose sale we presently have a record of is Haddo Pen, which was 'part-sold in lots and transferred by Evelyn Bazalgette to Benjamin Vickers on July 30, 1856'. The only other estate to which Evelyn may have secured title was the Elysium estate, which was mortgaged to him and which seems to have been under his control, overseen by the attorney George Kirlew. If the family were regarded as slave-owners it was not by choice.

It was not necessary to prove title to an estate to claim compensation under the Emancipation Act. If that had been the case, with the large number whose ownership was in dispute, it would have taken twenty years or more to settle all claims, which would have been unacceptable to the British government. All that was necessary was to put it a claim giving evidence of entitlement. Where there was a dispute, there were several claimants, and those who in the opinion of the board had just claims received compensation in proportion. So although the family were not slave-owners *per se*, they still received compensation for the loss of the labour of the slaves. They probably felt that this was their due, since where they had lent large sums to the actual owners this was the only way in which they got at least some of their money back, apart from the proceeds of the eventual sale of the estates, which in some cases were very small.

Chapter 24 - Louis' Children

Some of Louis' children have already appeared in the story, because they were somehow involved in his business ventures, but others have been hardly mentioned. By his first marriage to Catherine Métivier he had four children, the first being Louis, who was born on 31 May 1780 but not christened until 8 February 1784, when all of the children were christened together. According to the Reverend Evelyn Bazalgette's family Bible, young Louis died at about the age of five and was buried, like his mother, in the graveyard of Old Marylebone Church. Then there was his sister Louisa, who was born on 8 February 1781. We know very little of her life. It appears that she never married, and that she lived at 66, Albany Street, Regent's Park, dying there on 11 March 1867. By this time, the family had a vault in Kensal Green Cemetery, so she was buried there. The elder of the surviving sons, Joseph William, pursued a naval career which will be the subject of a further book. His younger brother John entered the army and was a lifetime officer, the pinnacle of his career being when he was made acting Governor General of Nova Scotia on two occasions from 30 May to 30 September 1851 and from 22 March to 5 August 1852. The first time he was standing in for Sir John Harvey, who had fallen ill and returned to England to recuperate. Harvey came back to Nova Scotia but then died, necessitating John's second term while a replacement was sought. Most of John's sons went into the army as well, though George joined the Royal Marine Light Infantry, serving as commander of the British garrison on San Juan Island during the Pig War. This branch of the family deserves a book in itself. One of John's descendants, Jack Bazalgette, wrote two books about his career which contain some family details, but that is all there seems to be. [*The Captains and the Kings Depart* and *Careering On*]

By his second marriage to Frances Bergman Louis had ten children, who were Frances Mary (b. 3 October 1788), Theresa (b. 21 August 1791), Louis (b. 13 September 1792), Daniel (b. 28 February 1793), Caroline (b. 1 February 1795), Cecilia (b. 5 October 1799), Evelyn (b. 20 October 1801), Sidney (b. 7 April

1806), Augustus (b. 18 October 1807) and Emmeline (b. 29 January 1813). Frances Mary died in June 1790, and was buried in the church of St. Marylebone. Theresa died in March 1792 and was buried in the same place. Louis has been mentioned already since he was a partner in Armstrongs and Bazalgettes. After siring an illegitimate daughter, Julia Augusta, by Ann Moxom (of neither of whom we know any more) he married Sarah Cooke at St. George's, Bloomsbury in 1837. Louis may have continued as a merchant after leaving the Armstrong partnership or may have just decided to live the life of a gentleman from then on. They lived at 34, Queen's Road, Bayswater (now known as Queensway) and had a daughter, Sarah Jane (b. 1837, d. 28 March 1928). She was known to the family as 'Great Aunt Jane' and never married. Louis left £150 per year to his wife Sarah, with the use of the house and contents while she lived, and the remainder to Jane. Louis died on 4th October 1879 and Sarah followed him to the grave just a month later.

Louis' second wife Frances (Fanny) continued to live at 86 Gloucester Place after his death. In the 1841 census the only occupants were Fanny (aged 70) and her daughter Emmeline (aged 25), with five servants: James Mayo (50), Mary Ann Davis (35), Sarah Inster (35), Elizabeth Todd (45), and Elizabeth Pyjit (25). Fanny passed away on 3 July 1847 of 'exhaustion from age.' She was seventy-eight years old, and her servant, Mary Ann Davis, was present at her death. *The Times* on 6 July briefly listed her passing 'on the 3rd Inst., at her residence in Glocester-place, Portman-square, Frances, widow of L. Bazalgette, Esq., late of Eastwick-park, in the county of Surrey, in her 79th year.' She was buried beside Louis in the family vault beneath St. Mary's Church, Marylebone.

No. 86, Gloucester Place and its remaining contents were auctioned by Fanny's executors and the following advertisements appeared in *The Times* of 12 February, 1848:

> No. 86, Glocester-place, Portman-square.-- Residence with possession, held for an unexpired term of 40 years, free of ground rent.

MESSRS. KEMP have received instructions from the Executors to SELL by AUCTION, on the Premises, on Wednesday, Febriary 16, at 1, the GROUND LEASE of a gentlemanly RESIDENCE, most desirably situate, No. 86, Glocester-place, Portman-square, comprising every convenience for a family, capital coach-house and stabling; held under Lord Portman for an unexpaired term of 40 years from Lady-day next, free of ground rent. Particulars at the Mart; on the premises; of Messrs, Gregory, Faulkner, Gregory and Skirrow, Bedford-row; and of Messrs' Kemp, Judd-street, Bruswick-square, who will give cards to view.

No. 86, Glocester-place, Portman-square.-- Furniture, 1,800 oz. of Plate, and Effects
MESSRS. KEMP will SELL by AUCTION, on the Premises, on Wednesday, February 16, and follwing day, at 12, by order of the Executors, the whole of the well-manufactured FURNITURE; comprising four post and tent bedsteads and furniture, excellent bedding, wardrobe, chests of drawers, rosewood sofa and occasional tables, large chimney and pier glasses and tables, handsome rosewood cheffonier with plate-glass back, couches, chairs, set of mahogany dining tables, breakfast table, eating-room chairs in morocco, sideboard table, sarcophagus, about 1,800 oz. of plate, including an elegant epergne, tea urn, tea kettle, salvers, candlesticks, King's pattern spoons & forks, &c.; a horizontal grand pianoforte by Broadwood & Sons, china dinner and dessert services, kitchen requisites, &c. To be viewed the day prior and morning of sale. Catalogues on the premises, and of the Auctioneers, Judd-street, Brunswick-square.

The furniture shows the grand style in which the family lived, sleeping in canopied four-poster beds and enjoying the use of some fine pieces of rosewood furniture. This is the last we see of the Broadwood grand piano, which had been bought in 1809 and which was annually moved so many times back and forth between Gloucester Place and Eastwick Park.

Mr. Martin Thackeray, Q.C., (1783-1864), who was for many years the vice-provost of King's College, Cambridge, was living in the house by 1851 with his wife Augusta, who was the daughter of the architect John Yenn, R.A. (1750-1821). Martin Thackeray was the brother of William Makepeace Thackeray, whose only son Richmond Thackeray was the father of the author and critic William Makepeace Thackeray. Martin bequeathed 86, Gloucester Place to his nephew, Joseph, but it was another nephew, the barrister Charles de la Pryme, who lived there until at least 1880. By 1897 it was occupied the Rev. Henry Russell Wakefield; it was the rectory of St Mary's, Marylebone by then, as it remains today (now numbered 73).

Daniel Bazalgette has received more attention in this book than perhaps he deserved, but he led an interesting life. His sister Caroline did not marry, and died on 18 July 1851, being buried with her parents in the vault in Marylebone church. Cecilia married Louis John Francis Twysden (he was the relative of Prinny's mistress Frances Twysden, Lady Jersey, who was mentioned before). His parents were Sir William Jervis Twysden, 7th Baronet, of Roydon Hall, East Peckham, Kent, and Frances Wynch. Cecilia and Louis had two sons, Louis John Francis (b. 1829) and Francis, who was born in 1831 and died at two days old, his mother dying at the same time. The surviving son, Louis John Francis Twysden, married Helen Mary Ann Bazalgette, one of the daughters of Captain Joseph William Bazalgette. Twysden succeeded in 1879, becoming 9th baronet. Helen died in 1908 and Louis then married Emily Offin in 1909 and himself died in May 1911.

The life of Evelyn, the Queen's Counsel, has also been well covered, but he is important because he was the family's lawyer. He also outlived most of the family, dying in March 1888. His brother Sidney married Maria Hand, the daughter of the vicar of Dunton in Essex, on 18 November 1831. After Maria's early death in 1833, he then married Caroline Sarah Montague on 23 April 1835. He died in Torquay in 1858, perhaps at Hesketh House, described later, and was buried in Kensal Green Cemetery. Then there was Augustus and finally Emmeline, a late arrival and therefore probably a favourite.

She also never married, and died on 4 May 1873 at 22 Chapel Street, Grosvenor Square.

At least one of Louis and Fanny's sons was a racehorse owner. The Racing Calendar for 1836 refers to 'Mr. Bazalgette of Mortimer, who kept a good stud of horses'. This has to be Sidney, because Mortimer Lodge, Stratfield Mortimer in Berkshire was his home. Augustus was also reputedly an owner, but only by family anecdote. There was a filly named Folly, who is listed in Weatherby's Stud book, volume sixty-four, as being owned by 'BAZALGETTE, —, Esq.', but tantalizingly without a first name or initial. The same publication in 1840 also has an entry for Folly - '1833 b. f. Folly, by Zinganee, Mr Bazalgette', under the name of her dam, which bore the unprepossessing name of The Shrew. This is also confirmed in the Racing Calendar for 1836, where Folly came second out of five in her maiden race at Guildford on Tuesday 19 July of that year:

> A Sweepstakes of 5 sov. each, with 25 added, for maiden horses; three yrs old, 7st. four, 8st.2lb. five, 8st. 10tb. six and aged, 9st. m. and g. allowed 3lb. two miles (5 subscribers).
> Mr Coleman's ch. c. Gorhambury, by Bedlamite, 3 yrs old —Wakefield............1
> Mr Bazalgette's b. f. Folly, by Zinganee, out of The Shrew, 3 yrs old. 2
> Mr Balchin's br. c. Guitar, by Chateau Margaux, out of Sola, 3 yrs old. 3

Unfortunately, no further trace of Folly has been found, and in fact most stud books do not list her at all. Her sire, the bay stallion Zinganee, was a descendant of Eclipse and was a very fine horse. He was born in 1825, out of Folly, by Young Drone, and was bred in the Burghley House stud of Brownlow Cecil, 2nd Marquess and 11th Earl of Exeter, in Northamptonshire. At the end of his first season he was sold to the trainer-jockey brothers Will and Sam Chifney, and Sam, with the exception of a few races after Zinganee was sold, was his jockey throughout his career. Sam had been Prinny's jockey until October 1791, when amid allegations of race-fixing the Prince pensioned him off and sold his own stables. Zinganee was a winner of the Newmarket Stakes, the Craven Stakes, the Oatlands Stakes and the Ascot Gold Cup and was sold to George IV in 1829. After several other good placings he was retired to Lord Chesterfield's stud at Bretby Park.

It is possible that Sidney and Augustus were in partnership in owning racehorses, but the only story of Augustus in this connection is the manner of his death. It is a family anecdote that he died in January 1849 after breaking the top off a bottle of champagne, intending to reward his winning horse with the contents, and cut himself, dying of tetanus. This is unlikely to be true. There is never any need to break the top off a bottle of champagne, since the cork pops out very readily. Instead of tetanus, his cause of death was in fact 'delirium tremens' which suggests that it was the contents of the bottle (and many others), rather than the bottle itself, which saw him off. He was buried with his parents in the Marylebone vault.

After Daniel Bazalgette died of lung cancer on 17 June 1838, his widow Margaret may have stayed on at Eastwick House in Little Hampton, Worcestershire for a while or rented it out. On 13 May 1841, she married Edward Rudge, who was a widower, and who had previously (on 28 July 1791) married Anne Nouaille, who died on 1 September 1836. Edward had been educated in Lincoln's Inn and Queen's College Oxford, and was very wealthy, a Fellow of the Royal Society and a noted botanist, as well as a J.P. and High Sheriff of Worcestershire. He owned a considerable amount of land at Evesham, and built the Abbey Manor House in 1816. He also owned part of the estate of Braybrooke, in Northamptonshire, and a London house: 8, Upper Wimpole Street in Fitzrovia.

At the end of August, 1841 Eastwick House was offered for rent in *The Times*.

THE VALE OF EVESHAM. - A comfortable Family Residence, withon one mile of the good market town of Evesham. -- To be LET, EASTWICK HOUSE; consisting of dining and drawing rooms, with small breakfast room, on the first floor; four bedrooms and two dressing rooms, with water closet, two large attics and two smaller, two kitchens, laundry with other offices, and good cellars; spacious court yard and drying ground, with capital coach-house and stables. The house stands on a pretty lawn, with pleasure garden and good kitchen ditto. It is situate at a convenient distance from the high road between Cheltenham and Leamington, 15 miles from the former and 25 miles from the latter watering place, and close to the mail road from Worcester to London, in connection with the G.T. Western Railroad. There is a pew in the parish church within a short walk. The whole to be let at a moderate rent, with rate and taxes optional, and a great part of the furniture, which is extremely good, may be taken at a valuation. Address, pre-paid, to James Denison, Esq., post-office, Evesham.

[*The Times*, Tuesday, 31 August 1841]

Three years later it was decided that Eastwick House would be offered for sale by Daniel's trustees, so it was advertised for auction by Mr. Thomas Murrell. This is a more detailed description:

The estate comprises 154 acres of excellent arable and pasture land, with a small portion of woodland. It has a commodious mansion house, called Eastwick House; comprising drawing room, dining room, breakfast parlour, spacious bed chambers, lock-up coach-houses, extensive stabling, and all other useful and necessary out-offices. There is a substantial farm house on the property, and also a newly-erected corn-mill, driving three pairs of stones, in good repair and possessing a never-failing source of water in all seasons, with a comfortable residence for a miller. The estate commands splendid views of beautiful scenery, bounded by the Cotswold and Bredon Hills. Earl Fitzhardinge's hounds hunt within six miles. Mr. Webb's "Terribles" meet in the immediate neighbourhood and the Worcestershire and Warwickshire foxhounds frequently throw off in the adjacent line of country. The state has a brook running through it, which is well stocked with fish, and might be made a valuable fishery. It empties itself into the far-famed Avon, which for some space flows past the Estate. [*The Times*, Monday, 15 July 1844]

The author posted a request on RootsChat for information about Eastwick House, in case anyone remembered it. He was delighted to hear from Jane Marshall, who had lived in the house as a child and also sent him some photographs. These show that this house was like a miniature version of its larger namesake. She said:

> I lived in half of Eastwick House with my parents for about 12 years, from 1957. My family rented the house from a Mr Lancaster and his wife; they had a daughter called Mary. I'm not sure when it was demolished. We left in 1969/70-ish, possibly a couple of years after that. The house was split in two when we were living there; we lived in the half that had twelve rooms; there were (in our half) two attics, on the first floor the biggest bathroom I've ever seen, a bath you practically needed a step ladder to get into (slight exaggeration), a shower and an airing cupboard (again very large). There were two doors either end; one of these led to the 'playroom' and back stairs. There was a long corridor leading off from the bathroom to a further large bedroom. On the same floor a large bedroom and a smaller one (dressing room). On the ground floor, a study, a very large sitting room/dining area, kitchen, wash room, boiler room and a pantry. Outside the back area were garages and the usual outbuildings, a wood at the back and extensive rear gardens. A coach house and stables - a blind man and his wife rented the house there. At the front were extensive lawns, a monkey puzzle tree and an orchard; the house front had a drive around a huge yew tree. At the side where Mr & Mrs Lancaster used to live were greenhouses and a lovely loggia. I have the original delft tiles that were inside the fireplace, depicting religious scenes (even a stoning!). [Email from Jane Marshall].

Edward Rudge died at the age of 83 on 3 September 1846 at the Abbey Manor House and was buried in its grounds with his first wife Anne. This left Margaret an even richer widow than the first time. When in London she actually lived at 14, Devonshire Place, close to her other London house, which she seems to have let to her uncle Evelyn, the barrister. At some time she bought Hesketh House in Torquay, which is at the eastern end of Hesketh Crescent, a palatial Georgian-style crescent facing the sea. Hesketh House later became 15, Hesketh Crescent, and it is still standing, being now subdivided into five holiday flats. Hesketh Place also houses in its central parts the Osborne Hotel, which survived a vandalistic Stuka attack during the second world war. Margaret and her daughter Frances Elizabeth spent their summers there it seems. The *Torquay Directory* of 9 March 1870 published a death notice for Margaret Rudge

> February 25, at No. 14, Devonshire Place, London, of congestion of the lungs, Margaret, widow of the late Edward Rudge, Esq., of Abbey Manor, Worcestershire, and 44, Wimpole-Street, London, aged 72.

Frances Elizabeth died just four-and-a-half years after her mother, on 21 December 1874, never seeing her *magnum opus* in print; her translation of the German edition of the two-volume 'Meditations on the Life and Doctrine of Jesus Christ', by the Austrian Jesuit Nicolaus Avancinus, was published the following year. In her will, she made Evelyn and Sir Joseph Bazalgette her executors, and made generous bequests and sometimes annuities to her various unmarried cousins, friends, servants, former servants and charities, though none to any of her American relatives. She also left 14, Devonshire Place and all its contents to Evelyn, and the residue of her estate to Joseph William 'as if he had been my child and heir' although he was a year older than she was. Evelyn Bazalgette was still living at 8 Wimpole Street according to the 1871 census, described as a 'barrister out of practice'. His staff at the time consisted of Frederick Edwards (footman), Mary Goodchild (cook) and Matilda Turpin (housemaid). He then moved to the house in Devonshire Place, where he lived for the rest of his life, dying in July, 1888. His nephew Joseph William executed his will, the value of his estate being £155,139/7/3. His obituary reads:

> Obiit Evelyn Bazalgette, QC, born 1801. He matriculated at Balliol College Oxford and took a first class in classics and a second in mathematics in 1822. Among his now distinguished contemporaries at Oxford may be mentioned the 7th Lord Shaftesbury, whose name appears in the first class of the same list, and Dr Pusey. He was admitted as a student of Lincoln's Inn in 1823 and was called to the bar in 1827. For many years he enjoyed an extensive Chancery practice and numbered among his contemporaries Lord Abinger, Lord Cairns, Lord Campbell, Lord Cottenham, Lord Cranworth, Lord Denman [son of one of the doctors who tried to cure his withered arm], Lord Hatherley, Lord Langdale, Lord Lyndhurst, Lord Romilly, Lord St Leonards, Lord Truro and Lord Westbury. He was created a Queen's Counsel in 1858 and invited to the bench of Lincoln's Inn in the same year. He was treasurer of Lincoln's Inn in 1878, one of the governors of King's College and one of the few surviving original members of the Oxford and Cambridge Club, established by Lord Palmerston and others in 1830.
> [Pump Court, the Temple newspaper and review, Volume 7]

Evelyn's house was offered for sale that same year:

> At a low reserve price.-- No. 14, Devonshire-place.-- Sale by order of the Executors of the late Evelyn Bazalgette, Esq., Q.C. -- One of the larger-fronted Houses, on the east side, with additions of an upper chamber storey, and within the last few years made modern by the introduction of plate-glazed sashes, bath room, handsome Minton tile paving to entrance-hall, stained glass landing windows, and other improvements. It forms a most attractive family residence, and occupies a position highly appreciated from being

central, and in a street that ranks next in width and cheerfulness to Portland-place, with quietude secured by the private end gates on the Marylebone-road.
[*The Times*, Saturday, 24 Nov 1888]

Eastwick Park (the one in Great Bookham) was again advertised for sale by auction, in three lots, in *The Times* in May, 1848 and also on 21 May 1881 and in April and June 1882. At this time it was described as 'in the Italian style', having a 76-foot salon, a cricket field and 'three vineries, peach, nectarine, pineapple and melon houses'. It was then sold in July 1882 to William Keswick M. P., and Barclay's furniture was auctioned off. Keswick had become head (or *Tai Pan*) of Jardine Matheson in 1874. Jardine, Matheson & Co were founded in 1832 and at that time were in the business of shipping tea and silk from China, funded by the shipping of opium from India to sell to the Chinese, though, like many other such companies, imperceptibly becoming over the years the respectable multi-national firm that they are today.

After Keswick's death in 1912, Eastwick was advertised regularly in *The Times* between 1914 and 1916 and was eventually purchased from Keswick's executors (presumably at a very advantageous price) by his son Henry, and then sold in 1918 to the Honourable (later Sir) Hippolyte Louis Wiehe du Coudray Souchon of Mauritius. Souchon was active in promoting the interests of Mauritius in agriculture and especially sugar production. He owned several race-horses (including one aptly named *Sugar Cane*) and also bred some prize Friesian bulls at Eastwick. He in turn sold it in 1922 to Percy Portway Harvey, a property speculator and estate agent with a somewhat shady past, who sold off some of the land for housing. Local residents purchased the remainder in the following year to safeguard the woodland on the common. The house and immediate grounds of Eastwick were bought leasehold by Henry Fussell in 1924 and it became a boys' private preparatory school, its name being changed to Southey Hall, after Southey Road, Worthing, the original home of the school before it became too small. In 1940 the staff and boys were evacuated to Fulford House, Dunscombe, near Exeter, and during the second world war Eastwick was used as a billet for Canadian troops. By the time the Canadians left in 1945 the banisters were gone (reputedly used for firewood) and the house was in a sorry state. The school returned and carried on until 1954, when the then headmaster, Fussell's son Denis, abruptly departed, apparently under a cloud. The school, which was in any case losing money, closed down shortly afterwards and the house was left to deteriorate further, until finally it was demolished in 1958 to make way for a housing estate and a junior school.

Pond House, Louis' former residence in Chiswick, was later occupied by members of the Ronalds family of Brentford, who owned a large market garden. Jane Ronalds was at Pond House in the 1851 Census when she was very elderly, and her son Francis, then in charge of the Royal Observatory at Kew and later to invent an electric telegraph, lived with her.

Many of the properties from the Chiswick Prebend Manor estates, some of which were previously owned by Louis, were offered in *The Times* for sale leasehold in February 1867. They were described as 'part of the property of the late Thomas How, esq.' Thomas How seems to have been a tea merchant and a steward of the Royal Orthopedic Hospital. Among those properties listed were Gordon House, which was just north of Louis' house, and which was later demolished to make way for a parade of shops, and Grosvenor House (i.e., Louis' Pond House), which was described as 'with offices and garden, in the occupation of Mrs Tutin, at £100 per annum' and 'a piece of nursery ground' which was probably what used to be Louis' adjoining paddock. From 1870 the house was home to St Agnes' Orphanage and Industrial Home for Girls. This establishment was described in Shaw's Local Government Directory for 1883 as 'For Training Ignorant and Troublesome Girls who have failed in Domestic Service'. Mary A. Hales, its 'Lady-Superintendant and Foundress', moved St Agnes' to 32a Fitzroy Square in 1880. Grosvenor House was again sold in 1900, probably to Stanley Victor Makower, who was called to the bar at Lincoln's Inn in 1895 but apparently never practised. He devoted his time to writing such works as *The Mirror of Music* and *Perdita*, which was a romantic biography of Mary

Robinson, who of course is mentioned earlier in this book as one of the Prince of Wales' first mistresses. Makower died at Grosvenor House at the age of 40 in 1911. The house is now just called No 2 Chiswick Lane and belongs to the Verona Sisters, who use it as a home for novice and retired nuns.

Louis, Fanny, Augustus and Caroline Bazalgette lay at peace in the crypt of St. Mary's Church, Marylebone for between a hundred-and-thirty and a hundred-and-fifty years, which by comparison with most inner London burial places was a very long time. The crypt was full by 1853 and the entrance was later bricked up. In April 1982 *The Times* announced that the then Rector, the Reverend Christopher Hamel Cooke, had conceived a plan to 'remove the dead and bring in the living' by converting the crypt into a healing and counselling centre. The families of the over 850 occupants were, if they could be traced, asked to authorise their removal and re-interment in a mass grave at Brookwood Cemetery in Surrey. Once this authority had as far as possible been given, the Parish employed the Farebrother Funeral Service of Kingston-Upon-Thames to remove and re-coffin the remains.

When the workmen broke through the bricked-up entrance, a grisly and chaotic sight met their eyes. Coffins and remains were strewn and piled all over the place in complete disorder. Some reasons for this disturbance are thought to be firstly the Dogger Bank Earthquake, which occurred early in the morning of 7 June, 1931, and which was the strongest tremor recorded in the United Kingdom since records began, measuring 6.1 on the Richter scale. Its effects were felt all over the British Isles and in parts of Europe. The shock caused some damage in the basement of Madame Tussaud's, just across Marylebone Road. In the Chamber of Horrors, poor Doctor Crippen's head split in half, with one half falling to the floor where it was smashed. Primo Carnera, the boxer, lost his head and several other figures were slightly damaged. The next likely cause of the disarray was the London Blitz in 1940. One of the first of many bombs to fall on the area obliterated Tussaud's Cinema, next to the waxworks. This surgical removal of the cinema made way for the construction later of the London Planetarium, which opened in 1958. Another bomb fell in the churchyard, blowing out most of the church windows. It is also likely that the constant vibration of heavy traffic along Marylebone Road contributed to the disintegration of the coffins, which in a damp and airless place were already rotten and fragile. Burials had begun soon after the present church was completed in 1817, and within a few years the vaults must have been pretty full, since they began to pile new coffins on top of the old, in an attempt to cram more into the space, and therefore the newer coffins would eventually crush those beneath. According to the records, no further coffins were however added to the Bazalgette vault, number eleven.

Farebrother's did their best to identify the remains, using not only the records of the Parish, but also the coffin-plates which were attached to many of the coffins. These consisted of a 'breast-plate', a finely engraved brass plate of a trapezoidal shape, which was screwed to the upper part of the inner coffin. In addition there were medium-sized lead breast-plates nailed in the same location on the outer casket and small blacked lead 'foot-plates', nailed to the foot of the outer coffin, for easier identification as one traversed the aisles of the crypt. The coffin plates were collected and placed in the safe-keeping of the Department of Typography and Graphic Communication at Reading University, where the style of lettering on the plates was studied. The remains were reverently reburied at Brookwood Cemetery in Surrey in 1983 and a handsome memorial erected. A special choral Eucharist was held at St Marylebone Church on 9 May 1983 to commemorate those who had been re-interred and to dedicate the new healing centre.

On 5 December 1996, the author and his fianceé Trish Walker went to Reading University and met with Bryony Newhouse, who had written a dissertation on the plates, and her Head of Department, Michael Twyman. They presented us with the Bazalgette coffin plates. There were ten plates altogether: four brass plates from the coffins of Louis, Frances, Augustus and Caroline, two medium-sized lead breast plates (for Frances and Caroline) and four small blacked lead foot-plates. These travelled with our effects across the Atlantic when we moved to Canada in 1998, but since we have no children we decided to carry the brass plates back to England

and give them to my brother Edward, as beautiful but slightly macabre mementos, to be handed down through the family.

Postscript

This book has been a very long time in the making, and as I have written already it started as a follow-on from genealogical research. The English Bazalgette dynasty begun by Louis continues to flourish, and many of its members have made successful and even distinguished careers. This book was always intended firstly for the family, to help them to know how, when and where it all started. Because of Louis's close association with the Prince of Wales and other historical figures it seems to have grown into a work of more general interest, and this I view as a bonus. The origins of the book make it something that has just grown rather than being designed, which means that its structure is somewhat unconventional. A biographer usually chooses his or her subject, or is awarded a commission, and then takes the necessary time to perform research. At some point the author decides on the style and structure of the story and the book is written. This was not my approach because at the outset I never had any intention to write a biography. A monograph maybe, but not a book intended for publication. It is hoped that despite this organic approach the book presents a fresh view of Georgian life, and that the reader considers it was worth the effort of reading it.

Acknowledgements

Acknowledgements usually end with a tribute to the author's long-suffering spouse, invariably prefixed by 'and last but not least'. In this case I will thank my wife Trish first, because if it were not for her this project would never have been begun, let alone finished. She was well qualified to teach me how to carry out research and to organize the data, and she started the first chronology upon which the book was built.

Since research began over twenty years ago I have seen an explosion in the amount of data available via the internet. This has brought me into contact with many people who have unselfishly helped, and since many of them replied to questions in forums such as Rootschat, I do not necessarily know their names. There are others whom I have probably forgotten. To all of these nameless people I extend my heartfelt thanks for their help, which I have tried where possible to reciprocate by helping others.

Those internet friends whom I can name and thank here are:

John Adey for Adey family information.
Antony Armstrong for sharing details of his Armstrongs.
Brett Ashmeade-Hawkins, for his encyclopaedic knowledge of Jamaica and its plantocracy.
My 5th cousin Simon Bazalgette for starting the bazalgette.com website and for passing on enquiries.
Dan Byrnes for help with merchants and slavery.
John Carter for Coutts family information and researching the *Ordre du Lys*.
David Collins for Lawrell and Sumner information and for reading a draft.
Hilary Davidson and Tim Long of the Museum of London and Daniel Milford-Cottam of the V & A for tailoring advice.
Simon Elliott - MacCrea family.
Peter FitzGibbon and Leonie Earwaker for Bergman family.

Charlotte Frost for information on Sir William Knighton and for finding Louis' passport application.
Harry Willis Fleming for South Stoneham House information.
Peter Fullerton and Ben Viljoen for Storer information.
Fiona Green for research in the British Library.
The Grosvenor Estates.
Baldwin Hamey for help with London street numbers.
Kathryn Kane for reading and critiquing the first draft and for sharing her knowledge of the period.
Colette King for searches in Mobile, Alabama.
Guy Knapton for help with Augustus and Sidney Bazalgette and the Montagus.
Anna Knowles for reading an early draft and for making encouraging noises.
Jean-Claude and Monique Lacroix of the *Association des Chercheurs et Généalogistes des Cévennes*, for help with Bazalgettes in Ispagnac and the origin of the name.
Christine Laget for information on the history of Ispagnac.
Joanne Major and Sarah Murden for sharing a useful piece of their research.
Lord Malmesbury for permission to reproduce a letter written by Louis to his ancestor.
Stan Mapstone - St. Leger family.
Jane Marshall for her memories of Eastwick House, Little Hampton.
Kelly McDonald for finding a letter that was of interest.
Simon Metcalf, the royal armourer.
John Moore, Vince Haysom and Helen Drucquer - Middleship family.
Patrick Payne for help with John Willet Payne.
Yves Rauzier - Bordeaux help.
Bruce Robertson for Van Nordens.
Elizabeth Rodgers and Guy Holborn - Lincoln's Inn.
Jenny Stiles for information on the Becher and French families.
Nicholas Storey for tailoring help and for reading a draft.
Jeanne Strang for help with *La Bazalgette*, amongst other things.

Janet Vogt – help with William Lilley.
Dr. Angus Whitehead for South Molton Street assistance.
Stephenie Woolterton for finding a tailoring account from Louis in William Pitt's papers.

There are many more I am sure and I apologize to anyone I may have forgotten.

There are some people who selflessly provided me with a great deal of their time and effort:
Margaret Anderson, who designed the front cover.
Sarah Jean Waldock, who designed the rear cover, and prepared the book for publication.
Tony Simpson, Carolyn Hammond, Shirley Seaton, Paul Kershaw and Celia Cotton for Chiswick research.
Tracey Earl - Archivist of Coutts Bank, for allowing us to photograph ledgers in the Strand and in Docklands, whither she ferried us in the chairman's customized London taxicab.
Graham Dalling for researching in Enfield.
The late Rear-Admiral Derek Bazalgette for sharing his papers.
The late Colin Glover for his papers. He was planning to write Louis' biography but sadly died before he could get very far with his research.

There were those whom I employed in far-flung places to do research for me, with excellent results:
Frédéric Deleuze - research in the Mende Archives.
Donna Evleth - Paris Archives.
Patricia Jackson - Jamaica research.
Dianne Strang - photographing Louis' accounts at TNA.
Alison Kenney - Westminster Archives.
The Royal Archives for their kind replies to my letters and for supplying copies of source documents.

My grateful thanks to you all.

C. F. W. B., Salmo, B.C., Canada – 2015

Appendix 1: Glossary of Fabrics and Colours

The following glossary covers terms that are encountered in the text and in Louis' accounts, including his spellings. Sources: Fairchild's dictionary of textiles; Cambridge History of Western Textiles; Western World Costume: an outline history by Caroline G. Bradley; Dictionary of Textiles by Louis Harmuth. This glossary was created by Sarah Jean Waldock, with the addition of entries from my rather smaller glossary. The author would like to thank her warmly for sharing it and permitting him to publish it here.

Alamode aka Mode: Thin lightweight and glossy plain weave, very soft, usually dyed black for mourning.

Allopeen: Mixture of wool/silk or mohair/cotton

Astrakhan aka Astracan: A loosely curled fur, a kind of karakul, made from the pelt of very young lambs originally bred near Astrakhan in Russia. Also a wool fabric with a pile cut and curled to look like this.

Baize aka Bays: Coarse loosely and plain woven woollen flannel with long nap used for lining bags etc., dyed usually green or red.

Barragon: A light corded cotton.

Bath Coating: Lightweight wide fabric with long nap that is bleached or coloured; preferred as a fabric for a coat over superfine by Beau Brummell according to the tailor Schweitzer.

Beaver: Felted woollen fabric with long nap used for coating. Also the underfur of the beaver used to make hats.

Blonde aka blonde lace: Unbleached silk bobbin lace that was creamy in colour. Later bleached or dyed, black blonde being popular during French Revolution. Usually a fine mesh ground with heavier thread making up the design, often floral.

Book Muslin: In 18th century folded with the book fold, doubled lengthwise then folded to make a compact package. Later either a soft muslin for tambour work or muslin stiffened to resemble French lawn.

Boue de Paris: A dark brown based on the colour of Paris mud.

Broadcloth: A cloth woven wider than a single man could weave it, originally woven by two men and a technique used only for the highest quality woollens, later with the advent of machinery any cloth that was broad, though generally a durable cloth.

Brocade: Silk patterned with a lustre face by jacquard weaving to produce a pattern in self colour or multicolour the warps carrying across on the underside so the fabric is not reversible but may be of very complex and rich design.

Buckram: Linen treated with size or gum and used for stiffening coats.

Calendared: Treated with rollers to create a shiny finish; or in earlier times rubbed manually with a hot glass implement - see also tabby and moiré

Calico aka Callico: Plain weave lightweight painted or printed cotton; from Calicut [Calcutta]. Later use in England implies plain white/cream cloth [bleached or unbleached] 22 OR 28 yards to the piece. 18th century calico was often cotton weft on a linen warp.

Cambric: Soft plain weave cotton or linen calendared for slight lustre, similar to muslin.

Camlet/Camblet: 18th and 19th century English and French plain woven or twilled fabric made with single or double warp of wool mixed with silk or goat's hair.

Carmelite: A dark brown colour as worn by monks of that order.

Cashmere: Fine, silky wool from the cashmere goat; used to make soft, light, warm shawls of great richness.

Cassimere: See Kerseymere.

Chain Tabby: (See Tabby) Tabby with a warp twisted to resemble a chain.

Chenille: A cotton wool or silk yarn having a pile protruding all around at right angles similar to a caterpillar; used as weft for fancy goods curtains and carpets, also for embroidery and fringes. It is woven in gauze weave with cotton or linen warp and silk wool or cotton filling; the warp threads are taped in groups and the filling beaten in very closely. After weaving the fabric is cut between the bunches of warps and the latter twisted forming the chenille.

Cloud: A cotton or silk which has had the warp printed before weaving so that when woven the pattern is clouded or marked with large spots.

Coating: Heavy fabric, usually wool, which can be used to make coats.

Corduroy aka Corderoy: A ribbed cotton uncut pile fabric, hard wearing, used for trousers and dresses.

Coquelicot aka Coquelico: Colour of the wild red poppy.

Corbeau: A blackish green colour like a crow feather. Can apply to other colours with a green cast.

Covered Buttons: Buttons made by covering a core of bone, horn, wood or metal with cloth, usually the same cloth as the garment.

Crepe: A silk fabric with a crinkled surface made by filling with alternate s-twist and z-twist yarns; used for mourning.

Damascen: Damson colour (dark purple)

Damask: A jacquard fabric which is reversible, may be self coloured or bi-coloured, the pattern being raised and in satin weave on one side, the negative pattern being so on the reverse.

Death Head aka Dthead: High-crowned cloth-covered buttons.

Diaper: Originally meaning diamond; soft absorbent cloth; huckaback.

Dimity aka Dimoty: Lightweight sheer cotton fabrics with 2, 3 or more warp cords woven together, often striped or checked.

Drab: Woollen coating in brownish grey; also cloths dyed in the colour called drab (a very dark beige and its variants).

Drap de...: Cloth of.... A French term.

Drugget: Ribbed wool and worsted cloth of the 18th century.

Droguet: Mixed wool and linen or silk dress fabric.

Duck: Broad term for strong plain weave fabrics usually cotton. Often used for canvas.

Duffield aka Duffel: A coarse woollen cloth having a thick nap or frieze. (from name of Duffel, a town of Brabant, between Antwerp and Mechli).

Eiderdown aka Elderdown: 1. Down of the eider duck; 2. A soft elastic knitted fabric made of thick soft spun yarn, heavily napped on one side; 3. A loose thick woollen fabric with a deep nap on one side.

Fearnought: A coarse heavy-duty woollen cloth used for seamen's clothing.

Flannel: From Welsh word for wool, a light or medium weight fabric of plain or twill weave with a lightly napped surface; woven in such a way to make a warm cloth with softly twisted and napped filling yarns.

Florentine (silk): A heavy silk often with stripes generally used for waistcoats. Ambiguous term; has other meanings.

French Lawn: A stiff, brittle lustrous finish applied to fine lawn fabrics.

French net: A net used much for evening gowns during the Regency period.

Fustian: Woollen fabric (initially a heavy worsted); after 17th century more increasingly of cotton. Heavy fabric, plain or with raised nap. May also be known as swansdown, moleskin or velveteen.

Galloon: Narrow ribbon or braid of cotton, wool or silk used for trimming men's hats, dresses or uniforms; may contain metal threads.

Gauze: Thin sheer open weave fabric made of silk or cotton. Term derives from city of Gaza.

Genoa Velvet: 1. A very fine thick all silk velvet having large patterns, made in Genoa Italy; 2. A weft pile cotton velvet having a one and two twill ground.

Gobelin aka Goblin (scarlet): A French woollen cloth (utilising the fast red dye invented by the Gobelin dyeworks, used for hunting pinks.) A cloth generally dyed in rich dark colours.

Haircloth: Uses hair other than wool in the weave and may have plain, satin or leno (open) weave; horsehair or camel usually.

Harateen: Furnishing fabric -18th and early 19th centuries; fine worsted warp and coarser filling to make rib effect, finished by watering and stamping.

Holland: Plain woven unbleached linen, originally from Holland.

Honeycomb Velvet: Woven to give a celled effect.

Irish Diamond: Rock crystal or marcasite found near Dublin.

Irish or Irish Linen: High quality linen.

Jaconet: Thin cotton material similar to muslin.

Jean: Cotton blend twill, lighter than drill.

Kersey: Durable woollen fabric much fulled and often finished with a slightly lustrous nap. May be twill. Used for overcoats, uniforms. From English town Kersey.

Kerseymere aka Cassimere: Medium weight twill weave soft textured wool fabric.

Lace: 1. Decorations in silver wires, or woven to make tissue or cloth of gold. 2. Bobbin, point or pillow lace made from fine yarns.

Lawn: Very fine sheer plain weave linen; French lawn is a stiff and brittle finish.

Limerick: Lambskin from very young or unborn lambs used for gloves.

Lustre/ lustre fabric: Dress fabric with cotton warp and heavier lustre fibre weft like mohair or alpaca.
Lutestring aka Lustring: Fine, glossy warp-ribbed silk dress fabric.

Mantua silk: Plain weave silk in black and other colours somewhat heavier than taffeta. Dress silk, sometimes furnishings.

Marcella: A fine figured cotton piqué.

Marsella: Heavy bleached linen fabric, twill weave, soft finish.

Merino: Wool derived from the merino sheep, a twilled worsted fabric, very fine cloth.

Moiré: French for the process of making watered effects on fabrics.

Moleskin: A very strong stout smooth cotton fabric made with one set of warp and two sets of filling of the same yarn spun two picks on the face and one pick on the back, the former combined with alternate warp ends forming a modified satin weave.

Muslin: Fine firm, plain weave cottons, lightweight. May be figured by having a heavier thread woven for lines, wavy lines or checked appearance, gold or silver with metallic thread woven in or printed with gold or silver leaf. Usually to be found in white or pastel in the Regency. 10 yards to the piece.

Nankeen aka Nankin: Durable firm textured cotton originally from Nanking, made from undyed brownish-yellow cotton.

Noisette aka Noiset: Hazel nut coloured.

Olivet: An oval button or piece of wood covered with silk or worsted and used for fastening a garment by means of a loop of braid.

Orlean: Lightweight fabric originated in England in the early part of the 19th century. It was woven usually in plain but also in five harness twill with a two ply cotton warp and worsted filling which completely covered the warp, and was dyed in the piece.

Paduasoy aka padaway: Group of heavy rich corded silk fabrics made in Padua Italy, popular in 17th and 18th centuries. Later (late 19th C) called repp.

Panion: A high quality black cloth imported from France.

Persian or Silk Persian: Lightweight plainweave silk lining fabric printed with large floral patterns; in use from 18th century.

Plaid: A tabby weave wool in the particular colours and arrangement of chequered pattern specific to the various highland clans. Found also in silk during the craze for plaid in 1789.

Plush aka Pluch aka Peluche: Originally a silk velvet or fustian.

Poplin: Durable plainweave fabric, usually a cotton broadcloth.

Puffs: Decorative gatherings of cloth often on the strings of breeches; pom-poms.

Ratteen aka Ratine: A coarse, loosely woven cloth, slightly nubby.

Russian duck: Fine bleached linen duck for summer garments.

Sarsanet aka sarcenet aka sarsnet etc.: In Regency usage, a fine thin silk fabric with a soft finish in plain or twill, after 19th century a plain weave piece-dyed cotton.

Satin aka Sattin: A smooth, lustrous silk fabric which may have a less lustrous back in the purest use of the term. Satin weave is achieved by the domination of warp yarns on the face.

Satin jean: Heavy durable cotton jean, highly twilled, with smooth glossy surface.

Satin Merino: Wool fabric with lustrous face and napped back, women's clothing early 19th century.

Satteen: Stout lustrous piece-dyed cotton fabric made in satin weave either in warp or filling flush. Also comes printed or in stripes, used for lining.

Saxon Blue: Dye made by dissolving indigo in oil of vitriol.

Saxon Green: Colour made by using yellow dye on Saxon blue fabric.

Serge: Twill with diagonal ridges on both sides. Worsted serge is used for uniforms, coats etc..

Shalloon: Twilled worsted fabric, made in England and France in 18th century.

Spring Silk: The higher quality silk is that produced in the Spring.

Superfine: Usually black woollen coat fabric much fulled and sheared for a soft finish; may also refer to kerseymere with silk or mohair included.

Spagnolet aka Spaniolet: See Espagnolette.

Stocking aka Stockinet(te): Any knitted fabric produced on a frame or machine, with a stretchy quality.

Swan(s)down: Twill weave cotton finished with a nap and used for underwear.

Tabby aka watered silk aka moiré: A watered effect caused by the finishing on a ribbed fabric where the crushing of some parts through rollers causes the play of light to give a rippled effect.
Tabbinett aka Tabinet: A fine drapery poplin of silk warp and wool filling with moiré finish.

Tambour: Embroidery in chain and other stitches over a sheer material stretched on a frame.

Tammy: In 18th and 19th centuries fine worsted dress fabric, high lustre finish.

Tissue: Gold or silver lamé cf. cloth-of-gold of earlier periods.

Toilinet: Plain poplin with a silk warp and woollen weft.

Velour aka Valure: Napped cloth similar to velvet.

Velveret: Cotton velvet often ribbed or printed with a pattern.

Velvet: Piled fabric, initially silk, woven on a epingle loom that lifts loops above the ground. The pile may be cut or left in loops, may be of different heights in patterns forming figured velvets, or parts of the pile voided (left showing a satin ground) by the original jacquard weave or by being etched out with acid. Brocaded velvet may have pile of different colours in a brocaded pattern.

Velveteen: A cotton velvet-like fabric but the pile is made with the filler not with the warp as in a true velvet.

Vigonia: Vicuña woven from the long soft brownish hair of the South American vicuña goat.

Worsted aka Worstead: Cloth woven from long combed wool.

Appendix 2: Georgian Tailoring Stitches
(As reproduced from the anonymous book *The Tailor*, 1801.)

And here it will be proper, before giving directions for sewing, first to enumerate the different kinds of stitches, and then to explain, as clearly as may be possible, the manner in which each of them is done. And, first, as to the different sorts of stitches, which are the basting-stitch, the back and fore-stitch, the back-stitch, the side-stitch, and the fore-stitch; also the back-pricking stitch, the fore-pricking stitch, the serging-stitch, the cross-stitch, and the button-hole stitch; besides which there is a distinct kind of stitch for hemming, filling, stotting, rantering, fine-drawing, prick-drawing, over-casting, and also for making what are called covered buttons. (The only difference between the pricking stitches, and the back-stitch and fore-stitch is, that the needle is not, as in them, turned up, and brought back through the cloth, but is first put entirely through, and then passed back again, so as to ensure a thorough hold being taken of the cloth on each side. It is used in thick fabrics, where great strength of workmanship is required).

The basting-stitch is a long and slight stitch, intended to be merely temporary, or to fasten together some of the inner and concealed parts of the garments. It is commonly used to keep the work in its proper position while being sewed.

The back and fore-stitch is made, as the name implies, by the union of back- stitching and fore-stitching; in this stitch the needle is first put through the cloth, and turned up in as short a space as is possible, so as to make a neat and strong stitch when completed; it is then put through the cloth again in the same place as at first, and again turned up, taking care that it passes through the cloth as nearly as possible within the same space as before. This being done, the first back-stitch is completed. The second stitch is made by passing the needle forward upon the surface of the cloth, but without taking hold of it, over a space equal to the length of the first stitch; the needle is then again put through the cloth, turned up, and brought back to the place where it was last put through, so as to form another back-stitch; which is followed by another putting of the needle forward, or, in plainer terms, another fore-stitch, and so on, in the same order, until the seam is finished. This kind of stitch is used for sewing linings, pockets, flannel garments, and other thin fabrics. There is no need to say much respecting the back-stitch, as this may be understood from what is said above respecting the first stitch in back and fore-stitching. This stitch is used for seams where strength is required; it is also sometimes used for ornament, instead of the side- stitch, but in this case it must be very neatly and regularly made.

The side-stitch is used for the edges of garments, to keep them from rolling over, or from being drawn out of shape. It is always intended for ornament as well as use, and requires a very quick eye and a careful hand to do it well. In this stitch the needle is passed through the cloth a little above or below the place from which it came out in the former stitch, but it must be at a very little distance from this place, or the sewing silk will be visible on the surface of the cloth, which is a great blemish, and yet it must be far enough away from where it came out to prevent its breaking through, in which case the stitch is lost, both as to use and ornament. Care must also be taken, that the stitches are at regular distances from each other, and that the whole of them are placed at the same distance from the edge of the cloth. In the fore-stitch, as has been already hinted, the needle, when drawn out from the seam, is always put forward, so that an equal quantity of thread, or a stitch of the same length, is visible on each surface of the cloth.

Serge-stitching is done by passing the needle through the cloth, from the under to the upper piece, throwing the thread over the edges of the cloth so as to keep them closely together. It is also used to join selvages together, as also to prevent taking up more space for seams than can be spared, when the pieces are barely large enough for the required purpose. It is not, however, much used by tailors, except where no great degree of strength is required.

The cross-stitch is formed by two parallel rows of stitches, so placed as that the stitch in the upper row is opposite to the vacant space in the lower one, the thread passing from one stitch to the other in diagonal lines. It is used for keeping open the seams of such garments as require washing, and also for securing the edges from ravelling out, in such fabrics as are too loosely made to allow of their edges being fastened down by the filling-stitch.

In the button-hole stitch, the needle is first put through the cloth from the inner to the outer surface, and before it is drawn out the twist is passed round the point of the needle, and kept in that position till the needle be drawn out to the full extent of the twist; this forms a kind of loop, called by tailors the "purl", at the top or edge of the opening, and, when regularly made, is both useful and ornamental. To increase the strength of this stitch, and also to aid in making it true or exact, a "bar" is formed on each side of the opening, before the hole is begun to be worked. This "bar", as it is called, is made by passing the needle from one end of the opening to the other (one, two, or more times), so as that there is a layer, if it may so be called, of twist stretching along its whole length (and on each side), upon which the whole is worked, the workman taking care to keep the "bar" as near to the edge of the opening as is possible, without allowing it to come over, in which case the button-hole will be neither strong nor neat.

There is not much need to say any thing about the hemming-stitch, as almost every lad will have had opportunities of seeing this used by his mother, his sisters, or other females. It may, therefore, suffice for this to say, that care must be taken to set it regularly, and also as closely together as may be either convenient or sightly. It must also be observed, that the needle is not to be deeply inserted, as it is necessary that the stitch should be as little visible as is possible on the other side of the cloth. The hand moreover must not be drawn in roughly, or by a snatch, but so gently as to prevent contracting the hem.

The filling-stitch is similar to that used in hemming; the chief difference being in the direction given to the needle. In hemming, its point is directed outwards, or from the workman, but in filling it is directed inwards, or towards him, and in each should be a little, but only a little slanted, in order to give the sewing a neat appearance. This stitch is used for sewing on facings, and when made with neatness, and without showing itself much on the outer side of the cloth, is considered to be ornamental, as well as useful.

Stotting (pronounced stoating) is the stitch used for joining pieces of cloth so neatly as that the join shall be but little visible, and yet strong enough to prevent the pieces from being easily parted. In this kind of seam the pieces of cloth are not laid the one upon the other, as in back-stitching, but are placed side by side, the edges being carefully fitted, so as to prevent any irregularity or roughness in the work. They are then sewn together by passing the needle half through the thickness of the cloth. Care must be taken to keep the stitches as near to each edge of the cloth as can be done without incurring the danger of its breaking through. The needle is put in on the nearest edge of the two, and must not be slanted in the direction given to it, but put as straight forward as possible. The stitch should be drawn close enough home to prevent the silk thread from showing itself on the right side of the cloth, but yet not so close as to draw the edges into a ridge. If the join be as neatly made as it may be, it will, when properly pressed, be barely perceptible. This stitch is used for joining the pieces of cloth of which facings, collar-linings, and other fillings-up of the inner sides of garments, are made, and also in other cases to preventing the taking up too much of the cloth by making a back-stitched seam.

Rantering, like stotting, is intended to conceal a join in the cloth. Here, however, it is requisite to make a strong as well as a neat joining; and, therefore, a seam is first sewn with a fore-stitch, and then the rantering-stitch is worked upon or over this seam. It should he worked with a very fine silk thread, or with twist that has had one of the strands taken out. The needle should be both long and slender, and must be passed forwards and backwards over the seam, so as to catch hold of its two sides, and draw them closely together; but, in doing this, care must be taken not to take a deep hold of the cloth - the nap or wool is all that should be taken hold of, and this must be done with a light hand, while the stitches must be placed close to each other, so that the seam may be well covered with wool; when this is done, the seam has to be "rubbed up", that is to say, it must be held between the forefinger and thumb of each hand, these being placed upon the fore-stitching, and its two edges brought as closely together as possible. The rantering must then be slightly carded or scratched, backwards and forwards, with the point of a needle, in order to bring the wool out again where it has been drawn in with the stitch; the seam is then ready for pressing, and, if this operation be properly performed, will be as much concealed as may be necessary; while it will be much stronger than if it had been merely back-stitched.

In fine-drawing, the stitch is formed in the same manner as in rantering, but there is a difference in the way of placing the pieces that are to be joined, i.e., if they be separate pieces, for this stitch is mostly used to close up places that have been accidentally cut, or torn; the two edges of the place requiring to be fine-drawn are first trimmed by cutting away the loose threads or ends of the cloth which may be upon them; they are then placed and kept in as level or flat a position as is possible, either with the fingers, nearest edge of the two, and must not be slanted in, or by fastening them to a piece of stiff paper. The needle should be both very small and long, and the thread used, whether it be of silk or twist, should be very slender. Greater care is here necessary than in rantering, to avoid taking a deep hold of the cloth; the needle should be passed forwards and backwards, over the opening, and the thread should be drawn no closer or tighter than is quite needful, in order to hide it in the wool. The stitches must be placed as near to each other as is possible, so as to prevent the edges of the cloth from being visible between them; if it be needful to make a strong as well as a neat joining, the fine-drawing should be repeated on the under side of the cloth, but here it will not be needful to put the stitches so close together. When the fine-drawing is done it must be pressed, but with as light a hand and in as short a time as is practicable, otherwise the sewing, however neatly done, will be visible, and so far as it is so, the design of the fine-drawing stitch will not be answered.

The stitch called prick-drawing is now but seldom used, yet it may be proper to notice it briefly. When this stitch is intended to be employed, the edges of the cloth are first stotted together, after which the needle is passed backwards and forwards in diagonal lines, under the stotting, so as to make the join more strong and durable, than it can be made by merely stotting the pieces together. This stitch is used where the cloth is very thick, or hard and unyielding, and, consequently, where the stotting-stitch would quickly give way without this support. It is also better than a back-stitched seam for cloths of this description, inasmuch as it can be made to lie more flat, and thus to be more neat in its appearance than a common seam.

Overcasting is used merely to secure the edges of thin and loose fabrics from "ravelling out". In using it, the edges of the cloth, whether it be woollen, linen, or cotton, are first trimmed clear of the loose threads; the needle is then passed through the cloth in a forward direction, at about the distance of one-eighth part of an inch from the edge of the cloth, and when drawn out it is carried (from the left to the right, and not, as in other stitches, from the right to the left) about a quarter of an inch; it is then again put through, and on being drawn out it is made to pass over the thread leading from the preceding stitch, so as to form a kind of loop on the edge; which loop secures the edge from becoming too much frayed, or ravelled.

In making cloth buttons, which formerly were almost universally worn, and probably will be again, it is necessary to see that the bone moulds over which the cloth is to be drawn, are all of the same size and thickness. Very thick moulds should be thrown aside, as also should such as are very thin; for the first will make the button too clumsy, and the last will - most likely - soon break. The coverings should then be cut in as near to a circular shape as is easily practicable, and should be cut of that size which will allow of the edges, when turned over the mould, nearly meeting each other. They are then to be slightly sewn round near the edge, and with a running stitch, either a serge or a fore-stitch, according as the material used may require; for if it be likely to ravel much it will be necessary to use the sergeing stitch. When this is done, the edge is gently drawn together, but no farther than will allow room for inserting the mould, which is then put in, as nearly in the middle of the covering as possible. The thread is then drawn tight, so as to bring the edges of the cover close together, and then the needle is passed over the gatherings from the near edge of the button to the opposite one, the maker taking care to keep regularly turning the button round with the forefinger and thumb of the left hand, so as to carry the sewing over every part of the gatherings. The bottom of the button will thus be composed of thread, and therefore may be far more strongly sewn on the garment than if it were fastened on by sewing it merely through the covering. [The Tailor: Anon, c. 1801]

Appendix 3: List of London Master Tailors in 1799

A report in *The Times*, of Saturday 27 January 1800 described a meeting of two hundred and thirty-four master tailors which had taken place on 22 December 1799 at the Freemason's Tavern in Great Queen Street. There was much agitation amongst the journeymen following the imposition of the Combination Act of that year, which prohibited workers from forming combinations (i.e., trade unions) to try to secure higher pay and better conditions. The resolution appended the names and addresses of the master tailors who attended the meeting, so it is therefore a useful reference list. Louis does not appear, as he had retired by then, and his business had been sold to Thomas Shepherd.

At a General Meeting of Master Taylors on Monday evening last, Mr. Smith in the Chair,
IT WAS RESOLVED,
1. That it appears to this Meeting, that, notwithstanding the public invitations and admonitions given by the Masters to the Journeymen Taylors, the Leaders and Advisors of the Journeymen still continue their dangerous and alarming conspiracy, to deter those who, amongst their own body, are willing and desirous to return to their duty, and their respective employers
2. That the advance of wages, now illegally demanded by the Journeymen of the Masters, is wholly out of their power to grant.
3. That the facility with which the Journeymen obtained an advance of wages in the year 1795, and at former periods, has enduced them to form the present conspiracy, a conspiracy of a more alarming nature than the Public at large are probably aware of, and which has involved the Master Taylors in a very perilous situation, the journeymen having it in their contemplation to prosecute them for having, in compliance with their demands, given them for a number of years, more wages than by Act of Parliament is allowed.

4. That it is the opinion of this meeting, that the Journeymen are extremely culpable by thus undeservedly distressing their Masters. As the same Act of Parliament grants them liberty at all times, under any grievance, to apply to the Lord mayor and Court of Aldermen of the City of London, who have full power vested in them, by virtue of the same act, to raise and regulate their wages whenever the exigencies of the time may require, to which decision the masters will cheerfully submit.
5. That inasmuch as the Journeymen are incorrigible, and do encourage and carry on their combinations in defiance of the law, to the great inconvenience of the public and stagnation of trade, the masters have, in consequence of their embarrassed situation, been obliged to apply to Parliament for relief.
6. That it is the resolution of this Meeting, that the measures adopted should be persisted in, even if the Journeymen should agree to return to their work at the late wages.
7. That it is the opinion of this Meeting, thay in order to destroy the combinations that exist among Journeymen Taylors, it is absolutely necessary to abolish public houses of call.
8. That, in order to set a great example to all Master Taylors, as well as to inform the Public in general of the unanimous determination of this Meeting, that the Resolutions of this Meeting shall be published, with the name of every person present.
9. That this Meeting do acknowledge, with the greatest gratitude, the kind indulgence they have experienced from the Nobility, Gentry and Public, in having suspended their orders, and they beg such further indulgencies as the existing circumstances may require.
10. That the Thanks of this Meeting be given to the Chairman for his candid and impartial conduct.
By Order of the Meeting, J. Mullett, Secretary.

Adams and Baker, Southampton-street, Covent Garden
Allan, Thomas, Bond-street
Anderson, Alexander, Union-street, Bond-street
Arbuthnot, Jos., Crown-court
Armstrong,-, Margaret-street, Cavendish-square

Atkinson, George, Castle-street, Leicester-fields
Bagster, George, Beaufort-buildings
Balard, Charles, Maddox-street
Barber,-, Haymarket
Barker, thomas, Basinghall-street
Barnes, Jos., Gracechurch-street
Barnes, Thomas, Broad-street, Carnaby-market
Bayley Christoper, Bedfordbury
Bayne, William, Cornhill
Beatly,-, Strand
Bell, John, Bateman-buildings
Bell, Matthew, Marybone-street, St. James's
Bichner, Otto, Soho-square
Binks, Christopher, King-street, Covent-garden
Bishop, Charles, Mount-street
Bower, Henry, Great Marlborough-street
Bowling, Nathaniel, Newcastle-court, Boswell-street
Brockleby and Co., 65, Margaret-street
Brown, George, Old Cavendish-street
Buck, Jarvis, 28, Arundel-street, Strand
Buckmaster, John, St. James's-street
Burgh, Charles
Callow, William, Greville-street, Hatton-garden
Callow, Paul, Arundel-street
Cameron, Angers, Noble-street, Cheapside
Cameron, John, Great Marlborough-street
Camppin,-, Greenland-dock
Cartwright, Thomas, Grosvenor-street
Cecil, Thomas, Jewin-street, Aldgate
Cepheld, Davidm Greek-street, Soho
Chambers, William, Charlotte-street, Portland-place
Christie, Samuel, Poland-street
Clark, John, Pancras-lane, Cheapside
Coe and Carr, White Hart-court, Bishopsgate
Cook, Thomas, King-street, Holborn
Cook, Thomas, Tavistock-street
Copley, John, Bolt-court, Fleet-street
Corner, Henry, Maddox-street
Couttee,-, Green-walk

Coward, William, Haymarket
Cox, Thomas, Leicester-place
Craven, William, Arundel-street
Creed, William, Finch-lane, Cornhill
Croft, Robert, Fleet-street
Cruett, John, Queen-street, Soho
Darley, Thomas, St. Michael's-alley, Cornhill
Davies, John, Cork-street
Davison, Anthony, Craven-buildings, Drury-lane
Deane, William, Argyle-street
Delin, Benjamin, Portland-street
Deraad, Walter, Marlborough-street, St. James's
Dietrichsen, Frederick, Rathbone-place
Dixon, Lindsey, Greek-street, Soho
Donaldson, John Staples-inn-buildings
Dunn, John, Bedford-street
Edward, Thomas, Hatton-garden
Edward, Joel, Greville-street, Hatton-garden
Edwards, T. and J., Broad-street, St. James's
Elliott, James, Berwick-street, Soho
Elliott, William, Berwick-street, Soho
Emmott, William, Leicester-fields
Evans, Richard, 194, Oxford-street
Fancook, Charles, Jermyn-street
Farrant and Co., Bedford-street
Filby, Miles, Pilgrim-street, Ludgate-hill
Finke and Co., Mortimer-street
Fisher, Robert, Bedford-street
Fisher, Peter, Castle-street, Leicester-fields
Ford, John, Strand
Forsyth, Alexander, Vere-street
Fortell, Jos., Suffolk-street
Fox, George, Henrietta-street
Fraser, Duncan. Titchfield-street, Oxford-street
Gerath, Casper, Church-street, Soho
Gibbs, James, Rupert-street, Soho
Gibson, John, Wells-street, Oxford-street
Glover, Thomas, Berners-street, Oxford-street
Goff, Richard, Adam-street, Manchester-square

Gordon, Alexander, Church-street, Soho
Graham, John, Cook's-court, Cary-street
Graham, William, Lothbury
Griffiths, Samuel, Old Boswell-court
Gwynne, David, Frith-street, Soho
Habberer, Poland-street
Hare, John, Little Stanhope-street, Mayfair
Hawkins, Thomas, Margaret-street
Hecking, Thomas, White Hart-court, Bishopsgate-street
Heron and Jones, South Molton-street
Heward, James, Chapel-court, Swallow-street
Hollier, Nicholson, Borough
Hood, James, Burlington-street
Horspool, Richard, Tavistock-street
Howell, John, King-street
Hunter, Thomas, Maddox-street
Hurd, Thomas, South-street
Inglish, James, Orange-street, Leicester-fields
Isaac, Thomas, Wimpole-street
Jackson, Thomas, Argyle-street
Jackson, James, Clement's Inn
Jennings, William, Covent-garden
Jones, Rice, Carlton-place
Keene, William, South Audley-street
Kemp, George, Great Pulteney-street
Key, John, Freeschool-street, Horslydown
King and Thompson, Little Maddox-street
Kolbe, John, 18, Broad-street, Soho
Laffan and Shee, Welbeck-street
Lamas, James, 4, Chapel-street, Lamb's Conduit-street
Lane, Richard, Charing-cross
Lanman, John, Hanover-street
Leverick, William, White's-alley, Chancery-lane
Lister, Richard, Little Stanhope-street, Mayfair
Little, Robert, 12, Garlick-hill
Lloyd, William, Beaufort-buildings
Logan, Samuel, South Molton-street
Lucas, Stephen, Greek-street, Soho
Lyne, George, Cecil-street, Strand

Mallam, Thomas, Shepherd-street, Mayfair
Matlers, William, Boyle-street
McCallan, Beaufort-buildings
McCarthy, Margaret-street, Cavendish-square
McKellar, Duncan, Cecil-street
McKenzie, Alexander, 4, Oxenden-street
McRonald, Alexander, Crown-street, Westminster
Meek, John, 17, Prince's-street, Bank
Meesk, Henry, Edward-street, Portland-place
Meyer and Co., 25, Mortimer-street
Micheson, Thomas, 10, Salisbury-street, Strand
Micklam, James, Wells-street, Oxford-street
Middleton, St. James's-street
Millar, John, Store-street
Milna, James, Grosvenor-street
Monkhouse, Thomas, Jermyn-street
Morrison, George, Parliament-street
Morse, William, Conduit-street
Moss, John, East-street, Red Lion-square
Nash, John, Salisbury-court, Fleet-street
Neil, Felix, Prince's-street, Hanover-square
Neupert, J. G., Poland-street, St. James's
Newman, Henry, Norfolk-street
Nix, James, Strand
Oliver, John, Warwick-street, Charing-cross
Onion, John, Essex-street
Orier, Thomas, Poland-street
Otley, Bond-street
Otto, Frederick, Berners-street, Oxford-street
Owen, Owen, Bond-street
Owen, David, Norfolk-street
Parkinson, James, Hatton-garden
Pearce, Sampson, Silver-street, Golden-square
Pearce, -, Greek-street, Soho
Penny, Stephen, King-street, Golden-square
Pepperill, Daniel, Featherstone-buildings
Philip, Robert, 52, Red Lion-street, Clerkenwell
Plagenberg, Mary-le-bonne-street
Pool, John, 30, Camomile-street

Popjoy, James, Water-lane, Blackfriars
Powell, James, 12, London-wall
Prosser, John, Strand
Pugh, William, 54, Berwick-street, Soho
Rait, James, 83, Minories
Rayner, Joseph, 81, Jermyn-street
Regnier, John, Leicester-fields
Rentz, Christopher, Great Pulteney-street
Ring, John, Borough
Robertson, David, Devonshire-street, Bishopsgate-street
Robertson, James, Whitechapel-road
Robertson, William, Duke-street, Portland-place
Ross, William, Broad-street, Carnaby-market
Russell, John, Blackfriar's-road
Sanders and Greece, Newport-street, Soho
Scarfe and Willis, Fleet-street
Schweitzer and Davison, Cork-street
Scott, Henry, Jermyn-street
Scott, Thomas, Kirby-street, Hatton-garden
Scott, Robert, Arundel-street, Strand
Sedgley, T., Bond-street
Shepherd, Thomas, 22 Grosvenor-street
Sheriff, Alexander, Newman-street
Shur, George, Wells-street, Oxford-street
Simms, William, King-street, Soho
Sizeland, John, Wimpole-street
Slater, Samuel, Surry-street, Strand
Smith, S., Litchfield-street, Soho
Smith, John, Craven-street, Strand
Smith, F., Prince's-street, Hanover-square
Sohaar, Charles, Great Pulteney-street
Somerville, William, Green-court, Cary-street
Soranson, Christopher, Newman-street, Soho
Staples, John, Hollis-street, Clare-market
Starck, Alexander, Buckingham-street
Stephen, William, Warwick-street, Charing-cross
Strachan, William, Oxendon-street
Stratton, Francis, Queen-square, Aldersgate-street
Strickland. Samuel, St. Martin's-lane, Leicester-fields

Stuart, John, Finch-lane
Taylor, John, 35, Bow-lane
Taylor, Thomas, Green-street, Leicester-fields
Taylor, Throgmorton-street
Tempany, William, High-street, Marylebone
Thomas, John, Devereux-court
Thompson, James, Adam-street, Manchester-square
Thompson, Peter, Frith-street, Soho
Thompson, Joseph, Cloysters
Toon, Daniel, Crown-street, Westminster
Trail, John, James-street, Golden-square
Twentyman, William, Davies-street, Grosvenor-square
Usher, John, Featherstone-buildings
Vantandaloe, Thomas, Great Titchfield-street
Vernon, -, Charing-cross
Vigurs, John, Southampton-street, Covent-garden
Wallace, David, Bridge-street, Westminster
Watkins, Robert, Mount-street
Welker, -, Warwick-street, St. James's
West, Joseph, Charles-street, Covent-garden
Weston, John, Featherstone-buildings
Wettig, Frederick, Duke-street, Portland-place
Weyrick, Henry, Berwick-street, Soho
Williams, Peter, George-street, Foster-lane
Williams, Richard, Philip-lane, London-wall
Wilson, Thomas, Store-street
Wilson, Samuel, East-street, Red Lion-square
Windlier, John and Henry, Rathbone-place
Winter, Sim., Bury-street, St. James's
Wood, George, Pall-mall
Wright, Robert, Cary-street
Wynn, William, Staples-inn-buildings
Young, Charles, Vine-street, St. James's
Young, Charles, Beaufort-buildings.

Appendix 4: Louis Bazalgette's Accounts to the Prince of Wales for 1790

This is a transcription of a specimen year only, as the full accounts occupy over 280 pages and therefore could not be included. The full accounts from 1786-1795 are available by email from the author. The running total is carried forward at the end of each page of the original and also at the end of each quarter. Note: These accounts are not crown copyright as they are not the work of a crown servant. The transcriptions I regard as my copyright and this should be acknowledged if they are used in any published work.

Date   Description   Cost   Total

January 1790
1   Altering a Hussar coat & new lining it with silk for Mr. Nutsell   5/-
    6 yds brown silk to line do. – 6/6   1/19/-
    Putting new welts & pockets to a scarlet quilting vest &
    edging the welts with fringe   2/6
    New pockets & black silk fringes   2/-
    Altering a black cassimere embroidered vest & for new
    pockets & welts &c.   2/-
    Additional embroidery to do.   10/-
    Altering a buff cassimere breeches   2/6
2   Altering a hunt frock, taking out the body lining & making
    a French riding sleeve to do.   6/-
    4 G. P. breast buttons – 8/-   2/8
    Altering a white spaniolet waistcoat and for new silk sleeves
    to do.   10/6
    Altering 22 diff't vests & putting welts & pockets to 15 of do.
    – 2/- each   2/4/-
    15 pair pockets & welts at 1/6 each   1/2/6
    Altering 3 pair cotton breeches   5/-   7/13/8
    To making a carmelite col'd cloth dress coat & waistcoat
    laced gold & gold loops & tassells to coat & all materials for
    Mr. Sackville, as the others   8/5/-
4   Taking out body and sleeve lining from a hunt frock & new
    lining the sleeves with sattin   3/-
    New sattin sleeve lining &c.   12/-

329

	Altering another scarlet coat	5/-	1/-/-
	To a fine Abergavenny flannell under vest with sleeves compleat		1/5/-
	To a fine white spaniolet vest with sleeves & all materials		2/4/6
	To a fine Welch flannell under vest with sleeves compleat		1/5/-
	Altering a sattin embroidered vest & for new welts & pockets	7/-	
	Altering 2 embroidered quilting vests & for new pockets &c.	6/-	
	Cleaning do. – 18d each	3/-	16/-
5	30 fine wove butt's – 2/6	6/3	
	Making a dark mixt beaver lapelled frock & all materials (own beaver)	1/11/9	1/18/-
	To a pair drab col'd cassimere breeches & all materials	2/-/-	
	Extra for embroidering do. in silks	18/-	2/18/-
	2 pair of drawers		15/-
	Altering 3 embroid'd sattin vests making new welts & po. to do. – 5/- each		15/-
	To making a cloth dress coat & waistcoat, laced & looped with gold & all materials as before for Mr. Weltje Junior		8/5/-
	Carried forward		37/-/2
	Embroidering new shirts with fishes, buckles &c. for a sattin waistcoat for Mr. Weltje Sen'r	1/10/-	
	New making up do. again. Sattin for shirts & to piece the sides &c.	15/-	2/5/-
6	15 round top plated butt's – 8/- 6 br.	11/4	
	Black velvet coller	10/-	
	Making a green mixt beaver frock & all materials (own beaver)	1/11/9	2/13/1
	To making a dress suit for Colonel Lake (own velvet & emb'd vest)	1/5/-	
	8 yds white sattin to line – 10/6	4/4/-	
	Silk sleeve lining, holl'd pockets	10/6	
	Backs body lining & pockets	8/-	
	Waistband lining & pockets	5/-	
	28 covered buttons – 2/6	5/10	
	28 breast do. – 1/3	2/11	
	Sewing silk & twist	5/-	7/6/3
	Altering 2 sattin embroid'd vests, making new welts & po. to do. & for welts &c. – 5/- each	10/-	
	Altering a black cassimere embroid'd do. & embroid'g the tops of lapells &c.	6/-	

	Paid for embroid'g do. & for the welts &c.	5/-	
	New forepart lining & interlining	2/6	
7	Altering 3 pair of breeches	9/-	
	Altering 4 embroid'd vests & putting new welts & po. to do. – 2/6 each	10/-	
	Stuff for welts & po. to 2 of them – 18d each	3/-	
	Altering 5 striped sattin vests, & making new welts & po. to do. – 2/6 each	12/6	2/18/-
	To a pair black silk stocking breeches & all materials as usual		2/14/-
	To a pair drab col'd cassimere do.		2/-/-
	Extra for embroid'g the cassimere ones		18/-
	4 pair drawers – 7/6		1/10/-
8	Altering a scarlet embroid'd vest & for linnen		2/6
	1 ½ yds buff spaniolet – 10/-	15/-	
	28 dthead butt's – 15d	3/-	
	Making a vest & all materials of do.	1/-/6	1/18/6
	To making a carmelite col'd cloth dress coat & waistcoat laced & looped with gold & all materials as usual for Mr. Soliel		8/5/-
	Blue velvet coller	10/-	
	16 silver engraved H. H. butt's – 3/6 each	2/16/-	
	6 breast do. – 2/- each	12/-	
	Making a Hampshire Hunt frock & all materials as usual (own blue cloth)	1/11/9	5/9/9
	Altering 3 str. sattin vests & making welts & po. to do. – 2/6 each	7/6	
	Altering a beaver frock	2/6	10/-
	To a fine flannell shirt compleat		1/5/-
	Altering a cassimere breeches	2/6	
9	Altering 2 frocks & putting a velvet coller on one of them		5/-
	Pea green velvet coller	10/-	
11	Altering a buff embroid'd vest	3/-	
12	Altering a 10th Dragoon coat & putting a new coller to do.		5/-
	Yellow cloth coller & silk to line	2/6	
	New buttoning a spotted sattin vest	1/-	
	24 covered buttons – 2/6	2/6	1/11/6
	Carried forward		78/6/9
13	New buttoning a str. beaver frock and putting a velvet coller on do.	6/-	
	18 rich steel buttons – 3/- each	2/14/-	
	Velvet coller &c.	10/-	
	New buttoning & putting a new coller as above on a		

	str. cloth frock	6/-	
	18 buttons as above – 3/- each	2/14/-	
	Velvet coller	10/-	7/-/-
	To a buff spaniolet waistcoat. Edges bound & compleat as before		2/1/6
15	To making a 10th Dragoon coat, laced & looped compleat as usual (own lace & cloth)		5/13/4
	New buttoning a str. frock & putting a velvet coller on do.	6/-	
	18 rich enamel butt's – 2/6 each	2/5/-	
	Velvet coller	10/-	3/1/-
	9 yds puce col'd & pink spot velvet – 42/-	18/18/-	
	28 rich embroid'd buttons – 3/- each	4/4/-	
	28 breast do. – 1/6	2/2/-	
	Making a velvet dress coat & breeches and silver tissue vest & coat cuffs all richly trim'd with a very rich applica, the coat all over the seams and the wais't all over & all materials as usual (own applica & vest & coat cuffs)	3/17/9	
	Paid for embroidering the applica on & making considerable additions to do.	50/-/-	79/1/9
	2 pair drawers		15/-
	To a buff spaniolet vest compleat as the last		2/1/6
16	Altering 2 pair buff breeches	2/-	
18	New lining an embroid'd dress suit with own white sattin	10/6	12/6
	Making a Hampshire Hunt frock and all materials as usual (own cloth & butt's)		1/11/9
	Putting a cloth coller on a blue coat & altering a velvet dress breeches		5/-
	16 plated breast buttons – 4/-	5/4	
	Flannell sleeves to a vest	3/6	
	Making a white duff'd waistcoat & all materials (own duff'd)	1/-/6	1/9/4
20	Altering a cotton stocking breeches		
21	9 yds puce, pink & green spot velvet – 42/-	18/18/-	
	Embroid'd white sattin vest in gold, silver &c.	9/9/-	
	28 covered buttons – 2/6	5/10	
	28 breast do. – 1/3	2/11	
	Making a dress suit of the above & all materials as usual	3/17/9	32/13/6
	2 pair drawers		15/-
	Altering a Hussar jacquet & waistcoat for Mr. Nutsell	2/6	

	Putting a large white velvet coller on a white spaniolet Waistcoat	1/6	
	Velvet coller	10/-	14/-
	1 ½ yds str. silk toilinet – 12/-	18/-	
	Silk binding for the edges	3/6	
	30 plated ball butt's – 10/-	1/5/-	
	Making a vest & all materials of do.	1/-/6	3/7/-
22	Altering 2 beaver frocks, 2 vests & 5 pair breeches	1/6	
	Black velvet coller to one coat	10/-	
23	Altering a 10th Dragoon coat and cotton stocking breeches & for coller lining to coat	6/6	2/2/6
	Carried forward		221/14/5
25	Altering 5 pair buckles		18/-
	To a Fox uniform frock & all materials as usual (own cloth)		4/10/9
27	Altering a blue cloth frock & putting on a large cloth coller & for cloth		3/6
	Altering a drab col'd cassimere breeches	1/-	
29	Altering 2 pair cotton stocking breeches	5/-	6/-
	Making 2 cassimere embroid'd vests (scarlet & black) & all materials as usual – 20/6 each (own foreparts)	2/1/-	
	Embroidering 3 dozen butt's to do. – 2/6	7/6	2/8/6
	Putting a velvet coller on a frock	1/6	
	Black velvet coller	10/-	
	Putting welts & pockets to 2 quilting vests & for welts, pockets &c. – 4/- each	8/-	
	Altering a blue cloth frock	2/6	1/2/-
	Altering a breeches		1/-
	To a pair nankeen col'd stocking breeches & all materials		1/16/-
	2 pair drawers		15/-
30	To a pair black silk stocking breeches & all materials		2/14/-
	2 pair drawers		15/-
	Cleaning 3 pair breeches – 18d each		4/6
	To a Fox uniform lapelled frock and all materials as usual (own cloth)		4/10/9
	1 ½ yds fancy silk toilinet 12/-	18/-	
	Silk binding for edges	3/6	
	36 plated ball buttons – 10/-	1/10/-	
	Making a wais't & all materials of do.	1/-/6	3/12/-
	Altering 2 frocks & 2 pair of cotton stocking breeches		8/-
	To a pair nankeen col'd cotton stocking breeches compleat as usual		1/16/-
	2 pair of drawers		15/-
	1 ½ yds str. toilinet – 12/-	18/-	

	Silk binding for the edges	3/6	
	30 plated buttons on bone – 4/-	10/-	
	Making a vest & all mat's of do.	1/-/6	2/12/-
	Fancy str. bagatelle foreparts	1/1/-	
	Making a vest & all materials of do.	1/-/6	2/1/6

February 1790

1   Altering a Fox uniform & new making up the coller & for stiffning &c.   2/6
    Altering a str. cloth frock & putting a coller on do. & for velvet   12/-
2   Putting new welts and pockets to 5 quilting vests & for stuff – 2/6 each   12/6   1/7/-
    A scarlet & green fleecy cotton piece   15/-
    Silk binding for the edges   3/6
    30 plated on bone buttons – 4/-   10/-
    Making a wais't & all mat's of do.   1/-/6   2/9/-
    To making a 10th Dragoon jacquet & waistcoat, laced & looped, lin'd allopeen & all materials as before   6/4/3
3   Altering 3 pair of breeches, lengthening the belts of a robe de chambre & letting a waistcoat out   7/6
    To a pair ribbed wors'd stocking bre's and all materials compleat   1/16/-
    2 pair drawers   15/-
        Carried forward   266/2/8
4   Altering a dress & a frock coat   5/-
    To a pair ribbed wors'd stocking breeches & all materials as usual   1/16/-
    2 pair drawers   15/-
    1 yard scarlet cloth (Goblin)   1/16/-
    Black silk binding   3/6
    3 dozen gilt ball butt's – 10/-   1/10/-
    Making a vest & all materials of do.   1/-/6   4/10/-
    Altering 2 pair velvet dress bre's & one pair black silk stocking breeches   5/-
    Repairing & buttoning a cass'e breeches   4/-
    12 fancy steel buttons – 2/6 each   1/10/-
    Altering a black cotton stocking breeches   2/6
    Altering a scarlet Hussar trowsers   5/-   2/6/6
6   To a pair white cotton stocking breeches compleat as usual   1/16/-
    To a pair black silk stocking do.   2/14/-
    4 pair drawers – 7/6   1/10/-
    Altering an embroid'd dress coat & wais't   4/-

	New buttoning a stocking breeches	1/-	
	10 fancy rich steel butt's – 3/6	1/15/-	2/-/-
6	24 wove butt's – 2/6 4 br.	5/6	
	Making a dark brown lapelled frock & all materials as usual (own cloth)	1/11/9	1/17/3
	1 yd scarlet cloth (Goblin)	1/16/-	
	28 wove butt's – 15d	3/-	
	Making a vest & all materials of do.	1/-/6	2/19/6
	To a pair flesh col'd cassimere breeches & all materials as usual		2/-/-
	2 pair of drawers		15/-
	To making a 10th Dragoon regimental coat and all materials as usual (own cloth & lace)		5/13/4
	Altering a regimental jacquet & 2 pair cotton stocking breeches	8/-	
	Cleaning 4 pair cotton stocking breeches – 18d each	6/-	14/-
	To a black silk masque		6/-
9	To a pair nankeen col'd cotton stocking breeches & all materials		1/16/-
	2 pair drawers - 7/6		15/-
	New lining a spotted velvet dress coat & waistcoat with your own light blue sattin		10/6
	To a Fox lapelled uniform frock compleat as usual (own cloth)		4/10/9
10	Altering a black silk breeches		2/6
	Scarlet emb'd cassimere shape in silks	3/3/-	
	3 dozen buttons – 15d	3/9	
	Making a vest &all materials of do.	1/-/6	4/7/3
	To a pair black silk stocking breeches		2/14/-
	10 fancy steel butt's – 3/- each		1/10/-
	2 pair drawers – 7/6		15/-
11	Embroid'd buff sattin shape in silver, stones & silk (own gold buttons & diamonds)	4/4/-	
	Making a vest & all materials of do.	1/-/6	5/4/6
	To a pair nankeen col'd cotton stocking breeches & all materials		1/16/-
	2 pair drawers – 7/6		15/-
	Altering 2 pair stocking breeches	6/-	
12	Altering two Generals frock coats & new lining the collers & for silk	6/-	12/-
	Carried forward		323/8/9
13	To making a Pages dress coat & wais't laced & looped with gold lace & all materials as before for Mr. [blank]		8/5/-

	To 6 fine white quilting waistcoats & all materials as usual – 32/6 each		9/15/-
	To 2 pair col'd cotton stocking breeches & all materials – 36/- ea		3/12/-
	4 pair drawers – 7/6		1/10/-
	Altering a 10th Dragoon jacquet & putting new wings to do.		4/-
	Putting new welts & pockets to 3 vests & for stuff	5/-	
15	Cleaning 7 pair breeches – 18d each	10/6	19/6
	To a black silk domino compleat		7/12/-
	A silk masque		6/-
	Making new welts & pockest to a plush velvet vest & for velvet & linnen	2/6	
16	Altering a brown frock, a scarlet waistcoat & cotton stocking breeches	5/-	7/6
17	To making a carmelite col'd vigonia dress coat & waistcoat, lin'd sattin, rich steel butt's, & all materials (own cloth, sattin lining & steel buttons)		3/9/9
18	To a pair black silk stocking breeches		2/14/-
	10 rich steel buttons – 3/-		1/10/-
	2 pair drawers – 7/6		15/-
	Making new welts & pockets to 2 buff vests & for stuff & pockets – 2/6 each	5/-	
	Altering 6 pair breeches (2 bla. silk and 4 cotton stocking) 2/6 ea	15/-	1/-/-
19	Putting new welts & pockets to 2 white dimoty vests & for dimoty & holland – 2/6 each	5/-	
	Altering 2 pair white & one pair buff cotton stocking breeches	5/-	10/-
20	24 round top plated butt's – 8/- 6 br.	18/-	
	Making a dark brown lapelled frock and all materials as usual (own cloth)	1/11/9	2/9/9
	1 ½ yds scarlet cassimere – 12/-	18/-	
	Black silk binding	3/6	
	3 dozen 4 gilt ball buttons – 10/-	1/13/4	
	Making a vest & all materials of do.	1/-/6	3/15/4
	To a pair nankeen col'd cotton stocking breeches & all materials		1/16/-
	2 pair drawers – 7/6		15/-
	To a fine white coating jacquet and trowsers lin'd flannell & all materials		3/3/-
	Altering a spaniolet vest & 2 pair cotton stocking breeches	6/-	
	Altering a Pages dress coat for Mr. Ford	4/-	

	Altering 5 pair of different col'd stocking breeches –		
	2/6 each	12/6	1/1/6
	Altering a blue Hussar jacquet and waistcoat for Mr. Nutsell, putting new cloth cuffs & coller to do., making the waistcoat longer & adding silver cord loops & 26 plated round top buttons to do. & for buttons & cloth (own cord)		3/3/-
23	24 covered butt's – 2/6 – 6 breast do.	5/8	
	Making a striped beaver lapelled frock & all materials as usual (own beaver)	1/11/9	1/17/5
	Carried forward		383/16/6
	Altering 2 pair cotton stocking breeches and putting on broad waistbands & for stuff – 5/- each		10/-
	To a pair dark col'd cotton stocking breeches with broad waistbands & all materials	2/-/-	
	2 pair of drawers	15/-	2/15/-
	Altering 3 frocks – 3/- each	9/-/	
	Putting black velvet collers of 3 more do. at 18d each	4/6	
	3 velvet collers at 10/- each	1/10/-	
25	Repairing & altering 2 pair breeches	5/-	
	Altering 2 pair do. & making very broad waistbands to do. & for stuff, linnen &c. – 5/- each	10/-	2/18/6
26	To making a Fox uniform lapelled frock & all materials as usual (own cloth)		4/10/9
	Embroid'd scarlet cassimere shape in silks	3/13/6	
	Embroid'd blue do.	3/3/-	
	Making 2 vests & all materials of do. – 20/6 each	2/1/-	8/17/6
	To 2 pair nankeen col'd cotton stocking breeches with very broad waistbands & all materials – 40/- each		4/-/-
	4 pair drawers – 7/6		1/10/-
27	24 wove butt's – 2/6 6 br.	5/8	
	Making a dark brown lapelled frock & all materials as usual (own cloth)	1/11/9	1/17/5
	Altering a cotton stocking breeches	2/6	
	Altering 2 pair silk breeches & putting broad silk waistbands to do. – 8/- each	16/-	
	Altering 7 pair diff't cotton stocking do. & putting broad waistbands to do. – 5/- each	1/15/-	
	Making new welts & pockets to 10 white dimoty vests & for welts & po. – 2/6 each	1/5/-	3/18/6
	Cleaning 6 quilting vests – 18d each	9/-	
	Cleaning 6 pair stocking breeches – 18d each	9/-	

March 1790

1	Altering 3 pair drab col'd cassimere breeches & putting broad waistbands on do. & for silk, linnen &c. at 8/- each	1/4/-	2/2/-	
2	1 ¾ yds rich striped black silk – 14/-	1/4/6		
	Making a wais't & all materials of do.	1/-/6	2/5/-	
	To a pair striped black silk breeches & for broad waistbands & all materials		3/-/-	
	2 pair drawers – 7/6		15/-	
	Repairing a black silk breeches & making broad waistbands to do. as before	8/-		
	Altering a black silk breeches	2/6		
3	Altering a black silk vest & making new welts to do. & for silk &c.	7/-		
	Altering 1 black silk & 5 pair of col'd breeches at 5/- each	1/10/-	2/7/6	
	To a pair of brettels		1/1/-	
4	1 ¾ yds rich striped sattin – 16/-	1/8/-		
	Making a vest & all materials of do.	1/-/6	2/8/6	
	To a rich striped sattin under waistcoat with sleeves lin'd with cotton & all materials as usual	3/13/-		
	To a coquelico vest as above	3/13/-	7/6/-	
	1 ¾ yds rich black silk – 14/-	1/4/6		
	Making a wais't & all materials of do.	1/-/6	2/5/-	
5	Altering 4 pair black silk breeches & for broad silk waistbands as before at 8/- each	1/12/-		
	Repairing & altg 2 pair breeches	3/-	1/15/-	
	Carried forward		439/19/2	
	To 2 pair black silk breeches (1 stocking) with very broad waistbands compleat at £3 each		6/-/-	
	4 pair drawers – 7/6		1/10/-	
	30 wove butt's – 2/6	6/3		
	Making a dark bottle green lapelled frock & all materials (own cloth)	1/11/9	1/18/-	
6	Altering 3 pair drab col'd cassimere breeches	6/-		
8	Altering 3 do. & putting new ribbon strings to the knees & for ribbon – 3/6 each	10/6	16/6	
	To a scarlet sattin under waistcoat without sleeves as before		2/10/-	
10	To making a great coat (own green cloth)	15/-		
	Silk sleeve lining & pockets	11/9		
	Large velvet coller	10/-		
	24 wove butt's – 2/6 6 breast	5/6		
	Sewing silk & twist	5/-	2/7/3	

	Altering an embroid'd coat & 2 vests	6/-	
	Altering 6 diff't pair of breeches – 2/- each	12/-	18/-
11	Making a sattin embroid'd vest with a velvet border & all materials (own shape)		1/-/6
12	To a silk toilinet shape	1/5/-	
	To 8 str. fancy do. – 18/- each	7/4/-	
	Silk binding & buttons – 6/- each	2/14/-	
	Making 9 vests of the above & all materials as usual – 20/6 each	9/4/6	20/7/6
	Putting a cloth coller on a blue coat & for cloth	2/6	
	Altering an embroid'd dress coat	2/-	
16	New buttoning a striped beaver frock	3/-	
	24 round top plated butt's – 8/-	16/-	
	Putting a cloth coller on a mixt cloth coat & for cloth	2/6	
	Altering a nankeen col'd cotton stocking breeches	4/-	1/10
17	24 wove butt's – 2/6 6 br.	5/8	
	Making a lapelled frock & all materials (own corbeau col'd cloth)	1/11/9	1/17/5
	To a pair black cotton stocking breeches with broad silk waistbands & all materials		2/-/-
	2 pair drawers – 7/6		1/10/-
19	Altering a pair black breeches		4/-
20	To a pair black silk stocking breeches & all materials		3/-/-
	10 rich steel butt's to do. – 3/- each		1/10/-
	2 pair drawers – 7/6		15/-
22	Putting a new coller to a buff silk vest & for silk		1/6
24	Altering 4 pair cotton stocking breeches – 5/- each		1/-/-
	Altering 4 embroid'd sattin waist's and piecing do. in the sides & for silk & additional embroidery – 10/6 each		2/2/-
25	To a pink silk under waistcoat with sleeves compleat as usual		3/13/-
	Carried forward		501/4/10
26	Putting new collers & new welts & pockets to 2 quilting vests & for stuff, linnen &c. – 3/- each		6/-
	1 ¾ yds rich buff silk – 14/-	1/4/6	
	Making a wais't & all materials of do.	1/-/6	2/5/-
	To a light blue silk under waistcoat with sleeves compleat as usual		3/13/-
27	Altering 2 pair ribbed stocking breeches		4/-
	24 round top plated butt's – 8/- 6 br.	18/-	
	Making a lapelled frock & all materials of do. (own striped silk cloth)	1/11/9	2/9/9
	Cleaning 4 pair white stocking breeches – 18d each		6/-

	To a buff silk waistcoat & all materials as above		2/5/-
	Silk binding & butt's to 2 vests – 6/- each	12/-	
	Making 2 fancy silk & cotton waistcoats & all materials as usual – 20/6 each (own foreparts to both)	2/1/-	2/13/-
	Altering 2 more quilting vests as at top – 3/- each		6/-
31	To making a fancy striped silk dress coat & waistcoat lin'd with white silk, rich stone set buttons & all materials (own outside, lining & buttons)		3/9/9
	Altering a slate col'd breeches		3/-
	To making a great coat (own mixt cloth)	15/-	
	Silk sleeve lining & pockets	11/9	
	24 wove butt's – 2/6 6 br.	5/8	
	Sewing silk & twist	5/-	1/17/5
	Ex'd J. L.		521/2/9

April 1790

1	New buttoning a green frock	3/-	
	24 high top plated butt's – 8/- 6 br.	18/-	
	Altering a cloth great coat	2/-	
2	Altering 2 pair cotton stocking breeches	8/-	1/11/-
	To making a great coat (own cloth)	15/-	
	3 ½ yds scarlet rattinett – 3/6	12/3	
	Scarlet velvet coller	10/-	
	Silk sleeve lining shaloon pockets	11/9	
	24 plain gilt buttons – 8/- 6 br.	18/-	
	Sewing silk & twist	5/-	3/12/-
	Altering a buff silk waistcoat & for new welts & pockets to do.		5/-
3	A velvet coller	10/-	
	Making a mixt cloth riding frock & all materials as usual (own cloth)	1/11/9	2/14/5
	Cleaning 6 pair drawers	1/6	
	Cleaning 3 buff vests – 18d each	4/6	
	New lining a blue cassimere embroid'd dress coat & waistcoat with your own silk serge	10/6	
	Taking the lining out of a Hussar jacquet & wais't & altering them. Cleaning the lining and putting it in again &c.	1/11/6	
	Altering 6 diff't dress coats & waistcoats at 5/- each	1/10/-	3/18/-
	To making a great coat	15/-	
	3 yds brown coating & for lining – 17/-	2/11/-	
	Silk sleeve lining &c.	11/9	
	24 wove butt's – 2/6 6 br.	5/10	
	Sewing silk & twist	5/-	4/8/7

	Putting black silk collers on two striped silk cloth frocks – 18d each	3/-	
	2 velvet collers – 10/- each	1/-/-	1/3/-
6	To making a great coat	15/-	
	7 yds mixt hunters cloth – 8/-	2/16/-	
	Silk binding for the edges	6/-	
	Silk sleeve lining &c.	11/9	
	14 wove butt's – 2/6 6 br.	3/9	
	Velvet coller	10/-	
	Sewing silk & twist	5/-	
	Box & booking	3/6	5/11/-
9	Altering a green frock & putting a velvet coller on do.	6/-	
	Black velvet coller	10/-	16/-
10	To a black worstead stocking dress suit lined with silk & trim'd with Brandenburgh loops and tassells & the waistcoat with rich lace & fringe & all materials as usual		27/7/8
	Altering 3 pair breeches – 3/- each	9/-	
12	To a pair black ribb'd wors'd stocking breeches & all materials	2/-/-	
	2 pair drawers – 7/6	15/-	
	Carried forward		54/10/9
13	Altering 2 pair cotton stocking breeches	10/-	
	Altering 2 black stocking dress coats & waistcoats	10/6	
	Altering a black cassimere & a black silk waistcoat & new welts & pockets to do. – 4/- each	8/-	
	Altering a black dress coat & waistcoat	6/-	1/14/6
	1 ¾ yds rich black silk – 14/-	1/4/6	
	Making a wais't & all materials of do.	1/-/6	2/5/-
	To a pair black cotton stocking breeches & all materials		2/-/-
	2 pair drawers – 7/6		15/-
15	Altering a striped dress coat & waistcoat & cotton stocking breeches	10/-	
17	Altering & repairing a cotton stocking breeches	3/-	
	Altering the collers & putting new welts & pockets to 76 different embroidered & plain white summer waist's & for new welts pockets & coller lining at 4/- each	15/4/-	15/17/-
	Making an embroidered dimoty waistcoat in gold & silks & all materials (own shape)		1/-/6
	To a Fox uniform lapelled frock & all materials as usual (own cloth)		4/10/9
	Altering the collers of 4 diff't under vests at 18d each	6/-	
	New binding the edges of a striped vest & for binding	3/6	9/6

	Altering 7 pair cotton stocking breeches – 2/- each		14/-
	To 2 under waistcoats with sleeves (pink & blue) lin'd with cotton & all materials at £3/13/- each		7/6/-
18	To a pink sattin do.		3/13/-
20	To 3 fancy toilinet waistcoats with silk binding & butt's & all materials as usual - £2/4/6 each		6/13/6
21	Scarlet (Goblin) cloth dress coat & waistcoat shape, richly embroidered in gold & purl & spangles		
	(own silk lining)	63/-/-	
	28 rich embroid'd buttons – 31/6	3/13/6	
	18 breast do. – 15/9	1/3/3	
	Making a dress coat & waistcoat & all materials as usual of do.	3/9/9	71/6/6
	To a Fox uniform lapelled frock & all materials as usual (own cloth)		4/10/9
	Making an embroidered silk waistcoat & all materials (own foreparts)		1/-/6
	2 fancy silk & muslin shapes – 31/6 each	3/3/-	
	Silk binding & buttons – 6/- each	12/-	
	Printed muslin wais't shape	1/18/-	
	28 silk buttons to do.	3/-	
	Making 3 vests & all materials of the above at 20/6 each	3/1/6	8/17/6
22	To 2 silk under vests (scarlet & blue) with sleeves lin'd flannell and all materials as usual - £3/13/- each		7/6/-
23	6 ½ yds blue cassimere – 10/6	3/8/3	
	Embroidering do. richly in silks	50/-/-	
	28 covered butt's – 2/6	5/10	
	18 breast do. – 1/3	1/10	
	Making a dress coat & waistcoat & all materials of as usual of the above (own silk lining)	3/9/9	57/5/8
24	Altg a dress coat & vest to fit Mr. Sackville		10/6
	Carried forward		169/3/11
	To a scarlet sattin under vest with sleeves lin'd flannell & all materials		3/13/-
26	Bottle green cassimere dress coat & wais't shape of white silk both richly embroidered in silver & stones	57/15/-	
	29 rich embroidered buttons – 21/-	2/9/-	
	18 breast do. – 10/6	15/9	
	Making a dress coat & waistcoat & all materials as usual	3/9/9	64/9/6
27	To 2 white quilting waistcoats & all materials as usual - 32/6 each		3/5/-
	To a Fox uniform lapelled frock and waistcoat compleat as usual (own cloth)		4/10/9

	Altering a cotton stocking breeches	4/-	
28	Altering 2 blue coats, one vest & 4 pair cotton stocking breeches	15/-	19/-
29	24 striped ribbon buttons – 5/- 6 br.	11/3	
	Making a striped cloth lapelled frock & all materials as usual (own cloth)	1/11/9	2/3/-
	Fancy cotton toilinet vest foreparts	10/-	
	Making a wais't & all materials of do.	1/-/6	1/10/6
	To a pair black silk stocking breeches & all materials as usual		3/-/-
	2 pair drawers – 7/6		15/-
	Putting new collers to 2 blue frocks & for cloth at 2/6 each		5/-
	To a pink silk under waistcoat with sleeves lin'd callico as usual		3/13/-
	Making a new coller & putting new backs to a str. silk cloth vest & for backs &c.		6/-
	To a fine white quilting waistcoat & all materials as usual		1/12/6
30	To a str. fancy toilinet waistcoat compleat as usual		2/4/6
	Altering 6 str. silk dress coats & waistcoats & new lining the collers of each at 12/- each		3/12/-
	To a pair nankeen col'd cotton stocking breeches compleat as usual		2/-/-
	2 pair drawers – 7/6		15/-
	Altering a blue coat & cotton breeches	6/-	

May 1790
1	Altering 2 pair cotton stocking breeches and for strings	11/-	
	Altering 9 dress vests & making the backs longer & for stuff – 3/- each	1/7/-	
	Altering 2 pair breeches at 2/- each	4/-	
	Altering 2 mixt frocks & putting a velvet coller on one & cloth one on the other – 6/- each	12/-	
	Velvet coller to one	10/-	
	Cloth for the other	2/6	
	Altering a laced jacquet & waistcoat for Mr. Sackville	1/6	3/14/-
	To 3 pair black silk drawers & all materials as usual - 12/- each		1/16/-
	24 covered butt's – 2/6 6 br.	5/8	
	Making a bottle green lapelled frock & all materials (own cloth)	1/11/9	1/17/5
	To 2 white quilting vests & all materials as usual - 32/6 each		3/5/-
	Box & booking to Newmarket		3/6

	Carried forward		278/13/7
4	To 3 white quilting vests as usual - 32/6 each		4/17/6
	Embroid'd white dimoty vest in silks	4/4/-	
	Emb'd str. muslin do. in gold	4/4/-	
	Making 2 vests & all materials – 20/6 each	2/1/-	10/9/-
	Piecing the backs & collers of 2 vests & for stuff &c. 18d each		3/-
6	24 round top plated butt's – 8/- 6 breast do.	18/-	
	Making a mixt cloth lapelled frock & all materials as usual (own cloth)	1/11/9	2/9/9
	10 ½ yds rich blue & crimson str. silk – 21/-	11/2/6	
	Embroid'd white silk vest in silver & silks	12/-/-	
	28 covered butt's – 2/6	5/10	
	28 breast do. – 1/3	2/11	
	Making a dress suit of the above & all materials as usual	3/17/9	27/9/-
	2 pair drawers – 7/6		15/-
7	Altering new buttoning and putting new cloth collers to 2 mixt cloth frocks – 9/- each	18/-	
	6 dozen wove butt's – 2/6	15/-	
8	24 round top plated butt's – 8/- 6 br.	18/-	
	Making a dark brown cloth lapelled frock & all materials (own cloth)	1/11/9	2/9/9
	To 6 pair fine nankeen breeches & all materials at 36/- each		10/16/-
	12 pair drawers – 7/6		4/10/-
	Striped black silk cloth dress coat & waistcoat shape, both richly embroidered in silks	47/5/-	
	6 ½ yds striped silk cloth – 21/-	6/16/6	
	28 covered buttons – 2/6	5/10	
	18 breast do. – 1/3	1/10	
	Making a dress coat & wais't & all materials of do. (own silk lining)	3/9/9	57/18/11
	1 ½ yds fancy toilinet – 12/-	18/-	
	Silk binding & buttons	6/-	
	Making a vest & all materials	1/-/6	2/4/6
10	24 wove butt's – 2/6 6 br.	5/8	
	Making a lapelled frock & all materials	1/11/9	1/17/5
	Altering 2 frocks at 2/6 each	5/-	
	Altering 6 diff't pair of breches & putting additional strings to do. & for strings &c. at 5/- each	1/10/-	1/15/-
11	To a crimson silk under waistcoat with sleeves lin'd with cotton & all materials		3/13/-
12	To a Fox uniform lapelled frock & all materials as usual (own cloth)		4/10/9

344

13	To a ditto		4/10/9
	Altering 2 pair nankeen breeches – 3/- ea		6/-
	To a pair buff wors'd stocking breeches & all materials as usual		2/-/-
	2 pair drawers – 7/6		15/-
	Altering a spotted silk dress coat & waistcoat to fit Mr. McEwen & for silk to line coat coller & cotton to piece the vest sides	10/6	
	Altering a blue frock & for new cloth coller	2/6	
	Altering 5 pair diff't breeches – 5/- each	1/5/-	1/18/-
	To a scarlet embroidered cassimere waistcoat shape sent home		3/13/6
14	Altering 4 dress coats, lengthening the collers & for silk & cloth – 2/6 each		10/-
	Carried forward		430/3/5
15	Altering 3 frocks & a black silk breeches		9/-
	To a pair drab col'd silk breeches comp't		3/-/-
	2 pair drawers – 7/6		15/-
	A black silk masque		6/-
	Altering 2 pair buff breeches – 2/- each	4/-	
	Cleaning 8 pair do. – 1/6 each	12/-	16/-
17	To a pair nutt colour silk bre's comp't	3/-/-	
	To a pair buff silk do.	3/-/-	6/-/-
	4 pair drawers – 7/6		1/10/-
	To a rose colour silk under vest with sleeves, lin'd with cotton & all materials as usual		3/13/-
	Altering a lapelled coat & 2 pair breeches	12/-	
	Making new collers & altering 12 dimoty vests & for dimoty & cotton – 2/- each	1/4/-	1/16/-
19	To a Fox uniform lapelled frock & all materials as usual (own cloth)		4/10/9
	To a blue & buff striped sattin under vest with sleeves compleat as usual		3/13/-
	Fancy str. jean for 3 shapes – 12/- each	1/16/-	
	Making 3 vests & all materials – 20/6 each	3/1/6	4/17/6
	Altering 4 pair breeches		6/-
	Fine white str. muslin shape	12/-	
	Fancy str. jean do.	12/-	
	Making 2 vests & all materials – 20/6 each	2/1/-	3/5/-
20	Altering 4 pair breeches & an under vest		9/-
21	To a pair buff worstead stocking breeches & all materials		2/-/-
	2 pair drawers – 7/6		15/-
	To 5 striped muslin vests as above – 32/6 each		6/2/6

25	Altering 2 pair wors'd breeches & for new strings – 5/3 each		10/6	
26	To a pair bottle green silk breeches & all materials		3/-/-	
	2 pair drawers – 7/6		15/-	
	Altering a ribbed wors'd stock'g breeches		6/-	
27	To 5 pair diff't colour silk breeches & all materials as usual - £3 each		15/-/-	
	10 pair drawers – 7/6		3/15/-	
	Altering a dress hunt frock & a drab col'd worstead stocking breeches	13/-		
	New blue velvet coller to coat	10/-	1/3/-	
	To 3 fancy silk under waistcoats with sleeves compleat as usual - £3/13/- each		10/19/-	
	2 pair drab col'd cassimere breeches compleat as usual - £2 each		4/-/-	
	4 pair drawers – 7/6		1/10/-	
29	Altering 4 blue frocks		4/-	
	To a Windsor dress coat with gold lace loops & all materials as usual (own cloth & lace)		5/6/9	
	To a Windsor frock do. (own cloth)		2/18/9	
	To a pair nankeen colour cotton stocking breeches as usual		2/-/-	
	2 pair drawers – 7/6		15/-	
	Altering the collers of 2 embroid'd vests & putting pockets to do. & for pockets		6/-	
31	Altering a drab col'd silk breeches		2/-	
	Altering a nankeen breeches		5/-	13/-
	Carried forward			527/3/2

June 1790

1	Putting a blue velvet coller on a blue coat & for velvet &c.		11/6	
	Altering 11 diff't colour frocks – 4/- each		2/4/-	
	Altering a striped silk breeches		4/-	2/19/6
2	24 wove butt's – 2/6 6 br.		5/8	
	Making a dark mixt lapelled frock & all materials (own cloth)		1/11/9	1/17/5
4	Garter blue str. rich silk coat & breeches, and white silk waistcoat & coat cuffs, all very richly embroidered in silver & stones & silk flowers, the coat on all the seams and the waistcoat all over		190/-/-	
	28 rich embroid'd buttons – 31/6		3/13/6	
	28 breast do. – 15/9		1/16/9	
	Making a Birthday dress suit and all materials compleat			

	of the above (own white silk lining)	3/17/9	199/8/-
	2 pair drawers		15/-
5	To a pair white silk drawers		12/-
	Altering 2 coats & 4 pair breeches		18/-
7	24 wove butt's – 2/6 6 breast do.	5/8	
	Making a lapelled frock & all materials (own dark mixt cloth)	1/11/9	1/17/5
	To a pair white cotton stocking breeches & all materials compleat		2/-/-
	To a pair nankeen col'd cotton do.		2/-/-
	4 pair drawers – 7/6		1/10/-
	Altering 2 pair silk breeches – 2/- each	4/-	
	Putting a blue cloth coller on a blue frock and for cloth	5/-	9/-
	To a Fox uniform frock & all materials as usual (own cloth)		4/10/9
	Altering 2 blue cloth frocks		6/-
9	24 wove butt's – 2/6 6 br.	5/8	
	Making a dark mixt cloth lapelled frock & all materials (own cloth)	1/11/9	1/17/5
10	Altering a green uniform coat & putting a new coller on do.	6/-	
	Black velvet coller	10/-	16/-
	1 ¾ yds rich buff silk – 14/-	1/4/6	
	Making a wais't & all materials of do.	1/-/6	2/5/-
11	Altering 12 embroid'd dimoty vests, new backs & embroid'd collers put to 2 of them & for cotton &c. 7/- each		4/4/-
	To a Brighton uniform frock double breasted & all materials as usual		10/18/3
12	Black & purple str. velvet coat & breeches & white silk waistcoat shape, all very richly embroidered in silks	50/-/-	
	28 covered buttons – 2/6	5/10	
	28 breast do. – 1/3	2/11	
	Making a dress suit and all materials of the above (own silk lining)	3/17/9	54/6/6
	2 pair drawers – 7/6		15/-
	Altering 7 diff't pair of silk breeches – 4/-		1/8/-
	Carried forward		822/16/5
	14 plated butt's 8/- 6 breast	11/4	
	Making a brown mixt cloth riding frock and all materials (own cloth)	1/11/9	
	Extra for double silk pockets	10/-	2/13/1
14	Cleaning 4 pair breeches – 18d each	6/-	
15	Altering 3 frocks to fit – 3/- each	9/-	
16	Altering a mixt frock & silk breeches	5/-	1/-/-

	2 yds rich pink & blue str. silk – 14/-	1/8/-	
	2 yds blue & buff do.	1/8/-	
	Buff & white jean shape	12/-	
	6 diff't silk & muslin shapes – 18/-	5/8/-	
	1 rich do.	1/5/-	
	Making 10 vests of the above & all materials as usual – 20/6 each	10/5/-	20/6/-
17	Altering 3 frocks & a pair breeches		11/-
	To a pair nankeen col'd cotton stocking breeches compleat	2/-/-	
	2 pair drawers – 7/6		15/-
18	Altering a cotton stocking breeches	4/-	
19	Altering 10 diff't col'd cloth frocks – 4/6 each	2/5/-	
	Altering 3 embroid'd vests & putting new collers to do. & for collers – 7/- each	1/1/-	
	Altering a black cotton stocking bre's & for new strings to do.	7/6	
	Altering a pair nankeen breeches	2/6	
	Cleaning 1 vest & 2 pair breeches – 18d each	4/6	
22	Altering 2 frocks – 3/- each	6/-	4/10/6
	To 12 fine white quilting vests & all materials as usual – 32/6 ea		19/10/-
24	To 12 fine white jean vests with sleeves & all materials as usual at £1/11/6 each for Mr. Vick	18/18/-	
	To 6 do. for Mr. Ince – 31/6 each	9/9/-	
	To 6 do. for Mr. Goldey – 31/6 each	9/9/-	
	To 6 do. for Mr. Taurade – 31/6 each	9/9/-	47/5/-
	Ex'd J. L.		921/7/-

July 1790

1	New lining a Brighton frock with buff cassimere & putting new buff cuffs & coller to do.	15/-	
	3 ½ yds buff cassimere – 10/-	1/15/-	
	Putting new collers to 2 frocks & for cloth &c. – 3/- each	6/-	2/16/-
	To 4 fine callico under vests with sleeves compleat at 31/6 each		6/6/-
	Altering the coller of a blue coat	3/-	
	Putting a buff cassimere coller on a green frock & for cassimere	3/6	
	Altering the collers of 2 frocks	4/-	
	Putting black velvet collers on 2 frocks & a cloth coller on one do.	6/-	
	2 velvet collers – 10/- ea	1/-/-	

	Cloth for 1 do.	2/6	1/19/-
	14 plated butt's – 8/- 6 breast	11/4	
	Making a blue riding frock and all materials (own cloth)	1/11/9	2/3/1
	To a pair black cotton stocking breeches & all materials		2/-/-
	2 pair drawers – 7/6		15/-
	Altering a dark green frock	3/-	
	Putting cloth collers on 2 frocks and for cloth &c. 3/- each	6/-	9/-
	24 wove butt's – 2/6 6 br.	5/8	
	Velvet coller	10/-	
	Making a mixt cloth lapelled frock & all materials (own cloth)	1/11/9	2/7/5
	Putting a velvet coller on a frock & for velvet		11/6
2	To a Fox uniform frock & all materials as usual (own cloth)		4/10/9
	Altering 12 embroid'd waistcoats & making new collers to do. & for embroidery &c. – 7/- each		4/4/-
	To a pair black silk stocking breeches & all materials		3/-/-
	2 pair drawers – 7/6		15/-
	Altering 7 diff't cloth frocks at 2/- each	14/-	
	Altering a cotton stocking breeches	2/-	16/-
	3 yds buff cassimere – 10/-	1/10/-	
	4 dozen 4 plain gilt butt's	17/4	
	Making 2 vests & all materials – 20/6 each	2/1/-	4/8/4
	To 2 buff silk waistcoats compleat as usual at £2/5/- each		4/10/-
	Altering 7 embroid'd vests as above – 7/- each	2/9/-	
	Altering a nankeen cotton stocking bre's & for broad waistband put to do.	8/-	2/17/-
3	24 wove butt's – 2/6 6 br.	5/8	
	Velvet coller	10/-	
	Making a light mixt cloth lapelled frock & all materials (own cloth)	1/11/9	2/7/5
	To a Fox uniform frock & all materials as usual (own cloth)		4/10/9
	Carried forward		51/6/3
	Fancy callico for 3 shapes – 10/- each	1/10/-	
	Making 3 vests & all materials of do. – 20/6 each	3/1/-	4/11/6
	To 3 silk under waistcoats with sleeves, lin'd callico compleat as usual - £3/13/- each		10/19/-
5	Embroidered quilting shape in silks	3/3/-	
	Making a vest & all mat's of do.	1/-/6	4/3/6

	Fancy callico foreparts	10/-	
	Making a wais't & all materials of do.	1/-/6	1/10/6
	24 wove butt's – 2/6 6 br.	5/8	
	Making a mixt cloth lapelled frock & all materials (own cloth)	1/11/9	1/17/5
	Altering 3 under waistcoats	4/-	
7	Altering 19 diff't pair of breeches & for broad waistbands -7/- ea	6/13/-	6/17/-
8	To a Brighton uniform coat & all materials as usual		10/18/3
9	Altering 7 diff't embroid'd waistcoats & for embroid'd collers as before – 7/- each		2/9/-
	To a scarlet dress hunt coat lin'd buff cassimere, gold lace loops & all materials as usual		10/12/9
	24 plated butt's – 8/- 6 breast	18/-	
	Blue velvet coller	10/-	
	Making a mixt brown cloth lapelled frock & all materials	1/11/9	2/19/9
	Altering 10 more pair breeches as the above & for waistbands – 7/- each	3/10/-	
	Putting velvet collers on 2 frocks & altering lapells &c. – 12/6 ea	1/5/-	
	2 velvet collers – 10/-	1/-/-	5/15/-
10	Altering & piecing the collers of 6 plain white vests & for stuff – 3/- each	18/-	
	Cleaning 2 pair of breeches – 18d each	3/-	1/1/-
	To a Brighton uniform frock as before		10/18/3
	24 wove butt's – 2/6 6 br.	5/8	
	Velvet coller	10/-	
	Making a light mixt cloth lapelled frock & all materials (own cloth)	1/11/9	2/7/5
	Altering a frock & an under waistcoat		4/-
	To 4 callico under waistcoats with sleeves at 32/6 each		6/6/-
13	Altering 6 more bre's as before – 7/- each	2/2/-	
14	Altering 8 emb'd vests as before - 7/- each	2/16/-	4/18/-
15	To 4 pairs black silk drawers & all materials as usual – 12/- each		2/8/-
16	Altering 3 nankeen breeches – 3/- each	9/-	
17	Altering 13 more emb'd vests as before - 7/- each	4/11/-	
	Altering 7 diff't frocks & putting velvet collers on 2 of them – 7/- each	2/9/-	
	2 velvet collers – 10/-	1/-/-	
	Altering 2 more embroidered vests as before & for collers &c. - 7/- each	14/-	
	Altering a blue frock, facing it with blue cloth & putting		

	scarlet cuffs & coller on do.	5/-	
	¾ yd blue cloth – 20/-	15/-	
	Scarlet cuffs & coller	3/6	
	Altering 2 under waistcoats	3/-	10/9/6
	Carried forward		152/12/1
20	Altering 2 frocks as the others & putting velvet collers on do. – 7/- each	14/-	
	2 velvet collers – 10/- each	1/-/-	
21	Altering 3 more frocks – 7/-	1/1/-	
	3 velvet collers – 10/- each	1/10/-	
	Altering 5 embroid'd vests as the others & for embroid'd collers - 7/- each	1/15/-	
	Altering a Windsor frock & for a new scarlet cloth coller	4/-	
	Putting a velvet coller on a dress uniform coat & for velvet	12/-	
	Embroidering the coller in gold	2/5/-	
	Altering a green frock in lapells & coller as the rest & for new cloth coller &c.	12/6	
23	Altering 4 under vests & a quilting one	4/-	
	Altering 2 more frocks as usual – 7/-	14/-	
	2 velvet collers to do. – 10/- each	1/-/-	
	Burnishing 26 silver buttons – 3d each	6/6	

August 1790

2	Altering 14 frocks in the collers – 2/- each	1/8/-	
	Altering 2 jocky vests – 2/- each	4/-	
	Repairing & altering 2 pair breeches	6/-	
	Altering 3 more frocks as the others – 7/-	1/1/-	14/17/-
	2 velvet collers – 10/- each	1/-/-	
	4 ½ dozen butt's to 2 frocks – 2/6	11/3	
	Making 2 lapelled frocks and all materials at £1/11/9 each (own green mixt & dark col'd cloth)	3/3/6	4/14/9
10	To making a Windsor dress coat & all materials as usual (own cloth & lace)		5/6/9
	Altering another do., putting new coller on do. & moving the lace loops &c.		8/6
11	To making a Windsor frock & all materials (own cloth)		2/18/9
	To 3 pair nankeen trowsers and all materials at 45/- each		6/15/-
	To 2 pair white cotton stocking breeches as usual – 40/- each		4/-/-
	4 pair drawers – 7/6		1/10/-

12	Altering a Windsor frock in lapells & putting new scarlet cuffs & coller to do.	8/-		
	Scarlet cloth cuffs & coller	3/6		
	Altering 3 mixt cloth frocks as the others – 7/-	1/1/-		
	3 black velvet collers at 10/- each	1/10/-		
	Putting a black velvet coller on a green frock & for velvet		12/-	
	Altering 2 more frocks as the rest – 7/- each	14/-		
	2 black velvet collers – 10/- each	1/-/-	5/8/6	
13	To paid expences of Mr. Smith going to Brighton and back &c.		5/5/-	
	Embroid'd dimoty vest in silks	3/13/6		
	Emb'd muslin do.	3/13/6		
	Emb'd fancy do. in silver & silks			
	Making 3 waistcoats of the above & all materials as usual – 20/6 each	3/1/6	15/3/-	
	Repairing a pair breeches & a pair trowsers		4/-	
	Carried forward		219/3/4	
14	Altering 9 diff't frocks & putting 4 velvet & 5 cloth collers on do. – 7/- each	3/3/-		
	4 velvet collers – 10/- each	2/-/-		
	5 cloth collers – 2/6 each	12/6		
	Altering 3 pair nankeen trowsers & for broad waistbands to do. – 6/6 each	19/6		
	Paid carriage & porterage of a large box from Brighton	18/-	7/13/-	
	24 wove butt's – 2/6 6 br.	5/8		
	Making a mixt green cloth lapelled frock & all materials as usual (own cloth)	1/11/9	1/17/5	
16	To 4 pink silk under waistcoats with sleeves compleat as usual - £3/13/- each		14/12/-	
	18 wove butt's – 2/6 6 br.	4/5		
	Black velvet coller	10/-		
	Making a mixt cloth frock & all materials	1/11/9	2/6/2	
	To a pair bottle green cotton stocking breeches compleat		2/-/-	
	2 pair drawers – 7/6		15/-	
	Altering 10 diff't frocks as the rest & putting 9 velvet & 1 cloth collers on do. at 7/- each	3/10/-		
	9 black velvet collers at 10/-	4/10/-		
	1 cloth coller	2/6		
	24 wove butt's – 2/6 6 br. to one coat	5/8	8/8/2	
	3 pair of brettels – 21/- each		3/3/-	
17	Altering 5 more frocks as above – 7/- each	1/15/-		
	3 black velvet collers at 10/-	1/10/-		
	1 cloth coller	2/6		

	10 Clarence uniform butt's – 15/9	13/1	
	Altering 5 diff't pair breeches & putting on broad waistbands & for do. – 7/- each	1/15/-	5/15/7
	To a pair buff striped cassimere breeches and all materials		2/5/-
	2 pair drawers – 7/6		15/-
	To a Fox uniform lapelled frock & all materials as usual (own cloth)		4/10/9
	To a pair black silk breeches & all materials compleat as usual		3/-/-
	2 pair drawers – 7/6		15/-
	To another black silk bre's & drawers		3/15/-
	Altering a nankeen colour cotton stocking breeches	2/-	
	Altering a scarlet frock & putting a velvet coller on do.	4/-	
	Black velvet coller	10/-	16/-
24	Altering a nankeen trowsers & for new broad waistband to do.		7/-
25	To a pair nankeen col'd cotton stocking breeches & all materials	2/-/-	
	To a pair buff wors'd stocking do.	2/-/-	4/-/-
	4 pair drawers – 7/6		1/10/-
26	18 wove buttons - 2/6	3/9	
	6 breast do.	8	
	Black velvet coller	10/-	
	Making a mixt cloth lapelled frock & all materials (own cloth)	1/11/9	2/6/2
	To a Fox uniform lapelled frock & all materials as usual (own cloth)		4/10/9
	Altering a frock & breeches		6/-
	Carried forward		294/10/4
	To 3 pair diff't col'd silk stock'g breeches compleat as usual - £3 each		9/-/-
	6 pair drawers – 7/6		2/5/-
	Altering the collers of 7 different col'd frocks at 2/- each		14/-
27	To 2 fine white quilting waistcoats as usual - 32/6 each		3/5/-
	Cleaning 6 pair breeches - 18d each	9/-	
	Altering 2 pair do.	6/-	15/-
28	To 3 quilting vests as above - 32/6 ea		4/17/6
29	To a Fox uniform frock & all materials as usual (own cloth)		4/10/9
	Fancy spotted callico foreparts	10/-	
	Making a vest & all materials of do.	1/-/6	1/10/6
	To 4 fine white quilting waistcoats as usual - 32/6 each		6/10/-
	To a pair nankeen colour cotton stocking breeches compleat		2/-/-
	2 pair drawers – 7/6		15/-

September 1790

1	To 3 quilting vests as above - 32/6 ea		4/17/6
	Altering 2 pair cotton stock'g breeches	6/-	
	Cleaning a pair do.	1/6	7/6
	To a pair drab col'd thickset breeches and all materials		2/-/-
	2 pair drawers – 7/6		15/-
2	To a pair buff ribbed wors'd stocking breeches as usual		2/-/-
	2 pair drawers – 7/6		15/-
	Large box & booking		3/6
4	To a pink silk under waistcoat with sleeves compleat as usual		3/13/-
	To a fine callico do. with sleeves		1/11/6
	Altering a 3 frocks & putting a velvet collers on do. - 4/- each	12/-	
	3 black collers at 10/- each	1/10/-	
	Altering 3 pair breeches - 3/- each	9/-	
	Cleaning 2 pair bre's & a pr. trowsers - 18d each	4/6	2/15/6
7	Altering a 3 blue frocks & putting a velvet collers on do. - 3/- ea	9/-	
	3 blue velvet collers	1/10/-	
	Altering 3 mixt cloth frocks & lining the collers with cloth at 3/- each	9/-	
	Altering 4 silk under vests 5 pair of breeches	12/-	
	Altering the collers of 2 mixt frocks	2/-	
	Altering 2 dark do. & making French riding sleeves to do. - 4/- each	8/-	
	Altering the lapells & collers of two blue frocks - 4/6 each		9/-
	Altering a pair of trowsers & putting new straps & buttons to do. & for buttons &c.	7/-	4/6/-
	Carried forward		356/12/7
	Altering the collers of 4 diff't colour frocks at 2/- each	8/-	
	Altering 3 embroid'd vests - 2/- each	6/-	
	Altering & repairing 2 pair breeches	7/-	
	Altering the lapells, collers &c. of two frocks at 8/- each	16/-	
	Altering 4 under vests & for linnen to put cross the bodys	10/6	
	Altering a pair of breeches & a pair of trowsers	7/-	
8	Altering 6 white waistcoats	6/-	
	Altering 3 pair cotton stocking trowsers and for broad waistbands at 7/- each	1/1/-	
9	Altering 2 pair nankeen trowsers	8/-	
	Cleaning a pair do.	1/6	4/11/-
10	To 2 pair olive col'd silk stocking breeches compleat		

	at £3 each	6/-/-	
	4 pair drawers – 7/6	1/10/-	7/10/-
11	14 wove butt's – 2/6 6 br.	3/9	
	Velvet coller	10/-	
	Making a lapelled frock & all materials of do.(own mixt green cloth)	1/11/9	2/5/6
	To a Fox uniform frock & all materials as usual (own cloth)		4/10/9
	Altering 2 under waistcoats & a cotton stocking breeches	6/-	
	Cleaning 6 vests & a pair trowsers - 18d each	10/6	
14	To a pair nankeen col'd cotton stocking breeches as usual	2/-/-	
	2 pair drawers	15/-	
15	To 2 do.	15/-	
	To a cotton stocking bre's as the last	2/-/-	
16	To a Shepherds cloth box coat to drive in. Edges bound, velvet coller, silk sleeve lining & all materials	5/-/-	
18	Altering 6 quilting vests	6/-	
	Altering a nankeen cotton stocking breeches & for new strings	5/-	11/-
20	2 ½ yds black cloth (panion) - 28/-	3/10/-	
	16 covered butt's – 2/6 6 br.	4/-	
	Making a broad lapelled frock & all materials of do.	1/11/9	
	Extra for making now gen'l mourning	10/-	5/15/9
	To another do. compleat & extra		5/15/9
	3 ½ yds black silk for 2 vests - 14/-	2/9/-	
	Making 2 vests & all mat's of do. - 20/6 each	2/1/-	
	Extra for mak'g now gen'l mourn'g - 5/- ea	10/-	5/-/-
	3 ½ yds black cloth (panion) - 28/-	4/18/-	
	Black velvet coller	10/-	
	24 covered buttons - 2/6 6 br.	5/8	
	Making a great coat & all materials	1/11/9	
	Extra for making now gen'l mourning	10/-	7/15/5
21	Black velvet coller to a great coat	10/-	
	Making a grey cloth great coat & all materials (own cloth)	1/11/9	
	Extra for making now gen'l mourning	10/-	2/17/5
	Carried forward		414/11/8
	4½ yds black cloth (panion) - 28/-	6/6/-	
	12 yds silk to line - 6/6	3/18/-	
	12 covered buttons - 2/6 6 br.	3/9	
	Making a weeper coat and waistcoat & all materials as usual	3/9/9	
	Extra for making now gen'l mourning	15/-	14/12/6
	To a pair of black silk stocking breeches & all materials	3/-/-	
	To a pair ribbed do.	3/-/-	

	Extra for making now gen'l mourning - 5/- each	10/-	
	4 pair drawers – 7/6	1/10/-	8/-/-
	Altering 3 pair of breeches and a pair trousers	18/-	
22	Altering a frock & breeches and making the coller lower 8/-		1/6/-
	To a pair black cassimere breeches & all materials	2/5/-	
	Extra for making now gen'l mourning	5/-	2/10/-
	2 pair of drawers		15/-
	To a pair of white silk drawers		12/-
	Altering a mixt cloth frock & repairing a cotton stocking breeches		3/-
	1 ½ yds black cassimere - 10/-	15/-	
	Making a vest & all materials of do.	1/-/6	
	Extra for making now gen'l mourning	5/-	2/-/6
	To 2 pair black cotton stocking breeches & all materials - 40/- ea	4/-/-	
	Extra for making now gen'l mourn'g - 5/- each	10/-	4/10/-
	4 pair drawers – 7/6		1/10/-
24	Altering 2 black frocks & putting velvet collers on do. - 2/- each	4/-	
	2 velvet collers - 10/- each	1/-/-	1/4/-
	2 ½ yds black cloth - 20/-	2/10/-	
	18 wove butt's – 2/6 6 br.	4/5	
	Making a lapelled frock & all materials for Mr. Du Paquet		18/6
	1 ½ yds black cassimere - 10/-	15/-	
	24 wove buttons - 15d	2/6	
	Making a vest & all materials for do.	15/-	
	To a pair black cassimere breeches for do.	1/12/-	
	Extra for making now gen'l mourning	1/-/-	7/17/5
	Box & booking	2/6	
	To a suit compleat as above for Mr. Jouard & extra		7/17/5
25	Cleaning 5 vests & 1 pair breeches - 18d each		9/-
30	Altering 2 great coats - 2/- each		4/-
	To making 2 black cloth lapelled frocks, buttons & all materials as before at £2/6/4 each (own cloth)	4/12/8	
	Extra for making now gen'l mourning	1/-/-	5/12/8
	Velvet coller to a great coat	10/-	
	24 wove butt's – 2/6 8 br.	5/8	
	Making a great coat & all materials (own mixt cloth)	1/11/9	
	Extra for making now gen'l mourning	10/-	2/17/5
	Altering 3 pair silk breeches		8/-
	2 pair black cass'e breeches - 45/- each	4/10/-	
	4 pair drawers	1/10/-	
	Extra for making now gen'l mourning	10/-	6/10/-

Ex'd J. L. 483/13/1

October 1790
4   5 yds mixt black & white cloth - 10/-   2/10/-
    Velvet coller   10/-
    16 wove butt's – 2/6 10 br.   4/5
    Making a lapelled frock & all mat's as usual   1/11/9   4/16/2
    6 ½ yds mixt cloth as above - 10/-   3/5/-
    Black velvet coller   10/-
    24 wove butt's – 2/6 10 br.   6/-
    Making a great coat & all mat's of the above as usual   1/11/9   5/12/9
    Extra for making them now gen'l mourning - 10/- each   1/-/-
    1 ½ yds black cassimere - 10/-   15/-
    Making a wais't & all materials of do.   1/-/6
    Extra for making now gen'l mourning   5/-   2/-/6
5   Black velvet coller   10/-
    16 wove butt's – 2/6 8 br.   4/2
    Making a riding frock & all materials (own black cloth) 1/11/9
    Extra for making now gen'l mourning   10/-   2/15/11
    To a pair black silk breeches   3/-/-
    To a pair black wors'd stocking do.   2/-/-
    4 pair drawers – 7/6   1/10/-
    Extra for making now gen'l mourning - 5/- each   10/-
7   Altering 2 stocking dress coats   10/6
    Altering & repairing a black cass'e breeches   3/-   13/6
8   To a black silk under vest with sleeves compleat as usual   3/13/-
    To a white sattin do.   3/13/-
    Extra for making now gen'l mourning - 5/- each   10/-
    Covering the body lining of 2 black vests with holland &
    altering a breeches & for holland &c. - 3/6 each   7/-
    Putting a black velvet coller on a black riding frock   2/-
    Black velvet coller   10/-   19/-
9   2 yds white spaniolet - 10/-   1/-/-
    Black binding for holes & edges   6/-
    15 black buttons   1/6
    Making a riding wais't of do. and all materials as usual 1/-/6
    To another do. compleat   2/8/-
    Extra for making now gen'l mourning 5/- each   10/-   5/6/-
    To a pair black silk stocking breeches   3/-/-
    Extra for making now gen'l mourning   5/-   3/5/-
    2 pair drawers – 7/6   15/-
    To a white sattin under vest as above   3/13/-
    Extra for making now gen'l mourning   5/-   3/18/-

	Altering a black wors'd breeches		2/6
	Black velvet coller	10/-	
	16 wove butt's – 2/6 8 br.	4/2	
	Making a riding frock & all materials (own black cloth)	1/11/9	
	Extra for making now gen'l mourning	10/-	2/15/11
	Altering a great coat & breeches	7/6	
14	Altering 2 black silk waistcoats & for new collers &c.	4/-	11/6
15	To a pair white silk drawers		12/-
	Altering 2 black frocks		6/-
	Carried forward		50/5/9
19	1 ¾ yds rich black silk - 14/-	1/4/6	
	28 wove buttons - 15d	2/11	
	Making a wais't & all materials of do.	1/-/6	
	Extra for making now gen'l mourning	5/-	2/12/11
21	To making a 10th Dragoon jacquet & wais't, laced & looped with silver lace loops & tassells for Cornet Leigh (your own lace, tassells &c.)	1/11/6	
	2 ¾ yds blue cloth - 20/-	2/15/-	
	2 ½ yds white rattinett to line - 2/6	6/3	
	Silk sleeve lining, holl'd pockets	10/6	
	Body lining to vest	6/-	
	6 dozen regimental butt's - 4/-	1/4/-	
	Sewing silk & twist	7/6	
	Yellow cloth cuffs, coller, edging &c.	4/9	7/5/6
22	To making a reg'l dress coat for do.	1/11/6	
	2 yds blue cloth - 20/-	2/-/-	
	Yellow cloth cuffs, coller & edging	4/9	
	5 yds allopeen to line - 3/6	17/6	
	20 reg'l butt's - 8/- 10 br - 4/-	16/9	
	Silk sleeve lining, holl'd pockets	10/6	
	Sewing silk & twist (own lace & parts)	5/-	6/6/-
	1 ½ yds white cassimere - 10/-	15/-	
	13 regimental butt's - 4/-	4/4	
	Making a wais't & all materials for do.	15/-	
	To a pair regimental cass'e bre's for do.	1/12/-	
	12 buttons as above	4/-	3/10/4
25	To a Shepherds coating driving coat compleat as before		5/-/-
26	Altering a generals coat to fit	10/6	
	Cleaning the coat & embroidery	10/6	1/1/-
28	Altering a 10th Dragoon dress coat		8/-
29	White quilting foreparts	12/-	
	Black silk fringe to do.	4/-	
	Making a wais't & all materials of do. (own glass & stone		

	buttons)	1/-/6	1/16/6
	Putting velvet collers on 2 mixt frocks & one scarlet one at 2/- ea	6/-	
	3 velvet collers - 10/- each	1/10/-	
	Altering a blue frock, making a French riding sleeve to do. & putting on a velv't coller	6/-	
	6 gilt buttons - 4/-	2/-	
	Velvet coller	10/-	2/14/-
30	Blue velvet coller	10/-	
	6 plated butt's - 8/- 6 breast	12/8	
	Making a riding frock & all mat's (own blue cloth)	1/11/9	2/14/5

November 1790

1	To 6 pair black silk drawers - 12/- each		3/12/-
	To a 10th Dragoon jacquet & wais't compleat as above for Cornet Leigh (your own lace, tassells & epaulets)		7/5/6
	To a 10th Dragoon dress suit for do.		9/16/4
	To making a great coat for do.	12/-	
	3 yds blue cloth - 20/-	3/-/-	
	1 ½ yds white shaloon - 2/6	3/9	
	Scarlet cloth coller	1/6	
	Silk sleeve lining & pockets	12/6	
	24 plated butt's - 6/- 6 br.	13/6	
	Sewing silk & twist	2/6	5/5/9
	5 yds silk cloth omitted 29th March - 21/-		5/5/-
6	To making a white spaniolet robe de chambre, lin'd flannell & all materials (own spaniolet & flannell)		1/11/10
	Carried forward		116/10/10
11	Fleecy cotton stocking	1/11/6	
	Silk serge sleeve lining	10/6	
	Making an under waistcoat of do., edges bound & all materials	8/-	2/10/-
	To a pair fleecy cotton stock'g drawers		15/-
	To 2 pair diff't colour thickset breeches compleat at 40/- each		4/-/-
	4 pair drawers - 7/6		1/10/-
13	Repairing a pair nankeen trowsers & for buttons	1/6	
16	Altering a blue frock	2/6	
	Box & booking	2/-	
18	Altering the loops of 2 Dragoon coats & taking the yellow cloth from under do. - 10/6 each	1/1/-	1/7/-
	To a pair (Vanbutchel) elastic brettels		6/6/-
19	To 3 fancy spaniolet vests and all materials as usual -		

	£2/6/6 ea		6/19/6
	To making 2 white spaniolet robe de chambre, lin'd flannell & all materials as usual - £1/11/10 each (own spaniolet & flannell)		3/3/8
22	To a scarlet & white striped under waistcoat with sleeves as usual		3/13/-
	Altering a frock & silk breeches	4/-	
23	Black velvet coller	10/-	
	16 wove butt's – 2/6 6 breast do.	4/-	
	Making a mixt green cloth lap'd frock & all materials (own cloth)	1/11/9	2/5/9
	To 2 scarlet & one fancy str. cassimere vests compleat as usual - £2/6/6 each		6/19/6
24	Making new collers to 12 quilting vests and for stuff - 2/6 each		1/10/-
	To a scarlet & white str. sattin under vest with sleeves as usual		3/13/-
25	To making a mixt green cloth lapelled frock exactly as one the 23d (own cloth)		2/5/9
	To a scarlet cassimere vest as usual	2/6/6	
	26 enamel china butt's - 2/- each	2/12/-	4/18/6
	Altering 2 sattin under waistcoats	6/-	
	Altering 2 blue frocks & putting velvet collers on do. - 6/- each	12/-	
	2 black velvet collers - 10/- each	1/-/-	
	Altering the collers of 2 quilting vests at 18d each	3/-	
	Altering a str. silk cloth dress coat & waistcoat	3/-	
	Altering the collers & lapells of 2 mixt frocks & putting new collers on do.	12/-	
	2 velvet collers - 10/- each	1/-/-	
	Altering the collers of 14 vests - 2/- each	1/8/-	
	Altering a black wors'd breeches	2/-	5/6/-
26	To a Princes uniform frock & all materials as usual (own cloth)		7/10/3
	To a pair black ribbed wors'd breeches		2/-/-
	2 pair drawers - 7/6		15/-
27	To a Fox uniform frock as usual (own cloth)	4/10/9	
	To a sca't cassimere vest as usual	2/6/6	6/17/3
	New buttoning a vest & for buttons		2/6
29	16 gilt butt's - 8/- 8 br.	12/8	
	Velvet coller	10/-	
	Making a frock & all materials (own blue cloth)	1/11/9	2/14/5
	Carried forward		193/16/11

	To a white quilting waistcoat & all materials as usual		1/12/6
	To a scarlet & white str. sattin under vest with sleeves as usual		3/13/-
	To making a Fox uniform as usual (own cloth)		4/10/9
	Altering a black wors'd stocking breeches	3/-	
30	New buttoning a sca't riding frock	3/-	
	16 plated butt's - 8/- 4 breast	12/-	
	Altering & putting collers to 7 frocks	1/4/-	
	4 velvet collers - 10/-	2/-/-	
	3 scarlet cloth do - 2/6 each	7/6	
	16 plated butt's - 8/- 4 br. to one blue frock	12/-	5/1/6
	To 2 fancy sattin under vests with sleeves as usual - £3/13/- ea		7/6/-

December 1790

2	To 6 fine white quilting vests as usual at 32/6 each		9/15/-
	2 velvet collers - 10/- each	1/-/-	
	30 wove butt's – 2/6 16 br.	8/-	
	Making 2 coating great coats and all materials as usual - £1/11/9 each (own coating)	3/3/6	4/11/6
3	To 6 fine white quilting vests as before at 32/6 each		9/15/-
4	1 ½ yds buff cassimere - 10/-	15/-	
	26 plain gilt buttons - 4/-	8/8	
	Making a wais't & all materials of do.	1/-/6	2/4/2
	New lining a blue frock	8/-	
	3 ½ yds buff cassimere - 10/-	1/15/-	
	Altering a mixt cloth frock	6/-	
	Altering 2 great coats and a frock - 3/- each	9/-	2/18/-
7	To a striped sattin under waistcoat with sleeves compleat as usual		3/13/-
9	Blue velvet coller	10/-	
	16 plated butt's - 8/- 6 br.	12/8	
	Making a blue riding frock & all materials (own cloth)	1/11/9	2/14/5
	Brown velvet coller	10/-	
	16 wove butt's – 2/6 6 br.	4/-	
	Making a Hunters cloth great coat & all materials (own brown cloth)	1/11/9	2/5/9
	To 3 spaniolet vests (scarlet white & buff) compleat as usual - £2/6/6 each		6/19/6
	To a pair black ribbed wors'd stock'g breeches		2/-/-
	2 pair drawers – 7/6		15/-
	Repairing a pair stocking breeches		1/-
10	6 ½ yds dark str. silk cloth - 25/-	8/2/6	

	26 very rich steel butt's - 10/6 each	13/13/-	
	18 breast do. - 6/6 each	5/17/-	
	Making a dress coat & waistcoat of do. & all materials	3/9/9	31/2/3
	To making a spaniolet robe de chambre & all materials (own spaniolet & flannell)		1/11/10
11	To making a short great coat (own blue cloth)	15/-	
	Silk sleeve lining &c.	11/9	
	Blue velvet coller	10/-	
	32 gilt breast butt's - 4/-	10/8	
	Sewing silk & twist	5/-	
	Making another do. as above with plated butt's	2/12/5	5/4/10
13	Two velvet collers (blue & black) - 1-/-	1/-/-	
	16 gilt butt's - 8/- 6 br. to blue coat	12/8	
	16 wove butt's - 2/6 6 br. to mixt coat	4/-	
	Making 2 lapelled frocks & all materials at £1/11/9 each (own cloth)	3/3/6	5/-/2
	Carried forward		306/12/1
14	To making a great coat (own cloth)	15/-	
	Silk sleeve lining &c.	11/9	
	Velvet coller	10/-	
	20 wove butt's - 2/6 6 br.	5/-	
	Sewing silk & twist	5/-	2/6/9
	To making a coating great coat and everything as above (own coating)		2/6/9
	Black velvet for 2 collers - 10/- each	1/-/-	
	16 wove butt's - 2/6 6 br. to mixt coat	4/-	
	18 plated butt's - 8/- 6 br. to dark col'd coat	14/-	
	Making 2 lapelled frocks & all materials at £1/11/9 each (own cloth)	3/3/6	5/1/6
	Altering 10 quilting vests		5/-
16	Light col'd velvet coller	10/-	
	14 wove butt's - 2/6 6 br.	3/9	
	Making a light mixt coating great coat & all materials (own coating)	1/11/9	2/5/6
	To making a pair of trowsers & all materials (own coating)		12/6
	Blue velvet coller	10/-	
	Gold binding for the edges of a coat	2/2/-	
	16 gilt engraved G. P. & feather butt's - 21/- 6 br.	1/13/3	
	Making a Kempshot Uniform frock & all materials (own blue cloth)	1/11/9	5/17/-
	1 ½ yds buff spaniolet - 10/-	15/-	
	12 buttons as above	10/6	
	Making a wais't & all materials of do.	1/-/6	2/6/-

	To a pair black silk stocking breeches & all materials	3/-/-	
	2 pair drawers – 7/6	15/-	
	To a white silk under waistcoat with sleeves lin'd thro' with the same and interlin'd thro with oiled silk and all materials compleat	3/5/-	
	Altering 2 short great coats and a black worstead breeches	5/-	
20	Altering a sca't vest & black silk bre's	2/-	
	Fancy str. silk cloth coat & breeches and white sattin vest all richly embroidered in silks (own lining)	50/-/-	
	28 covered butt's - 2/6	5/10	
	28 breast do. - 1/3	2/11	
	Making a dress suit of the above & all materials	3/17/9	54/6/6
	2 pair of drawers – 7/6		
21	Altering a wors'd stocking breeches	2/-	
	Altering the collers of 2 blue frocks	4/-	
22	Fancy str. silk cloth coat & waistcoat shape, both richly emb'd in silks (own sattin lining)	45/-/-	
	28 covered butt's - 2/6	5/10	
	18 breast do. - 1/3	1/10	
	Making a dress coat & waistcoat of the above & all materials as usual	3/9/9	48/17/5
	To 2 striped sattin under vests with sleeves compleat £3/13/- ea	7/6/-	
23	To 2 pair drab colour cassimere breeches & all materials - £2/5/- each	4/10/-	11/6/-
	4 pair drawers – 7/6		1/10/-
	Box & booking to Kempshot		3/6
	Carried forward		452/14/6
24	To a Fox uniform frock & all materials as usual (own cloth)		4/10/9
	Altering & putting velvet collers to a blue riding frock & a great coat	8/-	
	2 velvet collers - 10/- each	1/-/-	1/8/-
	To 2 pair black cassimere breeches & all materials - £2/5/- each		4/10/-
	4 pair drawers – 7/6		1/10/-
	To a pair drab col'd pantaloon bre's & all materials		2/12/6
	New buttoning a uniformfrock	3/-	
	22 Kempshot Uniform butt's - 21/- 10 br.	2/7/3	2/10/3
28	Blue velvet coller	10/-	
	16 gilt butt's - 8/- 6 br.	12/8	
	Making a riding frock & all materials as usual (own blue cloth)	1/11/9	2/14/5
29	To 6 diff't str. cassimere vests compleat at £2/6/6 each		13/19/-

30	To a Fox uniform frock & all materials as usual (own cloth)		4/10/9	
	To 2 pair buff ribbed wors'd stocking breeches & all mat's at 40/- each		4/-/-	
	4 pair drawers – 7/6		1/10/-	
	Altering a Kempshot frock	4/-		
	Making the waistbands broader of a cassimere breeches and for stuff	5/-		
	Buttoning a silk stocking breeches with your own steel buttons	1/-		
31	Altering a blue frock	3/-		
	Altering & new buttoning a blue coat	6/-		
	18 plain gilt butt's - 8/-	12/-		
	Altering 4 pair of breeches	9/-	2/-/-	
	2 velvet collers (brown & mixt colour) - 10/- each	1/-/-		
	3 dozen 4 wove butt's – 2/6 2 dozen breast	9/8		
	To making 2 great coats & all materials as usual - £1/11/9 each (own cloth)		3/3/6	4/13/2
	To a Princes uniform frock & all materials as usual (own cloth)		7/10/3	
	To 3 str. sattin under waistcoats with sleeves as usual £3/13/- ea		10/19/-	
	To a pair black silk stocking breeches compleat as usual		3/-/-	
	2 pair drawers – 7/6		15/-	
	Altering 2 pair breeches and putting new ribbon strings to one pair & for ribbon &c.		5/-	
	Ex'd J. L.		525/12/7	

Bibliography

Alger, John Goldsworth: Napoleon's British Visitors and Captives, 1801-1815
Anonymous: Prince of Wales's Lodge No. 259: List of members from the time of its constitution with notes of proceedings and circumstances of interest in connection with the Lodge and its members, Warrington & Co., 1910
Anonymous: The Tailor, published by Houlston and Stoneman, London, c. 1801
Anonymous: The Taylor's Complete Guide, or A Comprehensive Analysis of Beauty and Elegance in Dress, 1796
Ashton, John: Florizel's Folly, Chatto & Windus, 1899
Aspinall, A.: Correspondence of George Prince of Wales, Vols I-III
Astor, Jacques: Dictionnaire des Noms de Famille et des Noms de Lieu du Midi de la France, Editions du Beffroi, 2002
Banvard, John: The Private Life of a King Embodying the Suppressed Memoirs of the Prince of Wales
Bartlett, W.A.: The History and Antiquities of the Parish of Wimbledon, 1865
Bazalgette, Jean (Jean Bazal): *Mon Ancêtre Jean Louis: Compagnon De La Fayette*, Preface de Gilbert de Chambrun, Editions Cevennes Magazine, Les Grands Cévenols Ferce sur Sarthe, France 1977
Benjamin, Lewis Saul: The Beaux of the Regency
Blagdon, Francis W., Paris as it was and as it is, or A Sketch of the French Capital..., written by an English Traveller during the years 1801-2
Booth, Charles: Life and Labour of the People in London
Bourne, Kenneth: Palmerston, The Early Years 1784-1841
Brown, David: Palmerston
Butler, Kathleen Mary: The Economics of Emancipation: Jamaica & Barbados, 1823-1843
Campbell, Robert: The London Tradesman, being a Compendious view of All the Trades, Professions, Arts both Liberal and Mechanic, now practised in the Cities of London and Westminster, 1840

Chaix d'Est-Ange, Gustave: Dictionnaire des familles françaises anciennes ou notables à la fin du XIXe siècle, Vol III, 1903
Chambers, James: Charlotte & Leopold: The True Story of the Original People's Princess
Chambers, Robert and William: Chambers' Journal, Volume 51, 1874
Compaing, M.: L'Art du Tailleur, 1826
Cook, Sir Theodore Andrea: Eclipse and O'Kelly, Dutton. 1908
Crainz, Franco: An Obstetric Tragedy; The case of HRH The Princess Charlotte Augusta, 1977
Dickens, Charles: All The Year Round, Vol XII, 1864
Diderot & D'Alembert: Encyclopédie, ou dictionnaire raisonné des sciences, des arts et des métiers
Draper, Nicholas: The Price of Emancipation: Slave-ownership, Compensation and British Society at the end of Slavery
English Heritage: Survey of London, Vol 40
Farington, Joseph: Cave, Kathrin(Ed.): The Diary of Joseph Farington
Faulkner, James: An Historical and Topographical Account of Chelsea and its Environs, 1810
Flint, A. (pseudonym): The Tailor's Answer to the Late Attacks Upon their Profession from the Stage and Press With Critical Remarks on Jeremy Swell's Mock Heroic Poem
Foote, Samuel: The Tailors: a Tragedy for Warm Weather', 1767
Fortescue, S. E. D.: The Story of Two Villages: Great and Little Bookham, 1998
Frost, Charlotte: Sir William Knighton: The Strange Career of a Regency Physician, Authors Online, 2010
Galton, F.W.: Select Documents illustrating the History of Trade Unionism: 1. The Tailoring Trade
Goodrich, Hawthorne & Manning: Peter Parley's Universal History
Greville, Charles: Diaries
Gronow, Rees Howell: Reminiscences of Captain Gronow
Hall, Douglas: A brief history of the West India Committee, Caribbean University Press, 1971

Hamilton, Lady Anne: The Secret History of the Court of England
Hancock, David: Citizens of the World
Harden, Edgar F.: Thackeray's English Humorists and Four Georges
Haswell, Charles Haynes: Reminiscences of an Octogenerian of the city of New York (1816-1860)
Healey, Edna: Coutts – The Story of a Private Bank
Huish, Robert: Memoirs of George the Fourth, 1830
Irvine, Valerie: The King's Wife: George IV and Mrs Fitzherbert
Kingsley, Charles: Alton Locke, Tailor and Poet
Kloester, Jennifer: Tavendale, Graeme: Georgette Heyer's Regency World
Köhler, Karl; Von Sichart, Emma: A history of costume
Lean, E. Tangye: The Napoleonists
Leslie, Anita: Mrs. Fitzherbert, a Biography, Scribner, 1960
Major, Joanne and Murden, Sarah: An Infamous Mistress: The Life, Loves and Family of the Celebrated Grace Dalrymple Elliott, Pen and Sword, 2016
O'Byrne, William R.: Naval Biographical Dictionary, 1849
Parkinson, C. Northcote (Ed): The Trade Winds: a study of British overseas trade during the French wars, 1793-1815. London, Allen & Unwin, 1948
Ragatz, Joseph Lowell: The Fall of the Planter Class in the British Caribbean, New York, Century Co., 1928
St. Allais, Nicolas Viton de: Nobiliaire Universel de France, ou Recueil Général des Généalogies Historiques des Maisons Nobles de ce Royaume
Seligman, Kevin L.: Cutting for all!: the sartorial arts, related crafts, and the commercial paper pattern, 1996
Sichel, Walter Sydney: Sheridan, from new and original material, Houghton Mifflin, 1909
Smith, E.A.: George IV
Souter, J.: The Book of English Trades and Library of the Useful Arts, 1818
Stirling, A.M.W.: (compiler) The Letter-Bag of Lady Elizabeth Spencer-Stanhope Vol I
Stroud, Dorothy: Henry Holland, His Life and Architecture

Swell, Jeremy (pseudonym): The Tailor's Revolt
Thackeray, William Makepeace: The Four Georges: Sketches of Manners, Morals, Court and Town Life
Thackeray, W. M.: Sketches and Travels in London
Victoria County History: A History of the County of Middlesex, Vol VII, 1982
Walpole, B. C., Sheridan, Richard Brinsley: Recollections of the life of the late Right Honorable Charles James Fox
Walrond, Colonel: Some Old Archery Societies (Chapter XII)
Waugh. Norah: The Cut of Men's Clothes, 1600-1900, 1946
Wilkins, William Henry: Mrs. Fitzherbert and George IV
Wilks, Mark; History of the Persecutions endured by the Protestants of the South of France, and more especially of the Department of the Gard, during the years 1814, 1815, 1816, &c. including a Defence of their Conduct, from the Revolution to the Present Period: Longman, 1821
Willings, Heather: A Village in the Cevennes, 1979
Wright, G.N.: The Life and Reign of William the Fourth
Wroth, Warwick William: Cremorne and the later London gardens, 1907

Descendants of Claude Bazalgette
(Limited to six generations)

1. CLAUDE BAZALGETTE
1. sp: MARIE RAINAL
   2. JEANNE BAZALGETTE (b.1682)
   2 ETIENNE BAZALGETTE (b.1683)
   2 PIERRE BAZALGETTE (b.1685)
   2 sp: LOUISE GRIGNARD (m.1707)
     3 ETIENNE BAZALGETTE (b.1709;D.1757)
     3 sp: JEANNE DELEUZE (b.1715;M.1732)
       4 PIERRE BAZALGETTE (b.1739)
       4 MARIE BAZALGETTE (b.1743)
       4 GEORGES BAZALGETTE (b.1746;d.1795)
       4 sp: MARGUERITE BAUD
         5 ANTOINE BAZALGETTE
         5 JEAN BAZALGETTE (b.1779;d.1838)
         5 sp: MARIE CAMPREDON (b.1774;m.1808;d.1841)
           6 JEAN BAZALGETTE II dit BONAPARTE
           6 MAURICE-ANTOINE BAZALGETTE dit BONAPARTE   (b.1818;d.1902)
           6 sp: GERTRUDE DENDRE
           6 GERMAIN BAZALGETTE dit BONAPARTE
           6 FRANCOIS BAZALGETTE dit BONAPARTE
         5 PAUL BAZALGETTE
         5 ROSE? BAZALGETTE
       4 JEAN LOUIS BAZALGETTE (Louis) (b.1750;d.1830)
       4 sp: CATHERINE METIVIER (m.1779;d.1785)
         5 LOUIS BAZALGETTE (b.1780)
         5 LOUISA BAZALGETTE (b.1781;d.1867)
         5 JOSEPH WILLIAM BAZALGETTE CAPTAIN, RN (b.1783;d.1849)
         5 sp: THERESA PHILO PILTON (b.1796;m.1816;d.1850)
           6 THERESA PHILO BAZALGETTE (b.1817;d.1885)
           6 JOSEPH WILLIAM BAZALGETTE Sir, C.B. (b.1819;d.1891)
           6 sp: Maria Kough (b.1819;m.1845;d.1902)
           6 LOUISA BAZALGETTE (b.1820;d.1853)
           6 sp: ST LOUIS WELLS LUCAS (m.1841)

6 EMILY BAZALGETTE (b.1822;d.1824)
6 JULIA BAZALGETTE (b.1824;d.1902)
6 CECILIA BAZALGETTE (b.1826;d.1909)
6 HENRY GAMBIER BAZALGETTE (b.1828;d.1830)
6 HELEN MARY ANN BAZALGETTE (b.1829;d.1908)
6 sp: LOUIS JOHN FRANCIS TWYSDEN (b.1829;m.1856;d.1911)
6 EMMA BAZALGETTE (b.1830)
6 sp: WILLIAM CARNLEY (m.1851)
6 BENJAMIN CHARLES BAZALGETTE (b.1831;d.1831)
6 MATILDA ANNETTE BAZALGETTE (b.1833)
6 sp: CECIL DERMER BICKNELL (b.1837;m.1865)
6 CHARLOTTE JANE BAZALGETTE (b.1834;d.1836)
6 LAURA MARIA BAZALGETTE (b.1836;d.1908)
5 JOHN BAZALGETTE (b.1784;d.1868)
5 sp: SARAH CRAWFORD MAGDALEN VAN NORDEN (b.1794;d.1866)
6 HERBERT SAWYER BAZALGETTE (d.1852)
6 CECILIA JANE BAZALGETTE Cissy (d.1909)
6 CAROLINE EMMELINE BAZALGETTE (d.1891)
6 EVELYN BAZALGETTE Ensign (d.1857)
6 CATHERINE LOUISE BAZALGETTE
6 sp: JAMES ARTHUR CHARLES GORE Major
6 sp: JAMES FOX BLAND Major (b.1827;m.1858)
6 SARAH MAGDALEN BAZALGETTE (b.1817;d.1819)
6 JOHN VAN NORDEN BAZALGETTE (b.1819;d.1872)
6 sp: LUCY ELLEN OCTAVIA COCKSAGE (m.1863;d.1885)
6 LOUIS HOWE BAZALGETTE Lt. Col. (b.1820;d.1866)
6 DUNCAN BAZALGETTE Captain (b.1822)
6 WILLIAM JOSEPH BAZALGETTE LT COL (b.1824;d.1906)
6 JAMES ARNOLD BAZALGETTE Capt. (b.1829;d.1879)
6 sp: SARAH ELLEN CREELY (m.1869;d.1871)
6 sp: SOPHIA LOUISA ALMON (m.1872;d.1907)
6 GEORGE BAZALGETTE Major (b.1829;d.1885)
6 sp: LOUISE SEVILLE (m.1870;d.1918)
6 LOUISA CAROLINE BAZALGETTE (b.1830;d.1830)

6 SIDNEY AUGUSTUS BAZALGETTE Adjutant, Capt RA (b.1836;d.1869)
6 sp: LUCY CHAMBERLIN (m.1858)
4 sp: FRANCES BERGMAN (Fanny) (b.1768;m.1787;d.1847)
5 FRANCES MARY BAZALGETTE (b.1788;d.1790)
5 THERESA BAZALGETTE (b.1791;d.1792)
5 LOUIS BAZALGETTE (b.1792;d.1879)
5 sp: ANNE MOXOM
6 JULIA AUGUSTA BAZALGETTE (b.1816)
5 sp: SARAH COOKE (m.1837;d.1879)
6 SARAH JANE BAZALGETTE Jane (b.1837;d.1928)
5 DANIEL BAZALGETTE (b.1793;d.1838)
5 sp: MARGARET MacCREA (m.1817;d.1846)
6 FRANCES ELIZABETH BAZALGETTE (b.1820;d.1874)
5 CAROLINE BAZALGETTE (b.1795;d.1851)
5 CECILIA BAZALGETTE (b.1799;d.1831)
5 sp: LOUIS JOHN FRANCIS TWYSDEN (b.1808;m.1829)
6 LOUIS JOHN FRANCIS TWYSDEN (b.1829;d.1911)
6 sp: HELEN MARY ANN BAZALGETTE (b.1829;m.1856;d.1908)
6 FRANCIS TWYSDEN (b.1831;d.1831)
5 EVELYN BAZALGETTE Q.C. (b.1801;d.1888)
5 SIDNEY BAZALGETTE (b.1806;d.1858)
5 sp: MARIA HAND (m.1831;d.1833)
5 sp: CAROLINE SARAH MONTAGU (b.1814;m.1835;d.1876)
5 AUGUSTUS BAZALGETTE (b.1807;d.1849)
5 EMMELINE BAZALGETTE (b.1813;d.1873)

About the author

The author was born in a pacifist commune in Ashburton, Devonshire, towards the end of the second world war. His father Deryck Bazalgette was a conscientious objector who devoted his life to horticulture. His mother, Margaret Bonham, was a successful writer of short stories. He went first to Knowles Hill School in Newton Abbot. His parents divorced and his father remarried and moved the family to Surrey, where Charles went to a junior school in Virginia Water and then to the aptly-named Wallop School in Weybridge. For his secondary education he was lucky enough to get a grant to go to Dartington Hall School, back in Devonshire, where he was an indifferent student, preferring to play jazz and fish for trout in the nearby River Dart. On leaving school he worked at an art college and then in several public libraries, even going to library school in London before switching to a more lucrative job in computer programming. He has worked in the IT industry in a variety of roles for over forty years, discovering on the way a talent for intuitive technical problem solving, and still works from home for a major software company. He now lives near Salmo, a village in British Columbia, Canada, with his second wife Trish, who runs a bookstore and frames pictures. His interests are mainly in the past - research into family and social history but also the restoration of old buildings, furniture and clocks. He has always enjoyed writing (except essays at school) but has not done a great deal of it. He is fascinated by biography as a genre, and is currently researching the career of Louis' son Joseph William Bazalgette, who served as an officer in the British Navy for eighteen years during the Napoleonic Wars.